THE MASTER HANDBOOK OF
HIGH−LEVEL MICROCOMPUTER LANGUAGES

No.1733
$21.95

THE MASTER HANDBOOK OF
HIGH–LEVEL MICROCOMPUTER LANGUAGES

BY CHARLES F. TAYLOR

TAB BOOKS Inc.

BLUE RIDGE SUMMIT, PA. 17214

FIRST EDITION

SECOND PRINTING

Printed in the United States of America

Reproduction or publication of the content in any manner, without express
permission of the publisher, is prohibited. No liability is assumed with respect to
the use of the information herein.

Copyright © 1984 by TAB BOOKS Inc.

Library of Congress Cataloging in Publication Data

Taylor, Charles F. (Charles Floyd), 1946-
The master handbook of high-level microcomputer
languages.
Includes index.
1. Microcomputers—Programming.   2. Programming
languages (Electronic computers)   I. Title.
QA76.6.T3925   1984   001.64'24   83-24168
ISBN 0-8306-0733-1
ISBN 0-8306-1733-7 (pbk.)

Contents

Introduction   vii

1 What Is a High-Level Language?   1
Machine Languages—Assembly Languages—High-Level Languages—High-Level Versus Low-Level
Languages—Objective of this Book

2 General Features of High-Level Languages   5
Data Representation—The Assignment Statement—Arithmetic Expressions—Logical Expressions—
Input and Output—Control Structures—Data Structures—File Handling—Graphics—Summary

3 BASIC   19
Program Structure—Data Representation—The Assignment Statement—Arithmetic Expressions—Logic
Expressions—Input and Output—Control Structures—Data Structures—File Handling—Graphics—
Comprehensive Simple Program—Advantages and Disadvantages of BASIC—Availability—Summary

4 C   46
Program Structure—Data Representation—The Assignment Statement—Arithmetic Expressions—
Logical Expressions—Conditional Expressions—Input and Output—Control Structures—Data
Structures—File Handling—Graphics—Comprehensive Sample Program—Advantages and Disadvan-
tages of C—Availability—Summary

5 COBOL   86
Program Structure—Data Representation—The MOVE Statement—Arithmetic Expressions—Logical
Expressions—Input and Output—Control Structures—Data Structures—File Handling—Graphics—
Comprehensive Sample Program—Advantages and Disadvantages of COBOL—Availability—Summary

6 Forth   **126**

Program Structure—Data Representation—Arithmetic Expressions—Logical Expressions—Input and Output—Control Structures—Data Structures—File Handling—Graphics—Comprehensive Sample Program—Advantages and Disadvantages of Forth—Availability—Summary

7 FORTRAN   **160**

Program Structure—Data Representation—The Assignment Statement—Arithmetic Expressions—Logical Expressions—Input and Output—Control Structures—Data Structures—File Handling—Graphics—Comprehensive Sample Program—Advantages and Disadvantages of FORTRAN—Availability—Summary

8 LISP   **197**

LISP Programs and Functions—Data Types—The Assignment Function: SETQ—Arithmetic Expressions—Logical Expressions (Predicates)—Input and Output—Control Structures—Data Structures—File Handling—Graphics—Comprehensive Sample Program—Advantages and Disadvantages of LISP—Availability—Summary

9 Logo   **227**

Logo Programs and Procedures—Data Types—The Assignment Statement: MAKE—Arithmetic Expressions—Logical Expressions (Predicates)—Input and Output—Control Structures—Data Structures—File Handling—Graphics—Comprehensive Sample Program—Advantages and Disadvantages of Logo—Availability—Summary

10 Modula-2   **254**

Program Structure: The Module Concept—Data Representation—The Assignment Statement—Arithmetic Expressions—Boolean Expressions—Input and Output—Library Modules: Separate Compilation—Control Structures—Data Structures—File Handling—Graphics—Comprehensive Sample Program—Advantages and Disadvantages of Modula-2—Availability—Summary

11 Pascal   **297**

Program Structure—Data Representation—The Assignment Statement—Arithmetic Expressions—Boolean Expressions—Input and Output—Control Structures—Data Structures—File Handling—Graphics—Comprehensive Sample Program—Advantages and Disadvantages of Pascal—Availability—Summary

12 PILOT   **331**

Program Structure—Data Representation—Input and Output—The MATCH Statement—The COMPUTE Statement—Logical Expressions—Control Structures—Data Structures—File Handling—Graphics—Comprehensive Sample Program—Advantages and Disadvantages of PILOT—Availability—Summary

13 High-Level Languages Compared   **350**

Numerical Computation—Character Handling—Data Structures—Control Structures—Console Input/Output—File Input/Output—Subroutine Interface—Low-Level Operations—User Friendliness—Matching the Language and the Application—Conclusions

Index   **357**

Introduction

This is a book about computer languages, specifically high-level languages that are available for use on microcomputers. Ten different languages are presented and described.

BASIC	LISP
C	Logo
COBOL	Modula-2
Forth	Pascal
FORTRAN	PILOT

The purpose of the book is to provide in one location a description of each language, conveying the nature of each language along with its major features. Programming examples are interspersed liberally throughout. Along with the usual short examples, a longer, comprehensive sample program is provided at the end of each language chapter. You can thus see what a nontrivial program looks like in each language.

To make comparisons between languages easier, many of the programming examples are the same from language to language. You can thus see how the same program can be written in more than one language.

All of these languages are available for the Apple II series of microcomputers. (Some require the addition of an accessory plug-in circuit board with a supplemental Z80 microprocessor.) Most are available for the IBM Personal Computer. Most are also available for any microcomputer that supports the CP/M operating system (by Digital Research, Inc.)

The typical reader will probably know how to program in at least one high-level language (perhaps BASIC or FORTRAN), either on a microcomputer or on a larger machine. He or she will learn what each of the various languages has to offer and will be in a better position to choose a language appropriate for a particular application.

It is of course impossible to cover every feature of every language in such a short space. I have attempted to cover enough of the major features of each language so as to convey the essence of the language and to provide a valid basis for comparison. Features unique to a particular implementation of a language have been omitted when possible.

The first chapter addresses the question, "What is a high-level language?" The second chapter discusses in general terms the features commonly found in high-level languages. Its purpose is to provide a foundation for the chapters that follow and a basis for comparing languages. Chapters 3 through 12, the language chapters, form the heart of the book, with one chapter devoted to each language. The language chapters are presented in alphabetical order by the name of the language and may be read in any order. Chapter 13 provides a comparison of the various languages covered.

Chapter 1

What Is a High-Level Language?

At the heart of every microcomputer lies an integrated circuit called a *microprocessor*. This microprocessor makes up what is called the *central processing unit,* or *CPU,* of the microcomputer. All of the computation takes place in the CPU. In 1983, a microprocessor could be purchased for as little as $3.95 and was about the size of a man's thumb. Such a microprocessor contains as much computing power as the largest computers of 20 or 25 years ago. Such a computer then cost hundreds of thousands of dollars and occupied a large room. Times have changed.

Of course you cannot buy a microcomputer for $3.95, because a CPU is useless without such things as a power supply, input and output devices, memory, and various interface circuits. The total price is thus much higher, ranging from under $100.00 for the simplest microcomputers to over $10,000.00 for the more complex units.

MACHINE LANGUAGES

Common microprocessors available today include the Intel 8080A, 8085, 8086, and 8088; the Mostek 6502A; the Zilog Z80A; and the Motorola 6800, 6809, and 68000. Each microprocessor has its own language, or set of instructions that it understands, designed into the circuitry. Such a language is called a *machine language*. Machine languages are made up of 1s and 0s, or, binary numbers. These binary numbers are often written as hexadecimal (base 16) numbers, but even so, they are dreadfully hard for humans to use. Worse yet, each microcomputer speaks a different language. (There is some commonality between the 8080A, 8085, and Z80A, and between the 8086 and 8088; yet, there is no universal machine language.)

ASSEMBLY LANGUAGES

The next step above a machine language is an *assembly language*. In an assembly language a mnemonic is substituted for each machine language instruction. A mnemonic is made up of two or more letters and usually is an abbreviation for a phrase describing the action to be performed. Thus the

1

mnemonic INX means "INcrement the X register" in 6502 assembly language. The machine language equivalent is binary 11101000 or hexadecimal E8.

In order for an assembly language program to work, it must be translated into machine language. Fortunately this can almost always be done by a computer program called an *assembler*.

While INX is a definite improvement over 11101000 or E8, there is still essentially a one-to-one correspondence between machine language instructions and assembly language instructions. Machine and assembly languages are often called *low-level languages*. What this means is that it takes a lot of instructions to do a little processing, and the programmer has to know and keep track of numerous minute details.

Low-level language programming is difficult. It takes a lot of effort to learn a low-level language. A program written in a low-level language for one computer may not work on another computer. Today microcomputers are selling by the hundreds of thousands. People from every walk of life are buying and programming microcomputers. I think it is safe to say that this wouldn't be happening if only low-level languages existed today.

HIGH-LEVEL LANGUAGES

High-level languages were introduced on large computers in the late fifties. FORTRAN and COBOL were among the first such languages to be introduced. Since then numerous other high-level languages have appeared. These include BASIC, LISP, and Pascal, to name but a few.

How does a high-level language differ from a low-level language? In several ways. Fundamental to the distinction is that one statement in a high-level language is usually equivalent to many statements in a low-level language. The programmer can thus accomplish much more with much less effort.

High-level languages are usually more or less machine-independent. Thus a program written in COBOL to run on one computer can usually be made to run on another computer with only minor changes. Furthermore, a high-level language programmer doesn't have to be aware of and keep track of so many minute details about the computer he is using.

High-level languages are usually designed to be more readable than low-level languages. Suppose, for example that I wanted to add two numbers (A and B) together, giving a third number (C). In 6502 assembly language, this might look something like the following:

```
CLC          ;Clear the carry flag
LDA A        ;Load the accumulator with A
ADC B        ;Add B (with carry)
STA C        ;Store the result in location C
```

This example is short because I have assumed that the numbers in question, including the result, are integers between 0 and 255. If that were not true, the example would be much longer. In BASIC the example would look like this:

```
LET C = A + B
```

In COBOL it would look like this:

```
ADD A TO B GIVING C.
```

Even in this simple case, the high-level languages are much more readable. If I allowed the numbers to be much larger and included fractions, the assembly language example would become much more complex, while the high-level language examples would stay the same.

As is the case with assembly languages, high-level languages must be translated into machine language before a program can run. This is usually accomplished in one of two ways: with a *compiler* or with an *interpreter*. A compiler translates the program all at once. The result is a machine language program which can then be executed. An interpreter translates the program one line at a time, first translating the line and then executing it. The cycle is repeated for each line of the program.

Compiled programs usually run faster than interpreted programs. This is because each line of a compiled program is translated exactly once, regardless of how many times it is executed. A line of an interpreted program may have to be translated more than once if it is to be executed more than once. Interpreted languages, on the other hand, are sometimes easier to use because they do not require the extra compile step. Some languages, such as BASIC, are available on microcomputers in both interpreted and compiled versions. Most languages, however, are available only in one version or the other.

HIGH-LEVEL VERSUS LOW-LEVEL LANGUAGES

The primary advantage of low-level languages is execution speed. A program written in assembly language usually runs many times faster than a comparable program written in a high-level language.

Sometimes speed is critical. For example, a program that will be executed many times in a production environment must be fast. In such cases, the value of the speed advantage is questionable. It usually takes much longer to write and test a program in a low-level language than in a high-level language.

Another advantage of low-level languages is that they provide easy access to the inner workings of a particular machine. This is an advantage when software such as compilers and operating systems is being written.

High-level languages have advantages of their own. High-level languages are usually easier to learn and easier to use than low-level languages. The user need not be concerned about machine-specific details.

A programmer can usually be much more productive with a high-level language. The same operation usually requires fewer steps in a high-level language than in a low-level language. Studies have shown that programmers can usually produce the same number of lines of code per unit time, regardless of the level of language used. It therefore stands to reason that a programmer can effectively accomplish more with a high-level language than with a low-level language.

Because a given high-level language is usually available on many different kinds of computers, large and small, programs written in high-level languages are more portable than programs written in low-level languages. In other words, a program written in a high-level language can usually be run on a variety of different computers. Recall that low-level languages usually will run on only one kind of computer.

Finally, high-level language programs are usually more readable than low-level language programs. This is especially important for programs that must be maintained or modified after they are written, whether the maintenance is by the same programmer or by someone else. Unfortunately high-level language programs are sometimes so poorly written as to be difficult to read; nevertheless, the potential exists for high-level language programs to be much more readable than low-level language programs.

OBJECTIVES OF THIS BOOK

This book describes high-level languages from the point of view of the user. It discusses high-level languages in general in Chapter 2 and then discusses the particular features of various languages currently available for microcomputers. The emphasis is on portraying the "flavor" of each language to provide the reader with an idea of what programming in each language is like. The strengths and weaknesses of each language are explored.

Emphasis has been placed on the features of each language that are common to most implementations. Machine-dependent features such as graphics have been ignored whenever possible. (The major exception to this rule is Logo, in which graphics play a central role.) For the same reason this book will not cover such details such as how to create and run a program on a particular microcomputer. The user is referred to the instruction manual provided with the language for such details.

It is my firm conviction that there is not now, and probably never will be, a single language that is best for every application. Knowledge of more than one language can thus be an advantage because one language might be best for one application, another best for another application, and so on. What might be a long, convoluted program in one language might be trivial in another language. A programming language is a set of tools used to create computer programs. The programmer who limits himself or herself to only one programming language is thus a little like the carpenter who uses only a few tools; the job may get done, but it may not be done as well or as quickly as it might have been.

Chapter 2

General Features of
High-Level Languages

The purpose of this chapter is to describe the various features common to high-level languages in general and so to provide a framework for examining individual languages. This will also provide a convenient framework for making comparisons between the various languages.

DATA REPRESENTATION

Computers are often referred to as electronic data processing machines. All computers process data in one form or another. It is useful to examine the ways in which that data can be represented in high-level languages.

Constants

A *constant* is a data value that does not change. For example the number 12 is a constant; it will always represent the same number.

At the lowest level, computers store data in the binary system (base 2), because the 1s and 0s of the binary system correspond directly to the discrete states of digital electronic devices. When using a high-level language, the programmer need not be very much concerned with such details. What the programmer does need to know is that with some forms of data representation used by high-level languages, numbers that can be represented exactly in the decimal system (base 10) cannot be represented exactly in the binary system (base 2). This can cause some unexpected results; the reasons therefore will be discussed below.

Two forms of number representation that rely internally on the binary system are *integer* values and *real* values. An integer is a whole number written without a decimal point, such as 1, 2, and −5. A real number is a number written with a decimal point and/or an exponent, such as 1.0, 3.1415926, −2.8, or 1.2E5. The last number in the preceding list is read as "1.2 times ten to the fifth power." The E is used to signify powers of ten, corresponding to the *scientific notation* of mathematics.

Integers are represented exactly in computers, but they often have limited ranges. On a microcomputer, integers can typically range between −32768 and +32767. Their range is limited by the amount of memory used for their storage (typically

16 bits or 2 bytes) and by the form of their internal representation.

Real numbers are represented internally in two parts: an *exponent* and a *mantissa*. The number 1.234567890, as an example, would be represented internally as something like "0.123456E1." The "E1" is the exponent part and means "times ten to the first power." The "0.123456" is the mantissa. The last few decimal places were lost due to a restriction on the number of significant digits retained. The number of significant digits available is typically between 6 and 7 and is a function of how much storage is allocated to storing the mantissa. The exponent can typically range between plus and minus 38. This is a function of the number of bits allocated to storage of the exponent.

Another reason that real numbers are not always represented exactly inside the computer has to do with the fact that the internal representation is binary. The number one tenth is easily represented in the decimal system as 0.10, using a finite number of digits. The number one third, however, would require an infinite number of digits for an exact representation in the decimal system (0.333333 . . . . .). In the binary system, neither number can be represented exactly, using only a finite number of digits. The number "one tenth," for example, would look something like 0.09999999 . . . . . .

Some implementations of high-level languages on microcomputers support what are often called *double precision* real numbers. By allocating twice as much storage to such numbers, more significant digits (typically about 14) can be retained. This is often useful in statistical and other scientific applications.

For many applications of computers, integers and real or double precision numbers are adequate. The exception is for financial applications. Accountants like to see their ledgers balance to the penny; they have little sympathy for excuses such as, " . . . . but my computer doesn't represent all numbers exactly." The solution is to use an encoding scheme that represents numbers internally as binary encoded decimal numbers rather than as ordinary binary numbers. This is done at a sacrifice of storage efficiency. In binary, eight bits can rep-

resent numbers between 0 and 255, but in binary encoded decimal the same eight bits can only represent numbers from 0 to 99. The scheme by which this is accomplished is called *BCD*, for binary coded decimal. It permits the exact internal representation of decimal numbers. As you shall see, this feature is supported in only a few of the popular high-level languages.

So far only the representation of numbers has been discussed. Computers must also represent the letters of the alphabet and other characters. This is most commonly done using ASCII, the American standard code for information interchange. In ASCII the letter A is represented by the number 65, the digit 7 by the number 55, and the character % by the number 37. These are all examples of what are referred to as *characters*. A sequence of characters is called a *character string*, or simply a *string*. This type of data is also often referred to as *alphanumeric* data.

Some high-level languages also have a type of data called *logical* or *Boolean* (after George Boole, a nineteenth-century mathematician and logician). There are only two such data elements, true and false.

Variables

A variable in a computer language is often thought of as something mysterious out of a mathematical formula. A variable is not mysterious at all; it can be thought of as a place to store a data value. In fact, a variable is simply a name given to a particular place in the computer's memory where a value will be stored. The compiler or interpreter takes care of the details of setting aside and keeping track of the necessary memory for storing variables.

Variables are indispensable to all but the simplest computer programs. If it weren't for the availability of variables, you would have to write a new program for every different set of data you wanted to process. Thus you would need a new program to balance the same checkbook every month!

When a variable takes on a new value, it simply means that new value has been stored in the place allocated to that variable, displacing whatever was there before.

In most languages a particular variable can hold only one type of data (real, integer, or string). Some languages require that the user specify in advance what variables he or she intends to use and what type each of these variables is to be. Other languages have default (assumed) types based on the first or last letter of a variable's name.

High-level languages that are very particular about what types of variables are used, how they are declared, and how they are used are called *strongly-typed* languages. Pascal is an example of a strongly-typed language. Languages that are more lax about such matters are said to be *loosely-typed*. BASIC is an example of a loosely-typed language. There are advantages and disadvantages to each approach. Simply stated, loosely-typed languages are more forgiving, but strongly-typed languages provide better protection against stupid mistakes.

THE ASSIGNMENT STATEMENT

An assignment statement is used to assign a particular value to a variable. Most languages denote this operation by a symbol called an *assignment operator*. Most languages use either the equals sign, =, or a colon followed by an equals sign, :=, for the assignment operator. For example, suppose you wish to assign the value 5.1 to a real variable X. In Pascal you would write

X := 5.1;

in BASIC you would write either

LET X = 5.1

or, simply,

X = 5.1.

One reason Pascal and some other languages do not use the simpler = for an assignment operator is that the assignment operator doesn't really indicate equality. Suppose, for example, that you want to add 1 to X and store the result back in X. In BASIC or FORTRAN you could write

X = X + 1.

But how can X "equal" X + 1? It can't. It is good practice to read the assignment operator as "is assigned the value of," regardless of what symbol is used. The above would thus be read, "X is assigned the value of X plus 1." An alternate way to read it would be, "X takes on the value of X + 1."

ARITHMETIC EXPRESSIONS

The easiest way to describe an arithmetic expression is to give examples. First of all, a constant such as 1.2 is an arithmetic expression. A numeric variable such as X can be an arithmetic expression. In most high-level languages, an arithmetic expression followed by an arithmetic operator (+, −, etc.) followed by another arithmetic expression is also an arithmetic expression. Examples of this are X + 1, X + Y, and 2 * X. (The * means multiplication. The division operator is /.)

Arithmetic expressions can also contain parentheses. By repeated use of the above rules, more complex arithmetic expressions can be formed:

(X − Y)*(X + Y)
2*(3*(X + 4)/(Y − 5)))

Perhaps the key feature of arithmetic expressions is that they can be evaluated to a numeric value according to a given set of rules.

In the arithmetic expression

X + 2,

the X and the 2 are called *operands* and the + is called an *operator*. In most high-level languages the operator goes between the operands. This is sometimes called *infix* notation. A few high-level languages, such as LISP and Forth, use other forms of notation. LISP uses *prefix* notation (also called *Cambridge Polish* notation) in which the operator comes first followed by the two operands. In LISP the above expression would be written as

(+ X 2), or (PLUS X 2).

Forth uses *postfix* notation (also called *reverse Polish* notation) in which the two operands come first, followed by the operator. In this notation the above expression would be written as

X 2 +.

The word *Polish* in the descriptions of the above two kinds of notation is in honor of the Polish mathematician Jan Lukasiewicz (1878-1956), who pioneered prefix notation.

The expression is one of the key features that distinguishes high-level languages from low-level languages. In low-level language you can usually do only one thing at a time, that is, one operation per statement. An arithmetic expression in a high-level language permits the programmer to accomplish many calculations with only one statement.

LOGICAL EXPRESSIONS

If an arithmetic expression evaluates to an arithmetic value, then you can rightly expect that a *logical expression* evaluates to a logical value, that is, true or false. The most common form of logical expression involves relational operators such as $>$, $<$, $=$, $<=$, $>=$, and $<>$. The last three operators are read as "less than or equal," "greater than or equal," and "not equal," respectively. Thus

3 > 2

is a logical expression and evaluates to true.

If the variable X has the value 2 and the variable Y has the value 3, the expression

X + 2 = Y − 1

equates to false.

High-level languages also feature logical operators such as AND, OR, and NOT. The NOT operator changes the value of a logical expression from true to false or from false to true. Thus the expression

NOT (3 > 2)

evaluates to false, and

NOT (2 > 3)

evaluates to true.

The other two logical operators are a little more difficult to explain. First, note that each has two operands (NOT has only one). Each operand is a logical expression; one operand precedes and one follows the operator. The behavior of these operators is best described using truth tables. In the following truth tables, let A and B stand for logical expressions.

A	B	A AND B
-----	-----	------
TRUE	TRUE	TRUE
TRUE	FALSE	FALSE
FALSE	TRUE	FALSE
FALSE	FALSE	FALSE

Thus the logical expression A AND B is true if and only if A is true and B is true.

The following truth table describes the behavior of the OR operator.

A	B	A OR B
-----	-----	------
TRUE	TRUE	TRUE
TRUE	FALSE	TRUE
FALSE	TRUE	TRUE
FALSE	FALSE	FALSE

Thus the logical expression A OR B is false if and only if both A AND B are false.

More complex logical expressions can be constructed by combining simpler logical expressions. The liberal use of parentheses is advisable in order to eliminate any possibility of ambiguity.

INPUT AND OUTPUT

Processing data wouldn't be of much value if the results couldn't be printed out either on a screen or on a printer. In most languages, the statement that performs this function is called WRITE or PRINT or something similar. Most languages use the same or a similar statement whether the output device is a screen or a printer.

One way to give values to variables is, as we have seen, with the assignment statement. Another way is to read the values from the keyboard. In most languages the command to do this is called the READ statement or something similar. In BASIC, however, the appropriate command is called INPUT.

The various languages differ in how much control the user has over the format of the output. Useful formatting features include the ability to control the number of decimal places printed, the total number of columns allocated to a number, and so on.

Suppose you want a program to print "Enter Check Number:" and then to read the value into a variable called CKNR. In Pascal this would be accomplished as follows:

```
WRITE('Enter Check Number:   ');
READLN(CKNR);
```

In BASIC the same thing could be accomplished this way:

```
INPUT "Enter Check Number:   ";CKNR
```

Other languages have similar facilities.

Most languages also have facilities for reading data from the writing data to disk files. These facilities are discussed under the heading File Handling.

CONTROL STRUCTURES

The natural flow of control through a program is sequential. That is, each statement is executed in the order in which it is found, beginning with the first statement in the program and ending with the last. For all but the simplest applications, sequential flow of control by itself is inadequate. For most programs a more complicated control structure is needed.

Simple Selection: The IF-THEN-ELSE Statement

Consider, for example, a program that must calculate the pay of a worker. If that worker works 40 or fewer hours in a week, the pay is the number of hours worked times his/her wage rate. If the number of hours worked is more than 40, he/she is paid one-and-a-half times the regular wage rate for all hours in excess of 40. One way to calculate this is in FORTRAN 77 follows:

```
IF (HOURS .LE. 40) THEN
    PAY = HOURS * WAGE
ELSE
    PAY = 40 * WAGE + (HOURS − 40) *
    WAGE * 1.5
ENDIF.
```

(Note: the .LE. stands for less than or equal to.)

The beauty of the IF-THEN-ELSE construct is that what it does is almost self-explanatory. If the logical expression is true, it executes the statements following the THEN and then passes control to the statement following the ENDIF. Otherwise (ELSE), it executes the statements following the ELSE. In either case, the next statement to be executed is the statement following the ENDIF.

The IF-THEN-ELSE construct is extremely important in high-level languages. It allows the program to handle basic decisions, yet what happens next is clear. The reader is cautioned to avoid statements of the general form IF-THEN-GOTO whenever possible. The reason for this injunction is that it is difficult to follow the flow of control in programs that contain this type of statement because it is not always clear what happens next.

It should be pointed out that the ELSE part of the construct is optional. For example, suppose that a program is computing tax refunds for the

Internal Revenue Service and must set all amounts less than $1.00 to zero. This could be accomplished in FORTRAN 77 as

```
IF (AMT .LT. 1.00) THEN
   AMT = 0.0
END IF
```

or in the older versions of FORTRAN as

```
IF (AMT .LT. 1.00) AMT = 0.0.
```

Logically, this is equivalent to an IF-THEN-ELSE statement with an empty or null ELSE part.

The CASE Statement

The IF-THEN-ELSE statement allows two-way selection: the program selects one of two sets of statements to execute. Often it is necessary for the program to choose between more than two alternatives. The CASE statement provides a convenient way to do this.

CASE statements occur frequently in interactive programs. For example, suppose an educational program contained a multiple-choice question, such as, "Who is buried in Grant's Tomb?" In Pascal this could be programmed as follows:

```
WRITELN('Who is buried in Grant's
   Tomb?');
WRITELN('     1) Abraham Lincoln');
WRITELN('     2) General Grant');
WRITELN('     3) Groucho Marx');
WRITE('Select 1, 2, or 3:   );
READLN(I);
CASE I OF
   1:  WRITELN('Sorry, it was Grant.');
   2:  WRITELN('Right on!');
   3:  WRITELN('Sorry, it was Grant.');
END;
```

In this case exactly one of the responses will be printed; which one depends on the value typed in for the variable I.

The GO TO Statement

The GO TO or GOTO statement allows program control to be transferred to any arbitrary place in a program. At first thought, this might seem to be a great convenience. Experience has shown, however, that indiscriminant use of the GO TO statement can lead to programs that are hard to read, hard to debug, and hard to modify. It is the author's firm conviction that the GO TO statement is to be avoided whenever possible. In some languages, however, it is needed in order to emulate control structures such as REPEAT-UNTIL (introduced below) that are not directly implemented. This technique is often necessary in BASIC and FORTRAN.

Loops

One thing that computers do especially well is repetition. If you asked a person to add up the populations of all cities in the United States with populations between 10,000 and 25,000, that person would likely become bored with the task quickly and make mistakes; not so with a computer. Provided the computer was programmed properly and given access to the raw data, it would complete the task quickly, accurately, and without complaint.

The control structure that performs repetitive tasks in a computer language is called a *loop*. There are two major types of loops in high-level languages, the counted loop and the conditional loop.

Counted Loops. In a counted loop, the statements within the body of the loop are repeated a specified number of times. Each counted loop has a counter variable. At the beginning of the loop the counter is set to a specified initial value. After the body of the loop has been executed, the counter is incremented and compared to its specified upper bound. If the upper bound has not been exceeded, the body of the loop will be executed again. If the upper bound has been exceeded, control passes to the statement following the end of the loop.

All of this is easier than it sounds. Here is a simple example in the BASIC language. The program prints out the numbers from 1 to 10:

```
10   FOR I = 1 TO 10
20       PRINT I
30   NEXT I
40   END
```

In this example I is the counter variable. At the beginning of the loop, I is set to 1. The body of the loop (the statements between the line beginning with FOR and the line beginning with NEXT) is then executed. In this case the body of the loop is simply line number 20, and the number 1 is printed. At line 30, the bottom of the loop, the counter I will be incremented to 2 and then compared to the upper bound (in this case 10). Since 2 is less than 10, the body of the loop will be executed again and the number 2 will be printed. This cycle is repeated. When the number 10 is finally printed, the counter I will be incremented to 11. Because 11 is larger than 10 (the specified upper bound), execution will pass to statement 40, which terminates the program.

Conditional Loops. Another type of loop is the conditional loop, often called the *while* loop. Whereas the counted loop executes a group of statements a specified number of times, the conditional loop executes a group of statements until a specified condition is met.

Clearly, a conditional loop can do the work of a counted loop. Here is the above example repeated using a conditional loop:

```
10   I = 1
20   WHILE I <= 10
30       PRINT I
40       I = I + 1
50   WEND
60   END
```

(Note: some versions of BASIC, such as Applesoft, do not include the WHILE statement.)

In this case it took a few extra statements to do the same job with a conditional loop. This was a task better suited to a counted loop.

Suppose instead you want to read numbers from a keyboard until a 0 or negative number is encountered and to add up the numbers. This requires a little planning, as the WHILE loop tests the condition before it executes the loop for the first time. That is why the first read is outside the loop. Here is how this example could be done in BASIC:

```
10   SUM = 0
20   INPUT "ENTER X:   ";X
30   WHILE X > 0
40       SUM = SUM + X
50       INPUT "ENTER X:";X
60   WEND
70   PRINT "SUM = ";SUM
80   END
```

In line 10, SUM is initialized to 0. In line 20, the first value of X is read. Line 30 checks to see whether or not the current value of X is greater than 0. If it is, statements 40 and 50, which add X to SUM and get the next X, are executed. The loop is repeated until an X less than or equal to 0 is encountered. When that happens, control passes to statement 70.

A few languages offer a variant of the conditional loop in which the conditional testing takes place at the bottom of the loop rather than at the top, as is the case with the WHILE loop. In Pascal this variant is called the REPEAT-UNTIL loop. Here is the previous example in Pascal using the REPEAT-UNTIL construct:

```
SUM := 0;
REPEAT
  WRITE('ENTER X:   ');
  READLN(X);
  SUM := SUM + X
UNTIL X <= 0;
WRITELN('SUM = ';SUM);
```

The problem with this example is that it doesn't work as intended. See if you can find the problem before reading on.

The above example initializes the variable SUM to 0 and then repeats the three statements between REPEAT and UNTIL until the variable X becomes less than or equal to 0. The intent is to add up all the numbers in a list, not including the negative number used to stop the loop. The problem is that the value of X is added to SUM before X is tested. Thus when a negative number is entered to stop the loop, that number will be added to SUM before the loop is terminated.

Subroutines

Often it is convenient to divide programs into more-or-less self-contained segments or modules. Such modules are usually called *subroutines* or *procedures*. A subroutine or procedure is usually placed off by itself in a program, sometimes at the beginning of the program and sometimes at the end, depending on the language. Some languages permit the subroutines to be external to the program, perhaps on a system disk.

Subroutines are activated or called by a *CALL statement*. A CALL statement causes the subroutine to be invoked, and when the subroutine has finished, program control reverts to the statement following the CALL statement. The format of CALL statements varies from language to language. FORTRAN uses the word CALL followed by the name of the subroutine; BASIC uses GOSUB followed by a line number. In most other languages, a subroutine is invoked simply by writing its name.

There are several possible reasons for using a subroutine, including the following:

1. The use of subroutines permits large tasks to be divided into smaller, more manageable tasks. This is sometimes called the "divide and conquer" strategy. This strategy is a very important program design technique. Problems which seem otherwise unmanageable can often be handled easily when broken into appropriate modules.
2. Because a CALL statement can occur as many times as necessary in a program, the use of subroutines can often save considerable typing. For example, suppose a sort needs to be done twice in a program. If a subroutine is not used, the sort routine must be typed into the program twice, once in each place it is needed. If a sub-

routine is used, the sort routine need be typed into the program only once; it can be called as often as it is needed from other parts of the program.
3. If commonly-used routines are programmed in the form of subroutines, they can be easily transported from one program to another. Suppose you have written a good sorting subroutine for one program and now you need a sorting subroutine in another program. Chances are you will be able to reuse the original sorting subroutine. Programmers often develop libraries of commonly-used subroutines.

High-level languages usually use *parameters* and *arguments* to pass values back and forth between the subroutine and the calling program. Consider a subroutine designed to exchange the values of two numerical variables. Here is how such a subroutine might look in FORTRAN.

```
SUBROUTINE SWAP(X,Y)
   TEMP = X
   X = Y
   Y = TEMP
RETURN
END
```

The X and Y are called parameters of the subroutine. When the subroutine is called, the two variables to be exchanged might be named P and Q. Here is how a call to SWAP to exchange P and Q would look:

```
CALL SWAP(P,Q).
```

P and Q are referred to as arguments of the CALL statement. Later in the program, the variables R and S may need to be exchanged. The sort subroutine could be called again using R and S as arguments:

```
CALL SWAP(R,S).
```

Functions

Subroutines pass values using parameters and arguments, and are invoked by some form of CALL statement. Functions are similar to subroutines except in the manner in which they are invoked and in the manner in which values are returned to the invoking program.

Some functions are usually supplied as part of a language. These usually include functions for computing square roots, sines, cosines, and so on. Suppose you wanted to compute the square root of 4. In FORTRAN you would write

$$X = SQRT(4.0).$$

The SQRT is the name of a function built into FORTRAN for this purpose. The argument is 4.0. Note that the function is invoked by writing its name in an expression as if it were simply another variable. The result, in this case 2.0, is returned and used in the expression as if it were the value of a variable named SQRT. In this case, the result is assigned to the variable X.

Functions can be defined by the user in much the same manner as subroutines are defined. One difference is that the name of the function is usually treated as if it were a variable within the body of the function definition. This is how the value to be returned by the function to the invoking routine is usually determined. Using FORTRAN as an example, suppose a function is needed to return the larger of two integers. The code might appear as follows:

```
FUNCTION MAX(I,J)
  IF I .GE. J THEN
    MAX = I
  ELSE
    MAX = J
  ENDIF
RETURN.
END
```

(Note: older versions of FORTRAN do not include the IF-THEN-ELSE construct. The .GE. stands for greater than or equal to.)

The differences between functions and subroutines will be explored more fully in the chapters on individual languages.

Recursion

Another method of controlling the flow of program execution is called *recursion*. A function or subroutine is said to be recursive if it calls or invokes itself. Some languages such as FORTRAN and COBOL do not permit recursion. In other languages such as LISP and Logo, recursion is the most commonly used form of program control.

At first encounter, recursion seems mysterious to many beginning programmers—sort of like the snake that swallowed its own tail. Actually, recursion is simply another way of invoking repetition in a program. Of course the repetition would go on forever without some sort of escape mechanism. Recursive functions and subroutines must therefore check for termination conditions before invoking themselves again.

Certain applications are more naturally expressed using recursion rather than other forms of repetition. Computer language compilers use recursion. Many other applications can be written using either recursion or other forms of repetition. It is difficult to explain in a few words when recursion is most appropriate. Examples of recursive applications can be found in subsequent chapters.

DATA STRUCTURES

It is often convenient to be able to refer to a collection of related variables by a common name. For example, suppose you wanted to write a program to compute statistics describing the test scores of 26 students. You could use the letters A to Z with each letter representing one score. The resulting program would be tedious to say the least.

Arrays

A better solution is to use an *array*. Suppose the array name is SCORE. Then SCORE(1) would refer to the score of the first student, SCORE(2) to the score of the second student, and so on. The numbers in parentheses are called *subscripts*. SCORE is an example of an array with one subscript (even though that one subscript can take on various values).

Suppose that you needed a data structure in which to record the number of points scored in each of 20 games by each of 10 basketball players. An easy way to handle this situation is to use an array with two subscripts. Suppose the name of this array were POINTS. Then POINTS(1,3) would contain the number of points scored by the first player in the third game; POINTS(7,19), the number of points scored by the seventh player in the nineteenth game, and so on. Such an array is often called a *two-dimensional* array. In some languages, arrays can have more than two dimensions if needed.

Arrays are often used in conjunction with loops. Suppose, for example, that you want to set all the elements of the two-dimensional array POINTS to 0. This can be done easily using loops. Here is how it might look in BASIC:

```
10   FOR I = 1 TO 10
20      FOR J = 1 TO 20
30         POINTS(I,J) = 0
40      NEXT J
50   NEXT I
```

If the loop structure were not available, it could take 200 statements to accomplish the same thing.

The programmer must usually tell the compiler or interpreter in advance which variable names stand for arrays, how many subscripts each array has, and the range (permissible values) of each subscript. How this is done is peculiar to each language and will be covered for each language in the appropriate chapter.

Records

A limitation of arrays is that each element of the array must be of the same type, that is, integer, real, or alphanumeric (string). In the example above, POINTS was assumed to contain all integers. Suppose instead that you want to set up a grade book to keep track of the students in a class. You would need to record the name of each student and various numerical grades scored by that student. Note that name is an alphanumeric variable but that each grade is numeric. It is useful in this situation to have the concept of a *record*.

A record is a collection of related information,

where each element of the information may be of a different type. Suppose you wanted to set up a record called STUDENT, containing a student's name and his or her score on each of twenty tests. Each record should thus contain a string variable for the name, and an array with 20 numerical elements. Some languages, such as Pascal and COBOL, implement records directly. How this is done will be described in the appropriate chapters. With other languages, such as BASIC and FORTRAN, records must be simulated using *parallel arrays*. In this example, two arrays would be needed, a string array called NAME, and a numeric array called GRADES. NAME would be a one-dimensional array having as many elements as there were students. GRADES would be a two-dimensional array (similar to POINTS above), with the first subscript determining to which student the grade belongs, and the second subscript indicating on which test that grade was scored. Thus if Bill Smith were the fifteenth student, and he scored a 90 on his third test, NAMES(15) would contain "Bill Smith" and GRADES(15,3) would contain 90.

Arrays Revisited

One advantage of an array is that any element of that array can be addressed directly, independently of all other elements of the array. Thus you could refer to NAME(2) without referring to NAME(1). This feature is often quite useful.

Arrays may have disadvantages in certain situations. Suppose, for example, you have an array called NAME, containing the first names of 10 men. Suppose NAME(1) is Al, NAME(2) is Bob, NAME(3) is Carl, and so on. You want to keep the names in alphabetical order. Now suppose you have to add a new name, Bill, to the list. Bill should fit between Al and Bob. The problem is that to do so requires that Bob, Carl, and all other names be moved down one place in the list to make room for Bill. If NAME is part of a record (see the above example), the rest of the record (in this example the array GRADES) would have to be adjusted accordingly.

An analogous situation occurs when you want

to delete an element from an array. The elements following the deleted element may need to be moved forward to close the gap.

Lists

You have just seen that arrays have the advantage that individual elements are accessible independently and the disadvantage that adding to or deleting from an ordered array may be difficult. In some instances, you might be willing to give up independent access to elements (settling for sequential access) in exchange for ease in inserting and deleting elements. It turns out that there is a data structure called a *list* with just these properties.

The major properties of a list are that access is strictly sequential and that elements can be easily added to or deleted from the list. By allowing a list to be an element of another list, more complex data structures such as trees can be constructed. How this is done is beyond the scope of this book; you are referred to a book on data structures for more details.

In LISP and Logo, the list is the principle data structure. Some languages such as Pascal have facilities for the easy implementation of lists. With other languages such as BASIC and FORTRAN, lists must be implemented using arrays. How this is done will be illustrated below.

In general, an element can be added to a list at the beginning, at the end, or anywhere in the middle. The same goes for retrieving or deleting an element from the list. (Of course accessing interior elements requires sequential access.) A list with the property that elements can be added or deleted only from the ends (one at a time) is called a queue. If additions and deletions can take place at only one end, the queue is called a stack, or a *last in first out* (LIFO) queue. In the Forth language, the stack is the most important data structure.

As an example of how a list might be used in a program, suppose you wish to maintain a list of names in alphabetical order. The list initially contains the names Bob, Ernie, and Jim, who all work in an office. Jerry joins the organization and needs to

be added to the list between Ernie and Jim.

As described above, if you were to maintain the names in a simple array, you would need to move Jim to make room for Jerry. While this would work easily for such a short list, for longer lists it would be cumbersome. A better way would be to maintain the names as a linked list.

For this example, suppose that there can be a maximum of 5 names in the list. Several variables are needed to implement the list. An array of 5 elements is needed to hold the names themselves. Call this array NAME. Another array of 5 elements is needed to hold the *links* between names. Call this array LINK. Another name for a link is a *pointer*.

A pointer points to an element of an array if the value of the pointer is the value of the subscript of that element of the array. For example, if P is a variable being used as a pointer into array NAME and if it has the value 5, it points to array element NAME(5).

A variable is needed to point to the first (alphabetically) name in the list. Call this variable FIRST. FIRST is used to store the subscript of the first name. Similarly, the variable FREE will be used as a pointer to the first free (unused) record of the list.

Once the list has been entered, each link points to the next name in the list. For example, suppose FIRST points to element 3. To find the name in the list which follows NAME(3) alphabetically, look at LINK(3). If LINK(3) has value 1, that means that NAME(1) follows NAME(3) alphabetically.

A value is needed to signal the end of the list. This value is usually 0 or −1, depending on the language. For languages with arrays that always begin with subscript 1 (such as FORTRAN and COBOL), the value 0 is usually used. For languages with arrays that begin with subscript 0 (such as BASIC and C), the value −1 is usually used. For this example, the value 0 will be used. Thus if LINK(4) has the value 0, it means that there are no more names in the list to point to after NAME(4).

For our example, the list might initially look as follows:

```
FIRST = 1
FREE  = 4

      NAME      LINK

1     Bob       2
2     Ernie     3
3     Jim       0
4               5
5               0
```

Follow the links of the chain from FIRST; FIRST points to NAME(1), which is Bob. LINK(1) points to NAME(2), which is Ernie. LINK(2) points to NAME(3), which is Jim. LINK(3) has value 0, meaning that NAME(3) is the end of the list.

Each element of the list is often called a *record*. Recall the discussion above about records as implemented by parallel arrays. In this case, a record consists of a name and a link. The list of active records is sometimes called the *active list*.

There is another list called the *free list*. It is a chain of unused records. Following this chain from FREE, FREE points to record 4. LINK(4) points to record 5. Record 5 is the end of the free list. It is so designated because LINK(5) has value 0.

Now let us consider what happens when Jerry is added to the list. His name is written in record 4, because record 4 was the first record in the free list. The other pointers are adjusted so as to add record 4 to the proper place in the active list and to remove record 4 from the free list. Here is how the updated list looks:

```
FIRST = 1
FREE  = 5

      NAME      LINK

1     Bob       2
2     Ernie     4
3     Jim       0
4     Jerry     3
5               0
```

At first glance, the list now appears out of sequence. Following the chain from FIRST, however, you see that FIRST points to Bob (FIRST = 1); Bob points to Ernie (LINK(1) = 2); Ernie points to Jerry (LINK(2) = 4); Jerry points to Jim (LINK(4) = 3); and Jim is the end of the list (LINK(3) = 0).

After some time, Ernie retires and needs to be removed from the list. Record 2, the record occupied by Ernie, then needs to be removed from the active list and added to the free list. This is done by manipulating the links. Here is the result:

```
FIRST = 1
FREE  = 2

      NAME      LINK

1     Bob       4
2     Ernie     5
3     Jim       0
4     Jerry     3
5               0
```

Ernie appears to be still in the list. Following the active list from FIRST, however, reveals that he is not. Record 2 is now the first record in the free list. The fact that Ernie's name is still there is not a problem. The next name to be added will be written to the first record in the free list, which is now record 2. Ernie's name will then be overwritten.

Examples of the use of lists in various languages are included in the following chapters. These examples show the details of how a record is added to and deleted from a list.

FILE HANDLING

If the amount of data to be processed by a program is small, it can be typed in from the keyboard whenever it is needed. In many computer applications, however, the data must be carried forward from one run of the program to the next run, and the quantity of data soon becomes too large to type in every time. For this situation you need data files.

Computer programs used in business applications usually rely heavily on data files. Examples of such applications include general ledger, accounts receivable, accounts payable, inventory records, and other such programs. In selecting a language for such applications, the file handling features of the candidate languages should be examined closely.

Data files on microcomputers are most often kept on floppy disks. Some newer systems use hard disks. Floppy disks usually come in 8 inch and 5¼ inch sizes, but some new floppy disks are coming out in the 3¼, 3½, and 3.9 inch sizes. Floppy disks are convenient because they can be removed from the disk drive and stored in a safe place. Floppy disks typically hold from 100 kilobytes (a kilobyte is about 1 thousand characters) to 1.2 megabytes (a megabyte is about 1 million characters) of data.

Hard disks are not usually removable from the disk drive, but they provide faster access to the data, and each unit holds 5 megabytes or more. Hard disk drives also cost substantially more than floppy disk drives. This may change in the future, however.

Records

The concept of a record (discussed above) is very important in business and other applications that require file handling. It is very convenient to be able to read or write an entire record from or to the disk in a single operation. Consider, for example, a record that contains the name, address, and telephone number of an individual; to read such a record from the disk should require only one disk access.

COBOL was the first major language to handle records in files conveniently. Among the languages which have come later, PL/I, Pascal, C, Ada, and Modula 2 also provide facilities for dealing with records conveniently. Other languages make dealing with records less convenient.

Sequential Access

A *sequential access* file must be read (and written) sequentially from beginning to end. In other words, to read the thirty-second record in the file, the program must first read the first record, then the second, and so on, until it reaches the thirty-second record. In the earlier days of computing when files were kept mainly on magnetic tapes, this was the only way files could be organized. It was a restriction imposed by the physical characteristics of the storage medium. That physical restriction does not exist for disk files, but it is still convenient in some cases to organize disk files sequentially. This is usually the case when every record in the file must be processed during a run.

Direct-Access Files

Any record in a *direct-access* file can be accessed directly, without any other records in the file having to be accessed. For example, with a direct-access file, the program can access record 32 without previously accessing records 1 through 31. Direct-access files are frequently also called *random access* files. That is a slight misnomer, as most programmers prefer to access their files from predetermined rather than random locations.

To access a record in a direct-access file, the record number must be known. Thus the programmer must set up some means of keeping track of what information is in what record. This usually means maintaining an index of some sort.

Indexed Files

Some versions of COBOL (the more expensive versions) provide for the automatic maintenance of an index for a file. This can relieve the programmer of a significant burden. Unfortunately the version of COBOL described in this book lacks that feature.

GRAPHICS

Some microcomputer languages have built-in graphics features. Unfortunately there is no standard way to handle graphics on large or small computers. Even among different versions of BASIC, there is no standard way to handle graphics. How a particular version of a language handles graphics (if it does) is usually a function of the microcomputer on which it is implemented. For that reason, the graphics features of high-level languages are not discussed in this book.

There is one exception to the above rule—

Logo. All versions of Logo of which the author is aware share the same basic graphic capabilities. Furthermore, graphics is an important part of the Logo language. Thus, the chapter on Logo will include a discussion of Logo's graphic capabilities.

SUMMARY

This chapter has explored in general terms the distinguishing features of high-level languages. Familiarity with these features will make the understanding of specific languages easier. The chapter on a specific language will describe in more detail how these features are implemented in that particular language. This chapter has attempted to establish a framework for examining individual languages and for comparing one language to another.

Chapter 3

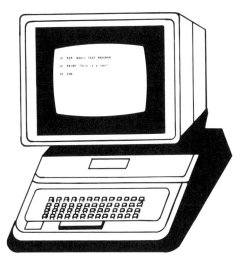

BASIC

The name BASIC is an acronym for Beginner's All-purpose Symbolic Instruction Code. The language was created in 1965 at Dartmouth College by John Kemeny and Thomas Kurtz. As the name suggests, it was intended as a simplified language, suitable for instructing beginners in computer programming.

BASIC is usually implemented as an interpretive language. What this means is that the program is translated into machine code a line at a time rather than all at once. The software that does this translation is called a BASIC *interpreter*. Because BASIC is a relatively simple language, a BASIC interpreter that occupies a relatively small amount of memory can be written.

In the early days of microcomputers (before 1976), there were very few high-level languages available that would fit in the limited memory available in a microcomputer. Intel had a language called PL/M (written by Gary Kildall), but it was most suitable for systems programming. Gordon Eubanks had written the forerunner of CBASIC as a

masters' thesis project at the Naval Postgraduate School in Monterey. CBASIC later proved popular for business applications, but PL/M never really caught on for general use.

In 1976, William Gates and Paul Allen wrote a BASIC interpreter for the Altair microcomputer. Finally there was a microcomputer high-level language for the masses. With their BASIC interpreter as the foundation, Gates and Allen founded Microsoft, Inc., which is today a leading microcomputer software house. Since then, their original BASIC interpreter has evolved into various versions known collectively as Microsoft BASIC. Microsoft BASIC and its various derivatives (including Applesoft, TRS-80 BASIC, and Commodore BASIC) have become the most widely-used versions of BASIC in the marketplace.

Today BASIC is by far the most widely-used high-level language in use on microcomputers. Many popular microcomputers, such as Apple, Radio Shack, and Commodore products, are sold with a BASIC interpreter in read only memory

(ROM). BASIC is also sold on disk for various computers, including those which run the CP/M operating system. Disk-based BASIC interpreters are usually more powerful than ROM-based BASIC interpreters.

Unfortunately the various versions of BASIC available for microcomputers differ somewhat from each other. The examples in this chapter were tested using Microsoft BASIC Version 5.2, running under the CP/M operating system on an Apple II microcomputer with an accessory Z80 processor card.

PROGRAM STRUCTURE

A BASIC program is simply a sequence of program statements. Each line of the program begins with a line number. A simple BASIC program that does nothing but display "This is a test" is shown in Fig. 3-1.

```
10   REM   BASIC TEST PROGRAM

20   PRINT "This is a test"

30   END
```

Fig. 3-1. A simple BASIC program.

Line 10 of the program is a remark or REM statement. It serves merely as a comment. Line 20 does the actual printing, and line 30 stops the program—pretty simple.

Statements in BASIC often occur one per line. Most versions of BASIC permit more than one statement per line, provided that the statements are separated by a special character, usually a colon (:). The default sequence of execution of a BASIC program is in order of increasing line numbers, regardless of the order in which the lines were typed.

Some versions of BASIC permit remarks to be placed on a line after the single quote (or apostrophe) symbol.

DATA REPRESENTATION

The more complete versions of BASIC support real, integer, double precision, and character string data types. Some versions lack either the real or the integer type, and many versions lack the double precision type.

Variables

Variable types in BASIC are usually distinguished by the last character of the variable name. If the last character of the variable name is a percent sign (%), then the variable is of the integer type. If it is a dollar sign ($), the variable is of the character string type. If it is a pound sign (#), the variable is of the double precision type. If it is an exclamation point (!) or anything else, the variable is assumed to be of the real type.

Some versions of BASIC allow the default type of a variable to be changed according to the first letter of the variable name. For example.

```
10   DEFINT I
```

would cause all variables beginning with the letter I to be integer variables unless otherwise specified.

BASIC variables are initialized automatically to 0 in the case of numeric variables and to the empty string in the case of character strings.

Constants

Numeric constants in a BASIC program can also be defined as specific types if they are followed by one of the symbols shown above (%, $, #, or !). Character strings are surrounded by double quotation marks.

Although there is usually no explicit Boolean or logical type of value in BASIC, the value 0 usually means false and the value −1 true in the appropriate context. This is discussed in more detail in the section on logical expressions.

THE ASSIGNMENT STATEMENT

The assignment operator in BASIC is the equals sign (=). In the original version of BASIC, all assignment statements had to begin with the keyword LET, as in

    20   LET X = 5.

In most versions of BASIC today, the LET keyword is optional and

    20   X = 5

will accomplish the same thing.

BASIC allows assignment between the various numeric variable types. The value of the expression on the right side of the assignment statement is automatically converted to the type of the variable on the left side before the assignment takes place. Common sense is the guide.

ARITHMETIC EXPRESSIONS

BASIC uses conventional infix notation (see Chapter 2) for its arithmetic expressions. The arithmetic operators are conventional (+, −, *, and /), except for the symbol for exponentiation, which is the up-arrow (↑). Parentheses have the usual meaning.

LOGICAL EXPRESSIONS

BASIC uses the usual logical operators as listed in Chapter 2; for example, <, and OR. Logical expressions normally evaluate to the logical values TRUE or FALSE, but BASIC has no explicit logical values. Logical values in BASIC are represented by numerical values. The value 0 usually represents FALSE, and the value −1 often represents TRUE, although this convention can vary between versions of BASIC. The logical expression

    5 > 2

thus evaluates to −1.

INPUT AND OUTPUT

The PRINT statement in Fig. 3-1 sends output to the system console. To output to the system printer, the LPRINT statement is used instead. Figure 3-2 is a simple example of the use of the LPRINT statement. (Applesoft BASIC and many other forms of BASIC used on microcomputers do not have LPRINT statements. Users of these systems are referred to their BASIC manuals for instructions on using a printer.)

Whether or not a PRINT or LPRINT statement causes a carriage return and line feed at its end is determined by the punctuation used. The statement

    10   PRINT "HELLO";

sends a carriage return and line feed to the screen. The statement

    10   PRINT "HELLO";

does not. The difference is the semicolon at the end. The semicolon suppresses the carriage return and line feed.

The statement

    10   PRINT Hello", "Hello", "Hello"

if repeated several times would print the word in three separate columns. The comma between items in the print list causes the printing to continue in the next column. The width of each column depends on the implementation.

The LPRINT statement responds to punctuation in the same way as the PRINT statement does.

The PRINT and LPRINT statements do not give the user very much control over the appearance of the output. As an example, they do not allow the user to control the number of decimal places to be printed for real numbers. The better versions of BASIC therefore provide the PRINT USING and LPRINT USING statements. The LPRINT USING statement is equivalent to the PRINT USING statement except that it directs its output to the printer, so only the PRINT USING statement will be described.

The PRINT USING statement uses a charac-

```
10    REM   TEST LPRINT

20    PRINT "This goes to the video screen."

30    LPRINT "This goes to the printer."

40    END
```

Fig. 3-2. A BASIC printer demonstration.

ter string enclosed in quotation marks to control the appearance of the output. For example,

```
10   X = 1/3
20   PRINT USING "##.###"; X
```

would print " 0.333" on the screen. The # symbol represents a numerical digit. The character string "##.###" means that the number is to be printed in a field six spaces wide (including the decimal point) and that three digits are to be printed to the right of the decimal point. If X had the value 172.945, the printed result would be "%172.95". The % sign in front of the number means that the number was too large to fit in the allotted number of spaces. (In this case only two spaces were allotted to the left of the decimal point.) The fractional part of the number was rounded to two decimal places before printing.

The PRINT USING statement can use various other symbols in the character string to specify such things as the leading dollar sign, plus or minus signs, and so on.

Data is read from the keyboard by the INPUT statement. The INPUT statement also allows the programmer to specify a prompt message to be printed on the screen to tell the user when to enter data and what to enter. For example.

```
10   INPUT "What is your name";NAME$
```

would print "What is your name?" (the question mark is automatically added) on the screen and then

wait for the user to enter his name. The name would be stored in the string variable NAME$.

The prompt is optional in the INPUT statement. The INPUT statement can be used to enter more than one item, separated by commas. For example.

```
10   INPUT X, Y, Z
```

would expect three numbers to be typed at the keyboard, separated by commas. If too many or too few items are entered, BASIC will respond with a message such as ?REDO FROM START. Because it is rather awkward to keep track of how many items to enter per line, it is usually better to ask for only one item per INPUT statement.

The program in Fig. 3-3 emulates an electronic typewriter, reading input from the keyboard and printing it on the system printer.

This program demonstrates the use of the INPUT statement and the LPRINT statement.

The program has one major deficiency: it won't accept text with commas. Commas cannot be used because of the way the INPUT statement separates multiple input items, as discussed above. If a comma is entered in a line of text, the message ?REDO FROM START results.

Because BASIC lacks the REPEAT-UNTIL construct described in Chapter 2, a conditional GOTO was used in line 100 to emulate the REPEAT-UNTIL construct. The IF and GOTO statements are discussed in more detail below.

To get around the problem of not being able to

```
10   REM   EMULATE AN ELECTRONIC TYPEWRITER

20   REM

30   PRINT "Welcome to your Electronic Typewriter."

40   PRINT

50   PRINT "Enter your text, followed by a $ in column 1."

60   PRINT

70   INPUT L$

80   LPRINT L$

90   INPUT L$

100 IF LEFT$(L$,1) <> "$" THEN GOTO 80

110 END
```

Fig. 3-3. BASIC Electronic Typewriter, Version 1.

enter text containing commas, the GET statement can be used. The GET statement reads data from the keyboard a character at a time. A second version of the Electronic Typewriter program is shown in Fig. 3-4. Notice that in lines 70 and 90 of the program, the GET is followed by a PRINT. If there was no PRINT, you would not be able to see what you were typing. Another detail that has to be attended to is that when a carriage return is entered, a line feed must be added. This is handled in line 95. A carriage return has an ASCII value of 13 and a line feed has an ASCII value of 10. These functions are represented in BASIC by CHR$(13) and CHR$(10), respectively.

Notice that in Fig. 3-4, a character is sent to the printer before the next character is read. Thus if the user types a character in error and tries to backspace over it to correct it, the error has already gone to the printer. Thus both the incorrect and the correct characters are sent to the printer.

Neither of these programs are thus complete enough to be very useful, but they do illustrate the behavior of the INPUT and GET statements. The interested user is encouraged to refine these programs to correct their deficiencies.

BASIC has a READ statement, but it differs from the READ statement of most other languages. For each READ statement, there must be a DATA statement in the program, and the READ statement takes its input from the DATA statement. For example,

```
10   DATA 3.14159, 2.71828
20   READ PI, E
```

would have the same effect as

```
10   PI = 3.14159
20   E = 2.71728.
```

```
10  REM   EMULATE AN ELECTRONIC TYPEWRITER, VERSION 2

20  REM

30  PRINT "Welcome to your Electronic Typewriter."

40  PRINT

50  PRINT "Enter your text, followed by a $ sign."

60  PRINT

70  GET L$:  PRINT L$;

80  LPRINT L$;

90  GET L$:  PRINT L$;

95  IF L$ = CHR$(13) THEN PRINT CHR$(10);:  LPRINT CHR$(10);

100 IF L$ <> "$" THEN GOTO 80

110 END
```

Fig. 3-4. BASIC Electronic Typewriter, Version 2.

CONTROL STRUCTURES

BASIC is a relatively simple language, having relatively few control structures. Some versions of BASIC have been extended to include such features as an ELSE clause in the IF statement and a WHILE statement. Other versions lack these features. The user who wishes to use the more complex control structures is thus forced to emulate them using simpler control structures such as the IF statement and the GOTO statement.

Simple Selection: The IF Statement

The simplest forms of BASIC allow only IF statements of the form

    40 IF X > 2 THEN 100.

If the condition is true, the next statement to be executed is statement number 100. Extensions to this form include the following:

    50 IF X > 2 GOTO 100
    60 IF X = 2 THEN GOTO 200
    70 IF X < 2 THEN X = 2: GOTO 300.

Statements 50 and 60 do exactly the same thing as statement 40. The THEN introduced in statement 60 allows a statement to follow, which in this case happens to be a GOTO statement. In statement 70, two statements follow the THEN (an assignment statement and a GOTO statement) separated by a colon. If the condition is true, both of these statements will be executed; otherwise neither will be executed and control will pass to the next line after line 70.

The next logical extension to the IF statement

is the ELSE clause. In the IF-THEN-ELSE construct, either the statement (or statements separated by colons) following the THEN or the statement (or statements) following the ELSE are executed, depending on whether the condition is true or false. Control is then passed to the next line in the sequence. Under no condition are both the THEN and the ELSE statements executed. Here is a simple example:

    80 IF DENOM = 0 THEN PRINT"Error—
        Division by Zero" ELSE PRINT NUM/
        DENOM.

This statement prints out an error message if the proposed denominator is zero; otherwise it prints out the result of the division.

A drawback of the IF-THEN-ELSE construct in many implementations of BASIC on microcomputers is that the statements following THEN and ELSE cannot be indented so as to visually show the structure of the statement. This deficiency is even more of a problem with nested IF statements such as the following:

    90 IF HOURS < = 40 THEN PAY = HOURS
    * RATE ELSE IF HOURS < = 50 THEN PAY
    = 40 * RATE + (HOURS − 40) * RATE * 1.5
    ELSE PAY = 40 * RATE + 10 * RATE * 1.5
    + (HOURS − 50) * RATE * 2.

The meaning of this statement can be ascertained after studying it carefully, but it is not immediately obvious. The ability to indent freely, as shown in Chapter 2, would allow BASIC programs to be made more readable.

Loops

The simpler forms of BASIC provide only one form of loop construct, the simple counted loop (the FOR statement). Many versions of BASIC also provide the WHILE statement, a form of conditional loop.

Counted Loops: The FOR Statement. The FOR statement of BASIC was described in Chapter 2 as an example of counted loops in general. An

example was given there, so the FOR statement will not be discussed further here.

Conditional Loops: The WHILE Statement. The WHILE statement of BASIC was also described in Chapter 2, and two examples were given there. It should be noted that not all versions of BASIC include a WHILE statement.

Recall that a WHILE loop tests its condition at the top of the loop. The conditional loop that tests its condition at the bottom of the loop is called the REPEAT-UNTIL loop. Very few versions of BASIC include a REPEAT-UNTIL loop.

The GOSUB Statement

The closest that BASIC comes to allowing the use of subroutines or procedures is the GOSUB statement. Like a subroutine or procedure call, the GOSUB statement transfers control to another part of the program. Control is returned to the statement following the GOSUB statement after the "subroutine" is completed, but the GOSUB statement allows no parameters. All variables in a BASIC program are *global*, which means that they can be accessed from any place in the program. It also means that subroutines can have no local variables not accessible from elsewhere in the program.

To illustrate the disadvantage of not being able to use parameters in a subroutine, suppose that a subroutine is needed to sort an array. Suppose the array in that subroutine is called X. Somewhere else in the program a subroutine is needed to sort an array called Y. Because there is no way to pass parameters directly, the Y array must be copied into the X array, the sort subroutine must be called, and then the resulting array must be copied back into the Y array.

Some languages require subroutines to be placed at the beginning of a program and some at the end of a program. With BASIC it doesn't matter. As a matter of good form, however, it is probably better to place them at the end.

Figure 3-5 contains a simple BASIC program that uses a GOSUB statement. The purpose of the subroutine is to check the range of the variables to be sure they are between 0 and 100. Variables less than 0 are set to zero, and variables greater than 100 are set to 100. The subroutine expects the variable to be checked to be named T. In order to check the variables X and Y, each is copied to T before the GOSUB and copied back from T afterward.

The GOSUB statement refers to the subroutine by the line number at which the subroutine begins, not by name. In this case line 1000 is a REM (remark), which identifies the purpose of the subroutine. It is good practice to identify subroutines in this manner; otherwise it is not always obvious just where a subroutine begins and what it does.

Note that the main program ends at line 140. The END at line 140 is important; otherwise execution would "fall through" to the subroutine at the completion at the main program. The subroutine begins at line 1000 and ends at line 1020.

```
10   REM   DEMONSTRATE A SIMPLE SUBROUTINE IN BASIC

20   MIN = 0

30   MAX = 100

40   INPUT "Type a number between 0 and 100"; X

50   T = X   'COPY

60   GOSUB 1000   'VERIFY RANGE

70   X = T   'RECOPY

80   INPUT "Type another number between 0 and 100"; Y

90   T = Y   'COPY

100  GOSUB 1000   'VERIFY RANGE

110  Y = T   'RECOPY

120  PRINT   'SKIP A LINE

130  PRINT "The two numbers are "; X; " and "; Y

140  END

1000   REM  Subroutine to verify that T >= MIN and T <= MAX

1010   IF T < MIN THEN T = MIN ELSE IF T > MAX THEN T = MAX

1020   RETURN
```

Fig. 3-5. A BASIC subroutine demonstration.

Subroutines are always terminated by a RETURN statement, which returns control to the main program upon completion of the subroutine.

In this instance the amount of computation performed by the subroutine is small, and there is little obvious gain in doing this computation in a subroutine rather than "in line" in the main program. There is some gain in clarity, however. When the reader encounters

```
100   GOSUB 100        'VERIFY RANGE
```

in a program, it is obvious that it is a call to a subroutine to check the range of the variable. The reader can then go on, concentrating on the main logic of the program. If the reader had instead encountered

```
100   If T<MIN THEN T=MIN ELSE IF T>
      MAX THEN T=MAX
```

he or she would have had to stop and try to figure out first what that statement does, and second, how it fits into the main scheme of processing. There is a definite advantage to restricting detail to subroutines.

Functions

The rules for using functions in BASIC are very different from those for using subroutines. First, a function must be defined before it is invoked; a subroutine can be defined anywhere in a program. Second, in most versions of BASIC a function is limited to one statement in length; a subroutine can be of any length. Third, a function is invoked by writing its name in an expression; a subroutine is invoked with a GOSUB statement. Fourth, a function may have parameters; a subroutine must rely on global variables.

The following is a simple BASIC function that computes the area of a circle of radius R:

```
10   DEF FN AREA (R) = 3.14159 * R * R.
```

The name of the function is AREA. Its parameter is R. The R in the function definition is independent of any other variable of the same name elsewhere in the program.

The function is invoked by writing its name together with a value of R in an expression, as in the following:

```
50   PRINT FN AREA (4)
60   PRINT FN AREA (6).
```

Statement 50 above will print the area of a circle with a radius of 4. Statement 60 will print the area of a circle with a radius of 6.

BASIC functions are sometimes useful in programs involving arithmetic computations, but in general, functions in BASIC are less useful than functions in other languages because of the limitations imposed on the use of functions in BASIC (as discussed above).

Recursion

BASIC does not officially support recursion; that is , a function or subroutine cannot invoke itself. Some implementations of BASIC, however, do support a limited degree of recursion, but recursion in BASIC is not dependable and therefore should be studiously avoided.

The ON . . . GOSUB Statement

BASIC does not have a CASE statement. (See Chapter 2 for a discussion of the CASE statement.) There are two statements in BASIC, however, that can be used to emulate the CASE statement. One is the ON . . . GOSUB statement. The other is the ON . . . GOTO statement, which is discussed later in this chapter.

The ON . . . GOSUB statement allows selection of exactly one subroutine out of several for execution. A simple illustration follows:

```
100   ON I GOSUB 1000, 2000,
      3000, 4000, 5000
110   END
```

The numbers 1000, 2000, 3000, 4000, and 5000 are the line numbers of subroutines elsewhere in the program. The variable I is assumed to be an integer between 1 and 5 in this case because exactly 5 subroutine line numbers are listed.

If I has the value 1, the subroutine at line 1000 will be executed because it is number 1 in the list of line numbers following the word GOSUB. If I has the value 2, the subroutine at line 2000 will be executed because it is number 2 in the list of numbers, and so on. In any case, following execu-

```
10   REM   HOW MANY DAYS IN A MONTH?

20   REM

30   INPUT "ENTER THE MONTH (1..12):  ", MONTH

40   IF MONTH < 1 OR MONTH > 12 THEN GOTO 30

50   ON MONTH GOSUB 100, 300, 100, 200, 100, 200, 100, 100, 200, 100,
     200, 100

60   PRINT "MONTH   ";MONTH;" HAS ";DAYS;" DAYS"

70   END

100 REM   SUBROUTINE FOR 31 DAY MONTHS

110 DAYS = 31

120 RETURN

130 REM

200 REM   SUBROUTINE FOR 30 DAY MONTHS

210 DAYS = 30

220 RETURN

230 REM

300 REM   SUBROUTINE FOR FEBRUARY

310 INPUT "ENTER THE YEAR:  ", YEAR

320 IF (YEAR MOD 4 = 0) THEN DAYS = 29 ELSE DAYS = 28

330 RETURN
```

Fig. 3-6. BASIC Calendar program.

tion of the appropriate subroutine, control will pass to line 110, which will end the program.

One common use of the ON . . . GOSUB statement is in interactive programs in which the user is given a menu of possible actions and must choose one. The program should check to be sure that the choice selected is within the appropriate range for the ON . . . GOSUB statement.

Figure 3-6 illustrates the use of the ON . . . GOSUB statement in a simple program that computes the number of days in a month.

Notice that in the program in Fig. 3-6 there are three subroutines. The subroutine at line 100 handles 31-day months; the subroutine at line 200 handles 30-day months; and the subroutine at line 300 handles February. The variable MONTH is read from the keyboard in line 30. Line 40 insures that MONTH is between 1 and 12. The ON . . . GOSUB statement in line 50 calls the appropriate subroutine to print out the number of days in that month and line 220 returns control to line 60.

The logic of the program depends on the order of the line numbers in the ON . . . GOSUB statement. Suppose MONTH is 1 (January). The first line number in the list is line 100, so the program does a GOSUB 100. The subroutine at line 100 handles 31-day months, which is correct in this case. Suppose MONTH is 9 (September). The ninth line number in the list is 200, so the program does a GOSUB 200. The subroutine at line 200 handles 30-day months, which is again correct. The reader should verify that the program produces correct results in every case.

When MONTH 2 (February) is selected, additional logic is required to determine whether or not it is a leap year. The necessary logic is in line 320.

The GOTO Statement

The GOTO statement transfers the flow of execution to a specified location in the program. That location can be anywhere in the program. The form of the statement is as follows:

```
100   GOTO 250.
```

After line 100, the next line to be executed will be line 250.

Unrestricted use of the GOTO statement in BASIC programs can result in programs that are difficult to read, difficult to understand, difficult to debug, and difficult to modify. The GOTO statement is often useful, however, as a means of emulating control statements not provided by BASIC. Some versions of BASIC, for example, do not provide a WHILE statement. In Chapter 2 the WHILE statement was illustrated with a short program segment that reads and sums positive numbers, stopping when a negative number or zero is input. Here is the same program segment using a GOTO statement to emulate the WHILE statement:

```
10    SUM = 0
20    INPUT "ENTER X: "; X
30    If X <= 0 THEN GOTO 70:
      REM Emulate WHILE loop
40       SUM = SUM + X
50       INPUT "ENTER X:   "; X
60       GOTO 30
70    PRINT "SUM = "; SUM
80    END
```

In a similar manner, the REPEAT . . . UNTIL control structure can be emulated. Note the REM in line 30, which indicates that a WHILE loop is being emulated. This makes it obvious what is being done. In the absence of remarks, the purpose of a GOTO statement is not always obvious.

The ON . . . GOTO Statement

The ON . . . GOTO statement is much like the ON . . . GOSUB statement. The difference is that a GOTO rather than a GOSUB is performed. In general, the ON . . . GOSUB statement is to be preferred to the ON . . . GOTO statement because with the former, the flow of the program must eventually return to the statement which follows. With the ON . . . GOTO, what will happen to program flow in the long run is not obvious.

DATA STRUCTURES

BASIC is rather limited in its support of data structures. The array is the only data structure supported directly. More complex data structures must be simulated.

Arrays

Arrays in BASIC are declared using the DIM statement. The following statement declares a one-dimensional array named A:

```
10   DIM A(50)
```

In this case the array A has one subscript (it is one-dimensional), and that subscript can take on values from 0 to 50. (Note that the lower limit is 0, not 1.)

BASIC allows simple variables and arrays to have the same name. Thus, following the above declaration, you could refer both to a nonsubscripted variable named A and to the array named A. BASIC would not confuse the two. You might, however.

Not all arrays need be declared in BASIC. Most versions of BASIC allow arrays to be used without being declared in a DIM statement provided that the value of the subscript does not exceed 10. It is bettter form, however, to declare all arrays.

Arrays in BASIC can have more than one subscript; that is, be more than one-dimensional. An example is the following array which has two subscripts:

```
20   DIM TABLE(5,10)
```

The array TABLE thus represents a two-dimensional table. The number of subscripts permitted in BASIC seems to vary from implementation to implementation. Applesoft BASIC claims to permit up to 88 subscripts. Microsoft BASIC, Version 5.2, seems to support approximately 12, which is more than enough. When you are using more than two or three subscripts, memory availability can quickly become a problem on microcomputers.

Records

Records must be simulated in BASIC. This is usually done using parallel arrays. To see how this

is done, let us consider an example.

In Chapter 2 we discussed a record containing a student's name and his scores on up to 20 tests. Suppose that there may be up to 30 students in the class. This scheme can be implemented in BASIC by using two arrays, a one-dimensional array of strings to contain the names and a two-dimensional array of real numbers to contain the scores. Their declarations in a BASIC program would look as follows:

```
10   DIM NAME$(30)
20   DIM SCORE(30,20)
```

Line 10 dimensions an array of 30 strings, one to contain the name of each student. Line 20 dimensions a two-dimensional array of 30 rows by 20 columns; each element of this array is a real number.

Each row of the array SCORE has an implicit relationship to an element of the array NAME$. The scores in row 10 of SCORE, for example, belong to the student whose name is in element 10 of the array NAME$, and so on. Thus the arrays NAME$ and SCORE are called *parallel*. The tenth element of NAME$ and the tenth row of SCORE together constitute one record.

Suppose that the name of student number 10 is Jones, and that he scored 88 points on the fourth test of the period. Then NAME$(10) would have the value "Jones" and SCORE(10,4) would have the value 88. To print these values, the following statement could be used:

```
100   PRINT NAME$(10), SCORE(10,4)
```

To print the scores on the fourth test for each of the students, the following could be used:

```
200   FOR I = 1 TO 30
210   PRINT NAME$(I), SCORE(I,4)
220   NEXT I
```

Linked Lists

BASIC arrays can also be used to simulate other advanced data structures such as linked lists, following the methodology outlined in Chapter 2.

In Chapter 2 the variable FIRST was used to point to the first record in the list, and the value 0 was used to indicate the end of the list. In BASIC, element 0 of the link array is available to point to the first record of the list, so the value -1 is used to indicate the end of the list. The value -1 of course cannot point to a real array element.

Here are the initializations necessary to set up in BASIC the linked list described in Chapter 2, with modifications as described in the preceding paragraph:

```
10    EL = -1          :
      REM End List marker
20    LL = 5           :
      REM List Length
30    DIM NAME$(LL)
40    DIM LINK(LL)      :
      REM LINK(0) points to first
50    REM name in linked list
60    FREE = 1     :
      REM First Free element in list
70    LINK(0) = EL     :
      REM List is initially empty
80    REM Now initialize free list
90    FOR I = 1 TO LL-1
100          LINK(I) = I + 1
110   NEXT I
120   LINK(LL) = EL
```

The comprehensive sample program at the end of the chapter shows the use of linked lists in an actual program. The algorithms for adding and deleting from linked lists are illustrated in that program.

FILE HANDLING

The use of statements that read from and write to disk files varies from one version of BASIC to another. The particular version discussed here is Microsoft BASIC, Version 5.2. This version runs under the CP/M operating system. The version of BASIC which comes with the IBM Personal Computer handles files in a very similar fashion. Users of other versions of BASIC should consult their reference manuals for differences from the details given here. The concepts will remain the same.

File Records

A file in BASIC may be thought of as a sequence of records stored on disk. A record may be thought of as a set of related data items, such as the name and address of an individual.

Files in BASIC may be set up for sequential access or for direct (random) access. Direct-access files may also be accessed sequentially, but sequential-access files may not be accessed directly. How file records are defined and manipulated varies between the two types of files in BASIC, so these topics will be covered in the appropriate paragraphs below.

Sequential Files

A file is called sequential if its records can be accessed only in sequence from beginning to end. Thus the second record of a sequential file can be accessed only after the first record. The file can be traversed only in the forward direction.

Figure 3-7 illustrates the use of a sequential file to store a list of names and ages on disk. The program prompts the user to enter the data from the keyboard, stores it on disk, and then reads it back and displays it on the video screen.

In line 40 the O shows that the file is being opened for output (writing to the disk). The #1 is a reference number used within the program to indicate which file is being referenced. If another file were opened, it would be referred to as #2. AGES.TXT is the name to be given to the file. It will appear in the directory of the disk.

Line 90 writes a record to the file. Each record will be separated by a carriage return and line feed. In this case, each record will consist of a name and the corresponding age. Because they are both character strings, they will be entered into the file surrounded by quotation marks.

The file is closed by line 110 after the user has finished entering names and ages. The file is reopened in line 130. The I means that it is to be opened for input (reading from the disk). When a

```
10   REM *** Illustrate the use of a sequential file to store

20   REM *** a list of names & ages.

30   REM

40   OPEN "O", #1, "AGES.TXT":    REM Open file for output

50   PRINT "ENTER NAMES AND AGES; AGE 0 TO QUIT."

60   PRINT

70   INPUT "NAME:   ", N$

80   INPUT "AGE:    ", A$

90   WRITE #1, N$, A$:            REM Write to disk file

100 IF A$ <> "0" THEN GOTO 60

110 CLOSE #1

120 REM Now read the file back in and display the records.

130 OPEN "I", #1, "AGES.TXT":    REM Open file for input

140 PRINT:  PRINT

150 INPUT #1, N$, A$

160 IF A$ <> "0" THEN PRINT N$, A$: GOTO 150

170 CLOSE #1

180 PRINT

190 PRINT "All done..."

200 END
```

Fig. 3-7. A BASIC sequential file demonstration.

sequential file is opened for input, the first record of the file read will be the first record of the file. If the file were a tape, we would say that the process of closing it (line 110) and reopening it (line 130), had caused the file to be "rewound" to its beginning.

Line 150 reads one record from the file. Line 170 closes the file after all records have been read from the disk and printed on the video screen.

In this context you should note that if an already-existing sequential file is opened for output, the pointer is initially positioned at the first record of that file. Any write commands would overlay the previous contents of the file unless preventive action were taken. The usual procedure for avoiding this problem when adding data to a sequential file is as follows:

1. Open AGES.TXT for input (the I mode).
2. Open a second file (#2) called TEMP.TXT for output (the O mode).
3. Sequentially read in each record from AGES.TXT and write it to TEMP.TXT, thus copying the file.
4. Close AGES.TXT and delete it. (Use the KILL command in Microsoft BASIC.)
5. Add the new data to TEMP.TXT.
6. Rename TEMP.TXT to AGES. TXT
7. Close the file.

Direct-Access Files

Recall that with sequential access, the records of a file must be accessed in sequence from beginning to end. It is often convenient to be able to directly access a particular record without accessing any other records. As an example, the user may need the 99th record of a 100-record file. With a sequential file, the first 98 records would have to be read first; with a direct-access file, the 99th record could be read directly without any other records being read.

The use of direct-access files is somewhat more complicated than the use of sequential files and requires that you learn several additional BASIC statements. These additional statements include the FIELD statement, the GET statement, the PUT statement, and the LSET statement. You must also learn several new BASIC functions in-

cluding MKI\$, MKS\$, MKD\$, CVI, CVS, and CVD functions.

The program in Fig. 3-8 illustrates the use of a direct-access file to store a list of names and ages. The program stores the records on disk in the order in which they are entered from the keyboard, but it permits the records to be retrieved in any order.

Line 40 shows how the file is opened for direct access. The R (for Random) indicates the access mode. The 24 is the length of each record in bytes or characters. Unlike the records of sequential files, the records of direct-access files must all be of the same length. Note that a file opened in the R mode is available for either input or output.

The FIELD statement in line 50 defines the fields or components of the record. In this case there are two fields, F1\$ and F2\$. Note that both are and must be character strings. Twenty bytes are allocated for F1\$ and four for F2\$; the total is 24, which matches the record length in the OPEN statement. These two fields together comprise what is known as the *file buffer*. All input to and output from the file must move through this buffer.

The LSET statement is used to move data into the file buffer. In the case of line 130, the move is straightforward; LSET left-justifies the string N\$ and pads it with blanks or truncates it, as appropriate, and moves it to F1\$. In line 140, the MKS\$ function must be used to convert the single-precision variable A to a string before it is moved to F2\$ with the LSET statement.

Once the buffer has been filled, it is written to the file with the PUT statement, as shown in line 160. The #1 in line 160 relates to the #1 in the OPEN and FIELD statements. The RECNR is the record number of the file into which the contents of the buffer is to be placed.

Conversely, the contents of a record are read into the buffer by the GET statement, as shown in line 300. The R in line 300 indicates the number of the record that is to be read. The contents of the buffer are moved into other program variables in lines 320 and 330. In line 330, F2\$ is converted back to single precision using the CVS function. Note that the records can be read in any order.

The file is closed in line 380, in the same way

```
10 REM ***   Illustrate the use of a direct-access file

20 REM ***   to store a list of names & ages.

30 REM

40 OPEN "R", #1, "DIRECT.TXT", 24

50 FIELD #1, 20 AS F1$, 4 AS F2$

60 RECNR = 0

70 PRINT "ENTER NAMES AND AGES; AGE 0 TO QUIT."

80 PRINT

90      RECNR = RECNR + 1

100     INPUT "NAME:   ", N$

110     INPUT "AGE:    ", A

120     REM Move data into file buffer

130     LSET F1$ = N$

140     LSET F2$ = MKS$(A)

150     REM Now write to disk file

160     PUT #1, RECNR

170 IF A <> 0 THEN GOTO 80

180 REM

190 REM Now allow selective recall of records

200 PRINT

210 PRINT "YOU WILL NOW BE ABLE TO DISPLAY RECORDS IN ANY ORDER "

220 PRINT
```

Fig. 3-8. A BASIC direct-access file demonstration. (Continued on page 35.)

```
230 PRINT "RECORD NUMBER MUST BE BETWEEN 1 AND "; RECNR; "."

240 PRINT "RECORD NUMBER = 0 CAUSES PROGRAM TO STOP."

250 PRINT

260 INPUT "RECORD NUMBER"; R

270     IF R < 1 THEN GOTO 380

280     IF R > RECNR THEN GOTO 260

290     REM Now get record R and fill buffer

300     GET #1, R

310     REM Now move from buffer into working variables

320     N$ = F1$

330     A  = CVS(F2$):  REM Convert from string to numeric

340     PRINT

350     PRINT N$, A

360     PRINT

370 GOTO 260

380 CLOSE #1

390 PRINT

400 PRINT "All done..."

410 END
```

that a sequential file is closed. Note that the difficulties encountered in updating an already-existing sequential file do not arise with direct-access files, because the program can begin writing anywhere in the file.

The comprehensive example at the end of the chapter also illustrates the use of direct-access files.

GRAPHICS

Several versions of BASIC on microcomputers offer graphics. Unfortunately, there is little in common between implementations. Each graphics package is designed for a particular hardware configuration. As an example, the graphics commands of Applesoft BASIC are totally different than those of Radio Shack BASIC. For that reason, the graphics capabilities of the BASIC language will not be discussed further in this book.

COMPREHENSIVE SAMPLE PROGRAM

The purpose of the comprehensive sample program is to tie together examples of the various BASIC constructs. In addition, it illustrates how a larger program ought to be organized. The previous programs in the chapter have been of such a size that the overall organization of the program has not mattered much. With larger programs, proper organization is essential. The comprehensive sample program is shown in Fig. 3-9. The purpose of the program is to establish and maintain a file of names and addresses. The program provides the capability of adding and deleting records from the file and of listing the file on the video screen or on a printer. The file is always maintained in alphabetical order by name. The file is never explicitly sorted, however; sorting is unnecessary because of the way the file is organized.

The file is organized as a linked list. The links are actually stored in a separate index file. As a record is added to the file, it is automatically placed in the proper place (alphabetically) in the index.

Notice that the main program is rather short, extending only to line number 410. Not counting remarks, declarations, or initializations, it consists of only 7 lines. Most of the work is done in subroutines. A directory of subroutines is at the end of the program, beginning with line 60000. The subroutine to open files, for example, is found at line 10000. The directory uses the GOTO 10000 to indicate the location of the subroutine. The number 10000 could have been put in a REM statement, but when it is in a GOTO statement it will automatically be updated if the program is renumbered. The GOTO 10000 is never executed.

The main program provides overall control for the program as a whole. It uses the menu subroutine to determine what the user wants to do and then transfers control to the appropriate subroutine. The process is repeated until the user chooses to end the session.

By now it should be obvious that the program was designed and constructed in modules, with the modules being implemented as subroutines. Taken by itself, each module is relatively simple. Each one is relatively short and has a single purpose. The longest subroutine has fewer than 50 statements; most are much shorter. Modular design thus makes the program much easier to write.

Many of the modules could have been coded "in line" instead of as subroutines. The menu subroutine is a good example. It is needed at only one place in the program. The body of the subroutine could have been incorporated into the main program at the appropriate place. The program is clearer, however, with the menu function as a separate subroutine. The main program is easier to read this way, provided that an appropriate remark is present to indicate the purpose of the GOSUB.

Writing a program of this length without using subroutines is possible, but experience has shown that programmers can deal much more effectively with many smaller pieces of a program than with one large piece.

There are several other features of the program in Fig. 3-9 which should be noted. First, note the subroutine called GET ENTRY, which begins at line 15000. The data input is set up so as to present the user with a form to fill out. The same function could have been accomplished with just a few INPUT statements, but extra effort to make the user interface more convenient often makes the difference between a mediocre and a good program.

Second, note the manner in which the names are maintained in alphabetical order. This is a practical example of the use of linked lists, which were discussed earlier in the chapter. There are actually two linked lists in use; one is a list of records in alphabetical order, and the other is a list of unused records (the "free list").

The records themselves are kept in a direct

```
100 REM    ***********************************************************
110 REM    ***                                                     ***
120 REM    ***   PROGRAM ADDRESS FILE                              ***
130 REM    ***                                                     ***
140 REM    ***      Create and maintain a file of names and        ***
150 REM    ***      addresses.  The file is maintained in          ***
160 REM    ***      alphabetical order at all times, using an      ***
170 REM    ***      index of pointers.  The index is maintained    ***
180 REM    ***      as a linked list.  A linked list of vacant     ***
190 REM    ***      records called the "free list" is also         ***
200 REM    ***      maintained.                                    ***
210 REM    ***                                                     ***
220 REM    ***      9/3/83                                         ***
230 REM    ***                                                     ***
240 REM    ***********************************************************
250 REM
260 MAXREC = 10                     :REM FILE CAPACITY; MODIFY AS REQUIRED
270 FILEA$ = "ADDRESS.TXT"          :REM FILE NAME
280 FILEI$ = "INDEX.TXT"            :REM INDEX FILE NAME
290 ENDLIST = 0                     :REM SENTINEL
300 DIM INDEX(MAXREC)
310 REM
320 REM             ***       MAIN PROGRAM     ***
330 REM
340 GOSUB 10000                      :REM OPEN FILES
350 GOSUB 12000                      :REM DISPLAY MENU
360 IF C = 5 THEN GOTO 400
370 ON C GOSUB 14000, 19000, 21000, 23000
380 REM APPEND, REVIEW, LIST FILE, OR DUMP FILE
390 GOTO 350
400 GOSUB 13000                      :REM CLOSE FILES
410 END
420 REM
9970 REM
9980 REM            ***       SUBROUTINES      ***
9990 REM
10000 REM           ***       OPEN FILES       ***
10010 REM
10020 OPEN "R", #1, FILEA$, 64
10030 FIELD #1, 12 AS F1$, 12 AS F2$, 20 AS F3$, 12 AS F4$, 2 AS
      F5$, 5 AS F6$
10040 REM
10050 ON ERROR GOTO 10500
10060 OPEN "I", #2, FILEI$
```

Fig. 3-9. BASIC Address Book. (Continued on page 38.)

```
10070 ON ERROR GOTO 0
10080 INPUT #2, FREE, FIRST     :REM POINTERS TO FREE LIST, FIRST RECORD
10090 FOR I = 1 TO MAXREC       :REM READ IN INDEX
10100    INPUT #2, INDEX(I)
10110 NEXT I
10120 CLOSE #2
10130 RETURN
10140 REM
10500 REM *** ERROR RECOVERY ***
10510 GOSUB 11000                      :REM INITIALIZE FILES
10520 RESUME
10530 REM
11000 REM          ***        INITIALIZE FILES          ***
11010 REM
11020 REM INDEX FILE MUST BE INITIALIZED
11030 OPEN "O", #2, FILEI$
11040 FREE = 1
11050 FIRST = ENDLIST
11060 WRITE #2, FREE, ENDLIST
11070 FOR I = 1 TO MAXREC - 1
11080    WRITE #2, I + 1            :REM INITIALIZE FREE LIST
11090 NEXT I
11100 WRITE #2, ENDLIST
11110 CLOSE #2
11120 RETURN
11130 REM
12000 REM          ***        MENU       ***
12010 REM
12020 REM PRINT MENU AND RETURN CHOICE AS C
12030 HOME:    PRINT CHR$(12)
12040 ROW = 5
12050 COL = 5
12060 VTAB ROW:  HTAB COL
12070 PRINT "1)   ADD TO FILE"
12090 ROW = ROW + 2:  VTAB ROW:    HTAB COL
12100 PRINT "2)   REVIEW FILE ON SCREEN"
12110 ROW = ROW + 2:  VTAB ROW:   HTAB COL
12120 PRINT "3)   LIST FILE TO SCREEN OR PRINTER"
12130 ROW = ROW + 2:  VTAB ROW:   HTAB COL
12140 PRINT "4)   DUMP FILE TO PRINTER"
12150 ROW = ROW + 2:  VTAB ROW:   HTAB COL
12160 PRINT "5)   QUIT
12170 COL = 1
12180 ROW = ROW + 2:   VTAB ROW:   HTAB COL
```

Fig. 3-9. BASIC Address Book. (Continued on page 39.)

```
12190 INPUT "SELECT 1, 2, 3, 4, OR 5:  ", C
12200 IF (C < 1) OR (C > 5) THEN GOTO 12190
12210 RETURN
12220 REM
13000 REM        ***       CLOSE FILES       ***
13010 REM
13020 REM WRITE INDEX FILE TO DISK AND CLOSE BOTH FILES
13030 OPEN "O", #2, FILEI$
13040 WRITE #2, FREE, FIRST
13050 FOR I = 1 TO MAXREC
13060   WRITE #2, INDEX(I)
13070 NEXT I
13080 CLOSE #2
13090 CLOSE #1
13100 RETURN
13110 REM
14000 REM        ***       APPEND RECORD TO FILE    ***
14010 REM
14020 GOSUB 15000                 :REM   GET ENTRY
14030 WHILE NOT FINISHED
14040   GOSUB 16000               :REM   INSERT
14050   GOSUB 15000               :REM   GET ENTRY
14060 WEND
14070 RETURN
14080 REM
15000 REM        ***       GET ENTRY          ***
15010 REM
15020 REM READ 1 RECORD FROM KEYBOARD
15030 HOME:   PRINT CHR$(12)              :REM CLEAR SCREEN
15040 START = 14
15050 ROW = 5:   COL = 1
15060 VTAB ROW:   HTAB COL
15070 PRINT "LAST NAME:";
15080 FLENGTH = 12
15090 GOSUB 25000                         :REM MARK OFF INPUT AREA
15100 ROW = ROW + 2:  VTAB ROW:   HTAB COL
15110 PRINT "FIRST NAME:";
15120 FLENGTH = 12
15130 GOSUB 25000                         :REM MARK OFF
15140 ROW = ROW + 2:  VTAB ROW:   HTAB COL
15150 PRINT "ADDRESS:";
15160 FLENGTH = 20
15170 GOSUB 25000                         :REM MARK OFF
15180 ROW = ROW + 2:  VTAB ROW:   HTAB COL
```

```
15190 PRINT "CITY:";
15200 FLENGTH = 12
15210 GOSUB 25000                          :REM MARK OFF
15220 ROW = ROW + 2:  VTAB ROW:  HTAB COL
15230 PRINT "STATE:";
15240 FLENGTH = 2
15250 GOSUB 25000                          :REM MARK OFF
15260 ROW = ROW + 2:  VTAB ROW:  HTAB COL
15270 PRINT "ZIP CODE:";
15280 FLENGTH = 5
15290 GOSUB 25000                          :REM MARK OFF
15300 ROW = 5:  COL = START + 1
15310 VTAB ROW:  HTAB COL
15320 INPUT "", LAST$
15330 FINISHED = (LAST$ = "")              :REM IF EMPTY
15340 IF FINISHED THEN RETURN
15350 ROW = ROW + 2:  VTAB ROW:  HTAB COL
15360 INPUT "", FIRST$
15370 ROW = ROW + 2:  VTAB ROW:  HTAB COL
15380 INPUT "", ADDRESS$
15390 ROW = ROW + 2:  VTAB ROW:  HTAB COL
15400 INPUT "", CITY$
15410 ROW = ROW + 2:  VTAB ROW:  HTAB COL
15420 INPUT "", STATE$
15430 ROW = ROW + 2:  VTAB ROW:  HTAB COL
15440 INPUT "", ZIP$
15450 RETURN
15460 REM
16000 REM          ***     INSERT          ***
16010 REM
16020 REM PLACE THE RECORD INTO THE INDEX AND WRITE IT TO DISK
16030 GOSUB 18000                          :REM GET FREE RECORD
16040 R = F
16050 LSET F1$ = LAST$                     :REM MOVE TO FILE BUFFER
16060 LSET F2$ = FIRST$
16070 LSET F3$ = ADDRESS$
16080 LSET F4$ = CITY$
16090 LSET F5$ = STATE$
16100 LSET F6$ = ZIP$
16110 PUT #1, R                            :REM WRITE TO DISK
16120 REM NOW INSERT RECORD R INTO THE INDEX
16130 P = FIRST                            :REM FIRST RECORD IN USE
16140 Q = 0
16150 IF P = ENDLIST THEN GOTO 16250
```

Fig. 3-9. BASIC Address Book. (Continued on page 41.)

```
16160    GET #1, P
16170    GOSUB 17000                      :REM COMPARE & FIND GREATER
16180    WHILE (P <> ENDLIST) AND (GREATER)
16190            Q = P
16200            P = INDEX(P)
16205            IF P=ENDLIST THEN GOTO 16230
16210            GET #1, P
16220            GOSUB 17000              :REM COMPARE
16230    WEND
16240 REM NOW INSERT INTO LINKED LIST
16250 INDEX(F) = P
16260 INDEX(Q) = F
16270 IF Q=0 THEN FIRST = F
16280 RETURN
16290 REM
17000 REM        ***      COMPARE          ***
17010 REM
17020 REM COMPARE FIRST$, LAST$ TO RECORD IN BUFFER
17030 GREATER = (LAST$ > F1$) OR ((LAST$ = F1$) AND (FIRST$ > F2$))
17040 RETURN
17050 REM
18000 REM        ***      GET FREE         ***
18010 REM
18020 REM RETURN THE NR OF THE NEXT FREE RECORD & REMOVE FROM FREE LIST
18030 F = FREE
18040 IF F=0 THEN PRINT: PRINT "ERROR!!! NO MORE FREE RECORDS!": END
18050 FREE = INDEX(FREE)
18060 RETURN
18070 REM
19000 REM        ***      REVIEW           ***
19010 REM
19020 REM STEP THROUGH FILE, 1 RECORD AT A TIME.  ALLOWS DELETION.
19030 HOME:  PRINT CHR$(12)               :REM CLEAR SCREEN
19040 R = FIRST
19050 Q = 0
19060 REM REPEAT UNTIL LOOP (SIMULATED)
19070 GET #1, R
19080    PRINT
19090    GOSUB 24000                      :REM PRINT RECORD R
19100    PRINT
19110    PRINT TAB(10) "1) GET NEXT RECORD"
19120    PRINT TAB(10) "2) DELETE THIS RECORD, OR "
19130    PRINT TAB(10) "3) QUIT?"
19135    PRINT
```

```
19140    REM REPEAT UNTIL LOOP (SIMULATED)
19150    INPUT "SELECT 1), 2), OR 3) ", C
19160             IF (C < 1) OR (C > 3) THEN GOTO 19150
19170    ON C GOTO 19180, 19210, 19240
19180    Q = R                                :REM GET NEXT RECORD
19190    R = INDEX(R)
19200    GOTO 19240
19210    INDEX(Q) = INDEX(R)                  :REM DELETE RECORD
19220    GOSUB 20000                          :REM PUT IN FREE LIST
19230    R = INDEX(Q)
19240    IF (R <> ENDLIST) AND (C <> 3) THEN GOTO 19070
19250 RETURN
19260 REM
20000 REM         ***      PUT FREE        ***
20010 REM
20020 REM PUT RECORD R BACK INTO THE FREE LIST
20030 INDEX(R) = FREE
20040 FREE = R
20050 RETURN
20060 REM
21000 REM         ***      LIST FILE       ***
21010 REM
21020 REM FIND OUT WHETHER TO LIST FILE TO SCREEN OR PRINTER
21030 REM THEN CALL LIST.
21040 HOME:   PRINT CHR$(12)                 :REM CLEAR SCREEN
21050 ROW = 5: COL = 10
21060 VTAB ROW: HTAB COL
21070 PRINT "LIST TO"
21080 ROW = ROW + 2
21090 VTAB ROW: HTAB COL + 5
21100 PRINT "1) SCREEN"
21110 ROW = ROW + 2
21120 VTAB ROW: HTAB COL + 5
21130 PRINT "2) PRINTER"
21140 ROW = ROW + 2
21150 VTAB ROW: HTAB COL
21160 INPUT "SELECT 1 OR 2:   ", D
21170 IF (D < 1) OR (D > 2) THEN GOTO 21160
21180 PRINT
21190 GOSUB 22000                            :REM LIST
21200 PRINT
21210 INPUT "TYPE <CR> TO CONTINUE",A$
21220 RETURN
21230 REM
```

Fig. 3-9. BASIC Address Book. (Continued on page 43.)

```
22000 REM        ***     LIST              ***
22010 REM
22020 REM LIST ALL ACTIVE RECORDS IN ALPHABETICAL ORDER
22030 REM LIST TO SCREEN IF D = 1, TO PRINTER IF D = 2.
22040 R = FIRST
22050 WHILE R <> ENDLIST
22060    IF D=1 THEN PRINT: GOSUB 24000 ELSE IF D=2 THEN LPRINT:
         GOSUB 26000 ELSE PRINT "ERROR IN SUBROUTINE LIST.  D = ";D
22070    R = INDEX(R)
22080 WEND
22090 RETURN
22100 REM
23000 REM        ***     DUMP              ***
23010 REM
23020 REM DUMP ENTIRE FILE TO PRINTER, INCLUDING EMPTY RECORDS
23030 REM AND INDEX FILE ENTRIES.  USEFUL FOR LEARNING HOW
23040 REM PROGRAM WORKS.
23050 PRINT: PRINT
23060 PRINT "BE SURE PRINTER IS ON...."
23070 LPRINT "FIRST FREE RECORD:            ";FREE
23080 LPRINT "FIRST RECORD ALPHABETICALLY:  ";FIRST
23090 FOR R = 1 TO MAXREC
23100    LPRINT
23110    LPRINT "RECORD          ";R
23120    GOSUB 26000                         :REM LPRINT RECORD R
23140    LPRINT "NEXT RECORD IS ";INDEX(R)
23150 NEXT R
23160 LPRINT
23170 RETURN
23180 REM
24000 REM        ***     PRINT RECORD    ***
24010 REM
24020 REM PRINT RECORD R ON THE SCREEN
24030 GET #1, R
24050 PRINT F2$;" ";F1$
24060 PRINT F3$
24070 PRINT F4$;" ";F5$;" ";F6$
24080 RETURN
24090 REM
25000 REM        ***     MARKOFF          ***
25010 REM
25020 REM MARK OFF DATA INPUT AREA
25030 HTAB START
25040 PRINT ":";
```

```
25050 FOR J = 1 TO FLENGTH
25060   PRINT " ";
25070 NEXT J
25080 PRINT ":";
25090 RETURN
25100 REM
26000 REM        ***       LPRINT RECORD    ***
26010 REM
26020 REM PRINT RECORD R ON THE PRINTER
26030 GET #1, R
26050 LPRINT F2$;" ";F1$
26060 LPRINT F3$
26070 LPRINT F4$;" ";F5$;" ";F6$
26080 RETURN
26090 REM
60000 REM  ************************************************************
60010 REM  ***                                                    ***
60020 REM  ***   DIRECTORY OF SUBROUTINES USED                    ***
60030 REM  ***                                                    ***
60040 REM  ************************************************************
60050 REM
60100 GOTO 10000         :REM   OPEN FILES
60200 GOTO 11000         :REM   INITIALIZE FILES
60300 GOTO 12000         :REM   MENU
60400 GOTO 13000         :REM   CLOSE FILES
60500 GOTO 14000         :REM   APPEND
60600 GOTO 15000         :REM   GET ENTRY
60700 GOTO 16000         :REM   INSERT
60800 GOTO 17000         :REM   COMPARE
60900 GOTO 18000         :REM   GET FREE
61000 GOTO 19000         :REM   REVIEW
61100 GOTO 20000         :REM   PUT FREE
61200 GOTO 21000         :REM   LIST FILE
61300 GOTO 22000         :REM   LIST
61400 GOTO 23000         :REM   DUMP
61500 GOTO 24000         :REM   PRINT RECORD
61600 GOTO 25000         :REM   MARKOFF DATA INPUT AREA
61700 GOTO 26000         :REM   LPRINT RECORD
```

Fig. 3-9. BASIC address book. (Continued from page 43.)

access file. The size of the file is established in line 260. It is set as 10 records for demonstration purposes. If you want to use this program for practical purposes, you should modify line 260 as appropriate.

The links that allow the maintenance of both linked lists are kept in a separate, sequential file. This file is kept in memory while the program is being run, and it is written back to disk at the end of the program. This is done for reasons of efficiency, but there is the disadvantage that if the program is interrupted (for example, by a power failure), you will be unable to access all the new records you entered during that session.

You may wish to add more features to this program. The modular structure makes this relatively easy to do. One suggestion is to add the ability to find the address of a particular individual and to display that address on the screen or write it to a printer.

The DUMP subroutine was included as a learning device. To understand more clearly how the program works, you should use this routine to print out the status of the file at various points during a session in order to see how additions and deletions are handled.

ADVANTAGES AND DISADVANTAGES OF BASIC

The BASIC language was designed for students. It is a simple language that has a relatively small number of different instructions. It is thus easy to learn all of the available instructions.

BASIC is usually implemented on microcomputers as an interpreted language. This makes program development simpler in the sense that it is easier to input a program and test it interactively than it would be if the language were implemented as a compiled language. The user can enter the program, test it, and correct errors all within the same environment. The result is a much friendlier programming environment.

With a compiled language, the user usually has to use a separate editor to input the text of the program, save the program to disk, and then use the compiler before he or she can test the program. Sometimes there are additional steps such as linking and loading. The result is a somewhat "user-hostile" environment.

On the negative side, most implementations of BASIC lack the full range of structured constructs such as the CASE statement, REPEAT-UNTIL, and so forth. These must often be emulated using IF and GOTO statements. BASIC also lacks local variables in subroutines and a means of passing parameters to subroutines.

Because BASIC is usually implemented as an interpreted language, BASIC programs usually run slower than equivalent programs in compiled languages. This is shown time and time again in programming benchmarks.

Most implementations of BASIC use binary integer and floating point arithmetic, which is fine for scientific and general applications, but inadequate for most business applications. As discussed in Chapter 2, BCD (decimal) arithmetic is desirable for business applications. Two versions of BASIC which do provide BCD arithmetic are CBASIC and Nevada BASIC.

In balance, BASIC is useful for writing relatively short programs for which execution speed is not of prime importance. Because of its user-friendliness, it is excellent for beginners.

AVAILABILITY

BASIC is the most widely-available language for microcomputers. Most microcomputers sold today, including those selling for under $100, are distributed with the BASIC language. BASIC compilers are also available. An excellent combination is a BASIC interpreter for program development and a compatible BASIC compiler for compiling the program for production work.

SUMMARY

BASIC is the most popular language in use today for microcomputers. Its popularity is due in part to its wide availability and in part to its ease of use. It is easy to learn, yet sufficiently powerful for many applications. It is particularly well-suited for beginners.

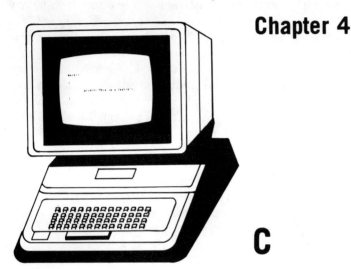

Chapter 4

C

The C programming language was designed and implemented by Dennis Ritchie at Bell Laboratories in Murray Hill, New Jersey, in 1972. It was based on the earlier language BCPL by Martin Richards and B by Ken Thompson. C was originally designed for and implemented on the UNIX operating system on the Digital Equipment Corporation PDP-11 minicomputer. C has since been implemented on numerous other computers, including microcomputers.

C is a general purpose high-level language, but it includes many low-level features as well. The low-level features permit bit-level manipulations such as are often needed in writing systems software such as operating systems. In fact, the UNIX operating system is now written mostly in the C language. Before the advent of C, operating systems had been written almost exclusively in assembly or machine language.

C is a very rich language, containing in particular many operators (including operators for incrementing, decrementing, and so on, as well as the usual arithmetic operators). This richness provides for several alternative ways to accomplish a given task, often including several shortcuts. In the hands of an expert, C is a very powerful language. It is also a very subtle language. Along with the subtleties and shortcuts, there are pitfalls for the unwary.

The features of C tend to encourage a particular style of programming, one that takes advantage of the richness of the language. Unfortunately, programs written in that style tend to be difficult to read for the uninitiated. This book will therefore attempt to present the essential features of the C language while avoiding many of the more subtle idioms of the language.

There are relatively few books available on the C language, compared to the number available on BASIC or Pascal. The definitive reference is *The C Programming Language*, by Brian W. Kernighan and Dennis M. Ritchie (Prentice-Hall, 1978). A newer book written at a more elementary level is *C Programming Guide*, by Jack Purdum (Que Corporation, 1983).

One of the first implementations of C on a microcomputer was Small C, published in *Dr. Dobb's Journal* in May 1980. Small C is now in the public domain. It lacks, however, many of the features normally found in C. Several companies have produced enhanced versions of Small C and sell them for relatively low prices (under $50). The programs in this chapter have been tested with one such compiler produced by the Code Works of Goleta, California. Code Works C lacks floating point variables, direct-access files, and several other features of standard C. Nevertheless it is useful for many purposes.

The Code Works C compiler, like several other microcomputer C compilers, produces an assembly language source file as output. This file must then be assembled and loaded using a separate assembler.

PROGRAM STRUCTURE

A C program consists of one or more functions. One function must be called *main*. This corresponds to the main program of other languages. (Functions are discussed in more detail below.)

A simple C program that prints "This is a test" is shown in Fig. 4-1. The first line is simply a comment identifying the program. By convention, this comment begins with the name of the file in which the source program is stored. In the next line, "main( )" identifies the beginning of the main program. The parentheses are necessary because main is actually a function, and function names in C must be followed by parentheses, even if empty. The body of the main program is enclosed by braces

({ and }). Note that they are placed so as to be easy to locate.

The actual work is done in the line that begins printf. The character string between the quotation marks is sent to the video screen by the standard library function printf. The only thing peculiar about this is the fact that the character string is terminated by the characters \ n (backslash-n), which represents a carriage return and line feed pair. One way to understand what this does is to note that two consecutive printf statements without the backslash-n would be printed on the same line.

It should also be noted that the printf statement ends with a semicolon. In C, the semicolon is a statement terminator, not a statement separator (as in Pascal), so it is always mandatory at the end of a statement.

Wherever one statement can appear in C, so can a group of statements. They must be surrounded by braces ({ and }). The braces correspond to the BEGIN and END of Pascal programs. The terseness of the C version is characteristic.

DATA REPRESENTATION

The C language supports the following data types: char (character), int (integer), float (floating point), and double (double precision). Additionally the int type can be modified with the prefixes long, short, or unsigned. The exact number of bits used to represent each variable type depends on the installation, but typically a char uses 8 bits; an int uses 16 bits; a long int uses 32 bits; a short int uses 16 bits; a float is a 32-bit floating point number, and a double is a 64-bit floating number. An unsigned int

```
/* fig41.c  --  Simple C Program */
main()

{

        printf("This is a test\n");

}
```

Fig. 4-1. A simple C program.

```
/*  fig42.c -- Illustrate constant declaration  */
#define  ENDLIST  (-1)

main()
{

        printf("The constant ENDLIST has value %d",ENDLIST);

}
```

Fig. 4-2. The use of a constant in C.

is always positive. Of these data types, the Code Works C compiler used for the examples in this chapter supports only char and int.

Constants

Integer constants in C follow the usual conventions discussed in Chapter 2, except that octal (base 8) and hexadecimal (base 16) constants can also be used. An octal constant is indicated by a leading 0. Thus 011 is an octal constant which is equal to the decimal constant 9. Similarly, hexadecimal constants are indicated by a leading 0x. The number 0x11 is the octal equivalent of 17 in decimal. Some implementations also allow binary (base 2) constants, prefixed by 0b.

Foating point constants follow the conventions concerning real numbers described in Chapter 2.

Constants of the char type are single characters surrounded by single quotes, for example, 'a'. A character contant has a numeric value corresponding to the numeric value of that character in the character set of the machine in use.

There are several special characters that can be represented by two character sequences beginning with a backslash: \ n is the newline character; \ t is the tab character; and \ 0 is the null character (hexadecimal 00). An aribitrary character can be represented by preceding it with a backslash. The backslash character itself is represented by \\ and the single quote by \'.

Arbitrary bit patterns can be represented by using the pattern '\ ddd', where the ddd represents one to three octal digits. The ASCII carriage re-

turn, for example, would be represented as '\ 012'.

String constants are delimited with double quotes. A string in C is terminated with the null character. (\0). Thus the character 'c' is only one character in length, but the string "c" is two characters in length, the second (unseen) character being the null character. The length of a string is determined by counting the characters before the null character.

Constants may be declared in C using #define. An illustration of the #define facility is given in Fig. 4-2. In this example the name of the constant is ENDLIST, and its value is −1. Everywhere that the name ENDLIST appears in the program text (except within quotation marks), the value −1 is substituted at the time the program is compiled. In this case the program merely prints out the value of ENDLIST. Note the %d within the character string in the printf statement. This tells printf to print the first item after the character string (in this case it is ENDLIST) at that place and to print that item as a decimal number. Notice that in this case the newline character (backslash-n) was omitted; observe the difference in the behavior of the cursor on your screen as you run this program, compared to its behavior when you run the program in Fig. 4-1.

Variables

Variables in C are declared at the beginning of a program. Functions, discussed below, may also have local variables not accessible from the main program or from other functions. A simple example of a variable declaration is shown in the example in

48

```
/* fig43.c -- Program Square; illustrate variable declarations    */
int side, area, perim;

main()

{

        side = 5;

        area = side * side;

        perim = side + side + side + side;

        printf("Area and perimeter of a square:\n\n");

        printf("Side:       %d\n", side);

        printf("Area:       %d\n", area);

        printf("Perimeter:  %d\n", perim);

}
```

Fig. 4-3. Variable declarations in C.

Fig. 4-3. The program computes and prints the area and perimeter of a square.

THE ASSIGNMENT STATEMENT

The assignment operator in C is the equals sign (=). The symbol used for testing equality is ==. The author of C decided that because the assignment operator is used more often, it should consist of only one keystroke, even if it meant that the equals sign would not mean equality. This tradeoff is wholly consistent with the philosophy of C, which favors conciseness over other considerations. In Pascal, on the other hand, the assignment operator takes two keystrokes and the symbol for testing equality one keystroke.

The assignment operator in C is not very particular about types. For example, it is common in C to assign a character value to an integer variable. Figure 4-3 shows three examples of assignment statements.

ARITHMETIC EXPRESSIONS

C uses conventional infix notation (see Chapter 2) for its arithmetic expressions. It uses the usual arithmetic operators (+, −, *, /), plus a modulus operator (%). The modulus operator produces the remainder after integer division; thus 5 % 2 is 1, and 10 % 4 is 2.

C, like Pascal, does not have an exponentiation operator. Exponentiation in C must be performed using repeated multiplication or using logarithms.

Figure 4-3 shows two simple arithmetic expressions used in computing the area and perimeter of a square.

C also has special operators for the common operations of incrementing and decrementing. The statement

    i++;

is, for example, equivalent to the statement

i = i + 1;

and the statement

i−−;

is equivalent to the statement

i = i − 1;.

The incrementing and decrementing operators can also be placed before the variable. Compare the two statements

j = i++;   /* A */
j = ++i;   /* B */.

Suppose that i initially has the value 5. Following statement A, j would have the value 5 and i the value 6. The incrementing thus takes place after the value of i is used in the expression. If i again has the value 5 before statement B is executed, both i and j would end up with the value 6. In that case, i would be incremented before its value is used in the expression.

The C language allows another form of shortcut when the value of a variable is to be modified by other than simple incrementing or decrementing. Consider the following statements:

amount += 5;   /* A1 */
amount = amount + 5;   /* A2 */
sales *= 2;   /* B1 */
sales = 2 * sales;   /* B2 */.

Statements A1 and A2 are equivalent, as are statements B1 and B2. Similar statements can be constructed using other arithmetic operators.

LOGICAL EXPRESSIONS

The relational operators in C are == (equals), != (not equals), > (greater than), >= (greater than or equals), < (less than), and <= (less than or equals). The logical operators are && (AND) and || (OR).

The logical operators are evaluated from left to right, and evaluation stops as soon as it can be determined whether the expression is true or false. This is sometimes convenient.

The C language also contains logical operators for manipulating variables at the bit level. These operators are valid only for char or integer variables. The following operators are provided: & (bitwise AND), | (bitwise OR), ⵁ (bitwise exclusive OR), ~ (one's complement), << (shift left one bit), and >> (shirt right one bit).

Some printers expect to find the high-order bit of a character set high, and some expect it low. The following statement would set the high bit of the character c high:

c |= 0x80;

the following would be sure that the high bit of the character is set low:

c &= 0x7f;.

In the former case, a bitwise OR is performed between the character c and the hexadecimal constant 0x80, which has all bits low (0) except the most significant bit, which is high (1). Note that the statement could have been written as

c = c | 0x80;.

In the latter case, a bitwise AND is performed between the character c and the hexadecimal constant 0x7f, which has the high-order bit low (0) and all other bits high (1).

CONDITIONAL EXPRESSIONS

A conditional expression evaluates to one of two values, depending on whether a given condition is true or false. It is a feature not often found in computer languages, whether they be high-level or low-level.

Suppose, for example, it is desired that a variable y evaluate to the value of x or zero, whichever is larger. The following shows one way to accomplish this:

$$y = x > 0 ? x : 0;.$$

If x is greater than zero, the value of the expression is x; otherwise it is 0. The general form of the expression is

$$<\text{log. exp.}> ? <\text{exp. 1}> : <\text{exp. 2}>.$$

If the logical expression is true, the value of the expression is the value of expression 1, which follows the question mark. If the logical expression is false, the value of the expression is the value of expression 2, which follows the colon.

INPUT AND OUTPUT

You have already seen the printf() function in Figs. 4-1, 4-2, and 4-3. Its purpose is, of course, to produce formatted output on the console (video screen). The C language has several other methods of sending output to the console and to the printer.

Technically speaking, the C language has no input and output statements. This is not apparent to the user, however, as input and output is implemented using standard functions provided with the compiler (such as printf()). The advantage of this approach is that C is thus more portable; as it moves to another environment, all the input and output functions that may need to be changed are together in one easily-accessible place.

The user should check the documentation provided with his or her C compiler to determine exactly which input and output functions are provided. Here is a typical list:

INPUT	OUTPUT
getchar( )	listchar( )
getkey( )	lists( )
gets( )	printf( )
scanf( )	putchar( )
	puts( )

Input and output functions that access files are discussed in a later section. Of the above functions, getchar( ), getkey( ), gets( ), and scanf( ) read from the console; printf( ), putchar( ), and puts( ) write to the console, and listchar(), and lists() write to the list device (printer).

First let us look at the print() function in more detail. The general form of the function is as follows:

printf (format, argument, argument, ...)

The format is a string containing text and possibly conversion specifications, which specify where and how the arguments are to be printed. In the following example, assume that a and b are integers:

printf("The sum of %d and %d is %d. /'n",a,b,a+b);

The arguments in this case are a, bbe, and a+b. Each is associated by position with a %d conversion specification. This specification means to print the corresponding argument as a decimal number. The output on the printer would look as follows, assuming a and b have the values 1 and 2, respectively:

The sum of 1 and 2 is 3.

Besides %d, there are several other permisible conversion specifications, as follows:

Specification	Format
%c	a single character
%s	a string
%u	an unsigned number
%o	an octal number
%x	a hexadecimal number
%e	floating point, scientific notation
%f	fixed point notation
%s	fixed or floating point, whichever is shorter

Compilers that do not support floating point numbers are not likely to support the %e, %f, or %s conversion specifications.

There is no direct counterpart of **printf()** for sending output to the printer. The same effect can be achieved, however, by using the sprintf() and the lists() functions in conjunction with each other. The program in Fig. 4-4 shows how formatted output can be sent to both the console and to the printer.

In the program in Fig. 4-4, MAXL is defined as a constant and used to dimension the string array str. It is given the value 81 to allow for an 80-character string plus the end-of-string character.

The printf() function is straightforward and was discussed previously. The sprintf() function produces a formatted character string like printf(), but stores it in a character string rather than sending it to the console. The function lists() then is used to send the formatted string to the list device (printer).

The function puts() sends a string to the console in the same manner that lists() sends a string to the list device. The functions putchar() and listchar() send a single character to the console and list device, respectively.

On the input side, the functions getchar() and gets() read a character and a string respectively from the console. The function getkey() is a nonstandard function that returns a character (like getchar()) if a key has been pressed; otherwise it returns −1.

The function scanf() corresponds to printf(). It reads characters from the console and converts them to the appropriate form according to the directions embedded in the control string, much as printf() converts output in the other direction. Unfortunately the discussion of scanf() requires knowledge of pointers, a topic not yet introduced in this book.

Notice that there is a function to read a character from the console and a function to read a string from the console, but no function to read an integer. Reading an integer can be accomplished

```
/* fig44.c -- Demonstrate Screen and Printer Output */
#define  MAXL    81

main()
{
        int a, b, sum;

        char str[MAXL];

        a = 2;
        b = 3;
        sum = a + b;

        /* First print to the console */

        printf("The sum of %d and %d is %d.\n\n",a,b,sum);

        /* Next build a formatted string for the printer */

        sprintf(str,"The sum of %d and %d is %d.\n\n",a,b,sum);

        /* Send the string to the printer */

        lists(str);
```

Fig. 4-4. Printer output in C.

```
/*   fig45.c -- Electronic Typewriter, Version 1 */
#define   CTRLZ             26
#define   MAXL              81

main()
{
        char str[MAXL];

        printf("Welcome to your Electronic Typewriter.\n\n");

        printf("Enter your text, followed by 'Control-Z'.\n\n");

        gets(str);
        while (str[0] != CTRLZ) {
                lists(str);
                gets(str);
        }
        printf("\nThat is all....\n");
}
```

Fig. 4-5. C Electronic Typewriter, Version 1.

easily by reading a string using gets() and then converting the string to an integer using the standard function atoi(). This is illustrated later in Fig. 4-7.

Figure 4-5 contains a program which emulates an electronic typewriter. It illustrates the use of the string input and output functions gets() and lists(). (Note: the while construct was discussed in Chapter 2 and is discussed further later in this chapter.) This program reads in line after line until a line consisting of the "Control-Z" character is encountered. Each line is echoed to the printer.

For comparison, the program in Fig. 4-6 does essentially the same thing using the functions getchar() and listchar(), which input and output text a single character at a time. Notice that the program in Fig. 4-5 is more forgiving of errors; it permits the user to backspace to correct errors.

The statement

c = getchar();

in the program of Fig. 4-6 reads a character from the console and assigns that character to the variable c.

Notice that the variable c is declared to be an integer rather than a character. This is because the function getchar() returns −1 when it encounters a control-Z and −1 is an integer, not a character. Notice also that the program in Fig. 4-6 can be terminated in the middle of a line by typing Control-Z, whereas to stop the program in Fig. 4-5 the Control-Z must be typed at the beginning of a line.

The user should compare the behavior of the two programs.

CONTROL STRUCTURES

The C language has a set of control structures comparable to that of Pascal and much richer than those of languages such as BASIC, COBOL, and FORTRAN. Most of the control structures of C encourage compliance with the principles of structured programming. Certain features, however, such as the break statement can easily be misused, violating the principle that a control structure should have a single entry point and a single exit point.

53

```
/*   fig46.c -- Electronic Typewriter, Version 2 */
#define  EOF            (-1)

main()
{
        int c;

        printf("Welcome to your Electronic Typewriter, Version 2.\n\n");

        printf("Enter your text, followed by 'Control-Z'.\n\n");

        c = getchar();
        while (c != EOF) {
                listchar(c);
                c = getchar();
        }
        printf("\nThat is all....\n");
}
```

Fig. 4-6. C Electronic Typewriter, Version 2.

The formats of the various control statements call for a single statement in many places. Where-ever one statement can appear in C, so can several statements grouped within braces ({ and }).

Simple Selection: if-else

The general format of this statement in C is as follows:

```
if (expression)
     statement 1;
else
     statement 2;
```

The expression in parentheses is evaluated. If it is true (nonzero), statement 1 is executed. If it is false (zero), statement 2 is executed. In no case are both statements executed.

Because in C the semicolon is a statement terminator, the semicolon after statement 1 is re-quired. This is contrary to the usage in Pascal.

As mentioned above, either statement 1 or statement 2 can be replaced by a group of state-ments within braces. Also, the else and statement 2 are optional.

Here is a simple if statement without an else part:

```
month++;
if (month > 12) {
    month = 1;
    year++;
}
```

This program segment increments the value of the month and then resets it to 1 and increments the year if the month was incremented past 12.

Here is an if statement with an else part:

```
if (month = 12) {
    month = 1;
    ++year;
} else
    ++month;
```

This achieves the same result as the previous example, but in a slightly different way. Which way is better is a matter of taste. There are two state-ments to be executed if the condition is true; they are enclosed between braces. There is only one statement to be executed if the condition is false.

Notice that the variable year in the if part and the variable month in the else part are incremented using the increment operator. Notice also that braces are required in the if part (because there are two statements to be executed) and not in the else part (because there is only one statement to be executed).

An if statement can be nested in C. Another way of saying this is to emphasize that statement 1 or statement 2 in the above skeleton format can also be another if statement. Here is an illustration showing the computation of a weekly payroll:

```
if (hours <= 40)
        pay = hours * rate;
else if (hours <= 50)
        pay = 40 * rate + (hours − 40) * rate *
        1.5;
else
        pay = 40 * rate + 10 * rate * 1.5 +
                (hours − 50) * rate * 2;
```

In this example, the employee is paid straight time for up to 40 hours per week; time-and-a-half for hours over 40 but less than 50, and double time for hours over 50 per week. Notice that the last else part is continued onto the next line. This makes no difference.

Multiple Selection: The switch Statement

The if statement allows selection between two alternative courses of action. If the else part is missing, the second course of action is simply to do nothing. There are sometimes situations when it is desirable to choose between more than two different courses of action. Nested if statements will work, but they become cumbersome for more than three or four alternatives.

The C language offers the switch statement for multiple selection. It is roughly analogous to the CASE statement discussed in Chapter 2, but there is an important difference. In the general CASE statement, each alternative is strictly mutually exclusive. There is no possibility for more than one

alternative to be executed. This is not the case in C. To make it that way, the break statement is needed. How the switch and break statements work together is illustrated in the program in Fig. 4-7.

The program in Fig. 4-7 reads in a number from 1 to 12 and then prints out the number of days in the corresponding month. The parentheses following the word switch contain an integer expression, in this case the variable month. Depending on the value of this expression, execution is passed to the appropriately labeled case. For example, if month had the value 11, control would be passed to the statement labeled case 11:. The statement days = 30; would be executed. The next statement is the break statement. This causes execution control to pass to the statement following the end of the body of the switch statement, which in this case is a printf statement at the end of the program. Had the break not been there, the next statement to have been executed would have been the statement labeled "case 2:.".

The break statement in general causes execution to pass the statement following the end of the current construct, whether that construct is a switch statement or one of the looping statements discussed below.

If month has value 3, for example, execution passes through to the "days = 31;" statement. If the value of month does not correspond to one of the labeled cases, execution is passed to the statement labeled default.

You should notice how the integer variable month is read in from the keyboard. It is first read in as a character string using the function gets( ); then it is converted to an integer with the standard function atoi( ). The name of this function is derived from the phrase "ASCII to integer." It will work only on computers that use the ASCII (American Standard Code for Information Interchange) character set. This includes most microcomputers but excludes most large IBM mainframes.

Loops

The C language has three kinds of loops: the for loop, which is a counted loop, and the while and

```
/*  fig47.c -- Days in month  */

#define   MAXL        81

main()
{
        int   month, days, year;
        char s[MAXL];

        printf("\nEnter the month (1..12):   ");
        gets(s);                  /*  Read in a string  */
        month = atoi(s);          /*  Convert string to an integer */
        switch (month) {
        case 1:
        case 3:
        case 5:
        case 7:
        case 8:
        case 10:
        case 12:    days = 31;
                    break;
        case 4:
        case 6:
        case 9:
        case 11:    days = 30;
                    break;
        case 2:     printf("\nEnter the year:   ");
                    gets(s);                /* Get string */
                    year = atoi(s);         /* Convert to int */
                    if ((year % 4) == 0)
                          days = 29;
                    else
                          days = 28;
                    break;
        default:    printf("\nSorry, month must be between 1 and 12.\n");
                    days = 0;
                    break;
        }
        printf("\n\nMonth %d has %d days.\n",month,days);
}
```

Fig. 4-7. C Calendar program.

do-while loops, which are conditional loops.

Counted Loops: The for Statement.
Chaper 2 contained a simple program in BASIC that printed out the integers from 1 to 10. The program of Fig. 4-8 accomplishes the same thing in C.

The controlling parameters of a **for** loop are contained within parentheses following the word **for**. As in Fig. 4-8, there are three parts within the parentheses, separated by semicolons. The first part is the initialization part—in this case, i=1. Thus the variable i starts with the value 1 on the first pass through the loop. The second part is the test part, in this case, i <= 10. This means that the condition i <= 10 must be true, or the control will pass outside the loop. The third part is the reinitialization part, in this case, i++. This means that after each iteration of the loop, the variable i is incremented, the test condition is checked, and if the test condition is true, the body of the loop is repeated.

```
/*    fig48.c -- Demonstrate the for
       loop    */
main()
{
        int i;

        for (i=1; i <= 10; i++)
                printf("%d\n", i);
}
```

Fig. 4-8. A C for loop demonstration.

The body of the loop is, in this case, a single printf()statement. In general it could be any statement, or a group of statements within braces.

Conditional Loops. A conditional loop repeats a statement or statements as long as a particular condition is true. The two kinds of conditional loops in C are the **while** loop and the **do-while** loop. The difference between them is that the **while** loop performs the test at the top of the loop, while the **do-while** performs the test at the bottom of the loop.

Because the **while** loop performs the test at the top, the body of the loop may not be performed at all if the condition is initially false.

Figure 4-9 shows how the task of the program

```
/*    fig49.c -- Demonstrate the
       while loop    */
main()
{
        int i;

        i = 1;
        while (i <= 10) {
                printf("%d\n", i);
                i++;
        }
}
```

Fig. 4-9. A C while loop demonstration.

in Fig. 4-8 can be performed using a **while** loop rather than a **for** loop. Notice that with the **while** loop, the intialization step (i = 1) must be performed outside the loop and that the reinitialization step (i++) must be performed within the body of the loop. Only the test condition is contained within the parentheses following the word **while**.

In this situation, the **for** loop of Fig. 4-8 was more appropriate than the **while** loop of Fig. 4-9. There are other situations, however, in which a **while** loop makes more sense. Suppose, for example, that a program is needed to read in integers from the console and sum these integers until their sum exceeds 100. The program must then print the sum and the number of integers that were included in the sum. The last integer read is not to be counted or summed. Such a program is shown in Fig. 4-10.

The variables count and sum are first set to zero. The first integer is read outside the loop. The **while** tests the termination condition, counts, sums, and reads in the next integer. The process is repeated as long as the sum is less than or equal to 100. After the loop terminates, the results are printed.

The same thing can be accomplished with a **do-while** loop, as shown in the program in Fig. 4-11. In this program some subterfuge is necessary to achieve the same result as in the previous program. Notice that count is initialized to −1 and then incremented back to zero on the first pass through the loop. There are several other minor differences.

```
/*   fig410.c -- Another while demonstration   */
        /*   Read in numbers until their sum exceeds 100 */

#define MAXL              81

main()
{
        int number, count, sum;
        char s[MAXL];

        count = 0;
        sum = 0;

        printf("Enter a series of numbers: \n");
        gets(s);
        number = atoi(s);
        while ((sum + number) <= 100) {
                count++;
                sum += number;
                gets(s);
                number = atoi(s);
        }

        printf("\n\n%d numbers were read.\n", count);
        printf("\nTheir sum is %d.\n", sum);
        printf("\nThe number %d was not counted.\n", number);
}
```

Fig. 4-10. Another C while loop.

In this case the **do-while** loop is less straightforward than the ordinary **while** loop. In other cases, the opposite is true. Which form of the conditional loop to choose is a function of the particular situation. That form which results in the most straightforward solution should be selected.

Functions

There are no subroutines or procedures in C, only functions. Because a function in C can do everything that a subroutine could do in another language, this is not really a disadvantage.

A function is a more-or-less self-contained module that can be invoked from anywhere in a program. A function usually returns a value associated with the name of the function, as described in Chapter 2.

In C a function can be invoked simply by writing its name; it can stand alone in a statement or it can be a part of an expression. In the stand-alone mode, it acts like a procedure; if it returns a value, that value is simply ignored.

You have already seen several examples of functions in C, including printf( ), sprintf( ), lists( ), gets( ), getchar( ), listchar( ), and atoi( ). These functions were furnished with the compiler. The documentation that comes with each C compiler includes a list of those functions furnished with that version of the compiler together with a description of what they do.

```
/*    fig411.c -- A do-while demonstration   */
        /*   Read in numbers until their sum exceeds 100   */
        /*   Version 2                                      */

#define   MAXL            81

main()
{
        int number, count, sum;
        char s[MAXL];

        count = -1;
        sum = 0;
        number = 0;

        printf("\nEnter a series of numbers:\n\n");
        do {
                count++;
                sum += number;
                gets(s);
                number = atoi(s);
        } while (sum + number <= 100);

        printf("\n%d numbers were read.\n", count);
        printf("\nTheir sum is %d.\n", sum);
        printf("\nThe number %d was not counted.\n", number);
}
```

Fig. 4-11. A C do-while loop demonstration.

Every C program contains at least one function, called main(). This function corresponds to the main program of other languages. The user can also write C functions. As a matter of fact, the use of functions to construct a C program in pieces is an excellent practice. Each function should perform a specific task or group of related tasks. The idea is that it is easier to write a large program if it is broken up into pieces (functions) of a moderate size.

Several examples of C functions are shown in the program in Fig. 4-12. The purpose of the program is to read in two numbers, print them out, exchange their values, and print them out again. These subtasks have been defined: reading in the numbers, printing them on the screen, and exchanging their values. A function was written to accomplish each of these subtasks.

Let us look at the function print2() first, as it is the simplest of the three. What the function does is simple: it takes two values given to it by the calling function (in this case the calling function is main()) and prints them, appropriately labeled. What is interesting is how it receives the values to print. The method used is called *pass by value*.

To understand what this means, first look at the definition of the function:

print2(x,y)
int x,y;

```
/*  fig412.c -- Demonstrate functions  */

     /*  Read and swap two integers  */

#define   CLEARSCREEN    "\033\052"
#define   MAXL           81
#define   CR             '\n'

main()
{
        int u,v;
        int c;

        do {
                puts(CLEARSCREEN);
                u = input("Enter first  variable:  ");
                putchar(CR);
                v = input("Enter second variable:  ");
                putchar(CR);
                print2(u,v);
                puts("Swapping....\n\n");
                swap(&u,&v);
                print2(u,v);
                printf("Again?  ");
                c = getchar();
        } while ((c=='y') || (c=='Y'));
}

input(prompt)
char prompt[MAXL];
{
        char s[MAXL];
        int i;

        printf("%s", prompt);
        gets(s);
        i = atoi(s);
        return(i);
}

print2(x,y)
int x,y;
{
```

Fig. 4-12. C Functions: the Swap program. (Continued on page 61.)

```
                printf("First    variable:    %d\n\n",x);
                printf("Second  variable:    %d\n\n",y);
}


swap(x,y)
int *x, *y;
{
                int temp;

                temp = *x;
                *x   = *y;
                *y   = temp;
}
```

The variables x and y are called *parameters* of the function. They are variables local to the function whose values are received from the calling function. When main() contains the statement

print2(u,v);

what happens is that the value of u is stored in the variable x, and the value of v is stored in the variable y while the function is executing. If the function contained the statement

x = 2*x;

the value of u would not be changed, because print() is in effect dealing with a copy of u, not with u itself.

In contrast to pass by value is *pass by reference*. This is illustrated by the function swap(). The purpose of swap() is to actually exchange the values of the variables passed to it, so pass by value would not work. With pass by value, no matter what was done to the variables in the function swap(), the variables in main() would remain unaffected.

Pass by reference works by passing a pointer to the function. A pointer can be thought of as containing the actual physical address in the computer's memory where the variable in question is stored. Thus when main() passes a pointer to swap(), it is telling swap() where it can find the variable so that swap() can change it if necessary.

In C the address of a variable is found by using the & operator. Thus

swap(&u,&v);

means that the addresses of the variables u and v are being passed to swap(). C uses the * operator to reverse the process; thus

temp = *x;

means that temp is to receive the value pointed to by x. In the heading of swap(),

swap(x,y)
int *x, *y;

means that x and y are pointers to variables of the integer type.

The function swap() uses the local variable temp to help carry out the exchange. Because you are using pointers, the function is actually exchanging the values of u and v in main(). A pointer can be thought of as a form of reference, thus making the phrase "pass by reference" more meaningful.

Pass by value is the usual way that ordinary variables and constants are passed to functions unless explicit use is made of addresses and pointers, as discussed above. Character strings are an exception. Character strings are always passed by reference in order to eliminate the overhead that would be required to make a copy of the string every time it is passed to a function.

When the compiler sees the statement

```
u = input("Enter first variable:");
```

it stores the character string in a convenient place and passes a pointer to that string to the function input(). No separate copy is made. The function input() need not use the "*" to acknowledge that it is receiving a pointer; it is understood.

The first two lines of the function definition are

```
input(prompt)
char prompt [MAXL];
```

The variable prompt is called a parameter of the function. It is declared to be a character string of length MAXL in the next line. (Note that MAXL is defined in the entire program.)

The function input() prompts the user and then reads an integer. It operates much like the INPUT statement of BASIC. The prompt is supplied by main(). The character string is printed on the video screen before the number is read. How an integer is read was discussed earlier.

We have not yet discussed how the value read in by input() is passed back to main(). Note that this value is stored in the local variable i. The statement

```
return(i);
```

causes the value of i to be passed back associated with the name of input(). Thus after

```
v = input("Enter second variable:");
```

is executed, v will have the value that was read

within input() and passed back by the return().

The program itself is straightforward. A main program often consists largely of a sequence of function calls, so if meaningful names are used for the functions, the program will be easy to read. Where meaningful names are not practical, appropriate comments should be included.

The statement

```
puts(CLEARSCREEN);
```

sends to the console the character sequence necessary to clear the screen. This sequence will vary from system to system.

Most of the main program is enclosed in a do-while loop so that the demonstration can be repeated easily.

Recursion

As discussed in Chapter 2, a function is said to be recursive if it invokes itself. How this is handled in C is illustrated by the program in Fig. 4-13, which demonstrates how a recursive function can be used to manipulate a character string.

The function takes a string of length N and prints it N times, dropping the first letter each time until there are no letters remaining. The result is a sort of triangle that can be read both horizontally and vertically. The function uses the standard C library function strlen(), which returns the length of the string.

A function was also needed to delete the first character from a string. Because such a function did not exist in the standard library supplied with this C compiler, it was necessary to write it. Rather than write a function that would serve only this purpose, a general purpose delete function was written that would delete a specified number of characters beginning with a specified position in the string.

The function that is recursive is called triangle(). When triangle() is called, the first thing it does is to check to make sure that the length of the string supplied to it is greater than zero. If not, triangle() returns without doing anything. If it is, triangle() prints the string, uses delete() to drop the first character, and then calls itself (triangle())

again. After the last character has been deleted, **strlen()** will return zero, and the function will return to where it was last called. Because this is the end of the function **triangle()**, the function will keep returning until it finally returns to **main()**. Because there is nothing left in **main()**, the program terminates.

It is easier to visualize how the program works after seeing it run. If you are still having trouble understanding the sequence of calls and returns, try adding

>   puts("triangle() entered");

as the first statement of **triangle()** and

>   puts("triangle() exited");

as the last statement of **triangle()**.

For variety, the **puts()** function was used to the exclusion of the **printf()** function in this program. With some compilers this can lead to a more compact program.

The Goto Statement

The goto statement is not often needed in C because of the rich variety of other control statements available. In other languages such as Pascal, the goto statement is sometimes used to escape from a loop before the loop has run its course. In C, the **break** statement can be used for that purpose. The problem with the **break** statement is that it will cause an exit from only one level of nesting. If it is necessary to escape from more than one level of nesting, the **goto** is necessary. This situation sometimes arises when an irreparable error is discovered deep inside a program and a quick exit is needed.

Some of the less expensive versions of C do not even support the **goto** statement, and it is not often missed. Nevertheless, for the record, I will discuss how it can be used in C.

A label must be defined to provide a destination for a **goto**. A label is simply an identifier followed by a colon. A label may precede any statement. A **goto** cannot jump out of a function; the target label must be in the same function as the **goto** that targets it. Here is the simple example of the use of a **goto** and the corresponding label:

```
/* Guessing game */
#define MAGIC   7
#define MAXL    81

main()
{
    char s[MAXL];
    int i;
start:  printf("Pick a number from 1 to 10");
    gets(s);
    i = atoi (s);
    i = ((i <1) || (i>10))
    if ((i<1) || (i>10))
        goto start;
    if (i==MAGIC)
        printf("You win! / n");
    else
        printf("You lose! / n");
}
```

The above program is rather simplistic and could have been programmed without the **goto** (by using **do-while**, for example), but it serves to illustrate the basic mechanics of the statement.

DATA STRUCTURES

Up to this point the C programs have used only integers, characters, and character strings. I will now introduce more advanced data structures such as arrays, structures, and linked lists.

Earlier I remarked that C is a rich language in that it provides a wide variety of control structures. C is also rich in its selection of data structures. The data structure called *structure* provides the user with the ability to define new data structures of arbitrary complexity.

Arrays

Arrays in C are treated in nearly the same way as are character strings. Character strings are, in fact, a special kind of character array that are terminated with the null character (binary zero).

```
/*  fig413.c -- Demonstrate recursion  */

        /*  Program manipulates a string recursively  */

#define   MAXL            81
#define   CLEARSCREEN   "\033\052"
#define   NULL          '\000'
#define   LF            '\012'

main()
{
        char s[MAXL];
        int  i;

        puts(CLEARSCREEN);
        puts("Type a string:\n");
        gets(s);
        for(i=1; i<=3; i++)       /*  Skip 3 lines  */
                putchar(LF);
        triangle(s);

}  /* end main() */

triangle(s)      /* Print a string, drop first char, repeat */
char s[MAXL];
{
        if (strlen(s)>0) {
                puts(s);
                delete(s,1,1);
                triangle(s);
        }

}   /*  end triangle()  */

delete(s,i,n)    /* Delete n chars, starting with i-th char of s */
char s[MAXL];
int i,n;
{
        int j,k;
        char t[MAXL];

        strcpy(t,s);     /*  Copies s to t */
        i--;             /*  Adjust char # to array subscript */
```

Fig. 4-13. Recursion in C. (Continued on page 65.)

```
    for(j=0; j<i; j++)          /*  Copy 1st part of string */
            s[j] = t[j];

    /*  Skip over deleted chars and copy the rest */
    for(k=i+n; k<MAXL-1 && t[k]!=NULL; j++, k++)
            s[j] = t[k];
    s[j] = NULL;                /*  Mark end of string */

}  /*  end delete() */
```

Arrays subscript in C are delimited by square brackets. Subscripts in C arrays always begin with 0. To create an array of 10 integers in C, the following declaration would be used:

int test[10].

Subscripts for this array would run from 0 to 9, not 1 to 10 as might be imagined. This peculiarity takes a little getting used to by programmers who have previously used other languages.

A two-dimensional array of 10 rows by 20 columns would be declared as

int test2[10][20];

Notice that two sets of brackets are required.

Earlier I mentioned that character strings are automatically passed to functions by reference rather than by value. The same is true for arrays. Otherwise the usage of arrays in C is similar to that in other languages. Examples showing the usage of arrays in C may be found in the following sections of this chapter.

Structures

In Chapter 2 I discussed the need for a record containing a student's name and his scores on up to 20 tests. Records in C are called *structures*. Suppose that there may be up to 30 students in the class. What is needed is an array of structures.

Here is how the declaration would look:

```
structure {
    char name[26];
    int score[20];
} student[30];
```

This structure allows for the name to have up to 25 characters (plus the null terminator) and for each student to have up to 20 test scores (numbered 0 to 19). If you want to have the test scores numbered from 1 to 20, the array must be dimensioned with 21 elements; element 0 can simply be ignored.

The name of the fourth student and the score he or she received on the seventh test would be printed as follows:

```
printf("%s %d \n", student[3].name,
        student[3].score[6]);
```

Notice the placement of the square brackets and the use of the "." to denote members of a structure. Recall that element 3 is the fourth element of the array of students and that element 6 is the seventh element of the array of scores.

Linked Lists

This section discusses how linked lists can be implemented as arrays of structures. Another method involving dynamic allocation of storage

65

exists, but it is considered to be an advance topic that is beyond the scope of this book.

The methodology illustrated here for implementing linked lists is especially the same as that discussed in Chapter 2 with several minor exceptions. Because array subscripts in C start with 0, the value -1 is used to mark the end of the list rather than the value 0. The first record in the list is stored as record 0 rather than as record 1. Also, rather than parallel arrays, one containing the name and the other the link, an array of structures is used.

The C declarations to set up the linked list are as follows:

```
#define EOL        (−1)
#define MAXLENGTH  5
#define NAMELEN     16
int first, free;
structure {
    char name[NAMELEN];
    int link;
} list[MAXLENGTH];
```

The constant EOL stands for *end-of-list* and is used to indicate that no more records follow in a list.

Following these declarations, the contents of record number 4 would be referred to as list[4].name and list[4].link.

The comprehensive example at the end of the chapter illustrates the use of linked lists in an actual C program, showing the details of how elements are added to and deleted from linked lists.

FILE HANDLING

A general-purpose high-level language must be able to write data to and read data from auxiliary storage devices. In the case of microcomputers, the most common form of auxiliary storage device is the floppy disk. A collection of data on a disk is called a *file*.

As mentioned earlier, the C language itself does not include any provision for input or output. Functions to handle input and output are customarily included in a function library provided with each C compiler. I have already examined functions that enable input from the console and output to the console and to a printer. In this section I will discuss functions to read from and write to disk files.

There is a more-or-less standard set of file input and output functions described *The C Programming Language*, by Kernighan and Ritchie. Not every C compiler, however, provides this standard set of file input and output functions. This book will discuss the particular set of functions provided with the Code Works C compiler.

The Code Works C compiler provides functions for character-oriented file input and output. Numbers and structures must be converted to characters before they can be written to a file. The compiler provides facilities for sequential file access, but not for direct or random file access.

Each file has associated with it a *file pointer*. In Code Works C, this **#define** is usually include in the program:

```
#define   FILE   char
```

The file pointer is then declared this way:

```
FILE   *fp;
```

The net result is that a file pointer is a pointer to a char. The file pointer is used to identify a particular file to the various input and output functions.

A file is opened using the **fopen()** function. For example,

```
fp = fopen("test.txt", "w");
```

opens a file called "test.txt" in the *write* or output mode and returns a file pointer for later use. This file pointer is assigned to the variable fp. To open a file for input, the mode is r for read. Code Works C also provides for the wb (write binary) and rb (read binary) modes. How these differ from w and r is discussed below with the **getc()** and **putc()** functions.

If an attempt is made to open a file in the w or wb mode and that file already exists, a new file will be created and the previous version of the file will be lost.

If an **fopen()** function fails for any reason, it

returns NULL (binary zero) instead of a pointer. It is good practice to check for such an occurrence.

Files are closed using the **fclose()** function. The correct usage is

    c = fclose(fp);

where c is a character and **fp** is a file pointer. The **fclose()** function returns NULL if an error occurs; otherwise it returns something else. What that something else is doesn't really matter.

When a character is sent to a file, an actual file output may not occur at that time. Instead the character may go to a **buffer**, which usually consists of 128 or more characters. When that buffer is full, the actual physical write to disk takes place. Closing a file automatically writes any characters remaining in the buffer to disk.

Sequential Files

A sequential file is a sequence of characters on a disk that are accessed one character at a time, from beginning to end. Except for the first character, no character can be accessed unless its immediate predecessor in sequence has just been accessed. In other words, character 4 can be accessed only after character 3, character 3 only after character 2, and so forth.

The function that writes a character to a file is called **putc()**. For example,

    a = putc(c, fp);

writes the character c to the file pointed to by fp. It returns and assigns to the variable a the character output if the write was successful; otherwise it returns EOF (end-of-file).

Ordinarily, **putc()** changes the newline character to a carriage-return/line-feed pair and ignores all NULL characters. If the file mode is wb instead of w, **putc()** will not do these things; it will write the data exactly as it receives it.

The function that reads a character from a file is called **getc()**. For example

    c = getc(fp);

reads a character from the file pointed to by fp and assigns it to c. If the end of the file has been reached, **getc()** returns EOF (−). For that reason, c must be an integer, not a character, as a character could not hold the value of EOF.

If the file was opened in the r mode, **get()** changes the text end-of-file character for CP/M (control-Z) to EOF. It also changes a carriage return to a newline character and discards the following character, which it assumes is a line feed. If the mode is rb, these editorial changes are not made and the characters in the file are read exactly as they are stored.

Most C libraries also include a function called **ungetc()**. This function puts a character back into a file after it has been read. It is sometimes useful when the program has read too far and needs to back up a character.

The program in Fig. 4-14 illustrates the use of sequential input and output. The program reads in a series of names and ages from the console and writes each to a sequential file. It then reads the names back from the disk, displaying each again on the console.

After the program clears the screen it opens a file called AGES. TXT for output (mode w). Following this there appears to be an infinite loop (while(FOREVER), where FOREVER has logical value true (−1)). This loop prompts the user to input a name and the corresponding age. If the user types a carriage return in place of a name, the first character of the string **name** will be the NULL character and a **break** will be executed to exit the loop.

The string **name** is read in using **gets()**. Because the variable **age** is an integer, it is first read into a temporary string and converted to an integer using **atoi()**.

A name and age pair is written to the sequential file by the function **putrec()**. The parameters of **putrec()** are **name**, **age**, and **fp**, the file pointer. The function **putrec()** in turn calls the function **putstr()** to write a string to the file. For the variable **name**, this is a straight pass-through. Because **age** is an integer, it must first be converted to a string. This is done using the standard function **sprintf()**.

```
/* fig414.c -- Sequential file of Names and Ages */
#define        CLEARSCREEN        "\033\052"
#define        EOF               (-1)
#define        FILE              char
#define        FN                "AGES.TXT"
#define        FOREVER           (-1)
#define        INPUT             "r"
#define        OUTPUT            "w"
#define        MAXL              81
#define        NEWLINE           '\n'
#define        NULL              '\000'

main()
{
        char name[MAXL], s[MAXL];
        int   age;
        FILE *fp;                        /* file pointer */

        puts(CLEARSCREEN);
        fp = fopen(FN,OUTPUT);           /* open file for output */

        /* Read in names & ages from keyboard & write to file */
        printf("\nEnter Names and Ages; <RETURN> to quit.\n\n");
        while (FOREVER) {
                printf("\nName:  ");
                gets(name);
                if (name[0]==NULL) break;
                printf("Age:   ");
                gets(s);                 /* read & convert to int */
                age = atoi(s);
                putrec(name,age,fp);     /* write to disk */
        }
        printf("\nInput complete; closing file %s.\n",FN);
        fclose(fp);

        /* Now read the file back and display on screen */
        printf("\nReopening file %s.\n",FN);
        fp = fopen(FN,INPUT);

        printf("\n\nHere are the names and ages from the file.\n\n");
        while (getrec(name,&age,fp)!=EOF) {
                printf("\n%s \t %d\n", name, age);
        }
```

Fig. 4-14. C sequential file usage. (Continued on page 69.)

```
                printf("\nClosing file %s.\n",FN);
                fclose(fp);

                printf("\nPress <space> to continue...");
                getchar();

}   /* end main() */

putrec(name, age, fp)                           /* write a record to file */

char name[];
int  age;
FILE *fp;
{
        char s[MAXL];

        putstr(name,fp);                        /* write string to file  */
        sprintf(s,"%d",age);                    /* convert int to string */
        putstr(s,fp);                           /* write string to file  */

}   /* end putrec() */

putstr(s,fp)                                    /* write a string to file */
char s[];
FILE *fp;
{
        int i;
        i = 0;

        while (s[i] != NULL) {
                putc(s[i],fp);                  /* put character to file */
                i++;
        }
        putc(NEWLINE,fp);                       /* newline to separate */

}   /* end putstr() */

getrec(name,age,fp)                             /* read a record from file */
char name[];
int  *age;
FILE *fp;
{
        char s[MAXL];
        int  c;
```

```
        c = getstr(name,fp);             /* get 1st string from file */
        if (c==EOF) return(EOF);
        c = getstr(s,fp);                /* get 2nd string from file */
        if (c==EOF)
                return(EOF);
        else {
                *age = atoi(s);          /* convert to int */
                return(0);               /* normal return  */
        }

}   /* end getrec() */

getstr(s,fp)                             /* read string from file */
char s[];
FILE *fp;
{
        int  c,i;
        i = 0;
        while ((c=getc(fp))!=NEWLINE) {
                if (c==EOF) {
                        s[i] = NULL;
                        return(EOF);
                } else {
                        s[i] = c;
                        i++;
                }
        }
        s[i] = NULL;
        return(0);

}   /* end getstr() */
```

Fig. 4-14. C sequential file usage. (Continued from page 68.)

The function putstr() writes the string to the file a character at a time using the standard function putc(). Because putc() suppresses the NULL character at the end of every string, a newline character is written to the file in its stead. The newline character is translated to a carriage-return/line-feed pair and serves to separate one string from another in the file.

After the last name and age pair are written to the file, the file is closed and reopened for input (mode r). Another while loop is used to read the data back in from the file and print it on the screen. Notice that when the file is opened for input, it is automatically positioned so that reading will start at the beginning of the file. The function getrec() is used to read in a name and age pair from the file. This function returns EOF when the end of the file is encountered, thus terminating the loop.

The function getrec() uses the function getstr() to read in a character string. Because name is a character string, there is no problem with it. Because age is an integer, its string representation must first be read into a temporary string variable and then converted to an integer using the standard function atoi().

The parameters of getrec() are name, age, and fp. Because name and age are to receive new values in this function, they must be passed by reference, not by value. Because name is a character string, it is automatically passed by reference. Because age is an integer, it must receive special handling in order to be passed by reference. This means that a pointer to age rather than age itself must be passed to the function. Thus the function is called as

```
getrec(name,&age,fp);
```

The parameter age in the function definition is declared as

```
int *age;
```

When age is given a value, it is referenced, using a pointer, specifically as

```
*age = atoi(s);
```

Failure to follow the rules of passing variables by reference is a common error among beginning C programmers.

The function getstr() uses the standard function getc() to read in a string a character at a time. When the newline character is encountered (the carriage-return/line-feed pair separating strings in the file), it is converted to the NULL character, thus terminating the string. Because of the parameter s of getstr(), the result is passed by reference. EOF is returned when the end of the file is encountered.

The final step is to close the file again.

Notice how the program is organized: the details of input and output are relegated to functions. Not only is the program easier to write this way, it is also easier to read and understand this way. This is because the logic of the main program can be followed more easily when the details are hidden away in functions.

Direct-Access Files

With a direct-access file, the program can access any record of the file independently of any other record. For example, record 2 can be accessed without first accessing record 1.

As was mentioned earlier, the Code Works C compiler does not support direct-access files. Full C implementations, however, usually provide the function seek() and/or lseek to permit direct access to files.

A direct-access file in C is treated as a sequence of bytes (or characters). The function seek() is used to position the file pointer at a particular place in the file. This position is measured relative to the beginning, the end, or the current position in the file. The offset is measured in numbers of characters. To use seek() the programmer must be able to compute the position of the desired record in the file. This requires extra bookkeeping.

The difference between seek() and lseek() is that in seek() the displacement is measured with an ordinary integer and with lseek() it is measured with a long integer. Thus seek() is useful only with files of up to 65,535 characters.

Because details of direct-access input and output tend to vary from compiler to compiler, the user should carefully check the documentation received with the compiler. It will cover, for example, the proper parameters to use for fopen().

Because direct-access files in C are character-oriented rather than record-oriented, it is less convenient to use direct-access files with C than with Pascal, COBOL, or FORTRAN. This deficiency can be overcome fairly quickly by creating functions to compute the location of a record in terms of characters, but with the other languages this function is automatically handled by the language.

GRAPHICS

The C language itself does not support graphics. There is no reason, however, why a particular implementation of C on a microcomputer

```
/* fig415.c -- Sequential file of Names and Addresses */
#define       CLEARSCREEN     "\033\052"      /* ESC "*" */
#define       EOF             (-1)        /* End Of File */
#define       EOL             (-1)        /* End Of List */
#define       FALSE           0
#define       TRUE            (-1)
#define       FILE            char
#define       FN              "ADDR.TXT"
#define       INPUT           "r"
#define       OUTPUT          "w"
#define       MAXL            81
#define       MAXRECORDS      10          /* Increase as necessary */
#define       NEWLINE         '\n'
#define       NULL            '\000'

struct {
        char lname[13];                         /*   12 chars + NULL */
        char fname[13];
        char address[21];
        char city[13];
        char state[3];                          /*   2 chars + NULL  */
        char zip[6];
} a[MAXRECORDS];

int link[MAXRECORDS], first, free;

FILE *fp;                               /* file pointer */

main()
{
        int c;
        openfile();
        do {
                c = menu();
                switch (c) {
                case 1:
                        append();
                        break;
                case 2:
                        review();
                        break;
                case 3:
                        listfile();
                        break;
```

Fig. 4-15. C Address Book. (Continued on page 73.)

```
                case 4:
                        dump();
                        break;
                case 5:
                        /* quit */
                        break;
                default:
                        break;
                }
        } while (c != 5);
        closefile();

}   /* end main() */

openfile()

{
        int i, c;
        fp = fopen(FN,INPUT);
        if (fp == NULL) {
                first = EOL;              /* indicate empty list */
                free  = 0;                /* first free record */
        } else {
                first = 0;
                i = 0;
                c = getrec(i);
                while ((c != EOF) && (i < MAXRECORDS-1)) {
                        i++;
                        c = getrec(i);
                }
                if (i == MAXRECORDS-1) warn();
                free = i;
                fclose(fp);
        }
        /* Initialize links to active records */
        for (i=first; i<free; i++)
                link[i] = i + 1;
        if (i>0) link[i-1] = EOL;
        /*  Now initialize free list */
        for (i=free; i<MAXRECORDS; i++) {
                link[i] = i + 1;
                a[i].lname[0]    =        /* multiple assignment */
                a[i].fname[0]    =        /* to blank out unused */
```

```
                    a[i].address[0] =          /* records              */
                    a[i].city[0]    =
                    a[i].state[0]   =
                    a[i].zip[0]     = NULL;
            }
            if (i==MAXRECORDS) link[i-1] = EOL;

}   /* end openfile()    */

menu()
{
        int row, col, c;
        char s[MAXL];
        puts(CLEARSCREEN);
        row = col = 5;
        gotoxy(col,row);                        /* position cursor */
        puts("1) Add to file");
        row += 2;                               /* add 2 to row */
        gotoxy(col,row);
        puts("2) Review file on screen");
        row += 2;
        gotoxy(col,row);
        puts("3) List file to screen or printer");
        row += 2;
        gotoxy(col,row);
        puts("4) Dump file to printer");
        row += 2;
        gotoxy(col,row);
        puts("5) Quit");
        col = 1;
        row += 2;
        do {
                gotoxy(col,row);
                printf("Select 1, 2, 3, 4, or 5:   ");
                gets(s);
                c = atoi(s);
        } while ((c < 1) || (c > 5));
        return(c);

}   /* end menu() */

append()                        /* add records to the file */
{
```

Fig. 4-15. C Address Book. (Continued on page 75.)

```
        int i,c;
        i = getfree();
        if (i==EOL) return(EOF);
        while (getentry(i)!=EOF) {
                insert(i);
                i = getfree();
                if (i==EOL) break;
        }

}   /* end append() */

getfree()                   /*  return rec nr of first free record */
{
        int i;
        i = free;
        if (i==EOL) {
                warn();
                return(EOL);
        } else
                return(i);

}   /*  end getfree() */

insert(i)                   /*  insert record into linked list in order */
int i;
{
        int p,q;
        if (free==EOL) {
                warn();              /*  no room to insert     */
                return;
        }
        free = link[i];             /*  delete from free list */
        p = first;
        q = EOL;
        while ((p!=EOL) && (greater(i,p))) {
                q = p;
                p = link[p];
        }
        link[i] = p;
        if (q==EOL)
                first = i;       /* new entry to head of list */
        else
                link[q] = i;
```

```
}   /*   end insert() */

getentry(i)                    /* read from keyboard into record i */
int i;
{
        int row, col, start;
        puts(CLEARSCREEN);
        start = 14;
        row = 5;
        col = 1;
        gotoxy(col,row);
        printf("Last Name:");    markoff(start,row,12);
        row +=2;  gotoxy(col,row);
        printf("First Name:");   markoff(start,row,12);
        row +=2;  gotoxy(col,row);
        printf("Address:");      markoff(start,row,20);
        row +=2;  gotoxy(col,row);
        printf("City:");         markoff(start,row,12);
        row +=2;  gotoxy(col,row);
        printf("State:");        markoff(start,row,2);
        row +=2;  gotoxy(col,row);
        printf("Zip Code:");     markoff(start,row,5);
        row = 5;  col = start + 1;
        gotoxy(col,row);
        gets(a[i].lname);
        if (a[i].lname[0]==NULL) return(EOF);
        row +=2;  gotoxy(col,row);
        gets(a[i].fname);
        row +=2;  gotoxy(col,row);
        gets(a[i].address);
        row +=2;  gotoxy(col,row);
        gets(a[i].city);
        row +=2;  gotoxy(col,row);
        gets(a[i].state);
        row +=2;  gotoxy(col,row);
        gets(a[i].zip);
        return(0);

}   /*   end getentry() */

markoff(col,row,n)                      /*   delimit input field boundary */
int col,n;
{
```

Fig. 4-15. C Address Book. (Continued on page 77.)

```
                int i;
                gotoxy(col,row);
                printf(":");
                for (i=0; i<n; i++)        /* n blank spaces */
                        printf(" ");
                printf(":");

}   /*   end markoff() */

review()                    /* print records to screen 1 at a time */
                            /* allows deletion of current record   */
{
                int q,r;
                char c;
                puts(CLEARSCREEN);
                if (first==EOL) return;
                r = first;
                q = EOL;
                do {
                        putchar('\n');
                        printrec(r);
                        putchar('\n');
                        do {
                                printf("G)et next record, ");
                                printf("D)elete this record, ");
                                printf("or Q)uit?   ");
                                c = getchar();
                                putchar('\n');
                        } while ((c!='G') && (c!='g') &&
                                 (c!='D') && (c!='d') &&
                                 (c!='Q') && (c!='q'));
                        switch (c) {
                        case 'G':                   /* get next */
                        case 'g':
                                q = r;
                                r = link[r];
                                break;
                        case 'D':                   /* delete   */
                        case 'd':
                                if (q==EOL) {
                                        first = link[r];
                                        putfree(r);
                                        r = first;
```

```
                       } else {
                               link[q] = link[r];
                               putfree(r);
                               r = link[q];
                       }
                       break;
               case 'Q':
               case 'q':
                       break;
               }   /* end switch */
        } while ((r!=EOL) && (c!='Q') && (c!='q'));

}   /* end review() */

putfree(r)        /* put r in free list */
int r;
{
        link[r] = free;
        free = r;

}   /* end putfree() */

listfile()                    /* list file to screen or printer */
{
        char c;
        int i;
        if (first==EOL) return;
        puts(CLEARSCREEN);
        printf("List to S)creen or P)rinter?  ");
        c = getchar();
        putchar('\n');
        switch (c) {
        case 'S':
        case 's':
                for (i=first; i!=EOL; i=link[i])
                        printrec(i);
                break;
        case 'P':
        case 'p':
                for (i=first; i!=EOL; i=link[i]) {
                        listrec(i);
                        listchar('\n');
```

Fig. 4-15. C Address Book. (Continued on page 79.)

```
                        }
                        break;
        default:
                        puts("Sorry, you must type 'S', 's', 'P', or 'p'.");
                        putchar('\n');
                        break;
        }
        putchar('\n');
        printf("Press any key to continue...");
        getchar();

}   /* end listfile() */

dump()                          /* dump file and pointers to printer */
{
        int i;
        char s[MAXL];
        sprintf(s,"first active = %d , first free = %d \n",first,free);
        lists(s);
        for (i=0; i<MAXRECORDS; i++) {
                        sprintf(s,"Record %d:",i);
                         lists(s);
                         listrec(i);
                         sprintf(s,"Link:   %d\n",link[i]);

                         lists(s);
                         listchar('\n');
          }

  }   /* end dump() */

 printrec(i)     /* print record i to the screen */
 int i;
 {
        printf("%s %s\n",a[i].fname,a[i].lname);
        puts(a[i].address);
        printf("%s, %s %s\n",a[i].city,
                a[i].state,a[i].zip);
        putchar('\n');

 }   /* end printrec() */

 listrec(i)         /* print record i on printer */
```

```
       int i;
       {
               char s[MAXL];
               sprintf(s,"%s %s",a[i].fname,a[i].lname);
               lists(s);
               lists(a[i].address);
               sprintf(s,"%s, %s %s",a[i].city,
                       a[i].state,a[i].zip);
               lists(s);

       }   /* end listrec() */

       closefile()              /* write list to disk and close out */
       {
               int i;
               fp = fopen(FN,OUTPUT);
               /* follow linked list */
               for (i=first; i!=EOL; i=link[i])
                       putrec(i);
               fclose(fp);

       }   /* closefile() */

       putrec(i)                               /* write a record to file */
       int i;
       {
               putstr(a[i].lname);
               putstr(a[i].fname);
               putstr(a[i].address);
               putstr(a[i].city);
               putstr(a[i].state);
               putstr(a[i].zip);

}   /* end putrec() */

putstr(s)                                 /* write a string to file */
char s[];
{
       int i;
       i = 0;
       while (s[i] != NULL) {
               putc(s[i],fp);               /* put character to file */
               i++;
       }
```

Fig. 4-15. C Address Book. (Continued on page 81.)

```
        putc(NEWLINE,fp);                    /* newline to separate */

}   /* end putstr() */

getrec(i)                                    /* read a record from file */
int i;
{
        int   c;
        c = getstr(a[i].lname);
        if (c==EOF) return(EOF);
        getstr(a[i].fname);
        getstr(a[i].address);
        getstr(a[i].city);
        getstr(a[i].state);
        getstr(a[i].zip);
        return(0);

}   /* end getrec() */

getstr(s)                                    /* read string from file */
char s[];
{
        int   c,i;
        i = 0;

        while ((c=getc(fp))!=NEWLINE) {
                if (c==EOF) {
                        s[i] = NULL;
                        return(EOF);
                } else {
                        s[i] = c;
                        i++;
                }
        }
        s[i] = NULL;
        return(0);

}   /* end getstr() */

greater(i,j)    /* return TRUE if a[i] > a[j] */
int i, j;
{
```

```
            int f1, f2;
            f1 = strcmp(a[i].lname,a[j].lname);
            f2 = strcmp(a[i].fname,a[j].fname);
            if ((f1)0 || (f1==0 && f2)0))
                    return(TRUE);
            else
                    return(FALSE);

}   /*  greater() */

warn()
{
            printf("\nWarning!!!  File is full!\n");
            printf("\nPress any key to continue...");
            getchar();

}   /*  end warn() */

gotoxy(col,row)                         /* position cursor    */
int col, row;                           /* hardware dependent */
{
            int offset;
            offset = 32;
            if (col ) 80) col = 80;
            if (row ) 24) row = 24;
            putchar('\033');            /* ESC */
            putchar('=');
            putchar(row + offset);
            putchar(col + offset);

}   /*  end gotoxy() */
```

Fig. 4-15. C Address Book. (Continued from page 81.)

with graphics capability could not include graphics functions. Because C supports low-level operations very well, the creation of such functions should be relatively easy.

COMPREHENSIVE SAMPLE PROGRAM

All the programs so far in this chapter have been relatively short and simple. Each has been intended to illustrate a particular feature of the language. The final program of this chapter is longer and more complex in order to portray more fully the nature of the language.

The comprehensive example program in this chapter is similar to that in most other chapters of this book in that it maintains a file of names and addresses in alphabetical order. It is different, however, in that it uses a sequential rather than a direct-access file. This is because of the limitations of the Code Works C compiler. It makes up for this lack of direct-access files by maintaining an array of structures in program memory.

The corresponding programs in other chapters

need only keep one or two records in memory at a given time. Each record is written to disk as it is entered. In the C program, the entire file is kept in memory and is written to disk only when the program is about to terminate. The impact of this is that the size of the file that can be handled by this C program is limited by the amount of available memory. A program using a direct-access file is limited not by the amount of memory, but by the amount of disk space available.

In this particular program the maximum size of the file is limited to 10 records by the constant MAXRECORDS. The reason for this will become clear later on. If the program is to be used for other than demonstration purposes, this upper limit can be easily changed.

The comprehensive example program is shown in Fig. 4-15. It has the capability to add records to the file, to delete records from the file, to display the file one record at a time, and to list the entire file on the screen or on a printer.

The file is maintained in alphabetical order at all times. As each record is added to the file, it is inserted in its proper place, eliminating the need for an explicit sort.

The data structure that permits the file to be maintained in alphabetical order without sorting is the linked list. As discussed earlier in the chapter, a linked list facilitates the insertion and deletion of records while maintaining the order of the list.

The data itself is stored in an array of structures. A separate array is used to store the links between record's. (The links could have easily been part of the structure.) A link points to a record by containing the value of that records's subscript.

The variable first is used to point to the first record in the file. It does so by holding the value of that record's subscript. The link corresponding to each record points to the next record in order. The corresponding link is the element of the array link with the same subscript as the record itself. A link value of −1 (EOL) indicates the end of the list.

Suppose that in a file that can hold 100 records, only 60 records are in use. Some way is needed to keep track of the unused records. One way to do this is to use a separate linked list called the *free list*.

The variable free points to the first record in the free list; subsequent free records are linked in the same manner as are the records in the active list.

The process of adding a record to the list consists of finding a record in the free list, removing it from the free list, and inserting it in its proper place in the active list. During all of this, the record itself does not move; the list insertion and deletion is accomplished by manipulating the links.

When the list is written to the disk, the records are put in sequence. There is therefore no need to store the links on disk. When the list is read into memory from disk, the links can be recreated easily because the records are already in the proper sequence.

Notice that certain of the variables in this program are declared outside of any function (before main()). This makes these variables *global* in scope. In other words, these variables may be accessed from any function in the program. They need not be redeclared in each function; in fact, any variable declared in a function with the same name as a global variable will prevent that global variable from being accessible in that function.

Global variables are useful for variables that must be referenced from several functions, such as the array of records and the array of links in this program. If they were not declared globally, they would have to be passed as arguments to each function that references them.

The overall structure of the program is illustrated by the structure chart of Fig. 4-16. In this chart, the names of functions that are called by another function are listed beneath and to the right of the calling function. Thus the functions openfile(), menu(), append(), and so forth are called by main(). The functions getfree(), getentry(), and insert() are called by append(); warn() is called by getfree(), and so on.

To make the operation of this program more understandable, a function called dump() is included. This function prints each record of the file and the corresponding links in the order in which they are stored in memory. To gain a better understanding of the data structures used in this program, you should enter several records, dump the file, and

```
        main()
              openfile()
                      getrec()
                              getstr()
              menu()
                      gotoxy()
              append()
                      getfree()
                              warn()
                      getentry()
                              gotoxy()
                              markoff()
                                          gotoxy()
                      insert()
                              warn()
                              greater()
              review()
                      printrec()
                      putfree()
              listfile()
                      printrec()
                      listrec()
              dump()
                      listrec()
              closefile()
                      putrec()
                              putstr()
```

Fig. 4-16. The structure chart for the Address Book Program.

then add and delete several records, dumping the file between each action. (The dump function as written requires a printer.) The reason that the constant MAXRECORDS was set to 10 was to keep the dump printout to a manageable size.

It is worth noting that the functions getstr() and putstr() in this program were borrowed from the program in Fig. 4-14.

ADVANTAGES AND DISADVANTAGES OF C

The C language was written by a professional programmer for use by professional programmers. It can be used by hobbyists, but it is probably not a good choice for beginners. Power and conciseness were design considerations; clarity of expression was not.

C provides a wide variety of control structures, including a for statement that is considerably more powerful than the corresponding statement in other languages. An example of its power can be found in the way it is used in the function closefile() of the program in Fig. 4-15.

C also provides facilities for manipulating bits and bytes. These facilities are useful for systems programmers who must deal with operating systems and such.

C is particularly useful for programs which read and manipulate characters. Examples include text editors and filters that convert certain characters (for example a program to convert each carriage return to a carriage-return/line-feed pair).

C allows the definition of data structures of arbitrary complexity using the **structure** facility.

Because C is usually implemented as a compiled language, programs written in C usually execute much faster than equivalent programs written in BASIC.

Programs written in C can usually be transported easily to other machines. Several major microcomputer software houses have begun to do all of their internal development in C for this reason. Software packages (including operating systems) written in C can be transported to new microcomputers as soon as a C compiler is available for that machine.

On the negative side, direct-access files are not as simple to use in most versions of C as in most other languages. Some versions of C have no direct-access file capability at all.

Most C compilers are relatively lax in their error-checking. For example, the compiler may not detect whether or not a function is being called with the proper number of arguments. Because C is a loosely-typed language, the compiler may not notice errors in program logic caused by mixed-mode assignments or arithmetic operations.

The concept of pointers in C is a very powerful one, but it requires the programmer to have a more detailed understanding of the underlying machine than ought to be the case. In my opinion, a high-level language ought to insulate the programmer from the underlying machine more than C does. The author of C readily admits (in Kernighan & Ritchie) that C is not a very high-level language.

The misuse of pointers can cause errors that are extremely difficult to detect.

Like Pascal, C lacks an exponentiation operator.

Most implementations of C on microcomputers provide very slow compilation speeds. The process of writing and running C programs is therefore less convenient than the corresponding process for BASIC or a language that compiles more quickly.

AVAILABILITY

There are many implementations of C available to microcomputer owners. Versions that run under CP/M, Apple DOS, IBM PC-DOS, CP/M-86, CP/M-68K, and Unix on various microcomputers are available. Some versions sell for as little as $35 and some for as much as $700.

The features of available C compilers vary greatly, so the potential buyer is cautioned to buy carefully. Some C compilers have floating points and long integers and some do not; some support direct-access files and some do not; some permit separate compilation of functions and some do not.

SUMMARY

C is a powerful language that is available for a wide variety of microcomputers. It is best suited for the intermediate to advanced programmer who already has a thorough understanding of the concepts of computers and computer programming and who needs the extra features provided by C.

C is an excellent choice for experienced assembly language programmers who wish to move to a high-level language. It is not a good choice as a first programming language for the beginner.

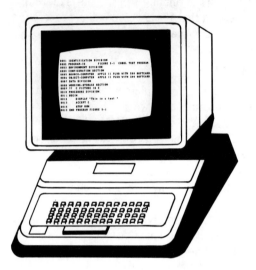

Chapter 5

COBOL

The name *COBOL* stands for COmmon Business Oriented Language. It is by far the most widely-used language today for business applications on large computers. A glance at the help wanted advertisements in a major metropolitan newspaper will reveal many more jobs available for COBOL programmers than for all other programmers combined. A language that is so widely used deserves a close look.

First of all, just what does it mean for a language to be "business oriented"? The obvious answer is that a business oriented language is a language that is suitable for business programs, but that just begs the question. How do business programs differ from other kinds of programs and why aren't languages such as BASIC and FORTRAN suitable for business programs?

First of all, business programs are oriented toward data files stored on magnetic disk or tape. A language for business programs must have efficient file-handling facilities. It should be able to read and

write data records simply and should handle both sequential and direct-access files.

Second, business programs must be able to handle dollars and cents exactly. Arithmetic must be exact. Floating point arithmetic is unacceptable for most business uses, as it has limited precision (usually about 7 decimal digits of precision). Integer arithmetic is exact and would be acceptable if it could handle larger numbers, but it cannot. Using integers to represent the number of cents, a 16-bit number could only handle amounts up to about $327.00. In short, a programming language should be able to perform exact decimal arithmetic involving large dollar amounts.

Most business programs involve storing, retrieving, and comparing data, with only simple arithmetic involved (addition, subtraction, multiplication, and division). A business programming language need not have advanced computational facilities.

Most general-purpose programming languages, such as BASIC, FORTRAN, Pascal, and C, provided excellent computational facilities. In fact these languages could be described as computationally-oriented. COBOL is not computationally-oriented nor does it need to be.

The general-purpose languages have facilities for handling files that vary in sophistication, but none of them has file-handling facilities as advanced as a full-blown COBOL implementation.

The general-purpose languages usually provide only floating point and integer arithmetic. COBOL provides decimal arithmetic. Some versions of BASIC and Pascal also provide decimal arithmetic, but they are in the minority.

In short, there is a whole class of problems for which the general-purpose programming languages are inadequate. This class of problems happens to be the largest group of problems that computers are called upon to solve. COBOL was designed for just this class of problems.

The roots of COBOL can be traced back to the early 1950's, to the work of Dr. Grace Murray Hopper. Dr. Hopper was one of the first persons to program an electronic computer, starting back in the early 1940's.

In the early days of computers, it was accepted as fact that computers had to be programmed in a very low-level language, using binary numbers (possibly disguised as octal or hexadecimal numbers) and possibly a few symbols. To be able to program using decimal numbers was a goal. Dr. Hopper believed that one ought to be able to program a computer in a language resembling English. She persisted in the face of much opposition, and the result was a language called Flow-Matic. Flow-Matic ran on a Univac computer beginning in 1956.

COBOL itself dates back to about 1960. Many of its ideas were borrowed from Flow-Matic. Dr. Hopper is sometimes called the mother of COBOL for her role in its development.

The current version of COBOL was adopted by the American National Standards Institute (ANSI) in 1974. Several implementations of COBOL are available for microcomputers, ranging in price from $39.95 to about $700.00. The version used for the examples in this chapter is Nevada COBOL by Ellis Computing. This is the $39.95 version, and therefore lacks some of the more advanced features of COBOL. It is nevertheless an excellent compiler and provides a sufficiently large subset of the language to be useful for practical applications as well as for illustrating the flavor of COBOL.

Despite the extent of its use on large computers, COBOL is relatively little-used on microcomputers. This is probably due to two facts: first, in the early days of microcomputers, BASIC was the most widely-available language and therefore the most widely-used despite its shortcomings. Second, it is easier to learn BASIC than it is to learn COBOL.

Now that COBOL is more widely-available for microcomputers, it seems likely that it will be used to a greater extent for future development of business applications on microcomputers for the same reasons that it is so widely-used on larger computers.

PROGRAM STRUCTURE

The structure of a COBOL program is more rigidly defined than that of most other languages. For an example of a minimal COBOL program, see Fig. 5-1. This program merely prints the message, "This is a test." on the screen.

A COBOL program is made up of four divisions, the identification division, the environment division, the data division, and the procedure division. Most languages have the equivalent of the data division and the procedure division, although they are not so rigidly defined. The data division contains all the variable declarations and the procedure division contains all the action statements.

The identification division is simply a place to put the name of the program, the author, the date written, and other documentary remarks. The environment division contains information about the computer on which the program is to run and when appropriate, information about external files.

One of the original design objectives of COBOL was portability from computer to computer. It was therefore decided to put all installation-specific information in a specific place

```
0001 IDENTIFICATION DIVISION.
0002 PROGRAM-ID.          FIGURE 5-1  COBOL TEST PROGRAM.
0003 ENVIRONMENT DIVISION.
0004 CONFIGURATION SECTION.
0005 SOURCE-COMPUTER.  APPLE II PLUS WITH Z80 SOFTCARD.
0006 OBJECT-COMPUTER.  APPLE II PLUS WITH Z80 SOFTCARD.
0007 DATA DIVISION.
0008 WORKING-STORAGE SECTION.
0009 77  C PICTURE IS X.
0010 PROCEDURE DIVISION.
0011 BEGIN.
0012     DISPLAY "This is a test.".
0013     ACCEPT C.
0014     STOP RUN.
0015 END PROGRAM FIGURE 5-1.
```

Fig. 5-1. A COBOL test program.

near the beginning of the program. In theory, to convert this program to run on another computer, one would only have to change the environment division and recompile it on the new computer.

COBOL programs were originally intended to be punched on cards for input to the computer via a card reader. Certain fields were intended to be punched in certain columns of the card. COBOL programs created using a text editor on a cathode ray tube display must still follow the same conventions. This is easily accomplished using the tab feature of most editors.

Columns 1 through 6 of a program contain sequence numbers. Column 7 is called the indicator area. An * in this column means the remainder of the line is to be taken as a comment or remark. Columns 8-11 are called the A-Field, and columns 12-72 the B-Field. Certain statements must start in the A-Field and others must start in the B-Field.

Nevada COBOL, the compiler on which the programs in this chapter were tested, supports the above column assignments, but also permits an alternate assignment. In the alternate assignment, sequence numbers go in columns 1-4, the indicator area in column 5, the A-Field in columns 6-9, and the B-Field in columns 10-70. The theory is that 4 digits of sequence numbers should be sufficient for programs written on a microcomputer. The programs illustrated in this chapter use the alternate column assignments.

The Nevada COBOL compiler is furnished with a utility program called Renumber, which creates the sequence numbers after the program is written, provided the programmer has left space in columns 1-4.

Notice that this program is written in upper case (except for characters within quotation marks). This is also a legacy from the early days of the language. The old key punches did not support lower case.

Examine the data division in the program in Fig. 5-1. Within the data division is the working-storage section, where independent variables are declared. (By independent variables, I mean those that are not part of a record.) The 77 in the A-Field of line 0009 is called the *level number*. Level 77 is used for independent variables. Other level numbers will be considered later. The name of the variable is C, it starts in the B-Field. The variable is described by its PICTURE.

The PICTURE of C is X. This means that its value can be any alphanumeric character, and that its width is one character. Other commonly used descriptors include 9 for a numeric digit, A for an alphabetic character or space, and V for an implied decimal point. These descriptors will be discussed more later on.

The Nevada COBOL compiler will not compile a program with an empty data division. An empty data division is so rare that this is not a serious problem.

The procedure division is organized into paragraphs. A paragraph label starts in the A-Field and the statements within the paragraph begin in the B-Field. This program contains only one paragraph, entitled BEGIN. The procedure division of a COBOL program must contain at least one paragraph.

The DISPLAY statement in line 12 displays the following character string on the video display screen. The STOP RUN statement in line 14 does exactly what it sounds like it does. The END PROGRAM statement in line 15 tells the compiler where to stop compiling.

COBOL uses periods at the end of division, section, and paragraph headings, at the end of variable declarations, and at the end of sentences. In this program each sentence contains only one statement, but in later programs, you will note more than one statement per sentence. Statements within a sentence are separated by a space, a comma, a semicolon, or by a carriage return.

All versions of COBOL that the author is aware of are true compilers rather than interpreters. This means that COBOL programs are likely to run much faster than similar programs written in an interpreted BASIC.

DATA REPRESENTATION

Data representations in COBOL differ from those in most other languages. This is because of COBOL's business orientation. COBOL has alphabetic, alphanumeric, and numeric data types. Alphanumeric data corresponds to character strings in other languages. Alphabetic data is similar, except that it is limited to the letters of the alphabet and the space character.

Data types in COBOL are defined by PICTURE clauses in the data division. the PICTURE for alphabetic data is A. A PICTURE of AAAAA represents a string of five alphabetic characters. An equivalent representation is A(5). The character B can also be included in an alphabetic PICTURE and represents a blank. Thus AAABAA represents a string of three alphabetic characters, a blank, and two more alphabetic characters.

The PICTURE for alphanumeric data is X. Thus XXXXX or X(5) represents a string of five characters, each of which can be any ASCII character.

Numeric data can be classified by its usage, which is DISPLAY, COMPUTATIONAL, or COMPUTATIONAL-3. This is indicated by the USAGE clause in the data division. This can be one of the following:

```
USAGE IS DISPLAY
USAGE IS COMPUTATIONAL
USAGE COMP
USAGE IS COMPUTATIONAL-3
USAGE COMP-3.
```

USAGE COMP is short for USAGE IS COMPUTATIONAL and USAGE COMP-3 is short for USAGE IS COMPUTATIONAL-3.

If the USAGE clause is omitted for numeric data, DISPLAY is assumed. DISPLAY data is stored as a sequence of ASCII characters, very much like a character string. The PICTURE clause allows for an implicit or actual decimal point and for a sign. The following PICTUREs represent numeric data:

```
S9(5)V99
S99999V99.
```

The two PICTUREs are equivalent. Each allows for a sign, five digits to the left of the (assumed) decimal point and two digits to its right. Unless explicit provision is made for the sign, there is no sign. Without the S in the picture of numeric data, any negative sign will be lost. This is a frequent problem for programmers who have programmed in other languages before learning COBOL. The solution is to always use the S unless you are sure the numbers cannot be negative.

The programmer can specify as many digits of precision as may be required for the application with DISPLAY data. This is a significant difference from other languages.

DISPLAY fields can also be edited. This is usually done in preparation for output. Here is an example:

$Z(5).99−.

This PICTURE will cause the number to be preceded by a dollar sign and to have five digits to the left of the decimal point with leading zeros suppressed, an actual decimal point, two digits to the right of the decimal point, and a trailing minus sign if the number is negative. If the number is positive or zero, no sign will print. There are additional editing characters, which can be found in any COBOL manual or text.

Whereas DISPLAY data is stored in ASCII (or whatever the native character is set of the host computer may be), COMPUTATIONAL data is stored in binary. In Nevada COBOL, COMPUTATIONAL data is stored as a 16-bit integer. COMPUTATIONAL data is therefore limited in magnitude to 32767. If the PICTURE of a COMPUTATIONAL data element is 99V999, however, Its maximum value is 32.767. The COMPUTATIONAL data type should be used sparingly on microcomputers and then only when speed of arithmetic operations is critical (which is almost never in COBOL).

COMPUTATIONAL-3 data is not a a part of standard COBOL, but is found in most COBOL implementations. It is sometimes referred to as *packed decimal*. In COMP-3, decimal digits are packed two to the byte, and the sign is stored in the rightmost half-byte. Unlike COMP data, COMP-3

data can be of arbitrary size. Arithmetic involving COMP-3 data is faster than arithmetic with DISPLAY data.

In summary, COBOL programs should use DISPLAY data as a matter of course. If computational speed is critical, then COMPUTATIONAL-3 data should be used. Only rarely should COMPUTATIONAL data be used.

Constants

COBOL does not support figurative constants in the same way as Pascal or C. It does, however, support the initialization of variables. This is done using the VALUE IS clause, as illustrated in the program in Fig. 5-2.

This program also contains an ACCEPT statement, which reads a character from the keyboard. This has the effect of waiting for the user to press the return key before allowing the program to terminate.

COBOL does support several symbolic constants such as ZERO, ZEROS, SPACE, and SPACES. The following declarations would initialize the variables A and B to zero and blank, respectively.

```
77 A    PIC 9(5) VALUE ZERO.
77 B    PIC X(5) VALUE SPACES.
```

Notice that PICTURE IS has been abbreviated to PIC and VALUE IS abbreviated to VALUE. Such abbreviation is common.

Variables

As mentioned before, variables in COBOL must be declared in the data division before they are used. Several more examples of variable declarations are shown in the program in Fig. 5-3.

This program reads a dollar amount from the console, computes sales tax (at the rate of 6%), and prints the result on the screen in edited format. How the ACCEPT and DISPLAY statements work

```
0001 IDENTIFICATION DIVISION.
0002 PROGRAM-ID.      FIGURE 5-2   ILLUSTRATE USE OF INITIALIZATION.
0003 ENVIRONMENT DIVISION.
0004 CONFIGURATION SECTION.
0005 SOURCE-COMPUTER.  APPLE II PLUS WITH Z80 SOFTCARD.
0006 OBJECT-COMPUTER.  APPLE II PLUS WITH Z80 SOFTCARD.
0007 DATA DIVISION.
0008 WORKING-STORAGE SECTION.
0009 77  STRING          PICTURE IS X(30)
0010                     VALUE  IS "This is a character string.".
0011 77  C              PICTURE IS X.
0012 PROCEDURE DIVISION.
0013 BEGIN.
0014     DISPLAY STRING.
0015     ACCEPT C.
0016     STOP RUN.
0017 END PROGRAM FIGURE 5-2.
```

Fig. 5-2. COBOL data initialization.

is discussed in the section on input and output. The MOVE statement is discussed in the next section.

THE MOVE STATEMENT

The MOVE statement of COBOL corresponds roughly to the assignment statement of other languages, but in some ways it is more powerful and in other ways, less.

As an example of the increased power of the MOVE statement, moving an unedited numeric data item to an edited numeric field causes the appropriate editing to take place. This is illustrated in lines 25, 27, and 29 in Fig. 5-3.

The MOVE statement can be used to move the figurative constants SPACE, SPACES, ZERO, and ZEROS to a variable when needed. This will set that variable to blanks or zero, as appropriate.

Another way in which the MOVE statement is powerful is that it can have multiple destinations, as in

MOVE ZERO TO A, B.

This MOVE statement sets both A and B to zero.

Later in the chapter, you will see that the MOVE statement can be used to move groups of related data all at once.

On the negative side, the MOVE statement can handle only constants and variables; it cannot handle expressions. Arithmetic must be performed by the appropriate ADD, SUBTRACT, MULTIPLY, or DIVIDE statement, not by a MOVE statement. These statements are discussed in the following section.

ARITHMETIC EXPRESSIONS

Most other languages use the symbols +, −, *, and / for addition, subtraction, multiplication, and division respectively. The philosophy of COBOL is to make the program as much like the English language as possible, so COBOL uses the words ADD,

```
0001 IDENTIFICATION DIVISION.
0002 PROGRAM-ID.       FIGURE 5-3  SIMPLE COMPUTATIONS.
0003*                          USE OF NUMERIC VARIABLES.
0004 ENVIRONMENT DIVISION.
0005 CONFIGURATION SECTION.
0006 SOURCE-COMPUTER.  APPLE II PLUS WITH Z80 SOFTCARD.
0007 OBJECT-COMPUTER.  APPLE II PLUS WITH Z80 SOFTCARD.
0008 DATA DIVISION.
0009 WORKING-STORAGE SECTION.
0010 77  COST           PICTURE IS 99V99.
0011 77  TAX-RATE       PICTURE IS 9V99
0012                    VALUE   IS 0.06.
0013 77  TAX-AMOUNT     PICTURE IS 999V99.
0014 77  TOTAL-COST     PICTURE IS 999V99.
0015 77  PRINT-LINE     PICTURE IS $ZZ9.99.
0016 77  C              PICTURE IS X.
0017 PROCEDURE DIVISION.
0018 BEGIN.
0019     DISPLAY "COMPUTE SALES TAX."
0020     DISPLAY " ".
0021     DISPLAY "ENTER COST  XXXX:  ".
0022     ACCEPT COST.
0023     MULTIPLY COST BY TAX-RATE GIVING TAX-AMOUNT ROUNDED.
0024     ADD COST TO TAX-AMOUNT GIVING TOTAL-COST.
0025     MOVE COST TO PRINT-LINE.
0026     DISPLAY "COST:   ", PRINT-LINE.
0027     MOVE TAX-AMOUNT TO PRINT-LINE.
0028     DISPLAY "TAX:    ", PRINT-LINE.
0029     MOVE TOTAL-COST TO PRINT-LINE.
0030     DISPLAY "TOTAL:  ", PRINT-LINE.
0031 END-OF-JOB.
0032     ACCEPT C.
0033     STOP RUN.
0034 END PROGRAM FIGURE 5-3.
```

Fig. 5-3. COBOL numeric computation.

SUBTRACT, MULTIPLY, and DIVIDE instead.

Line 24 shows an example of an ADD statement. The equivalent statement in BASIC or FORTRAN would be something like the following:

TOTAL-COST = COST + TAX-AMOUNT.

Suppose you did not want to use another variable such as TOTAL-COST, but simply wanted to add TAX-AMOUNT to COST. This could be done as follows:

ADD TAX-AMOUNT TO COST.

Line 23 shows an example of a MULTIPLY statement. Notice the ROUNDED clause. Rounding of numbers to the nearest penny is something that is required frequently in business oriented problems, so the ROUNDED feature is included as a part of the language.

Not shown is the ON SIZE ERROR clause, which permits the program to check for a result too large for the receiving data field and to jump to an error routine.

Some implementations of COBOL offer the COMPUTE statement, which allows arithmetic to be performed using the usual arithmetic operators (+, −, and so on).

LOGICAL EXPRESSIONS

The relational operators in COBOL are IS EQUAL TO, =, IS GREATER THAN, >, IS LESS THAN, <, IS NUMERIC, and IS ALPHABETIC. The English-language versions and the symbolic versions are equivalent; which to use is a matter of preference. The logical operators are AND, OR, and NOT.

Logical expressions in COBOL are used in much the same way as in other languages. The IS NUMERIC and IS ALPHABETIC expressions are not usually found in other languages, but their operation is predictable. They are often useful for editing input data. Here is an example:

IF MONTH IS NUMERIC
    ADD 1 TO MONTH.

COBOL handles compound conditions in two ways. One way is the same way as most other languages, for example

(A > B) AND (A < C).

Another way that this could be handled in COBOL is as follows:

A > B AND
    < C.

This would be clearer in words:

A IS GREATER THAN B AND LESS THAN C.

The first variable need not be repeated in each comparison if it does not change.

INPUT AND OUTPUT

You have already seen examples of the ACCEPT and DISPLAY statements for console input and output in Fig. 5-1, 5-2, and 5-3. The ACCEPT statement in line 22 of the program in Fig. 5-3 requires a closer look.

The field into which data is being read is COST. The PICTURE for COST is 99V99. COST is therefore a 4-digit number (the implied decimal point doesn't count). For the ACCEPT statement of Nevada COBOL to work properly, the user of the program must type exactly 4 digits at the console when prompted, with leading zeros if necessary. The decimal point is not entered; it is understood. In other words, "3000" would be read as 30.00.

If you type more than 4 digits, the extra digits are ignored. If you type fewer than 4 digits, the digits typed are left-justified in the field COST, and whatever was previously in the right-most digits of COST stays there. In other words, you may get garbage.

To remind the user to type exactly 4 digits, the DISPLAY statement in line 21 shows a template of XXXX.

The only justification the author can think of for such a strange way of handling console input is that it is an anachronism left over from the days of card input. More sophisticated COBOL compilers likely have a solution to the problem. In the meantime, it is something that can be gotten used to, albeit grudgingly.

The program in Fig. 5-4 illustrates how to handle printer output in Nevada COBOL. Notice the input-output section of the environment division. This connects the local name PRT to the external device called PRINTER. This associates the PRINTER with a file called PRT. In other words, the program is made to think that the printer is a file. This is a common device in several other languages as well, including Pascal.

In the file section of the data division, a file description (FD) is given for the file PRT. The format of this FD may vary slightly from compiler to compiler. Notice that the FD identifies a DATA RECORD called PRINT-LINE. This is analogous to a print buffer. PRINT-LINE is defined just below as a level 01 item with PICTURE X(80).

To the beginner there is little apparent logic in how to set up for printer output. It varies from system to system and is best learned by rote. The easiest way is to find an example that works.

The actual output to the printer is accomplished in two steps. First the data to be output is MOVEd to PRINT-LINE; then the WRITE statement is used as in line 28. In this case alphanumeric data was moved to PRINT-LINE, which has PICTURE X(80). Numeric data can also be moved to alphanumeric fields such as PRINT-

```
0001 IDENTIFICATION DIVISION.
0002 PROGRAM-ID.        FIGURE 5-4   USE OF A PRINTER.
0003 ENVIRONMENT DIVISION.
0004 CONFIGURATION SECTION.
0005 SOURCE-COMPUTER.   APPLE II PLUS WITH Z80 SOFTCARD.
0006 OBJECT-COMPUTER.   APPLE II PLUS WITH Z80 SOFTCARD.
0007 INPUT-OUTPUT SECTION.
0008 FILE-CONTROL.
0009     SELECT PRT ASSIGN TO PRINTER.
0010 DATA DIVISION.
0011 FILE SECTION.
0012 FD  PRT
0013     LABEL RECORDS ARE STANDARD
0014     VALUE OF FILE-ID IS "PRINTER"
0015     DATA RECORD IS PRINT-LINE.
0016 01  PRINT-LINE     PICTURE IS X(80).
0017 WORKING-STORAGE SECTION.
0018 77  STRING-1       PICTURE IS X(80)
0019                    VALUE IS "This goes to the video screen.".
0020 77  STRING-2       PICTURE IS X(80)
0021                    VALUE IS "This goes to the printer.".
0022 77  C              PICTURE IS X.
0023 PROCEDURE DIVISION.
0024 BEGIN.
0025     OPEN OUTPUT PRT.
0026     DISPLAY STRING-1.
0027     MOVE STRING-2 TO PRINT-LINE.
0028     WRITE PRINT-LINE.
0029 END-OF-JOB.
0030     ACCEPT C.
0031     STOP RUN.
0032 END PROGRAM FIGURE 5-4.
```

Fig. 5-4. COBOL printer use.

94

LINE provided that the USAGE is DISPLAY. COMP and COMP-3 fields should first be moved to a numeric field with USAGE DISPLAY before being moved to PRINT-LINE.

The printer can be made to double space as follows:

```
WRITE PRINT-LINE BEFORE
ADVANCING 2 LINES.
```

For triple spacing, substitute 3 for 2, and so on. For printers with top-of-form capability, you can write

```
WRITE PRINT-LINE BEFORE
ADVANCING PAGE.
```

Sometimes a programmer needs to use the DISPLAY statement to print something on the screen and wishes to leave the cursor at the end of the line. This is done by typing something like

```
DISPLAY PRINT-LINE WITH NO ADVANCING.
```

CONTROL STRUCTURES

COBOL has a fairly limited set of control structures compared to more modern languages such as Pascal. The user is forced to use the GO TO statement more frequently than would be necessary if the more advanced control structures were available.

Simple Selection: IF-ELSE

The general format for the IF statement in COBOL is as follows:

```
IF logical expression
    statement-1
ELSE
    statement-2.
```

Statement-1 can be a series of statements as long as none of them is terminated by a period. Statement-2 can also be a series of statements. The scope of the IF statement is determined by the placement of the final period following statement-2.

Statement-1 or statement-2 can also be NEXT SENTENCE, which is merely a place-holder. ELSE NEXT SENTENCE is redundant and may be omitted.

The Nevada COBOL compiler does not permit nested IF statements. In other words, neither statement-1 nor statement-2 can be another IF statement. This is not a restriction of COBOL compilers in general.

Here is a simple example of an IF statement without an ELSE part:

```
ADD 1 TO MONTH.
IF MONTH > 12
    MOVE 1 TO MONTH;
    ADD 1 TO YEAR.
```

Here is an example of an IF statement with an ELSE that accomplishes the same thing:

```
IF MONTH = 12
    MOVE 1 TO MONTH;
    ADD 1 TO YEAR;
ELSE
    ADD 1 TO MONTH.
```

Which of the two examples is the preferred way to accomplish the task is a matter of taste.

Multiple Selection

The COBOL equivalent of the CASE statement is the GO TO-DEPENDING ON statement, discussed below.

Loops and Subroutines

COBOL has only one loop statement, the PERFORM statement. The PERFORM statement has several variants, however. The simple PERFORM statement is much like a subroutine call, most closely resembling the GOSUB of BASIC. PERFORM-TIMES is like a counted loop, and PERFORM-UNTIL is like a conditional loop.

Simple Subroutines: The PERFORM Statement. Earlier I pointed out that the procedure division of a COBOL program consists of a sequence of paragraphs. Each paragraph is identified by a paragraph name, which begins in the A-Field. The body of the paragraph begins in the B-Field. The end of one paragraph is marked only by the beginning of the next paragraph or by the END PROGRAM statement.

Each paragraph in a COBOL is a potential subroutine. A subroutine is invoked by a PER-FORM statement as illustrated below:

PERFORM PARA-1.

In this example, PARA-1 is the name of a paragraph.

Another form of the PERFORM statement is as follows:

PERFORM PARA-1 THRU PARA-3.

In this example, PARA-1, PARA-3, and all intervening paragraphs are treated as a single subroutine. There is no explicit return statement in COBOL. The end of the subroutine is the end of the last-named paragraph.

There are no parameters in this simple form of subroutine in COBOL. All variables within the program are global in scope.

An example showing two simple subroutines is given in Fig. 5-5. The program clears the screen and prints a message in the center of the screen. One subroutine clears the screen, and the other positions the cursor. You are cautioned that the details of these subroutines will vary from microcomputer to microcomputer; these particular subroutines were written and tested on an Apple II Plus with a Microsoft Softcard and an ALS Smarterm II 80-column video display card.

Notice the use of 01, 02, and 03 levels in the working-storage section of the data division. The 02 levels are subordinate to the preceding 01 level and the 03 levels are subordinate to the preceding 02 level. One purpose of this is to group related data together. Another is to permit multiple data elements to be MOVEd together, as in the CLEAR-SCREEN subroutine.

In lines 14, 15, 19, and 20 of Fig. 5-5, the 03-level data elements are all given the name

FILLER. How can they be accessed? The FILLER data elements are part of larger groups, in one case the 02-level data element CLEAR and in the other case the 02-level data element CURSOR PO-SITION. When the respective 02-level data elements are MOVEd or DISPLAYed, the FILLER data elements go along as part of the group.

The two subroutines are placed following the STOP RUN statement and before the END PRO-GRAM statement. Recall that statements with an * immediately following the sequence number are comment lines.

In this program each subroutine is PER-FORMed only once. In larger programs, a subroutine can be PERFORMed as often as needed, but it need be defined only once.

COBOL also supports separately-compiled subroutines that are invoked by the CALL statement. This type of subroutine does support parameters. Separately-compiled subroutines are considered to be an advanced topic and are beyond the scope of this book.

Counted Loops: PERFORM-TIMES. In most languages a loop consists of a control line (for example, the FOR statement of BASIC or Pascal), a body of one or more lines, and possibly a terminal line (for example the NEXT statement in BASIC). The body of the loop almost always follows the control line.

COBOL is different. The body of the loop is a separate paragraph, possibly located elsewhere in the program. In fact, executing a loop in COBOL is akin to PERFORMing a subroutine multiple times.

The simplest loop in COBOL is the PER-FORM-TIMES loop. An example is given in the program in Fig. 5-6. This program simply prints the integers from 1 to 10 on the video screen, double spaced.

Conditional Loops. Another form of the PERFORM statement provides the COBOL version of the conditional loop. The named paragraph is PERFORMed until a certain condition becomes true. If the condition is initially false, the paragraph will not be PERFORMed at all.

An example of the PERFORM-UNTIL statement is shown in Fig. 5-7. The program produces

```
0001 IDENTIFICATION DIVISION.
0002 PROGRAM-ID.        FIGURE 5-5   USE OF PERFORM.
0003 ENVIRONMENT DIVISION.
0004 CONFIGURATION SECTION.
0005 SOURCE-COMPUTER.  APPLE II PLUS WITH Z80 SOFTCARD.
0006 OBJECT-COMPUTER.  APPLE II PLUS WITH Z80 SOFTCARD.
0007 DATA DIVISION.
0008 WORKING-STORAGE SECTION.
0009 01  SCREEN-DATA.
0010     02  OFFSET      PIC 9999   VALUE 7967.
0011     02  MAX-ROW     PIC 99     VALUE 24.
0012     02  MAX-COL     PIC 99     VALUE 80.
0013     02  CLEAR.
0014         03  FILLER  PIC X      VALUE ""1B"".
0015         03  FILLER  PIC X      VALUE "*".
0016     02  ROW         PIC 99     USAGE COMP.
0017     02  COL         PIC 99     USAGE COMP.
0018     02  CURSOR-POSITION.
0019         03  FILLER  PIC X      VALUE ""1B"".
0020         03  FILLER  PIC X      VALUE "=".
0021         03  XY      PIC 99     USAGE COMP.
0022 77  C               PIC X.
0023 PROCEDURE DIVISION.
0024 BEGIN.
0025     PERFORM CLEAR-SCREEN.
0026     MOVE 12 TO ROW.
0027     MOVE 30 TO COL.
0028     PERFORM POSITION-CURSOR.
0029     DISPLAY "Hello There!" WITH NO ADVANCING.
0030 END-OF-JOB.
0031     ACCEPT C.
0032     STOP RUN.
0033 CLEAR-SCREEN.
0034     DISPLAY CLEAR WITH NO ADVANCING.
0035 POSITION-CURSOR.
0036*    FIRST CHECK FOR LEGAL SCREEN COORDINATES.
0037     IF ROW < 1        MOVE 1 TO ROW.
0038     IF ROW > MAX-ROW MOVE MAX-ROW TO ROW.
0039     IF COL < 1        MOVE 1 TO COL.
0040     IF COL > MAX-COL MOVE MAX-COL TO COL.
0041*    NOW COMPUTE NECESSARY VALUES.
0042     MULTIPLY 256 BY COL GIVING XY.
0043     ADD ROW    TO XY.
0044     ADD OFFSET TO XY.
0045*    OUTPUT TO SCREEN.
0046     DISPLAY CURSOR-POSITION WITH NO ADVANCING.
0047 END PROGRAM FIGURE 5-5.
```

Fig. 5-5. The COBOL PERFORM statement.

```
0001 IDENTIFICATION DIVISION.
0002 PROGRAM-ID.        FIGURE 5-6   ILLUSTRATE USE OF A COUNTED LOOP.
0003 ENVIRONMENT DIVISION.
0004 CONFIGURATION SECTION.
0005 SOURCE-COMPUTER.  APPLE II PLUS WITH Z80 SOFTCARD.
0006 OBJECT-COMPUTER.  APPLE II PLUS WITH Z80 SOFTCARD.
0007 DATA DIVISION.
0008 WORKING-STORAGE SECTION.
0009 77  COUNTER        PIC 99.
0010 77  C              PIC X.
0011 PROCEDURE DIVISION.
0012 BEGIN.
0013     MOVE 1 TO COUNTER.
0014     PERFORM PRINT-COUNTER 10 TIMES.
0015 END-OF-JOB.
0016     ACCEPT C.
0017     STOP RUN.
0018 PRINT-COUNTER.
0019     DISPLAY COUNTER.
0020     DISPLAY SPACE.
0021     ADD 1 TO COUNTER.
0022 END PROGRAM FIGURE 5-6.
```

Fig. 5-6. A counted loop in COBOL.

```
0001 IDENTIFICATION DIVISION.
0002 PROGRAM-ID.        FIGURE 5-7   ILLUSTRATE USE OF A CONDITIONAL LOOP.
0003 ENVIRONMENT DIVISION.
0004 CONFIGURATION SECTION.
0005 SOURCE-COMPUTER.  APPLE II PLUS WITH Z80 SOFTCARD.
0006 OBJECT-COMPUTER.  APPLE II PLUS WITH Z80 SOFTCARD.
0007 DATA DIVISION.
0008 WORKING-STORAGE SECTION.
0009 77  COUNTER        PIC 99.
0010 77  C              PIC X.
0011 PROCEDURE DIVISION.
0012 BEGIN.
0013     MOVE 1 TO COUNTER.
0014     PERFORM PRINT-IT UNTIL COUNTER > 10.
0015 END-OF-JOB.
0016     ACCEPT C.
0017     STOP RUN.
0018 PRINT-IT.
0019     DISPLAY COUNTER.
0020     DISPLAY SPACE.
0021     ADD 1 TO COUNTER.
0022 END PROGRAM FIGURE 5-7.
```

Fig. 5-7. A conditional loop in COBOL.

98

```
0001 IDENTIFICATION DIVISION.
0002 PROGRAM-ID.        FIGURE 5-8   ILLUSTRATE USE OF A CONDITIONAL LOOP.
0003*                                A MORE COMPLEX EXAMPLE.
0004 ENVIRONMENT DIVISION.
0005 CONFIGURATION SECTION.
0006 SOURCE-COMPUTER.   APPLE II PLUS WITH Z80 SOFTCARD.
0007 OBJECT-COMPUTER.   APPLE II PLUS WITH Z80 SOFTCARD.
0008 DATA DIVISION.
0009 WORKING-STORAGE SECTION.
0010 77   NUM          PIC 99.
0011 77   COUNT        PIC 999.
0012 77   SUM          PIC 999.
0013 77   TEMP         PIC 999.
0014 77   D-LINE       PIC ZZZ.
0015 77   C            PIC X.
0016 PROCEDURE DIVISION.
0017 BEGIN.
0018     MOVE ZERO TO COUNT, SUM.
0019     PERFORM READ-IT.
0020     PERFORM SUM-IT UNTIL TEMP > 100.
0021     MOVE COUNT TO D-LINE.
0022     DISPLAY D-LINE, " NUMBERS WERE READ.".
0023     MOVE SUM   TO D-LINE.
0024     DISPLAY "THEIR SUM IS ", D-LINE, ".".
0025     MOVE NUM   TO D-LINE.
0026     DISPLAY "THE NUMBER ", D-LINE, " WAS NOT COUNTED.".
0027 END-OF-JOB.
0028     ACCEPT C.
0029     STOP RUN.
0030 READ-IT.
0031     DISPLAY SPACE.
0032     DISPLAY "Enter a Number XX:   "
0033             WITH NO ADVANCING.
0034     ACCEPT NUM.
0035     ADD NUM TO SUM GIVING TEMP.
0036 SUM-IT.
0037     ADD 1 TO COUNT.
0038     ADD NUM TO SUM.
0039     PERFORM READ-IT.
0040 END PROGRAM FIGURE 5-8.
```

Fig. 5-8. Another conditional loop in COBOL.

exactly the same output as the program in Fig. 5-6.

In this trivial example, there is little advantage to using the PERFORM-UNTIL rather than the PERFORM-TIMES. Another example, which better illustrates the utility of the PERFORM-UNTIL statement, is shown in Fig. 5-8.

The program in Fig. 5-8 reads a series of two-digit numbers until their sum exceeds 100. It then prints the count of the numbers included in the sum, the sum itself, and the number that would have made the sums go over 100.

The PERFORM-UNTIL statement is in line 20. The body of the loop is the paragraph entitled SUM-IT. SUM-IT happens to call the subroutine READ-IT, using an ordinary PERFORM statement.

More complete implementations of COBOL allow a VARYING clause to be added to the PERFORM statement. The statement

PERFORM PARA-A VARYING INX
FROM 1 BY 1 UNTIL INX > 10.

is roughly equivalent to the FOR statement of Pascal and BASIC.

Functions

The COBOL language does not support functions.

The GO TO Statement

The GO TO statement is needed rather more frequently in COBOL than in some other languages such as Pascal and C. Sometimes it is more convenient to simulate a **while** loop with its body in line than to use a PERFORM-UNTIL.

The program in Fig. 5-9 is a rewrite of the program of Fig. 5-8 using GO TO statements rather than a PERFORM-UNTIL. The coding is straightforward and needs little comment.

As illustrated in this example, the object of a GO TO statement is a paragraph name.

The GO TO-DEPENDING ON Statement

The GO TO-DEPENDING ON statement permits the emulation of a CASE statement, as described in Chapter 2. The program in Fig. 5-10 shows how this is done.

Between the GO TO (line 21) and the DEPENDING ON (line 35) is a list of paragraph names, each of which is the name of a month. Control is transferred to one of them based on its relative position in the list and on the value of the variable MONTH. If MONTH has value 1, control is transferred to the first paragraph named in the list (January); if MONTH has a value of 10, control is transferred to the tenth paragraph named in the list (October), and so on.

In this case, 12 paragraph names are listed. If MONTH is not between 1 and 12, control would be passed to the next statement, which in this case is statement 36. Statement 37 then transfers control back to the beginning to read in another value for MONTH.

There is a paragraph for each month. The paragraphs are listed in the GO TO-DEPENDING ON statement in order so that the appropriate paragraph is selected for each month. Within each paragraph the appropriate name is transferred to the character string MONTH-NAME, and the appropriate number of days, to the variable DAYS. At the end of each paragraph except the last is a GO TO END-CASE, which ensures that only one of the paragraphs is executed for a particular value of MONTH.

For most months the action is simple. For February, however, action is required to determine whether or not the year is a leap year. The rule is that years evenly divisible by 4 are leap years.

In more complete implementations of COBOL, the remainder after division can be computed directly, as in

DIVIDE 4 INTO YEAR GIVING QUOTIENT
REMAINDER REMAIN.

In this program the remainder had to be computed indirectly.

DATA STRUCTURES

COBOL allows the construction of a wide variety of data structures. The relationships between

```
0001 IDENTIFICATION DIVISION.
0002 PROGRAM-ID.  FIGURE 5-9  ILLUSTRATE USE OF THE GO TO STATEMENT.
0003 ENVIRONMENT DIVISION.
0004 CONFIGURATION SECTION.
0005 SOURCE-COMPUTER.  APPLE II PLUS WITH Z80 SOFTCARD.
0006 OBJECT-COMPUTER.  APPLE II PLUS WITH Z80 SOFTCARD.
0007 DATA DIVISION.
0008 WORKING-STORAGE SECTION.
0009 77  NUM           PIC 99.
0010 77  COUNT         PIC 999.
0011 77  SUM           PIC 999.
0012 77  TEMP          PIC 999.
0013 77  D-LINE        PIC ZZZ.
0014 77  C             PIC X.
0015 PROCEDURE DIVISION.
0016 BEGIN.
0017     MOVE ZERO TO COUNT, SUM.
0018 LOOP.
0019     PERFORM GET-NUM.
0020     ADD NUM TO SUM GIVING TEMP.
0021     IF TEMP > 100 GO TO PRINT-IT.
0022     ADD 1 TO COUNT.
0023     MOVE TEMP TO SUM.
0024     GO TO LOOP.
0025 PRINT-IT.
0026     MOVE COUNT TO D-LINE.
0027     DISPLAY D-LINE, " NUMBERS WERE READ.".
0028     MOVE SUM   TO D-LINE.
0029     DISPLAY "THEIR SUM IS ", D-LINE, ".".
0030     MOVE NUM   TO D-LINE.
0031     DISPLAY "THE NUMBER ", D-LINE, " WAS NOT COUNTED.".
0032 END-OF-JOB.
0033     ACCEPT C.
0034     STOP RUN.
0035 GET-NUM.
0036     DISPLAY SPACE.
0037     DISPLAY "Enter a Number XX:   "
0038              WITH NO ADVANCING.
0039     ACCEPT NUM.
0040 END PROGRAM FIGURE 5-9.
```

Fig. 5-9. The GO TO statement in COBOL.

```
0001 IDENTIFICATION DIVISION.
0002 PROGRAM-ID.        FIGURE 5-10   COMPUTE NUMBER OF DAYS IN A MONTH
0003*                                 USING GO TO-DEPENDING ON.
0004 ENVIRONMENT DIVISION.
0005 CONFIGURATION SECTION.
0006 SOURCE-COMPUTER.   APPLE II PLUS WITH Z80 SOFTCARD.
0007 OBJECT-COMPUTER.   APPLE II PLUS WITH Z80 SOFTCARD.
0008 DATA DIVISION.
0009 WORKING-STORAGE SECTION.
0010 77  MONTH          PIC 99.
0011 77  DAYS           PIC 99.
0012 77  YEAR           PIC 99.
0013 77  MONTH-NAME     PIC X(10).
0014 77  REMAIN         PIC 9(5).
0015 77  QUOTIENT       PIC 9(5).
0016 77  TEMP           PIC 9(5).
0017 77  C              PIC X.
0018 PROCEDURE DIVISION.
0019 BEGIN.
0020     MOVE SPACES TO MONTH-NAME.
0021     DISPLAY "ENTER THE MONTH (01..12):   "
0022     ACCEPT MONTH.
0023     GO TO JANUARY,
0024          FEBRUARY,
0025          MARCH,
0026          APRIL,
0027          MAY,
0028          JUNE,
0029          JULY,
0030          AUGUST,
0031          SEPTEMBER,
0032          OCTOBER,
0033          NOVEMBER,
0034          DECEMBER
0035       DEPENDING ON MONTH.
0036 NONE-OF-THE-ABOVE.
0037     GO TO BEGIN.
0038 JANUARY.
0039     MOVE "JANUARY"   TO MONTH-NAME.
0040     MOVE 31 TO DAYS.
0041     GO TO END-CASE.
0042 FEBRUARY.
0043     MOVE "FEBRUARY"  TO MONTH-NAME.
```

Fig. 5-10. COBOL Calendar program, Version 1. (Continued on page 103.)

```
0044      DISPLAY "ENTER THE YEAR (00-99):    "
0045          WITH NO ADVANCING.
0046      ACCEPT YEAR.
0047      DIVIDE 4 INTO YEAR GIVING QUOTIENT.
0048      MULTIPLY 4 BY QUOTIENT GIVING TEMP.
0049      SUBTRACT TEMP FROM YEAR GIVING REMAIN.
0050      IF REMAIN IS EQUAL TO 0
0051          MOVE 29 TO DAYS
0052      ELSE
0053          MOVE 28 TO DAYS.
0054      GO TO END-CASE.
0055 MARCH.
0056      MOVE "MARCH"      TO MONTH-NAME.
0057      MOVE 31 TO DAYS.
0058      GO TO END-CASE.
0059 APRIL.
0060      MOVE "APRIL"      TO MONTH-NAME.
0061      MOVE 30 TO DAYS.
0062      GO TO END-CASE.
0063 MAY.
0064      MOVE "MAY"        TO MONTH-NAME.
0065      MOVE 31 TO DAYS.
0066      GO TO END-CASE.
0067 JUNE.
0068      MOVE "JUNE"       TO MONTH-NAME.
0069      MOVE 30 TO DAYS.
0070      GO TO END-CASE.
0071 JULY.
0072      MOVE "JULY"       TO MONTH-NAME.
0073      MOVE 31 TO DAYS.
0074      GO TO END-CASE.
0075 AUGUST.
0076      MOVE "AUGUST"     TO MONTH-NAME.
0077      MOVE 31 TO DAYS.
0078      GO TO END-CASE.
0079 SEPTEMBER.
0080      MOVE "SEPTEMBER" TO MONTH-NAME.
0081      MOVE 30 TO DAYS.
0082      GO TO END-CASE.
0083 OCTOBER.
0084      MOVE "OCTOBER"    TO MONTH-NAME.
0085      MOVE 31 TO DAYS.
0086      GO TO END-CASE.
0087 NOVEMBER.
```

```
0088        MOVE "NOVEMBER"   TO MONTH-NAME.
0089        MOVE 30 TO DAYS.
0090        GO TO END-CASE.
0091 DECEMBER.
0092        MOVE "DECEMBER"   TO MONTH-NAME.
0093        MOVE 31 TO DAYS.
0094 END-CASE.
0095        DISPLAY MONTH-NAME, " HAS ", DAYS, " DAYS.".
0096        DISPLAY "                         AGAIN?  (Y/N):   "
0097            WITH NO ADVANCING.
0098        ACCEPT C.
0099        IF C IS EQUAL TO "Y" OR EQUAL TO "y"
0100            GO TO BEGIN.
0101 END-OF-JOB.
0102        STOP RUN.
0103 END PROGRAM FIGURE 5-10.
```

Fig. 5-10. COBOL Calendar program. Version 1. (Continued from page 103.)

the various elements of a data structure are determined hierarchically by the level numbers in more-or-less outline form.

Each element of a data structure is of course described by its PICTURE clause, which permits the construction of heterogeneous as well as homogeneous structures. In a homogeneous data structure, each data element has the same PICTURE. In a heterogeneous data structure, different elements can have different PICTUREs.

Tables

Tables in COBOL correspond to arrays in other languages. Specifically, a table is a homogeneous array. Suppose we wished to construct a table containing the name of each of 30 students. An appropriate declaration in the data division would be as follows:

```
01 STUDENTS.
   02 NAME OCCURS 30 TIMES PIC X(20).
```

The name of the first student would be referred to as NAME (1); the name of the second student as NAME (2); and so on. Each name would be a character string of up to 20 characters.

More examples of tables are given in the program in Fig. 5-11. This is a rewrite of the program in Fig. 5-10, showing an alternative way of computing the number of days in a month. Each of the two programs produces exactly the same results.

The program in Fig. 5-11 shows a common COBOL technique for initializing tables. First, a structure called TABLE-1 is defined with each element being FILLER with PICTURE X(10). Each is initialized in turn to the appropriate month name.

Immediately following, in line 23, you see TABLE-2 REDEFINES TABLE-1. This means that TABLE-2 is another name that refers to exactly the same place in computer memory as does TABLE-1. Line 24 states that NAME has a PICTURE of X(10) and OCCURS 12 TIMES. In TABLE-1 each element has a PICTURE of X(10), and there are 12 of them. The two tables therefore occupy exactly the same area of memory, and each element of NAME coincides with the appropriate element of TABLE-1. NAME (5) then has the value "MAY   ", NAME (9) has the value "SEPTEMBER", and so on.

The same technique is used to initialize the table DAYS-IN with the appropriate number of days in each month.

The data division of this program is longer than that of the previous program; the overall program is shorter and the procedure division is much shorter. Most of the work is done with table look-ups in lines 55 and 56. Additional computation is still needed to handle leap years.

In Chapter 2 I used a two-dimensional integer array called POINTS to record the number of points each of 20 students in a class scored on each of 10 tests. In COBOL this would be a two-dimensional table, declared as follows:

```
01  TWO-DIMENSIONAL-TABLE.
    02  STUDENT OCCURS 20 TIMES.
        03  POINTS OCCURS 10 TIMES PIC
            999.
```

The score achieved by student number fifteen on the third test would be referred to as POINTS (15,3).

Although the declaration of tables in COBOL is quite different from the declaration of arrays in most other languages, their use is quite similar.

Records

In Chapter 2 I described a record containing a student's name and the scores achieved by that student on up to 20 tests. The basic record would be declared as follows in COBOL:

```
01 STUDENT-RECORD.
   02 NAME        PIC X(20).
   02 SCORE       OCCURS 20 TIMES,
                  PIC 999.
```

Now suppose that the equivalent of an array of 30 of these records were required. The declaration would change as follows:

```
01 STUDENT-RECORDS
   02 STUDENT OCCURS 30 TIMES.
      03 NAME     PIC X(20).
      03 SCORE    OCCURS 20 TIMES,
                  PIC 999.
```

The name of the 25th student would be referred to as NAME (25), and the score of the same student on the 5th test would be referred to as SCORE (25,5).

Notice that this structure contains both names (PIC X)20)) and scores (PIC 999). It is therefore heterogeneous. The Nevada COBOL compiler does not permit an OCCURS clause for an 01 level data item, hence the form shown above.

By using the appropriate level numbers and OCCURS clauses, data structures of arbitrary complexity can be defined in COBOL.

Linked Lists

The linked list is a useful data structure for maintaining ordered lists of data. Chapter 2 explained how a linked list can be implemented with parallel arrays. Linked lists can be implemented in COBOL using a table of records. The methodology is, however, quite similar.

The following COBOL data division declarations will support such a list:

```
01 TABLE-1.
   02 ELEMENT      OCCURS 5 TIMES.
   03 NAME         PIC X(10).
   03 LINK         PIC 9.
77 FIRST           PIC 9.
77 FREE            PIC 9.
77 MAX-RECORDS     PIC 9 VALUE 5.
77 END-OF-LIST     PIC 9 VALUE 0.
```

For a list of more than 9 records, the PICTUREs of the various pointers would have to be enlarged from 9 to the appropriate size.

The comprehensive example program at the end of the chapter illustrates the use of linked lists in an actual program. In that example the elements of the list are stored on disk rather than in a table in memory. The example shows the details of how to add records to and delete records from a linked list.

FILE HANDLING

Business applications usually involve the maintenance of files on external storage devices such as magnetic disks. A business-oriented language must therefore be able to handle files easily.

```
0001 IDENTIFICATION DIVISION.
0002 PROGRAM-ID.        FIGURE 5-11   COMPUTE NUMBER OF DAYS IN A MONTH
0003*                                 USING TABLES.
0004 ENVIRONMENT DIVISION.
0005 CONFIGURATION SECTION.
0006 SOURCE-COMPUTER.   APPLE II PLUS WITH Z80 SOFTCARD.
0007 OBJECT-COMPUTER.   APPLE II PLUS WITH Z80 SOFTCARD.
0008 DATA DIVISION.
0009 WORKING-STORAGE SECTION.
0010 01   TABLE-1.
0011      02  FILLER     PIC X(10)          VALUE "JANUARY    ".
0012      02  FILLER     PIC X(10)          VALUE "FEBRUARY   ".
0013      02  FILLER     PIC X(10)          VALUE "MARCH      ".
0014      02  FILLER     PIC X(10)          VALUE "APRIL      ".
0015      02  FILLER     PIC X(10)          VALUE "MAY        ".
0016      02  FILLER     PIC X(10)          VALUE "JUNE       ".
0017      02  FILLER     PIC X(10)          VALUE "JULY       ".
0018      02  FILLER     PIC X(10)          VALUE "AUGUST     ".
0019      02  FILLER     PIC X(10)          VALUE "SEPTEMBER  ".
0020      02  FILLER     PIC X(10)          VALUE "OCTOBER    ".
0021      02  FILLER     PIC X(10)          VALUE "NOVEMBER   ".
0022      02  FILLER     PIC X(10)          VALUE "DECEMBER   ".
0023 01   TABLE-2 REDEFINES TABLE-1.
0024      02  NAME       PIC X(10)          OCCURS 12 TIMES.
0025 01   TABLE-3.
0026      02  FILLER     PIC 99             VALUE 31.
0027      02  FILLER     PIC 99             VALUE 28.
0028      02  FILLER     PIC 99             VALUE 31.
0029      02  FILLER     PIC 99             VALUE 30.
0030      02  FILLER     PIC 99             VALUE 31.
0031      02  FILLER     PIC 99             VALUE 30.
0032      02  FILLER     PIC 99             VALUE 31.
0033      02  FILLER     PIC 99             VALUE 31.
0034      02  FILLER     PIC 99             VALUE 30.
0035      02  FILLER     PIC 99             VALUE 31.
0036      02  FILLER     PIC 99             VALUE 30.
0037      02  FILLER     PIC 99             VALUE 31.
0038 01   TABLE-4 REDEFINES TABLE-3.
0039      02  DAYS-IN    PIC 99             OCCURS 12 TIMES.
0040 77   MONTH          PIC 99.
0041 77   DAYS           PIC 99.
0042 77   YEAR           PIC 99.
0043 77   MONTH-NAME     PIC X(10).
```

Fig. 5-11. COBOL Calendar program, Version 2. (Continued on page 107.)

```
0044 77  REMAIN          PIC 9(5).
0045 77  QUOTIENT        PIC 9(5).
0046 77  TEMP            PIC 9(5).
0047 77  C               PIC X.
0048 PROCEDURE DIVISION.
0049 BEGIN.
0050     DISPLAY "ENTER THE MONTH (01..12):  "
0051     ACCEPT MONTH.
0052*    VALIDATE INPUT.
0053     IF MONTH < 01 OR > 12 GO TO BEGIN.
0054*    TABLE LOOK-UPS.
0055     MOVE NAME    (MONTH) TO MONTH-NAME.
0056     MOVE DAYS-IN (MONTH) TO DAYS.
0057*    CHECK FOR LEAP YEAR IF MONTH IS FEBRUARY.
0058     IF MONTH NOT = 2 GO TO PRINT-RESULTS.
0059         DISPLAY "ENTER THE YEAR (00-99):   "
0060             WITH NO ADVANCING;
0061         ACCEPT YEAR;
0062         DIVIDE 4 INTO YEAR GIVING QUOTIENT;
0063         MULTIPLY 4 BY QUOTIENT GIVING TEMP;
0064         SUBTRACT TEMP FROM YEAR GIVING REMAIN;
0065         IF REMAIN IS EQUAL TO 0
0066             ADD 1 TO DAYS.
0067 PRINT-RESULTS.
0068     DISPLAY MONTH-NAME, " HAS ", DAYS, " DAYS.".
0069     DISPLAY "                    AGAIN?  (Y/N):  "
0070         WITH NO ADVANCING.
0071     ACCEPT C.
0072     IF C IS EQUAL TO "Y" OR EQUAL TO "y"
0073         GO TO BEGIN.
0074 END-OF-JOB.
0075     STOP RUN.
0076 END PROGRAM FIGURE 5-11.
```

File handling is in fact one of COBOL's great strengths.

COBOL provides three major kinds of files: sequential, random (direct-access), and indexed. As discussed in Chapter 2, a random or direct access file provides access to any record in the file based on the relative position of that record in the file (i.e., the record number). An *indexed file*, on the other hand, provides access to any record of the file based on the value of that record.

Indexed files are a very powerful tool, particularly in a business context. Nevada COBOL unfortunately does not support indexed files, so they will not be illustrated in this book. The user is referred to one of the many available COBOL textbooks for further information on indexed files.

A linkage between the file names used in a program and the outside world must be established in the environment division of a COBOL program. As this varies for sequential and direct-access files,

```
0001 IDENTIFICATION DIVISION.
0002 PROGRAM-ID.  FIGURE 5-12  DEMONSTRATE USE OF A SEQUENTIAL FILE.
0003 ENVIRONMENT DIVISION.
0004 CONFIGURATION SECTION.
0005 SOURCE-COMPUTER.  APPLE II PLUS WITH Z80 SOFTCARD.
0006 OBJECT-COMPUTER.  APPLE II PLUS WITH Z80 SOFTCARD.
0007 INPUT-OUTPUT SECTION.
0008 FILE-CONTROL.
0009     SELECT AGE-FILE
0010         ASSIGN TO DISK,
0011         ORGANIZATION IS SEQUENTIAL,
0012         ACCESS IS SEQUENTIAL.
0013 DATA DIVISION.
0014 FILE SECTION.
0015 FD AGE-FILE,
0016     LABEL RECORDS ARE STANDARD,
0017     VALUE OF FILE-ID IS "AGES.TXT",
0018     DATA RECORD IS ENTRY.
0019 01  ENTRY.
0020     02  NAME            PIC X(20).
0021     02  AGE             PIC 99.
0022 WORKING-STORAGE SECTION.
0023 77 C            PIC X.
0024 PROCEDURE DIVISION.
0025 BEGIN.
0026     OPEN OUTPUT AGE-FILE.
0027     DISPLAY "ENTER NAMES & AGES; <RETURN> TO QUIT."
0028     DISPLAY SPACE.
0029 INPUT-LOOP.
0030     MOVE SPACES TO NAME.
0031     DISPLAY "NAME:      ".
0032     ACCEPT  NAME.
0033     IF NAME = SPACES GO TO END-INPUT-LOOP.
0034     DISPLAY "AGE:  (XX) ".
0035     ACCEPT AGE.
0036     WRITE ENTRY.
0037     DISPLAY SPACE.
0038     GO TO INPUT-LOOP.
0039 END-INPUT-LOOP.
0040     CLOSE AGE-FILE.
0041*    NOW REOPEN & READ BACK, DISPLAYING EACH RECORD.
0042     OPEN INPUT AGE-FILE.
0043     DISPLAY "HERE ARE THE NAMES AND AGES FROM THE FILE.".
```

Fig. 5-12. COBOL sequential file usage. (Continued on page 109.)

```
0044 OUTPUT-LOOP.
0045     DISPLAY SPACE.
0046     MOVE SPACES TO NAME.
0047     READ AGE-FILE RECORD AT END GO TO END-OF-JOB.
0048     DISPLAY ENTRY.
0049     GO TO OUTPUT-LOOP.
0050 END-OF-JOB.
0051     CLOSE AGE-FILE.
0052     DISPLAY SPACE.
0053     DISPLAY "PRESS <RETURN> TO CONTINUE...".
0054     ACCEPT C.
0055     STOP RUN.
0056 END PROGRAM FIGURE 5-12.
```

it will be illustrated in the appropriate section below.

File buffers must be defined in the data division. Examples will be given in the sections on sequential and direct-access files.

Files must be CLOSEd at the end of a program.

Sequential Files

Sequential files in COBOL can have either fixed-length records or variable-length records. Only fixed-length records are covered in this section. A program that uses a sequential file to maintain a list of names and ages is shown in Fig. 5-12.

Notice that the basic parameters of the file are established in the input-output section of the environment division, lines 0007 to 0012. These statements give the file a name for use later in the program (AGE-FILE), assign it to disk, and establish its organization and access method (SEQUENTIAL).

The file is defined further in the FILE SECTION of the DATA DIVISION, lines 0014 to 0021. The external name of the file is established as AGES.TXT. This is the name you will see in the disk directory after the program has been run.

Line 0018 identifies the file buffer as ENTRY, which is defined in the following lines. This buffer may be thought of as both a place where data is stored on its way to and from the file, and as a template that defines the format of each file record. In this case each record consists of a character string called NAME, and a numeric variable called AGE. The record is 22 characters long; NAME is 20 characters in length and AGE is 2 characters in length.

With fixed-length records, there are no intervening characters between records in the file. With variable-length records, some delimiting characters are required, usually a carriage return and line feed character pair.

The file is opened for output in line 0026. The data is read into the file buffer from the keyboard in lines 0032 and 0035, and written to the file in line 0036.

After the requisite number of records have been written, the file is closed in line 0040. It is reopened for input in line 0042. The next READ statement in line 0047 will read the first record of the file, as the file is always "rewound" to its beginning by an OPEN statement.

After each record has been read in from the file and written out to the video screen, the file is closed again. The program as a whole is quite simple. It is important to note how the file is defined in the environment division and data division. The details of how this is done can vary from compiler to compiler, so the compiler documentation should be carefully checked.

```
0001 IDENTIFICATION DIVISION.
0002 PROGRAM-ID.          FIGURE 5-13   SETUP FOR ADDRESS BOOK.
0003*                                   INITIALIZE FILES.
0004 ENVIRONMENT DIVISION.
0005 CONFIGURATION SECTION.
0006 SOURCE-COMPUTER.   APPLE II PLUS WITH Z80 SOFTCARD.
0007 OBJECT-COMPUTER.   APPLE II PLUS WITH Z80 SOFTCARD.
0008 INPUT-OUTPUT SECTION.
0009 FILE-CONTROL.
0010     SELECT ADDRESS-FILE ASSIGN TO DISK,
0011          ORGANIZATION IS SEQUENTIAL,
0012          ACCESS MODE IS  SEQUENTIAL.
0013     SELECT INDEX-FILE ASSIGN TO DISK,
0014          ORGANIZATION IS SEQUENTIAL,
0015          ACCESS MODE IS  SEQUENTIAL.
0016 DATA DIVISION.
0017 FILE SECTION.
0018 FD   ADDRESS-FILE
0019     LABEL RECORDS ARE STANDARD,
0020     VALUE OF FILE-ID IS "B:ADDRESS.TXT",
0021     DATA RECORD IS ADDRESS-RECORD.
0022 01  ADDRESS-RECORD.
0023     02  NAME.
0024         03  LAST-NAME     PIC X(12).
0025         03  FIRST-NAME    PIC X(12).
0026     02  ADDRESS           PIC X(24).
0027     02  CITY              PIC X(18).
0028     02  STATE             PIC XX.
0029     02  ZIP               PIC X(10).
0030     02  PHONE-NR          PIC X(14).
0031 FD   INDEX-FILE
0032     LABEL RECORDS ARE STANDARD,
0033     VALUE OF FILE-ID IS "B:INDEX.TXT",
0034     DATA RECORD IS INDEX-RECORD.
0035 01  INDEX-RECORD          PIC 999.
0036 WORKING-STORAGE SECTION.
0037 77  FILE-SIZE     PIC 999.
0038 77  POINTER       PIC 999.
0039 77  END-OF-FILE   PIC 999 VALUE 0.
0040 77  C             PIC X.
0041 PROCEDURE DIVISION.
0042 BEGIN.
0043     DISPLAY "WARNING:  THIS PROGRAM INITIALIZES B:ADDRESS.TXT."
```

Fig. 5-13. COBOL Address Book Setup program. (Continued on page 111.)

```
0044     DISPLAY "IT WILL DESTROY AN EXISTING B:ADDRESS.TXT."
0045     DISPLAY SPACE.
0046     DISPLAY "DO YOU WISH TO CONTINUE?  (Y/N)".
0047     ACCEPT C.
0048     IF C NOT = "Y" AND NOT = "y" GO TO END-OF-JOB.
0049     DISPLAY SPACE.
0050     DISPLAY "HOW MANY RECORDS SHOULD BE ALLOCATED? (XXX):  ".
0051     ACCEPT FILE-SIZE.
0052     OPEN OUTPUT ADDRESS-FILE.
0053     MOVE SPACES TO ADDRESS-RECORD.
0054     PERFORM PUT-ADDRESS-RECORD FILE-SIZE TIMES.
0055     CLOSE ADDRESS-FILE.
0056     OPEN OUTPUT INDEX-FILE.
0057*    WRITE FIRST-ACTIVE RECORD INDEX.
0058     MOVE END-OF-FILE TO INDEX-RECORD.
0059     WRITE INDEX-RECORD.
0060*    WRITE FIRST-FREE RECORD INDEX.
0061     MOVE 1 TO INDEX-RECORD.
0062     WRITE INDEX-RECORD.
0063*    NOW BUILD THE CHAIN OF FREE RECORDS.
0064     MOVE 2 TO POINTER.
0065 LOOP-1.
0066     IF POINTER ) FILE-SIZE GO TO END-LOOP-1.
0067     MOVE POINTER TO INDEX-RECORD.
0068     WRITE INDEX-RECORD.
0069     ADD 1 TO POINTER.
0070     GO TO LOOP-1.
0071 END-LOOP-1.
0072     MOVE END-OF-FILE TO INDEX-RECORD.
0073     WRITE INDEX-RECORD.
0074     CLOSE INDEX-FILE.
0075 END-OF-JOB.
0076     DISPLAY SPACE.
0077     DISPLAY "PRESS <RETURN> TO CONTINUE...".
0078     ACCEPT C.
0079     STOP RUN.
0080 PUT-ADDRESS-RECORD.
0081     WRITE ADDRESS-RECORD.
0082 END PROGRAM FIGURE 5-13.
```

Direct-Access Files

With Nevada COBOL a file must already exist before it can be opened for direct-access. This is accomplished by using a program to create the file using sequential file access. An example of such a program is shown in Fig. 5-13.

This program is very similar to the program in Fig. 5-12 in form. It interrogates the user for the number of records to be written, then writes the number of blank records to the file B:AD-DRESS.TXT. The file description for that file is identical to that of the following program (see Fig. 5-14) and was in fact taken from that program using a text editor. It could have been defined simply as

```
01  ADDRESS-RECORD  PICTURE  X(92)
            VALUE SPACES.
```

Creating this file serves to allocate the proper amount of space on the disk for the file.

The other file initialized by this program is called B:INDEX.TXT. It is a sequential file. Its organization will be discussed in the section covering the comprehensive sample program at the end of the chapter.

Once a file has been established using a program such as that in Fig. 5-13, it can be accessed from another program as a direct-access file. In order for that to happen, the file must be declared as a direct-access file. The following shows the required statements for a simple example:

```
ENVIRONMENT DIVISION.
   . . .
INPUT-OUTPUT SECTION.
FILE-CONTROL.
     SELECT FILE-1 ASSIGN TO DISK,
     ORGANIZATION IS RELATIVE,
     ACCESS MODE IS RANDOM,
     RELATIVE KEY IS FILE-1-KEY
DATA DIVISION.
FILE SECTION.
FD FILE-1
   LABEL RECORDS ARE STANDARD,
   VALUE OF FILE-ID IS "FILE1.TXT",
   DATA RECORD IS FILE-1-RECORD.
```

```
01 FILE-1-RECORD PIC X(80).
WORKING-STORAGE SECTION.
77 FILE-1-KEY PIC 999.
```

This example would establish a direct-access file with the internal (to the program) file name of FILE-1 and external file name of FILE1.TXT. Each record of the file would consist of 80 alphanumeric characters. Data to be written to the file would be MOVEd to FILE-1-RECORD.

Notice the clause that defines the RELATIVE KEY as FILE-1-KEY. This is a data element defined later in the WORKING-STORAGE SECTION. To write something to the thirtieth record of the file, you could do the following:

```
MOVE "This goes in record 30"
      TO FILE-1-RECORD.
MOVE 30 TO FILE-1-KEY.
WRITE FILE-1-RECORD
      INVALID KEY DISPLAY
"INVALID KEY:  ",
            FILE-1-KEY.
```

Moving the value 30 to FILE-1-KEY causes the subsequent WRITE statement to write the contents of FILE-1-RECORD in record 30 of the file. The INVALID KEY clause is required, and in this case it causes a message to be displayed to the console if record 30 of the file does not exist.

The READ statement works the same way: to read a particular record from a direct-access file, first MOVE the record number to the RELATIVE KEY field; then use the READ statement.

The comprehensive example program that follows illustrates the use of a direct-access file in a nontrivial program.

GRAPHICS

COBOL does not support graphics.

COMPREHENSIVE SAMPLE PROGRAM

The program in Fig. 5-14 maintains a computerized address book. It records names, addresses, and telephone numbers in a direct-access file. The file is organized so that it is logically

```
0001 IDENTIFICATION DIVISION.
0002 PROGRAM-ID.         FIGURE 5-14  ADDRESS BOOK.
0003****************************************************************
0004*                                                              *
0005*    Comprehensive Example Program.                            *
0006*                                                              *
0007*         Maintains an ordered file of names and addresses.    *
0008*         The program in Figure 5-13 must be run to            *
0009*         initialize the files before this program is run      *
0010*         the first time.                                      *
0011*                                                              *
0012*         File size is now set to 010 records.  To expand,     *
0013*         you must modify lines 59 and 109 of this             *
0014*         program and re-run the program in Figure 5-13.       *
0015*                                                              *
0016****************************************************************
0017 ENVIRONMENT DIVISION.
0018 CONFIGURATION SECTION.
0019 SOURCE-COMPUTER.   APPLE II PLUS WITH Z80 SOFTCARD.
0020 OBJECT-COMPUTER.   APPLE II PLUS WITH Z80 SOFTCARD.
0021 INPUT-OUTPUT SECTION.
0022 FILE-CONTROL.
0023     SELECT PRT ASSIGN TO PRINTER.
0024     SELECT ADDRESS-FILE ASSIGN TO DISK,
0025         ORGANIZATION IS RELATIVE,
0026         ACCESS MODE IS RANDOM,
0027         RELATIVE KEY IS ADDRESS-KEY,
0028         FILE STATUS IS  ADDRESS-FILE-STATUS.
0029     SELECT INDEX-FILE ASSIGN TO DISK,
0030         ORGANIZATION IS SEQUENTIAL,
0031         ACCESS MODE IS  SEQUENTIAL.
0032 DATA DIVISION.
0033 FILE SECTION.
0034 FD   PRT
0035     LABEL RECORDS ARE STANDARD,
0036     VALUE OF FILE-ID IS "PRINTER",
0037     DATA RECORD IS PRINT-LINE.
0038 01  PRINT-LINE            PIC X(80).
0039 FD   ADDRESS-FILE
0040     LABEL RECORDS ARE STANDARD,
0041     VALUE OF FILE-ID IS "B:ADDRESS.TXT",
0042     DATA RECORD IS ADDRESS-RECORD.
0043 01  ADDRESS-RECORD.
0044     02  NAME.
0045         03  LAST-NAME      PIC X(12).
```

Fig. 5-14. COBOL Address Book. (Continued on page 114.)

```
0046          03  FIRST-NAME        PIC X(12).
0047     02  ADDRESS              PIC X(24).
0048     02  CITY                 PIC X(18).
0049     02  STATE                PIC XX.
0050     02  ZIP                  PIC X(10).
0051     02  PHONE-NR             PIC X(14).
0052 FD  INDEX-FILE
0053     LABEL RECORDS ARE STANDARD,
0054     VALUE OF FILE-ID IS "B:INDEX.TXT",

0055     DATA RECORD IS INDEX-RECORD.
0056 01  INDEX-RECORD             PIC 999.
0057 WORKING-STORAGE SECTION.
0058 01  INDEX-TABLE.
0059     02  LINK         OCCURS 010 TIMES      PIC 999.
0060 01  ADDRESS-FILE-STATUS.
0061     02  AFS-KEY-1            PIC X.
0062     02  AFS-KEY-2            PIC X.
0063 01  COMPARE-BUFFER.
0064     02  COMPARE-NAME         PIC X(24)      VALUE SPACES.
0065     02  COMPARE-NR           PIC 999        VALUE ZERO.
0066 01  PRINT-RECORD.
0067     02  PR-NAME.
0068          03  PRN-FIRST       PIC X(12).
0069          03  FILLER          PIC X          VALUE SPACE.
0070          03  PRN-LAST        PIC X(12).
0071     02  PR-CITY.
0072          03  PRC-CITY        PIC X(18).
0073          03  FILLER          PIC XX         VALUE ", ".
0074          03  PRC-STATE       PIC XX.
0075          03  FILLER          PIC X          VALUE SPACE.
0076          03  PRC-ZIP         PIC X(10).
0077     02  PR-HEADERS.
0078          03  FILLER    PIC X(16)
0079                        VALUE "FIRST-ACTIVE: ".
0080          03  PRH-FA    PIC 999.
0081          03  FILLER    PIC X(19)
0082                        VALUE "   FIRST-FREE:    ".
0083          03  PRH-FF    PIC 999.
0084     02  PR-NUMBER.
0085          03  FILLER    PIC X(17)
0086                        VALUE "RECORD NUMBER:   ".
0087          03  PRN-NUMBER      PIC 999.
0088     02  PR-LINK.
0089          03  FILLER          PIC X(8)
0090                              VALUE "LINK:  ".
```

Fig. 5-14. COBOL Address Book. (Continued on page 115.)

```
0091         03  PRL-LINK        PIC 999.
0092 01  SCREEN-DATA.
0093     02  OFFSET       PIC 9999   VALUE 7967.
0094     02  MAX-ROW      PIC 99     VALUE 24.
0095     02  MAX-COL      PIC 99     VALUE 80.
0096     02  CLEAR.
0097         03  FILLER   PIC X      VALUE ""1B"".
0098         03  FILLER   PIC X      VALUE "*".
0099     02  ROW          PIC 99     USAGE COMP.
0100     02  COL          PIC 99     USAGE COMP.
0101     02  CURSOR-POSITION.
0102         03  FILLER   PIC X      VALUE ""1B"".
0103         03  FILLER   PIC X      VALUE "=".
0104         03  XY       PIC 99     USAGE COMP.
0105 01  POINTERS.
0106     02  P            PIC 999.
0107     02  Q            PIC 999.
0108     02  R            PIC 999.
0109 77  MAX-RECORDS      PIC 999    VALUE 010.
0110 77  ADDRESS-KEY      PIC 999.
0111 77  FIRST-ACTIVE     PIC 999.
0112 77  FIRST-FREE       PIC 999.
0113 77  END-OF-LIST      PIC 999    VALUE 0.
0114 77  REC-NR           PIC 999.
0115 77  I                PIC 999.
0116 77  CASE-NR          PIC 9.
0117 77  C                PIC X.
0118 PROCEDURE DIVISION.
0119 BEGIN.
0120     PERFORM CLEAR-SCREEN.
0121     DISPLAY "WELCOME TO YOUR ADDRESS BOOK."
0122     DISPLAY SPACE.
0123     DISPLAY "INITIALIZING..."
0124     OPEN OUTPUT PRT.
0125     PERFORM INIT-INDEX.
0126     OPEN I-O ADDRESS-FILE.
0127 MAIN-LOOP.
0128     PERFORM MENU.
0129     GO TO CASE-1,
0130          CASE-2,
0131          CASE-3,
0132          CASE-4,
0133          CASE-5
0134      DEPENDING ON CASE-NR.
0135 NONE-OF-THE-ABOVE.
```

```
0136        GO TO MAIN-LOOP.
0137 CASE-1.
0138        PERFORM APPEND.
0139        GO TO END-CASE.
0140 CASE-2.
0141        PERFORM REVIEW.
0142        GO TO END-CASE.
0143 CASE-3.
0144        PERFORM LIST-FILE.
0145        GO TO END-CASE.
0146 CASE-4.
0147        PERFORM DUMP.
0148        GO TO END-CASE.
0149 CASE-5.
0150        DISPLAY "CLOSING FILES...".
0151 END-CASE.
0152        IF CASE-NR NOT = 5 GO TO MAIN-LOOP.
0153 CLEAN-UP.
0154        CLOSE ADDRESS-FILE.
0155        CLOSE PRT.
0156        PERFORM SAVE-INDEX.
0157 END-OF-JOB.
0158        PERFORM WAIT.
0159        STOP RUN.
0160 INIT-INDEX SECTION.
0161   II-1.
0162        OPEN INPUT INDEX-FILE.
0163        READ INDEX-FILE AT END DISPLAY "ERROR READING INDEX.TXT",
0164                               GO TO END-OF-JOB.
0165        MOVE INDEX-RECORD TO FIRST-ACTIVE.
0166        READ INDEX-FILE AT END GO TO II-3.
0167        MOVE INDEX-RECORD TO FIRST-FREE.
0168        MOVE 1 TO I.
0169   II-2.
0170*       SIMULATE WHILE STATEMENT.
0171        IF I > MAX-RECORDS GO TO II-3.
0172        READ INDEX-FILE AT END GO TO II-3.
0173        MOVE INDEX-RECORD TO LINK (I).
0174        ADD 1 TO I.
0175        GO TO II-2.
0176   II-3.
0177        CLOSE INDEX-FILE.
0178   II-EXIT.  EXIT.
0179 MENU SECTION.
0180   M-1.
0181        PERFORM CLEAR-SCREEN.
```

Fig. 5-14. COBOL Address Book. (Continued on page 117.)

```
0182      MOVE 5 TO ROW, COL.
0183      PERFORM POSITION-CURSOR.
0184      DISPLAY "1)  ADD TO FILE" WITH NO ADVANCING.
0185      ADD 2 TO ROW,          PERFORM POSITION-CURSOR.
0186      DISPLAY "2)  REVIEW FILE ON SCREEN" WITH NO ADVANCING.
0187      ADD 2 TO ROW,          PERFORM POSITION-CURSOR.
0188      DISPLAY "3)  LIST FILE TO SCREEN OR PRINTER"
0189          WITH NO ADVANCING.
0190      ADD 2 TO ROW,          PERFORM POSITION-CURSOR.
0191      DISPLAY "4)  DUMP FILE TO PRINTER" WITH NO ADVANCING.
0192      ADD 2 TO ROW,          PERFORM POSITION-CURSOR.
0193      DISPLAY "5)  QUIT" WITH NO ADVANCING.
0194      MOVE 1 TO COL.
0195      ADD 2 TO ROW.
0196  M-2.
0197      PERFORM POSITION-CURSOR.
0198      DISPLAY "SELECT 1, 2, 3, 4, OR 5:  " WITH NO ADVANCING.
0199      ACCEPT CASE-NR.
0200      IF CASE-NR < 1 OR > 5 GO TO M-2.
0201  M-EXIT.  EXIT.
0202 APPEND SECTION.
0203  A-1.
0204      PERFORM CLEAR-SCREEN.
0205      IF FIRST-FREE = END-OF-LIST
0206          DISPLAY "NO ROOM IN LIST...",
0207          PERFORM WAIT,
0208          GO TO A-EXIT.
0209      MOVE 1 TO COL.
0210      MOVE 5 TO ROW.
0211      PERFORM POSITION-CURSOR.
0212      DISPLAY "LAST NAME    :              :"
0213          WITH NO ADVANCING.
0214      ADD 2 TO ROW,          PERFORM POSITION-CURSOR.
0215      DISPLAY "FIRST NAME   :              :"
0216          WITH NO ADVANCING.
0217      ADD 2 TO ROW,          PERFORM POSITION-CURSOR.
0218      DISPLAY "ADDRESS      :                       :"
0219          WITH NO ADVANCING.
0220      ADD 2 TO ROW,          PERFORM POSITION-CURSOR.
0221      DISPLAY "CITY         :                  :"
0222          WITH NO ADVANCING.
0223      ADD 2 TO ROW,          PERFORM POSITION-CURSOR.
0224      DISPLAY "STATE     :  :"
0225          WITH NO ADVANCING.
0226      ADD 2 TO ROW,          PERFORM POSITION-CURSOR.
0227      DISPLAY "ZIP          :              :"
```

```
0228          WITH NO ADVANCING.
0229      ADD 2 TO ROW,           PERFORM POSITION-CURSOR.
0230      DISPLAY "PHONE NUMBER :              :"
0231          WITH NO ADVANCING.
0232*     READ IN ADDRESS-RECORD FROM SCREEN.
0233      MOVE SPACES TO ADDRESS-RECORD.
0234      MOVE 5 TO ROW.
0235      MOVE 15 TO COL.
0236      PERFORM POSITION-CURSOR.
0237      ACCEPT LAST-NAME.
0238      IF LAST-NAME = SPACES GO TO A-EXIT.
0239      ADD 2 TO ROW,           PERFORM POSITION-CURSOR.
0240      ACCEPT FIRST-NAME.
0241      ADD 2 TO ROW,           PERFORM POSITION-CURSOR.
0242      ACCEPT ADDRESS.
0243      ADD 2 TO ROW,           PERFORM POSITION-CURSOR.
0244      ACCEPT CITY.
0245      ADD 2 TO ROW,           PERFORM POSITION-CURSOR.
0246      ACCEPT STATE.
0247      ADD 2 TO ROW,           PERFORM POSITION-CURSOR.
0248      ACCEPT ZIP.
0249      ADD 2 TO ROW,           PERFORM POSITION-CURSOR.
0250      ACCEPT PHONE-NR.
0251      PERFORM INSERT-RECORD.
0252      GO TO A-1.
0253  A-EXIT.   EXIT.
0254  REVIEW SECTION.
0255  R-1.
0256      PERFORM CLEAR-SCREEN.
0257      DISPLAY "REVIEWING FILE...".
0258      DISPLAY SPACE.
0259      IF FIRST-ACTIVE = END-OF-LIST
0260          DISPLAY "NO RECORDS TO REVIEW...",
0261          PERFORM WAIT,
0262          GO TO R-EXIT.
0263      MOVE FIRST-ACTIVE TO R.
0264      MOVE END-OF-LIST  TO Q.
0265  R-2.
0266*     SIMULATE REPEAT-UNTIL.
0267          MOVE R TO ADDRESS-KEY.
0268          READ ADDRESS-FILE
0269              INVALID KEY PERFORM INVALID-KEY.
0270          PERFORM LIST-RECORD.
0271  R-3.
0272          DISPLAY SPACE.
```

Fig. 5-14. COBOL Address Book. (Continued on page 119.)

```
0273          DISPLAY "G)ET NEXT RECORD, D)ELETE THIS RECORD, ",
0274              "OR Q)UIT?   ".
0275          MOVE SPACE TO C.
0276          ACCEPT C.
0277          IF C NOT = "G" AND
0278              NOT = "D" AND
0279              NOT = "Q" AND
0280              NOT = "g" AND
0281              NOT = "d" AND
0282              NOT = "q"        GO TO R-3.
0283          IF C = "G" OR = "g"
0284*             GET NEXT RECORD
0285              MOVE R TO Q,
0286              MOVE LINK (R) TO R,
0287              GO TO R-4.
0288          IF C NOT = "D" AND NOT = "d" GO TO R-EXIT.
0289*             DELETE THIS RECORD
0290              IF Q = END-OF-LIST
0291                  MOVE LINK (R) TO FIRST-ACTIVE,
0292                  PERFORM PUT-FREE,
0293                  MOVE FIRST-ACTIVE TO R
0294              ELSE
0295                  MOVE LINK (R) TO LINK (Q),
0296                  PERFORM PUT-FREE,
0297                  MOVE LINK (Q) TO R.
0298  R-4.
0299      IF R NOT = END-OF-LIST GO TO R-2.
0300  R-EXIT.  EXIT.
0301 PUT-FREE SECTION.
0302* PUT RECORD R BACK INTO THE FREE-LIST.
0303  PF-1.
0304      MOVE FIRST-FREE TO LINK (R).
0305      MOVE R TO FIRST-FREE.
0306  PF-EXIT.  EXIT.
0307 LIST-FILE SECTION.
0308  LF-1.
0309      PERFORM CLEAR-SCREEN.
0310      IF FIRST-ACTIVE = END-OF-LIST
0311          DISPLAY "NO RECORDS IN FILE TO LIST...",
0312          PERFORM WAIT,
0313          GO TO LF-EXIT.
0314      DISPLAY "LIST FILE TO S)CREEN OR P)RINTER?   ".
0315      ACCEPT C.
0316      IF C NOT = "S" AND
0317          NOT = "s" AND
```

```
0318            NOT = "P" AND
0319            NOT = "p"        GO TO LF-1.
0320      MOVE FIRST-ACTIVE TO R.
0321   LF-2.
0322      MOVE R TO ADDRESS-KEY.
0323      READ ADDRESS-FILE
0324            INVALID KEY PERFORM INVALID-KEY.
0325      IF C = "S" OR C = "s"
0326            PERFORM LIST-RECORD,
0327            DISPLAY SPACE,
0328      ELSE
0329            PERFORM PRINT-REC.
0330      MOVE LINK (R) TO R.
0331      IF R NOT = END-OF-LIST GO TO LF-2.
0332      PERFORM WAIT.
0333   LF-EXIT.  EXIT.
0334 DUMP SECTION.
0335   D-1.
0336      PERFORM CLEAR-SCREEN.
0337      DISPLAY "DUMPING FILE...".
0338      MOVE SPACES TO PRINT-LINE.
0339      MOVE FIRST-ACTIVE TO PRH-FA.
0340      MOVE FIRST-FREE   TO PRH-FF.
0341      MOVE PR-HEADERS TO PRINT-LINE.
0342      WRITE PRINT-LINE.
0343      MOVE 1 TO I.
0344   D-2.
0345      MOVE I TO PRN-NUMBER, ADDRESS-KEY.
0346      MOVE SPACES TO PRINT-LINE.
0347      MOVE PR-NUMBER TO PRINT-LINE.
0348      WRITE PRINT-LINE.
0349      READ ADDRESS-FILE RECORD INVALID KEY DISPLAY "INVALID KEY".
0350      PERFORM PRINT-REC.
0351      MOVE LINK (I) TO PRL-LINK.
0352      MOVE SPACES TO PRINT-LINE.
0353      MOVE PR-LINK TO PRINT-LINE.
0354      WRITE PRINT-LINE.
0355      MOVE SPACES TO PRINT-LINE.
0356      WRITE PRINT-LINE.
0357      ADD 1 TO I.
0358      IF I NOT > MAX-RECORDS GO TO D-2.
0359      PERFORM WAIT.
0360   D-EXIT.  EXIT.
0361 INSERT-RECORD SECTION.
0362   IR-1.
```

Fig. 5-14. COBOL Address Book. (Continued on page 121.)

```
0363      PERFORM GET-FREE.
0364      MOVE REC-NR TO ADDRESS-KEY.
0365      WRITE ADDRESS-RECORD
0366          INVALID KEY PERFORM INVALID-KEY.
0367      MOVE NAME TO COMPARE-NAME.
0368      MOVE REC-NR TO COMPARE-NR.
0369*     FIND THE PROPER PLACE IN THE LIST AND ADJUST LINKS.
0370      IF FIRST-ACTIVE = END-OF-LIST
0371*         LIST WAS PREVIOUSLY EMPTY
0372          MOVE END-OF-LIST TO LINK (COMPARE-NR),
0373          MOVE COMPARE-NR TO FIRST-ACTIVE,
0374          GO TO IR-EXIT,
0375      ELSE
0376          MOVE FIRST-ACTIVE TO P,
0377          MOVE END-OF-LIST  TO Q.
0378  IR-2.
0379      MOVE P TO ADDRESS-KEY.
0380      READ ADDRESS-FILE
0381          INVALID KEY PERFORM INVALID-KEY.
0382      IF P = END-OF-LIST OR
0383          COMPARE-NAME ( NAME GO TO IR-3.
0384      MOVE P TO Q.
0385      MOVE LINK (P) TO P.
0386      IF P NOT = END-OF-LIST GO TO IR-2.
0387  IR-3.
0388*     AT THIS POINT, Q POINTS TO PREDECESSOR OF COMPARE-NR,
0389*         AND P TO ITS SUCCESSOR.
0390      MOVE P TO LINK (COMPARE-NR).
0391      IF Q = END-OF-LIST
0392          MOVE COMPARE-NR TO FIRST-ACTIVE
0393      ELSE
0394          MOVE COMPARE-NR TO LINK (Q).
0395  IR-EXIT.  EXIT.
0396 INVALID-KEY SECTION.
0397  IK-1.
0398     DISPLAY "INVALID KEY:   ", ADDRESS-KEY.
0399     PERFORM WAIT.
0400  IK-EXIT.  EXIT.
0401 GET-FREE SECTION.
0402  GF-1.
0403     MOVE FIRST-FREE TO REC-NR.
0404     MOVE LINK (FIRST-FREE) TO FIRST-FREE.
0405  GF-EXIT.  EXIT.
0406 PRINT-REC SECTION.
0407  PR-1.
```

```
0408     MOVE SPACES TO PRINT-LINE.
0409     WRITE PRINT-LINE.
0410     MOVE FIRST-NAME TO PRN-FIRST.
0411     MOVE LAST-NAME  TO PRN-LAST.
0412     MOVE PR-NAME TO PRINT-LINE.
0413     WRITE PRINT-LINE.
0414     MOVE SPACES TO PRINT-LINE.
0415     MOVE ADDRESS TO PRINT-LINE.
0416     WRITE PRINT-LINE.
0417     MOVE SPACES TO PRINT-LINE.
0418     MOVE CITY  TO PRC-CITY.
0419     MOVE STATE TO PRC-STATE.
0420     MOVE ZIP   TO PRC-ZIP.
0421     MOVE PR-CITY TO PRINT-LINE.
0422     WRITE PRINT-LINE.
0423     MOVE SPACES   TO PRINT-LINE.
0424     MOVE PHONE-NR TO PRINT-LINE.
0425     WRITE PRINT-LINE.
0426 PR-EXIT.  EXIT.
0427 SAVE-INDEX SECTION.
0428  SI-1.
0429     OPEN OUTPUT INDEX-FILE.
0430     MOVE FIRST-ACTIVE TO INDEX-RECORD.
0431     WRITE INDEX-RECORD.
0432     MOVE FIRST-FREE   TO INDEX-RECORD.

0433     WRITE INDEX-RECORD.
0434     MOVE 1 TO I.
0435  SI-2.
0436*    SIMULATE WHILE LOOP.
0437     IF I ) MAX-RECORDS GO TO SI-3.
0438     MOVE LINK (I) TO INDEX-RECORD.
0439     WRITE INDEX-RECORD.
0440     ADD 1 TO I.
0441     GO TO SI-2.
0442  SI-3.
0443     CLOSE INDEX-FILE.
0444 SI-EXIT.  EXIT.
0445 LIST-RECORD SECTION.
0446  LR-1.
0447     DISPLAY SPACE.
0448     DISPLAY FIRST-NAME, " ", LAST-NAME.
0449     DISPLAY ADDRESS.
0450     DISPLAY CITY, ", ", STATE, " ", ZIP.
0451     DISPLAY PHONE-NR.
0452  LR-EXIT.  EXIT.
```

Fig. 5-14. COBOL Address Book. (Continued on page 123.)

```
0453 CLEAR-SCREEN SECTION.
0454  CS-1.
0455      DISPLAY CLEAR.
0456  CS-EXIT.  EXIT.
0457 POSITION-CURSOR SECTION.
0458  PC-1.
0459*     FIRST CHECK FOR LEGAL SCREEN COORDINATES.
0460      IF ROW < 1        MOVE 1 TO ROW.
0461      IF ROW > MAX-ROW MOVE MAX-ROW TO ROW.
0462      IF COL < 1        MOVE 1 TO COL.
0463      IF COL > MAX-COL MOVE MAX-COL TO COL.
0464*     NOW COMPUTE NECESSARY VALUES.
0465      MULTIPLY 256 BY COL GIVING XY.
0466      ADD ROW    TO XY.
0467      ADD OFFSET TO XY.
0468*     OUTPUT TO SCREEN.
0469      DISPLAY CURSOR-POSITION WITH NO ADVANCING.
0470  PC-EXIT.  EXIT.
0471 WAIT SECTION.
0472  W-1.
0473      DISPLAY SPACE.
0474      DISPLAY "PRESS <RETURN> TO CONTINUE...".
0475      ACCEPT C.
0476  W-EXIT.  EXIT.
0477 END PROGRAM FIGURE 5-14.
```

always in alphabetical order. No sorting is performed; each record is inserted in the proper place when it is added to the file. The program permits records to be added to the file, deleted from the file, displayed on the video screen, or listed on a printer.

As a record is added to the file, it is written using direct access to the first available location in the file. The data structure that supports this technique is a linked list. (Linked lists are discussed in detail in Chapter 2.) The links are kept in a table during execution and in a separate file between runs.

The format for the address file is defined in lines 0043 through 0051. Extra space was left in the zip code field for future expansion. The telephone number field allows room for parentheses around the area code, that is (123) 456-7890.

The program allows the user to dump the contents of the file and the links to a printer. This facilitates understanding the logic underlying the file structure and following the steps involved in adding records to and deleting records from the file. To keep the volume of printing down, the program is originally set up to maintain a file of 10 names and addresses. The program in Fig. 5-13 must be run before the program in Fig. 5-14 in order to create the files and allocate the appropriate amount of file space.

The number of records allowed in the file can be changed by modifying lines 0059 and 0109 of the program. Following this, the program must be recompiled and the file allocation program must be run again. The program can handle up to 999 records without further changes. To go beyond that number would require changing all the PIC 999 fields to PIC 9999 or larger.

The organization of the program in Fig. 5-14 can be seen more easily by consulting the structure chart shown in Fig. 5-15. This chart shows by indentation which subroutines call which other subroutines. Subroutines called by several other subroutines are shown separately.

In previous examples, the body of subroutines called by the PERFORM statement were simply paragraphs. In this program the concept of a SECTION is introduced. A SECTION lies between the

```
            MAIN PROGRAM

        INIT-INDEX
        MENU
        APPEND
            INSERT-RECORD
                GET-FREE
        REVIEW
            LIST-RECORD
            PUT-FREE
        LIST-FILE
            LIST-RECORD
            PRINT-REC
        DUMP
            PRINT-REC
        SAVE-INDEX

    Common Use Subroutines

        WAIT
        POSITION-CURSOR
        CLEAR-SCREEN
        INVALID-KEY
```

Fig. 5-15. The structure chart for the Address Book program.

DIVISION and the paragraph in the COBOL hierarchy. A SECTION is a grouping of paragraphs. A SECTION that is to be PERFORMED ends with the EXIT statement in a paragraph by itself. This style is followed consistently in this program.

The program displays a menu of options to the user and then waits for an answer. The appropriate subroutine is PERFORMed, depending on the selection. This process is repeated until the QUIT option is selected.

The format of reading a data record from the console is worth noting. The subroutine APPEND clears the screen, displays a skeletonized record, and then accepts input from delimited areas of the screen. The effect is like filling out a form.

The program as it stands can be useful for maintaining a list of names and addresses to be printed out. Addition of the capability to search the file based on name, city, or other field would make the program even more useful.

ADVANTAGES AND DISADVANTAGES OF COBOL

It is interesting to compare the COBOL program in Fig. 5-14 with the corresponding program in the C language (Fig. 4-15). Both have about the same number of lines (477 lines for the COBOL program and 465 for the C program), but the COBOL program consists of 11,389 characters (not counting blanks and tabs) compared to 6,858 for the C program.

Clearly, COBOL is not very concise. It is tempting to criticize COBOL because of its wordiness, but this is not necessarily a valid criticism. Wordiness is in itself neither good nor bad. A serious evaluation of COBOL must probe more deeply.

The two major strengths of COBOL are its ability to handle data in a wide variety of forms and structures and its ability to handle files.

The importance given by COBOL to data is symbolized by the fact that COBOL has a separate DATA DIVISION. There is an increasing recognition in the data processing industry that the data to be processed is more important than the algorithms with which it is processed. Most other computer languages were designed for ease of expressing algorithms; COBOL was designed for ease of describing data.

The importance of data requires that much of it be stored in files, and the facilities that COBOL provides for file handling are excellent. In addition to the sequential and direct-access files described in this chapter, the more complete implementations of COBOL provide for indexed files. This can be a major advantage in many applications. Full COBOL implementations also provide a built-in sort facility.

The MOVE statement of COBOL is very powerful when compared to the assignment statement of other languages. Whole structures can be MOVEd in one statement. Data can also be converted from COMPUTATIONAL to DISPLAY format with a MOVE statement.

On the negative side, COBOL is notably weak in its control structures. To emulate a *while* statement requires a PERFORM statement with the body of the loop stored elsewhere, or a GO TO statement.

COBOL also lacks the concept of an arithmetic expression as found in most other languages. COBOL can do arithmetic to be sure, but a statement like

$$IF\ A > (B + C)\ .\ .\ .\ .$$

is impossible in COBOL. To accomplish this in COBOL, one would have to first do

ADD B TO C GIVING TEMP,

then

$$IF\ A > TEMP\ .\ .\ .\ .$$

COBOL handles basic arithmetic very well, but it has problems with more complicated mathematics such as exponentiation and trigonometry. Simple arithmetic, however, is all that is needed in most business applications.

Also on the negative side, all variables in a COBOL program are global, with the exception of variables used in separately compiled subroutines invoked by the CALL statement. (The CALL statement was not discussed in detail in this chapter.) A subroutine invoked by a PERFORM statement must rely only on global variables.

Programming in COBOL is not particularly difficult compared to programming in other languages, but it can be tedious.

AVAILABILITY

COBOL implementations for computers running the CP/M-80, CP/M-86, PC-DOS, and MS-DOS operating systems are widely available at costs ranging from $29.95 and up. Most are priced in the $500 to $700 range. Nevada COBOL, available for the CP/M-80 operating system at $39.95, is an excellent buy, although it is not without its shortcomings.

SUMMARY

COBOL is the most widely-used computer language on large computers. It has powerful facilities for the handling of data and data structures, both within a program and in external files.

All in all, COBOL is an excellent language for its intended purpose, business-oriented data processing. It is not suitable for applications that require extensive mathematical calculations.

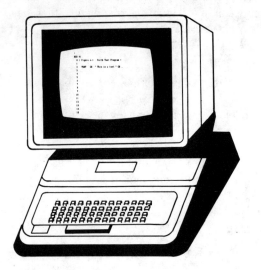

Chapter 6

Forth

The language Forth was developed by Charles H. Moore in the late 1960's and early 1970's. It is therefore of about the same vintage as C, Logo, Pascal, and PILOT. Forth is very popular among a small but enthusiastic group of microcomputer users.

The name Forth has an interesting derivation. Programming languages are sometimes categorized by generation. The first generation of programming languages consists of machine languages. Assembly languages became the second generation. Machine and assembly languages are both computer-specific and are collectively called *low-level languages*. The third generation of programming languages includes FORTRAN, COBOL, and Pascal—in fact all the languages covered in this book. They are also called *high-level languages*. Moore thought that his new language was so much superior to earlier languages that it should be classified as a "fourth-generation language." He wanted to call it "Forth", but the com-

puter on which he was working (an IBM 1130) permitted only 5 characters in a word, so "Fourth" was truncated to "Forth".

Forth is many things:

- ☐ Forth is a high-level language
- ☐ Forth is a low-level language
- ☐ Forth is an operating system
- ☐ Forth is a programming philosophy

One of the distinguishing characteristics of a high-level language is that it is not machine-specific. A Pascal program written for one computer will (at least in theory) run on any other computer that has a Pascal compiler. In that sense, Forth is a high-level language; implementations of Forth are available for most microcomputers and for many minicomputers.

Another, related, characteristic of a high-level language is that the programmer need not be concerned with the architecture of the computer he or she is using. By the architecture of the computer, I mean such details as stacks, registers, and the computation of addresses for array elements. While it is true that the Forth programmer doesn't have to worry about the computer's stacks and registers, he or she does have to contend with the architecture of "the Forth Machine", and does have to worry about the computation of addresses for array elements.

The Forth Machine is a *virtual* machine. It is the image of how the computer appears to the Forth programmer. It exists in software and stands between the programmer and the actual physical machine. The problem is that the programmer has to be concerned with nearly the same level of detail with the Forth Machine as he or she would with the actual physical machine. In that sense Forth is a low-level language.

The Forth Machine consists of the following:

☐ The parameter stack
☐ The return stack
☐ The Dictionary
☐ Secondary (disk) storage

I have left out several predefined areas, but the point is that there are specific places for most things in the Forth Machine, and it is up to the programmer to keep track. Each of these parts of the Forth Machine will be discussed in turn in the pages that follow.

Forth is an operating system in the sense that it performs a number of tasks within the language that are normally performed by the operating system. The most obvious of these is disk file management. The Forth disk file management scheme is very simple; in fact it doesn't even include a disk directory. The disk is divided into blocks of 1024 bytes each. Each block has a number. It is up to the user to keep track of what is in each block and to load and save blocks by number.

Forth is also a programming philosophy, perhaps even a state of mind. The Forth philosophy is that computer memory and computer time are scarce resources, and that the programmer should go out of his or her way to conserve these resources. Forth is designed to afford the user maximum control over these resources. The Forth philosophy encourages the use of programming tricks that save computer time or memory. Some-times this cleverness comes at the expense of clarity. The Forth philosophy encourages mental gymnastics; Forth programmers are fond of showing each other one- or two-line programs and issuing the challenge, "I'll bet you can't figure out what this does!"

Forth is often used in industrial control applications, that is, for programming small microprocessors that control machines in real time. These machines might be household appliances or industrial robots. For these applications at least, time and memory are often at a premium, so the Forth philosophy is appropriate.

Forth is a controversial language. Forth divides people into three groups:

☐ Those who love Forth
☐ Those who hate Forth
☐ Those who have never heard of Forth

It is difficult to know anything about Forth and still remain indifferent about it. There are a number of books about Forth on the market. All were written by those who love Forth. (Why would anyone who hates Forth bother to write a book about it?) I have tried to remain objective in this chapter; you can be the judge of whether I have succeeded.

The programs in this chapter were written and tested on an Apple computer using MVP-FORTH, a product of Mountain View Press. MVP-FORTH complies with the FORTH-79 Standard.

PROGRAM STRUCTURE

The basic structural unit in Forth is the word. A word in Forth corresponds to a function or procedure in other languages. Even the basic operators such as +, −, and so on are implemented as Forth words.

A Forth program is made up of one or more Forth words. The usual procedure is to break a task up into smaller and smaller pieces until each is manageable and then to implement each piece as a Forth word. The interactive nature of Forth facilitates implementing and testing each word independently.

A simple FORTH program that prints, "This is a test" on the screen is shown in Fig. 6-1. This program is implemented as the Forth word TEST.

```
;
SCR #1
   0 ( Figure 6-1:  Forth Test Program )
   1
   2 : TEST   CR ." This is a test." CR ;
   3
   4
   5
   6
   7
   8
   9
  10
  11
  12
  13
  14
  15
```

Fig. 6-1. A Forth test program.

A detailed analysis of this word definition follows. Because of the significance of spaces and quotation marks in Forth, individual words will be delimited by braces, {and}, within the text. The braces are not part of the Forth words being presented.

Comments in forth are delimited by parentheses. Note that the left parenthesis is separated from the rest of the text by a space. This is necessary because the left parenthesis is actually a Forth word. All Forth words, including punctuation marks, must be separated from each other and from other text by one or more spaces. The comment for this program serves to identify the example.

The initial colon { : } is itself a Forth word and is used to initiate the definition of another Forth word. The definition is terminated by the semicolon { ; } at the end of the line. Notice that the colon and semicolon are separated from the adjacent words by a space.

The name { TEST } is the name given to the word. To execute the word after it has been defined, simply type

TEST

at the terminal. The { CR } emits a carriage return and causes the output to appear on a line by itself. The Forth word {."} initializes the printing of the following character string. Because it is a Forth word, it is separated from the text by a space. The character string is terminated by the next quotation mark, ". The quotation mark that terminates a character string is a delimiter, not a Forth word, and therefore does not need to be separated from the preceding text by a space.

That is all there is to our example. The program can be typed in directly from the keyboard or indirectly through the Forth editor. If it is typed in directly, no record is kept of the source text. Creating Forth words with the editor is generally preferable because it preserves a copy of the source text. The numbers on the left of the listing were added by the editor.

The Forth editor is used to create a Forth screen. A Forth screen consists of 1024 characters, arranged as 16 lines of 64 columns each. Each Forth screen is saved as a numbered block on disk and retrieved by its number.

A Forth word is compiled by entering it at the keyboard or by loading it from a Forth screen (using the word { LOAD }). When a word has been successfully compiled, it is entered into the *Forth Dictionary*.

The Forth Dictionary contains the definitions of all Forth words, whether they were furnished with the system or supplied by the user. When a Forth word is compiled, it is added to the end of the dictionary. When Forth searches the dictionary for a word, it starts at the end and searches backwards sequentially. If a word is defined more than once in the dictionary, only the most recent definition will be found. The names of the words in the Forth dictionary can be viewed on the screen by typing the word { VLIST }.

One consequence of the way words are added to the dictionary is that during the development cycle, when a word is being developed, several versions of the word may be compiled. If the word has been compiled six times, it will appear in the dictionary six times. Of course only the most recent definition will be found, but the earlier definitions become *garbage*. Forth therefore provides the { EMPTY } word, which deletes all user-defined words from the dictionary, leaving only predefined words. It is good practice to include { EMPTY } at the beginning of a program so that earlier versions of the program can be deleted before the new version is added.

A typical Forth program consists of a series of word definitions. The lower-level definitions appear first so that they can be incorporated in the higher-level definitions that follow. The highest-level definition appears last. This corresponds to the main program of most other languages.

DATA REPRESENTATION

The basic data types in Forth are characters (8-bit), normal integers (16-bit), unsigned integers (16-bit), and double-precision integers (32-bit). The logical data type does not exist as such, but zero is recognized as false, and anything else is recognized as true in the appropriate context.

The range of normal integers is from -32768 to $+32767$. Unsigned integers can range from 0 to 65535. Double-precision integers can range from $-2,147,483,648$ to $+2,147,483,647$.

The FORTH-79 standard does not support floating-point numbers, but some Forth implementations do. (MVP-FORTH does not.) Some Forth enthusiasts will argue that it is an advantage not to support floating-point numbers because floating-point arithmetic is much slower than fixed-point (integer) arithmetic, and anything that is worth doing can be done in one way or another with fixed-point arithmetic anyway (possibly with double precision).

Although Forth supports the data types described above, there is no such thing as a type declaration. Forth is very loosely-typed; it is up to the programmer to keep track of what type of data his program is dealing with.

The Parameter Stack

Data in most languages is stored in memory locations called variables. While Forth supports variables, they play only a secondary role. Data in Forth programs is most often stored on a *stack*.

A stack is a Last-In, First-Out (LIFO) list. It can be likened to one of the spring-loaded plate dispensers found in many cafeterias. A plate is placed on top of the stack, and those below sink beneath its weight. Only the plate on top of the stack is accessible at a given time. When a plate is removed from the stack, the next plate rises to the top of the stack and becomes accessible.

There are no springs in Forth stacks; it is all done with pointers, but the effect is the same. Only the number at the top of the stack can be accessed. Numbers come off the stack in the reverse of the order in which they went on. Thus is you place the numbers 1, 2, and 3 on the stack in that order, they would come off as 3, 2, and 1.

There are two stacks in the Forth Machine, the parameter stack (often called simply the stack) and the return stack. Each stack element has 16 bits, and is usually a 16-bit integer, although it could be a character (padded to 16 bits), or half of a 32-bit integer.

The parameter stack is so called because it is used as a means for passing parameters to a Forth word. (Recall that a Forth word corresponds to a function or subroutine in other languages.) The parameter stack has other uses as well. The top of the stack is used in much the same way as an accumulator is used in assembly langauges: It is the site for processing arithmetic expressions and a conduit for data on its way to or from such places as memory, the video screen, the return stack, the printer, disk files, and so on.

A number is placed on the stack simply by typing it, whether directly from the keyboard or within a program. The Forth word { . } removes a number from the top of the stack and prints it on the screen. Thus if a user types 3 4 . at the keyboard, Forth will respond, 4 OK. (OK is the system's signal that it has successfully processed your command and is awaiting another.) The 3 and the 4 placed on the stack; then the { . } word removed the 4 and printed it. If the user typed . again, Forth would respond with 3.

A way to see what is on the stack without removing anything is to use the Forth word { .S }. This word is useful during the program development process, because it is important to keep track of what each Forth word does to the stack. The Forth community has even developed a special notation for documenting how a particular word affects the stack. As an example, the stack effects of the word { . } can be described as follows:

$$(n -)$$

The n to the left of the — indicates that { . } expects to find a number on the top of the stack. The fact that there is nothing to the right of the — indicates that the number is removed from the stack.

Several stack manipulation words are worth discussing here. These words and their stack effects are listed below:

.R	(n1 n2 —)
SWAP	(n1 n2 — n2 n1)
DUP	(n — n n)
ROT	(n1 n2 n3 — n3 n2 n1)
OVER	(n1 n2 — n1 n2 n1)
DROP	(n —)

{ .R } prints the number n1 right-justified in a field n2 characters wide. { SWAP } simply exchanges or swaps the two top elements of the stack. Before the execution of { SWAP }, n2 was on top of the stack; after execution, n1 is on top. { DUP } simply duplicates the value of the top element on the stack. { ROT } exchanges the values of the first and third elements of the stack. { OVER } duplicates the value of the second item on the stack and places it on the top of the stack. { DROP } simply discards the top element of the stack.

The Return Stack

The Forth Machine has another stack, called the *return stack*. Forth words are stored in the Dictionary. When a Forth word is executed, control passes to that word in the Dictionary. The system must keep track of where to return to find the next word to execute in the program. The system uses the return stack for this purpose.

The system also uses the return stack to keep track of loop counter variables. In addition, the return stack is available to the programmer for temporary storage of data. Because of the other uses of the return stack, the programmer must be careful not to leave data on the return stack too long (not past the end of the execution of a word) and to be extra careful within the body of a loop.

The Forth word { > R } moves the top element of the parameter stack to the top of the return stack. The complementary word { R> } moves the top element of the return stack to the top of the parameter stack. Both of these words remove the element from the source stack. By contrast, { R@} copies the top of the return stack onto the parameter stack without removing the element from the return stack.

Constants

Forth supports the use of named constants. These are useful for storing data that doesn't change during the course of a program. Programs that use named constants are easier to read, because a meaningful name can be used, and easier to modify, because the value appears only once in the program.

Suppose that a program needs to refer to the minimum age for voting. A constant called V.AGE can be declared and initialized for this purpose as follows:

18 CONSTANT V.AGE

Notice that the value comes before the word { CONSTANT }. This is typical of Forth and occurs because 18 is a parameter of the word { CONSTANT } and is passed to { CONSTANT } via the parameter stack.

Constants are stored in the dictionary. Once a constant has been declared, its value is retrieved and placed on the stack whenever its name appears. Also, once a constant has been declared, its value can never be changed.

Variables

Variables must also be declared in Forth, and are also stored in the Forth dictionary. The primary difference between a variable and a constant is that the value of a variable can be changed as often as needed in a program.

Suppose that a variable called SUM is to be used. It is declared as follows:

VARIABLE SUM

Data is assigned to a variable using the store word {!}. To set the value of SUM to 0, you would write the following:

0 SUM !

When the Forth intepreter encounters the number 0, it places it on the stack. The interpreter next looks up the address of the variable SUM and places it on the stack. The interpreter then passes control to the word {!}, which uses the address at the top of the stack (the address of SUM) to store the value next on the stack (0 in this case).

To recall the value of the variable SUM, the word fetch {@} is used, as in the following:

SUM @

The address of SUM is placed on the stack, then {@} retrieves the value stored at that address.

Double Precision

As mentioned earlier, Forth supports double-precision (32-bit) data. Double-precision numbers can be either signed or unsigned. Because they take up 32 bits, they are stored on the stack as if they were two single-precision numbers. The low-order 16 bits go first, with the high-order 16 bits following on top.

There are separate stack operators for double-precision numbers. Some of these words and their stack effects are listed below:

D.	(d —)
D.R.	(d n —)
DDROP	(d —)
D@	(addr — d)
D!	(d addr —)

DCONSTANT	(d —)
DVARIABLE	(—)
DSWAP	(d1 d2 — d2 d1)
DOVER	(d1 d2 — d1 d2 d1)

These words are similar in operation to their single-precision counterparts and therefore need no further explanation.

There is also a class of words that begin with 2. These words are similar in operation to the above-listed words, but they are used to manipulate the top two elements of the stack even when they are two separate single-precision numbers. These words include the following:

2!	(d addr —)
2@	(addr — d)
2CONSTANT	(d —)
2VARIABLE	(—)
2DROP	(d —)
2DUP	(d — d d)
2OVER	(d1 d2 — d1 d2 d1)
2SWAP	(d1 d2 — d2 d1)

Again, the operation of these words is analogous to the operation of their single-precision counterparts.

ARITHMETIC EXPRESSIONS

Forth uses *Reverse Polish notation*, sometimes called *postfix* notation, for arithmetic expressions. (See Chapter 2 for a discussion of the various forms of notation.) In postfix notation the numbers to be operated on come first, followed by the operator. For example, the numbers 2 and 3 would be added as follows:

2 3 +

Here is what happens as this expression is evaluated: First the number 2 is placed on the top of the stack; then the number 3 is placed on the stack. The two top elements on the stack are then 2 and 3. The {+} operator adds the two top elements of the stack and leaves the result at the top of the stack. As indicated by the notation, the operator {+} is a

Forth word and is stored in the dictionary just as other Forth words are.

Other Forth arithmetic operators include { − }, { * }, { / }, and { MOD }. These operators perform subtraction, multiplication, integer division, and the modulus (remainder after integer division) operations, respectively. The operator { /MOD } provides both the integer quotient and the remainder. Each of these operators take the top two elements of the stack as operands and leave the result at the top of the stack. In the case of { /MOD }, both results are left on the stack.

Figure 6-2 illustrates the use of arithmetic expressions in Forth. Two words are defined in Fig. 6-2. Each word expects to find a number on the stack. That number is taken as X in the expression, "A times the square of X plus B times X plus C,"here A is 3, B is 5, and C is 1. Each word prints the result on the screen.

The constants A, B, and C, which are used in the expressions, are declared explicitly in lines 4, 5, and 6. This makes the functions themselves easier to read and makes the program easier to modify.

The first word, { FN1 }, is written in the usual Forth style. No variables are used; all data is stored and manipulated using only the two stacks. The expression was factored into a simpler form before being programmed. This is consistent with Forth style: the premise is that the programmer should factor the problem into the form most convenient for Forth so that the resulting program will be compact and efficient.

First a duplicate is made of X and moved to the return stack for temporary storage. Next the X remaining on the stack is multiplied by A and 5 is added. Then the X from the return stack is brought back and multiplied by the previous result. Finally, C is added, and the result printed.

The second word, { FN2 }, is programmed in a style more often found in programs written in languages such as BASIC, FORTRAN, and Pascal. A variable, which is declared in line 3 is used. The word FN2 itself is defined in lines 10 through 14. The first step is to store the value found on the stack in the variable X. In line 11, X is retrieved, squared, and multiplied by A. In line 12, X is again retrieved, multiplied by B, and added to the previous result. In line 13, C is added. The result is printed in line 14.

A separate set of Forth words exist for performing arithmetic operations involving double-precision numbers. These include the following:

```
SCR #2
 0 ( Figure 6-2:  Arithmetic Expressions in Forth )
 1 (              3 X SQUARED + 5 X + 1            )
 2
 3  VARIABLE X
 4  3 CONSTANT A
 5  5 CONSTANT B
 6  1 CONSTANT C
 7
 8  : FN1   DUP )R A * B + R) * C + . ;
 9
10  : FN2   X !
11          X @ DUP * A *
12          X @ B * +
13          C +
14              . ;
15
```

Fig. 6-2. Arithmetic expressions in Forth.

D+   (d1 d2 — d3)
D—   (d1 d2 — d3)
DABS (d1 — d2)

In the case of { D+ }, the double-precision number d3 is the sum of the double-precision numbers d1 and d2. In the case of { D— }, d3 is the difference rather than the sum. { DABS } produces the absolute value of a double-precision number.

LOGICAL EXPRESSIONS

A logical expression produces the value true or the value false, which are represented in Forth by 1 and 0, respectively. In the appropriate context, any nonzero value is taken as representing true.

Like arithmetic expressions, logical expressions in Forth are written using postfix notation. For example, to test whether 3 is greater than 2, you would write the following:

3 2 >

Like arithmetic operators, relational operators such as { > } are Forth words and take their operands from the stack. The above expression is thus testing whether the next-to-the-top element of the stack (3) is greater than the top element (2). Because this is true, { > } will leave the truth value (1) on top of the stack.

The relational operators in Forth include the following:

>	greater than
<	less than
=	equal
0=	zero equal
0<	zero less than
0>	zero greater than

Notice that there are special operators used for making comparisons with zero. These operators require only one operand from the stack. The first three operators listed require two operands from the stack. Each of the six leaves 0 (false) or 1 (true) on the stack.

The logical operators in Forth are { AND },

{ OR }, and { NOT }. Both { AND } and { OR } require two operands. { AND } produces a 1 (true) if and only if both operands are nonzero; otherwise it produces a 0 (false). { OR } produces a 0 (false) if and only if both operands are zero; otherwise it produces a 1 (true). { NOT } requires only one operand. If that operand is zero, { NOT } returns a 1 (true); if the operand is nonzero, { NOT } returns a 0 (false). { NOT } is equivalent to { 0= }.

You may have noticed the absence of operators to test for less than or equal, greater than or equal, and not equal. The test for greater than or equal has the same meaning as not less than, and could be accomplished as in the following example:

5 4 < NOT

This example would leave a 1 at the top of the stack because 5 is greater than or equal to (not less than) 4.

If the above procedure seems awkward, you can define a new Forth word to accomplish the same thing as follows:

: >=   < NOT ;

The new word { >= } will then behave exactly as if it were built into the language. Similarly, you can define words to test less than or equal and not equal as follows:

: <=   > NOT ;
: <>   = NOT ;

These are good examples of the extensibility of Forth.

There are also separate words for use in logical expressions involving double-precision numbers. These include the following:

D>	greater than
D<	less than
D=	equal to
D0=	equal to zero

The usage of these words is analogous to that of

their single-precision counterparts. Each leaves a 0 (false) or 1 (true) on the stack.

INPUT AND OUTPUT

This section discusses how Forth programs read data from the keyboard and write data to the terminal (or video screen) and the printer. Disk file input and output is discussed in the section on File Handling.

You have already seen two Forth words for terminal output, { . } and { ." } (pronounced dot and dot-quote, respectively). { . } of course prints the number at the top of the stack to the terminal, followed by a space. The number is removed from the stack as it is printed. { ." } prints all characters up to the next quote, as in Fig. 6-1.

Other simple output words include the following:

Word	Stack Effect
CR	(—)
EMIT	(n —)
BL	(— 32)
SPACE	(—)
SPACES	(n —)
TYPE	(addr n —)

{ CR } simply outputs a carriage return and a line feed. { EMIT } outputs the character whose ASCII value is at the top of the stack. To output the bell character (Control-G) for example, type the following:

7 EMIT

{ BL } places the ASCII equivalent of a blank on the stack. { SPACE } outputs a single blank. The same result could be achieved by the following sequence:

BL EMIT

{ EMIT } in this case takes as its input the ASCII blank left on the stack by { BL }. { SPACES }

outputs the number of spaces indicated by the number at the top of the stack.

The operation of { TYPE } is more complicated. It expects to find a number (n) at the top of the stack and an address (addr) below that. { TYPE } outputs n characters beginning at address addr. { TYPE } is often used in conjunction with number formatting commands, as described below.

The most common formatting words are { <# }, { # }, { #S }, { HOLD }, and { #> }. { <# }, pronounced variously as "bracket-number" or "less-sharp," marks the beginning of a formatting sequence, and { #> } marks the end of the sequence. Here is a simple example of a formatting sequence:

<# # # 46 HOLD #S #>   TYPE

What this sequence does is to print a number with two decimal places. The number to be printed is taken from the stack and is expected to be a double-precision unsigned number. It is first converted to a character string and then printed by { TYPE }. The formatting operators leave the proper arguments on the stack for { TYPE }.

A double-precision number can be put on the stack in several ways, including the following:

1,250
1250.
1250   0

Inclusion of a punctuation mark such as a period (.), comma (,), slash (/), dash (-), or colon (:) marks a number as double-precision. The third example consists of two single-precision numbers and causes the high-order part of the number to be set to zero. As mentioned earlier, a double-precision number can be printed directly from the stack by using the word { D. }.

The number is converted a character at a time, right to left. The first two occurrences of { # } convert the digits that are to the right of the decimal. The 46 is the decimal representation of the ASCII value for the period (.). { HOLD } inserts

```
SCR #6
  0 ( Figure 6-6:  Demonstrate Text Input )
  1
  2 : HELLO
  3    CR
  4    ." What is your first name?  "
  5    QUERY
  6    BL TEXT
  7    CR ." Hello, "
  8    PAD COUNT TYPE ." !  It is a pleasure to meet you."
  9    CR ;
 10
 11
 12
 13
 14
 15
```

Fig. 6-3. The function to print dollars and cents.

that character into the character string being created. The { #S } converts the remaining digits to the left of the decimal.

A more complicated character conversion is shown in the program in Fig. 6-3. The Forth word { .$ } expects to find a double-precision number on the stack. That number can be positive or negative. { .$ } prints out that number with a leading minus sign if the number is negative (no sign if it is positive), a dollar sign, and two decimal places. The sign is handled by the word { SIGN }, which is at the end of the definition. Recall that digits are converted from right to left.

There are no explicit commands that direct output to the printer. How this is done depends on the implementation. In the Apple version of MVP-FORTH, the { PR# } word is used to activate and deactivate the printer. The expression

    1 PR#

activates the printer, provided that the printer interface card is plugged into the Apple slot #1. The printer is deactivated by the following expression:

    0 PR#

If an 80-column display card is plugged into the Apple slot #3, then the expression

    3 PR#

serves to deactivate the printer. The use of the printer is illustrated in the program in Fig. 6-4.

Forth contains words for the input of characters and character strings. Input of a number requires that a character string be read in and then converted to a number. A program that demonstrates this process is shown in Fig. 6-5. This program reads in two numbers from the keyboard and prints out their sum.

The word { QUERY } reads in a string of up to 80 characters and places it in a special area called the *terminal input buffer*. The word { WORD } has as its input the blank character. It scans the terminal input buffer until it finds the blank, and transfers the substring ending with the blank to a safe place in memory. It leaves the address of that place on the stack. The word { NUMBER } uses the address on the stack to find that substring and converts it to a double-precision number, which it places on the stack.

This process is repeated, so two double-

135

```
SCR #4
  0 ( Figure 6-4:  Use of the Printer in Forth )
  1
  2 : PRINT
  3      1 PR#
  4      ." This goes to the printer." CR
  5      3 PR#
  6      CR  ." This goes to the screen."  CR
  7      ;
  8
  9
 10
 11
 12
 13
 14
 15
```

Fig. 6-4. The use of the printer in Forth.

```
SCR #5
  0 ( Figure 6-5:  Demonstrate Input Commands )
  1
  2 : ADD2   QUERY BL WORD NUMBER
  3          QUERY BL WORD NUMBER
  4          D+
  5          D. ;
  6
  7
  8
  9
 10
 11
 12
 13
 14
 15
```

Fig. 6-5. A demonstration of input commands.

precision numbers will be put on the stack. The word { D+ } adds them, and { D. } prints the result.

An example of simple character input is shown in Fig. 6-6. A typical exchange using this program follows:

HELLO	(User)
What is your first name?	(Forth)
MARY	(User)
Hello, MARY! It is a pleasure to meet you.	(Forth)

```
SCR #6
  0 ( Figure 6-6:  Demonstrate Text Input )
  1
  2 : HELLO
  3      CR
  4      ." What is your first name?  "
  5      QUERY
  6      BL TEXT
  7      CR ." Hello, "
  8      PAD COUNT TYPE ." ! It is a pleasure to meet you."
  9      CR ;
 10
 11
 12
 13
 14
 15
```

Fig. 6-6. A demonstration of text input.

The word { QUERY } in this program functions in the same way as in the previous program. This time { TEXT } is used instead of { WORD }. Note that { TEXT } also takes the blank character as a deliminter. It transfers the substring to a special location called the PAD. This is a scratch pad area and is guaranteed to be at least 64 bytes long. The word { PAD } puts the address of this area on the stack. The word { COUNT } counts the number of characters and sets up the stack for the word { TYPE }, which types the name at the console.

Notice that handling input and output in Forth requires a fairly detailed understanding of the inner workings of the Forth machine.

CONTROL STRUCTURES

Forth supports a wide variety of control structures. It supports IF statements, various kinds of loops, the equivalents of functions and procedures, and recursion. The only significant omission is a CASE statement. (See Chapter 2 for a discussion of the CASE statement.) Forth in particular encourages a modular approach to program structure and design.

Forth control structures rely heavily on the parameter stack for inputs and in many cases on the return stack for intermediate operations. How the stacks are used will be discussed below.

Simple Selection: IF-ELSE-THEN

The general format for this statement is as follows:

```
condition IF
    statement(s)
ELSE
    statement(s)
THEN
```

The Forth format differs from the format most often found in high-level languages in several ways. First, the condition precedes the word { IF }. This is to be expected, as { IF }, like other Forth words, takes its arguments from the stack. The other major difference is the use of the word { THEN } to mark the end of the construct. Some implementations of

Forth also accept the word { ENDIF } as a synonym for { THEN }.

The above illustration shows the IF construct properly indented in order to clearly show the structure. There is an unfortunate tendency among some Forth programmers to compress such constructs into a single line.

A program to demonstrate an IF statement is shown in Fig. 6-7. The program computes and prints the gross weekly wages of a worker when the overtime rate is one-and-one-half times the basic rate for between 40 and 50 hours per week, and double the basic rate for work in excess of 50 hours per week.

```
SCR #7
  0 ( Figure 6-7:  Compute Weekly Pay in
Forth )
  1
  2 800 CONSTANT RATE
  3 : HOURS DUP
  4    40 < IF
  5       RATE M*
  6    ELSE DUP 50 < IF
  7       40 - RATE 3 2 */ M*
  8       40 RATE M* D+
  9    ELSE
 10       50 - RATE 2* M*
 11       RATE 3 2 */ 10 M* D+
 12       40 RATE M* D+
 13    THEN THEN
 14    CR ." Weekly pay is " .$ CR ;
 15
```

Fig. 6-7. The computation of weekly pay in Forth.

There are several points to note about this program. First, the basic pay rate of $8.00 per hour is stored as 800, an integer constant. Second, there are several new words introduced. { M* } takes two 16-bit numbers as arguments, multiplies them and produces a 32-bit result. Double precision is needed in this problem because weekly pay can exceed $327.67, which would be stored as 32767 pennies. (Recall that 32767 is the maximum possible value for a 16-bit integer.)

137

Because the number 1.5 cannot be represented directly as an integer, some other way must be used to compute 1.5 times the basic pay rate. One way is to multiply by 3, then divide by 2. This can be done in one operation, using the word { */ } as in the following expression:

RATE 3 2 */

This is the expression used in line 7 of Fig. 6-7.

The other word in this example that has not been used before is { 2* }. This is merely a shorthand for the expression "2 *."

The word { HOURS } expects to find the number of hours worked on the stack. Here are a few sample results:

30 HOURS	Weekly pay is $240.00
40 HOURS	Weekly pay is $320.00
45 HOURS	Weekly pay is $380.00
50 HOURS	Weekly pay is $440.00
55 HOURS	Weekly pay is $520.00

The program uses nested IF statements. The various branches of the IF statements leave the result on the stack as a double-precision number. The result is converted to a dollars-and-cents representation using the { .$ } word shown in Fig. 6-3. This is a good example of how Forth words are often reused in the definition of other Forth words.

Counted Loops

Forth supports counted loops with the DO-LOOP structure. The format of this structure is as follows:

limit start DO
    statement(s)
LOOP

A simple example is shown in the program in Fig. 6-8. This program prints the numbers from one to ten.

The loop counter I is maintained on the return

```
SCR #8
 0 ( Figure 6-8:  The DO Loop )
 1
 2 : 1TO10
 3      11 1 DO
 4           CR I.
 5      LOOP ;
 6
 7
 8
 9
10
11
12
13
14
15
```

Fig. 6-8. The DO loop.

stack. The Forth word { I } copies the value of the loop counter to the parameter stack. The initial value of the loop counter is taken from the top of the parameter stack, and the upper limit for the loop counter is taken as the next item on the parameter stack. These are represented by "start" and "limit," respectively, in the format illustration above.

The loop counter is incremented by one at the end of each pass through the loop. The loop counter is compared to the upper limit, and if it is less than the upper limit, the body of the loop is executed again. If the loop counter equals or exceeds the upper limit, control is passed to the first statement following the end of the loop. Because the test is performed at the bottom of the loop, a DO loop is always executed at least once.

Notice that two Forth words { DO } and { LOOP }, make up the counted loop construct just described. They work as a team. Notice also that the loop counter is incremented by one at the end of each iteration. If it is necessary, the word { +LOOP } can be substituted for { LOOP }. When this is done, the loop counter is incremented by whatever value is on the stack when { + } is encountered. The following variation of the program in Fig. 6-8 will count from 2 to 10 in increments of 2:

```
: SKIP
    11  2  DO
        CR  I  .
    2   +LOOP  :
```

Conditional Loops

There are two basic forms of conditional loop in Forth: the BEGIN . . . UNTIL loop and the BEGIN . . . WHILE . . . REPEAT loop. The BEGIN . . . UNTIL loop is very similar to the REPEAT . . . UNTIL loop in Pascal, and the BEGIN . . . WHILE . . . REPEAT loop is much like the WHILE look in Pascal, BASIC, and other languages.

Each of these loop forms is controlled by a condition left on the stack. That condition is the result of a logical expression, such as those discussed earlier in this chapter. In the case of the BEGIN . . . UNTIL loop, it is the { UNTIL } word that checks for the condition. The loop is repeated as long as the condition is false. In the case of the BEGIN . . . WHILE . . . REPEAT loop, it is the { WHILE } word that looks for the flag. If the condition is false (zero), control is immediately passed to the statement following the REPEAT. Otherwise, the { REPEAT } word causes the loop to repeat.

Figure 6-9 contains two programs. Each counts to 10, as did the program in Fig. 6-8. One uses a BEGIN . . . UNTIL loop, and the other uses a BEGIN . . . WHILE . . . REPEAT loop.

Unlike the program in Fig. 6-8, these two programs do not use the return stack. As a result, the { I } word cannot be used to obtain the loop index. All of the counting has to be done within the loop. Notice that each program ends with the word { DROP } . The process of testing a Forth word should include checking to see what is left on the stack after the word is executed in order to avoid unintentionally leaving extraneous data on the stack.

The process of counting to ten is done more easily with a counted loop than with a conditional

```
SCR #9
  0 ( Figure 6-9:  Conditional Loops )
  1
  2 : RLOOP
  3     1 BEGIN
  4         CR DUP .
  5         1+ DUP
  6         11 =
  7     UNTIL DROP ;
  8
  9 : WLOOP
 10     1 BEGIN
 11         CR DUP .
 12         DUP 10 (
 13     WHILE
 14         1+
 15     REPEAT DROP ;
```

Fig. 6-9. Conditional loops.

loop. There are many other situations, however, in which a conditional loop is more natural. An example of this situation was given in Chapter 2.

The word { LEAVE } causes a loop to be exited before the next iteration. This is similar to the break command in the C language. When used, it is almost always found within the body of an IF statement.

Recursion

A Forth word is recursive if it refers to itself in its definition. Recursion can be a useful control structure in certain types of programs. A common example is the calculation of the factorial function.

The factorial of a positive integer is a mathematical function that is defined recursively. The factorial of zero is defined as 1. The factorial of a number N is defined as the product of that number and the factorial of N-1. Thus the factorial function is defined in terms of itself.

Different versions of Forth implement recursion in different ways. The MVP-FORTH implementation requires a little subterfuge. There is a flag in the dictionary definition of each Forth word called the *smudge bit*. When a Forth word is being defined, this smudge bit is set to indicate that the word has not yet been successfully compiled until such time as it actually has been. This prevents incorrectly-defined words from being found in the dictionary. As a result, when the recursive word is being defined, it cannot find itself in the dictionary. The Forth word { SMUDGE } is used to toggle the smudge flag so that the recursive word can in fact find itself.

{ SMUDGE } must be enclosed between brackets so that it will be executed during compilation rather than compiled as part of the word definition. Because the flag has been toggled, it must be toggled again after the word has been successfully defined in order to return it to its normal state. All of this is illustrated in the program in Fig. 6-10.

The program is used as follows:

```
4 FACTORIAL     (User)
24 OK           (Forth)
```

The argument precedes the name of the function, as is usual in Forth. The program first takes the absolute value of its argument to protect against negative arguments. The factorial of a negative number is not defined, and without this safeguard, an at-tempt to calculate the factorial of a negative number could result in an infinite loop.

The IF-ELSE-THEN construct checks to see whether or not the argument is 0. What happens then is best explained by example. Suppose that the original number is 3. Because 3 is not equal to 0, the ELSE branch is taken. This branch tries to multiply 3 by 2 FACTORIAL. This invokes FACTORIAL again, because the factorial of 2 is not yet known. In a similar manner, the function tries to calculate the factorial of 2 in terms of the factorial of 1. The factorial of 1 is calculated in terms of the factorial of 0. This time around, the function can finally calculate a value directly; it returns 1. Now 2 factorial can be calculated. Given 2 factorial, 3 factorial can be calculated, and the process is finished.

The program in Fig. 6-10 is of limited useful-ness as it stands. The factorial function increases rapidly; the factorial of 8 is too large to fit in a 16-bit integer. You might find it a useful exercise to con-vert the program to double-precision.

DATA STRUCTURES

Forth provides support for advanced data structures such as arrays, lists, and so forth, but at a rather primitive level. It is true that complex data

```
SCR #10
 0 ( Figure 6-10  Recursive Factorial Function )       EMPTY
 1
 2 : FACTORIAL
 3      ABS
 4      DUP 0= IF
 5                  DROP 1
 6          ELSE
 7                  DUP 1-
 8              [ SMUDGE ] FACTORIAL
 9                  *
10          THEN ;
11   SMUDGE
12
13
14
15
```

Fig. 6-10. The recursive factorial function.

structures can be programmed in Forth, but the same can be said of assembly language. Like assembly language, Forth makes the programmer do most of the work.

Arrays

One-dimensional arrays can be implemented in Forth without too much difficulty. With the addition of a few user-defined words, it is fairly easy.

The Forth word { VARIABLE } associates a variable name with a storage location in the dictionary and allocates two bytes of storage. The word { ALLOT } is used to add more storage space to the most-recently-defined variable. For example, suppose that an array called WEEK is needed and that it must have room for seven 16-bit integers. It would be declared as follows:

```
VARIABLE WEEK
12 ALLOT
```

Fourteen bytes of storage are needed for seven 16-bit integers. The { VARIABLE } word provides two of the 14 bytes. The { ALLOT } word provides the remaining 12.

This method of allocating space for arrays forces the programmer to count bytes. It would be better if the programmer could simply indicate how many elements the array should contain. With a little work, a new Forth word that will allow such declarations can be created.

One way to improve matters is to define a Forth word as follows:

```
: DIMENSION  1−  2*  ALLOT ;
```

This word expects to find the number of elements the array is to contain on the stack. The number of bytes to allot is computed by subtracting one and multiplying by 2. Using this new word, the array WEEK could be declared as follows:

```
VARIABLE WEEK
7 DIMENSION
```

This spares the programmer from having to figure out how many bytes to allot.

When a variable name appears in a Forth program, it causes the address of the appropriate memory location to appear on the stack. The seven array elements are usually thought of as being numbered from 0 to 6. The addresses of the seven elements of the array WEEK can be visualized as follows:

Element	Address
0	WEEK
1	WEEK + 2
2	WEEK + 4
3	WEEK + 6
4	WEEK + 8
5	WEEK + 10
6	WEEK + 12

To retrieve the value of the fourth element of WEEK (element number 3), you could write the following:

```
6  WEEK  +  @
```

The process of computing the addresses of array elements can be simplified considerably by creating a new Forth word:

```
: ADDR  SWAP  1−  2*  + ;
```

With this word, you no longer have to number the items 0 to 6; you can use the more natural 1-to-7 numbering scheme. Using this new word, the fourth element of WEEK can be retrieved as follows:

```
4  WEEK  ADDR  @
```

The word { ADDR } can also be used to compute the address for storing data into the array. For example, the following would store the number 10 in the second element of the array WEEK:

```
10  2  WEEK  ADDR  !
```

```
SCR #11
  0 ( Figure 6-11:  Array Handling Words )
  1
  2 : DIMENSION   1- 2* ALLOT ;
  3
  4 : ADDR    SWAP 1- 2* + ;
  5
  6 : ARRAY
  7     CREATE 2*  ALLOT
  8     DOES)    ADDR ;
  9
 10
 11
 12
 13
 14
 15
```

Fig. 6-11. Array handling words.

The use of arrays in Forth is made much easier using the new words { DIMENSION } and { ADDR } . There is another, simpler way to accomplish the same thing using the word pair { CREATE } and { DOES> }. With this method you can create a new defining word called ARRAY, which can then be used to declare any number of arrays. How this is done is shown in Fig. 6-11.

The word { ARRAY } can be used to declare the array WEEK as follows:

7 ARRAY WEEK

If another array called MONTH is required, it could be declared by the following:

30 ARRAY MONTH

No separate VARIABLE declaration is needed when { ARRAY } is used.

The following would retrieve the fourth element of the array WEEK:

4 WEEK @

The method for storing 7 in the fifth element of WEEK is as follows:

7 5 WEEK !

As you may have deduced, the code between = CREATE } and { DOES > } is used at the time the array is declared; it allocates the appropriate number of bytes of storage. The code following { DOES } is executed when the name of the array is used in an expression. In this case you simply used the previously-defined word { ADDR } to calculate the appropriate address.

If you have access to Forth on a computer, you can use the words { FILL } and { DUMP } to experiment with arrays. The expression

1 WEEK 14 0 FILL

will fill the array WEEK with zeros. The contents of the array can be displayed on the screen by typing the following:

1 WEEK 14 DUMP

This sequence displays the contents of memory for 14 bytes beginning with the first element of WEEK. If you zero-fill an array and then dump it after performing a store operation, it will be easy to see the results of the operation.

Character Strings

The arrays discussed above have all consisted of 16-bit data elements. Forth can also handle arrays consisting of 8-bit data elements. These are useful for storing characters. Arrays of characters are commonly called character strings.

Forth character strings are usually stored with the length of the string in the first byte. This means that Forth character strings can hold up to 255 characters, because 255 is the largest number that can fit in one byte.

The Forth word used to store an 8-bit character is { C! }. The word to retrieve an 8-bit character and place it at the top of the stack is { C@}. If you adopt the convention that the length of a character

142

string is in element 0 of the array, and that the nth character is in element n, the array will have n + 1 elements. Using techniques similar to those used above for integer arrays, you can define a word to create character arrays as follows:

```
: CARRAY
    CREATE 1+ ALLOT
    DOES>  SWAP
           + ;
```

Using this word, a character array called STRING capable of holding 80 characters would be created as follows:

```
80   CARRAY STRING
```

The following would retrieve the tenth character in STRING:

```
10   STRING   C@
```

To store the letter A in the first character position of STRING, you would type the following:

```
65   1   STRING   C!
```

The number 65 is the ASCII representation for A.

The following sequence would retrieve the letter A from STRING and print it as a character:

```
1   STRING C @ EMIT
```

The word { EMIT } converts the number 65 back to the letter A and prints it.

Forth provides several words that make the manipulation of character strings easier. One useful function is to initialize a character string to all blanks. This can be done as follows:

```
0   0   STRING   C!
1   STRING   80   BL   FILL
```

The first line sets the character count to zero. The first 0 is the value that is stored, and the second zero is the subscript of the character array STRING

that indicates where the character count resides. The second line stores 80 blanks beginning with the address STRING +1. Some versions of Forth have a word called { BLANK } or { BLANKS }, which could be used to accomplish the same task in a slightly simpler way:

```
0   0   STRING   !
1   STRING   80   BLANK
```

The word { CMOVE } can be used to move characters from one string to another. Suppose you have two character strings, 1STRING and 2STRING. The contents of 1STRING can be copied into 2STRING as follows:

```
0   1STRING   0   2STRING   81   CMOVE
```

The expression 0 1STRING leaves the address of the beginning of the first string on the stack. Similarly, 0 2STRING puts the address of the second string on the stack. The number 81 is the number of characters to move, counting the character-count byte.

The word { COUNT } can be used to separate the character count from the rest of the string. This separation sets up the stack for other commands that require the character count to be on the stack. The action of { COUNT } can be summarized by the following:

```
( addr   —   addr+1   n )
```

Before { COUNT } is executed, the address on the stack is the address of the count byte. After { COUNT } is executed, the address of the first character is in the second position of the stack and the count itself is on the top of the stack.

A word that requires the stack to be set up in this manner is { TYPE }. The contents of STRING can be displayed on the screen in the following manner:

```
0   STRING   COUNT   TYPE
```

Another word that requires the stack to be set

up the same way is { −TEXT }. The sequence

   0 1STRING COUNT 0 2STRING
   COUNT −TEXT

will compare the two strings. If they are equal, a zero will be left on the stack. If the contents of { STRING } are less than the contents of { 2STRING }, a negative numbber will be left on the stack. Otherwise, a positive number will be left on the stack. The − at the beginning of { −TEXT } stands for not. It is used to indicate that it returns zero (false) for a positive (true) result.

Two-Dimensional Arrays

Forth has no direct provision for arrays with more than one dimension. Two-dimensional arrays can be handled, but it is left up to the programmer to figure out how.

The handling of two-dimensional arrays can be greatly simplified by creating a Forth word to take care of the necessary details. Such a word, called { 2ARRAY }, is shown in Fig. 6-12.

The word { 2ARRAY } allows a two-dimensional array to be declared, as in the following:

   3 5 2ARRAY TABLE

This creates a 3 row by 5 column array of integers named TABLE. The number of columns is stored in a variable called NC, because it will be needed in the computation of addresses for individual array elements. (Because a single variable is used, all arrays declared using 2ARRAY within a given program must have the same number of columns.)

The { DOES> } portion of the word { 2ARRAY } expects to find the subscripts and the name of the array on the stack. The two { ROT } words move the subscripts ahead of the array name on the stack. The displacement in bytes from the beginning of the array is computed using the algorithm shown in lines 10 through 14 in Fig. 6-12. Note the use of the number of columns in the computation.

Suppose the array TABLE has been declared to be a 3 by 5 array as described above. The following two sequences would first store the number 10

```
SCR #12
  0 ( Figure 6-12:  Two-Dimensional Array
    Setup )
  1
  2 VARIABLE NC
  3
  4 : 2ARRAY
  5    CREATE            ( ROW COL 2ARRAY NAME )
  6          DUP NC !    ( SAVE NR OF COLUMNS )
  7          * 2* ALLOT  ( ALLOCATE SPACE )
  8    DOES>             ( R C NAME )
  9          ROT ROT
 10          1- SWAP     ( COLUMN DISPLACEMENT )
 11          1- NC @ *   ( ROW DISPLACEMENT )
 12          +           ( TOTAL DISPLACEMENT )
 13          2*          ( 2 BYTES PER INTEGER )
 14          + ;         ( ADD TO BASE ADDRESS )
 15
```

Fig. 6-12. A two-dimensional array setup.

in row 2, column 3 of the array and then retrieve and print the number:

   10 2 3 TABLE !
   2 3 TABLE ?

Figure 6-13 shows the use of nested DO loops in conjunction with the two-dimensional array TABLE. The word { TFILL } fills each element of the array with the product of its row and column numbers. The word { TPRN } prints out the contents of the array in a tabular format. Note the use of the words { I } and { J } in the inner loops. The word { I } returns the value of the current loop counter from the return stack. The word { J } returns the value of the next outer loop counter from the return stack. The expression 5 .R causes the top of the stack to be printed right-justified in a field 5 characters wide.

Records

Chapter 2 illustrated the concept of a record with the example of creating a record to a student's name and his or her scores on up to 20 tests. If there

```
SCR #13
  0 ( Figure 6-13:  Use of Two-Dimensional Arrays )
  1
  2  3 5 2ARRAY TABLE
  3
  4 : TFILL    4 1 DO
  5                    6 1 DO
  6                         J I * J I TABLE !
  7                    LOOP
  8           LOOP ;
  9
 10 : TPRN     4 1 DO CR
 11                    6 1 DO
 12                         J I TABLE @
 13                         5 .R
 14                    LOOP
 15           LOOP CR ;
```

Fig. 6-13. The use of two-dimensional arrays.

are 30 students in the class, this information will be needed for each one. One set of information consisting of a name and the corresponding scores constitutes a *record*.

Forth does not directly support the concept of a record. Forth does, however, provide the means to define records of various kinds. It is left up to the programmer to figure out how.

The first step is to decide on a record layout. One possibility is the following:

Name   Positions 1-30
Scores   Positions 31-70

The name field would allow for up to 30 characters. A count byte is not necessary for the name field because it will always be of the same fixed length, padded with trailing blanks if necessary. Because each score is assumed to be a 16-bit (2-byte) integer, and there are up to 20 scores, 40 bytes are needed for scores. The record length is therefore 70 bytes.

To be able to use records conveniently, three capabilities are needed:

☐ The capability to allot the required memory
☐ The capability to access the desired record
☐ The capability to access the desired field within a record

Forth words to carry out each of these tasks can be defined using many of the techniques illustrated in the preceding sections of this chapter. The details are omitted here, but they will be shown in the comprehensive example program at the end of the chapter.

Linked Lists

As with other advanced data structures, linked lists are not directly supported in Forth. Because of the flexibility provided by Forth, there are several ways in which a linked list could be implemented. Perhaps the simplest way is to implement a linked list as an array of records, with one field of each record used as a link or pointer. Suppose the first record should point to the third record. This would be accomplished by setting the link field of the first record to 3. This way of implementing a linked list was explained in more detail in Chapter 2.

The comprehensive sample program at the end of this chapter illustrates the use of linked lists and shows in detail how records are added to and deleted from linked lists.

FILE HANDLING

One of the things that computers do well is storing data. Because of the limited amount of memory in most computers, external storage is required in order to store an appreciable amount of data. On microcomputers the external storage medium is usually a floppy disk.

A collection of data stored on a disk is called a file. One of the measures of the usefulness of a high-level language is how well it handles the storage of data in files. This section will describe how Forth handles files.

Forth treats a disk as if it were an extension of regular memory. The disk is conceptually divided up into blocks of 1024 bytes each. How many blocks there are on a disk depends on the system; with MVP-FORTH on an Apple II, there are140 blocks per disk. Forth maintains two or more buffers in memory, each large enough to hold one block. The Forth program acts as if it were writing directly to a block on disk, but it is really writing to a buffer in memory. The Forth system takes care of moving data between a buffer and the disk. The programmer has three responsibilities in this area:

1. To specify which block number is being addressed.
2. To use the { UPDATE } word after a block has been modified, so that the system will know that the buffer must be saved
3. To use the { SAVE-BUFFERS } word before changing the disk or turning off the system, so that Forth will be sure that all buffers have been saved to disk

Blocks in Forth are addressed by number, not by name. The programmer must keep track of which blocks comprise which files. The equivalent of an OPEN command is either the { BUFFER } or the { BLOCK } command, depending on whether the file to be opened is a new file or an existing file. The command

30   BUFFER

opens a new file; it establishes a buffer in memory associated with block number 30, but it does not read in any data from the disk. The command

30   BLOCK

on the other hand, not only establishes a buffer associated with block number 30, it also reads the contents of that block into the buffer.

The equivalents of the CLOSE command are the { UPDATE } and { SAVE-BUFFERS } words discussed above.

All Forth files are direct-access files. A program can access any byte of any file at any time. Direct-access files can be addressed sequentially if desired.

File Records

A file consists of logical units called records. As indicated previously, a record can consist of a single byte or it can consist of a sequence of bytes that contain related information. A record can be of fixed or variable length; this chapter will discuss only fixed record lengths.

Forth leaves the organization of records to the programmer. All details associated with writing records to disk and reading records from disk must be handled by the programmer.

Sequential File Access

A file is said to be accessed sequentially if the records of the file are accessed in sequence from beginning to end. Figure 6-14 contains an example of a program that creates a file of names and ages, and then reads the file back from disk and displays it on the screen.

The program consists of four Forth words. Three are executed directly from the keyboard, and one is treated as a subroutine. The word { INIT } initializes the file to all blanks. The word { MAKE } prompts the user for keyboard input and creates the file. The word { PRINT } reads the file back from disk and prints its contents on the screen. The word

146

{ GETREC } computes the address of a given record and is used as a subroutine.

Three constants are declared: ADDR is set to 50, which is the block number in which this file is stored. Each record is 32 bytes in length; 30 bytes are allocated to the name and 2 bytes to the age. There is room for a maximum of 32 records of 32 bytes in length in a block of 1024 bytes, so the constant MAXREC is set to 32. The constant EOL is set to 13, the ASCII representation of the carriage return character.

A program of this complexity requires a detailed, almost line-by-line explanation. Line 0 of Screen #14 is simply a comment that identifies the program. Line 2 causes Screen #15 to be loaded. Before discussing the word { MAKE } in Screen

```
SCR #14
  0 ( Figure 6-14:  Sequential Name and Age File )
  1
  2 15 LOAD
  3
  4 : MAKE                       ( READ FROM KBD & WRITE FILE )
  5      MAXREC 0 DO
  6              CR ." Enter Name:  "
  7              QUERY EOL TEXT
  8              PAD C@ 0= IF LEAVE ELSE
  9                  PAD 1+ I GETREC PAD C@ CMOVE
 10                  CR ." Enter Age:     "
 11                  QUERY BL WORD NUMBER DROP
 12                  I GETREC 30 + !
 13              THEN
 14      CR LOOP
 15      UPDATE SAVE-BUFFERS ;

SCR #15
  0 ( Part of Figure 6-14 )
  1
  2 50 CONSTANT ADDR              ( BLOCK NR )
  3 32 CONSTANT MAXREC           ( MAX NR OF RECORDS )
  4 13 CONSTANT EOL              ( END-OF-LINE CHAR )
  5
  6 : INIT    ADDR BUFFER 1024 BLANK ;
  7 : GETREC   32 * ADDR BLOCK + ;
  8 : PRINT CR
  9      MAXREC 0 DO
 10          CR I GETREC DUP DUP
 11          C@ BL = IF LEAVE ELSE       ( DONE? )
 12              30 TYPE
 13              30 + @  3 .R             ( GET AGE )
 14          THEN CR
 15      LOOP ;
```

Fig. 6-14. A sequential name and age file.

#14, let's discuss the words { INIT } and { GET-REC } in Screen #15.

The word { INIT } in Screen #15 initializes the file to all blanks. The sequence ADDR BUFFER puts the address of the buffer for the block number on the stack. The sequence 1024 BLANK causes 1024 blanks to be stored beginning at that address. This fills the buffer.

The word { GETREC } at line 7 of Screen #15 expects to find the record number on the stack. (Record numbers range from 0 to 31.) Its purpose is to compute the address of the first byte of that record. It does this by multiplying the record number by the record length (32) and adding the starting address of the block (ADDR BLOCK). { GETREC } leaves the record address on the stack for use by other routines.

Now let's return to the word { MAKE }, which begins in line 4 of Screen #14. Line 5 is the beginning of a DO loop, which counts from 0 to 31, the range of possible record numbers. Line 6 prompts the user to type in a name. That name is read by the { QUERY } of line 7. The sequence EOL TEXT transfers the text from the input buffer to the PAD, using the end-of-line character (carriage return) as an end-of-text marker.

Line 8 checks the first character of the PAD to see whether or not it is zero. If it is, the character count is zero. That means that the user typed an immediate carriage return instead of a name in response to the name prompt. This causes the word { LEAVE } to be executed, which in turn causes an exit from the loop before the next iteration. If the character count is not zero, lines 9 through 12 are executed.

In line 9, the word { CMOVE } moves the name from the PAD to the appropriate location in the file buffer. The source address is PAD + 1. The destination address is computed by passing the loop counter (which is the record number) to { GETREC }. The number of bytes to move is retrieved from the count byte at location PAD.

Line 10 prompts the user to type the age. Line 11 reads in the age using { QUERY }. The sequence BL WORD NUMBER converts the number from a character string to double-precision number and places the result on the stack. The word { DROP } converts the number back to single precision. The sequence "I GETREC" of line 12 computes the address of the beginning of the record. Adding 30 computes the address of the age field within the record. The { ! } word stores the age at the appropriate buffer location.

Line 13 marks the end of the IF statement, and line 14 marks the end of the DO loop. Line 15 marks the block as having been updated ({ UPDATE }) and then causes the contents of the buffer to be written to disk ({ SAVE-BUFFERS }).

The word { PRINT }, which begins at line 8 of Screen #15, can be used to print the contents of the file on the screen. The DO loop between lines 9 and 15 again spans the range of possible record numbers, with a provision for an early exit ({ LEAVE }) if the end of the file is found.

Line 10 computes the address of the beginning of record I, makes two extra copies of the address, and leaves them on the stack. The first copy of this address is used to retrieve the first character of the record. This character is checked to see whether or not it is blank, which would indicate the end of the file. (Recall that the file was initialized to all blanks.) If it is not blank, the next copy of the record address is used in conjunction with 30 TYPE to print the contents of the name field in the record to the screen.

Line 13 uses the final copy of the record address from the stack, adds 30 to compute the start of the age field, retrieves the age from the buffer, and then prints it right-justified in a 3-character field. Lines 14 and 15 terminate the IF statement and the DO loop, respectively.

This program created a file that was confined entirely to one block of the disk. Files can span more than one block, but the use of more than one block necessitates more program overhead to keep track of the various blocks. The comprehensive example program at the end of the chapter illustrates the use of a file that spans more than one block.

Direct-Access Files

The file described in the previous section was accessed sequentially even though Forth files all have direct-access capability. The sequence was controlled by the DO loop, which counted in record number sequence. The record number was fed to { GETREC }, which calculated the starting address of the appropriate record. There is nothing to stop {GETREC} from computing the starting address of any record in any sequence. { GETREC } functions like the SEEK procedure of some other languages.

The comprehensive example program at the end of the chapter will illustrate the use of a direct-access file by a Forth program.

GRAPHICS

Forth itself does not support graphics. Because Forth is so easily extended, and because of the ease with which Forth can handle low-level data (bits and bytes), adding a graphics capability to Forth is relatively simple. The MVP-FORTH implementation for the Apple II series includes high-resolution graphics. Because graphics are not "native" to Forth, they will not be discussed further here.

COMPREHENSIVE SAMPLE PROGRAM

The examples in this chapter have been relatively short; each has been intended to illustrate some facet of the language. In order to more accurately portray the nature of the Forth language, a longer, more complex example is needed. Such a program is shown in Fig. 6-15.

The program in this figure maintains an address book on disk, or more precisely, a disk file containing names, addresses, and telephone numbers. The program provides the capability to create a new file, to add records to a file, to delete records from a file, and to display the contents of the file on the video screen or on a printer.

The program maintains the file in alphabetical order by name. As a record is added, it is physically placed in the next available place in the file. The logical order of the file is maintained using pointers to implement a linked list. No sorting is required; each record is linked in the proper place in the list as it is added to the file.

Each record is 80 characters in length. The first 78 characters make up the actual data, that is,

the name, address, and so forth. These data are stored as ASCII characters. The last 2 positions of the record hold the link field, which is stored as an integer. Each record has a logical record number. If record 4 is linked to record 7, the link field of record 4 has the value 7. This is the method of implementing linked lists that was explained in more detail in Chapter 2.

Each disk block in Forth consists of 1024 characters. There is therefore room in each block for 12 records of 80 characters each, with some space left over. The extra space in the first block is used to store the two pointers FIRST and FREE, which point to the first active record and the first free record in the file respectively. The program as written allows for 15 records, enough to span 2 blocks. The word RECORD is used to translate from a logical record number (0, 1, 2, . . .) to a physical disk address (block number and displacement within the block).

The details of file length, record length, and field length within a record are all defined in the constant declarations near the beginning of the program. To change any of these parameters, it is only necessary to change the appropriate constants and recompile the program.

The program is loaded by typing 16 33 THRU. To run the program, type BOOK. The program is completely menu driven. To initialize a file, select menu item 1. To open a previously existing file, select 2. To close a file that has been modified, select 7. The other options are similar. There are built-in safeguards to keep you from listing a file which has not been opened and making other illogical selections.

The organization of the program is illustrated by the structure chart shown in Fig. 6-16. The "main program" is the word called { BOOK }. A word which serves as a subroutine is shown indented below the word which calls it. { BOOK } calls MENU, OPEN, APPEND, REVIEW, LISTFILE, DUMPFILE, and CLOSE; REVIEW calls PRINTREC and PUTFREE, and so on.

The DUMP option allows the user to examine the structure of the file, including the pointers. By using this option after various add and delete

```
SCR #16
   0 ( FIGURE 6-15:  THE ADDRESS BOOK PROGRAM IN FORTH )
   1
   2 ( This program maintains a list of names, addresses, and    )
   3 ( telephone numbers in a disk file.                         )
   4
   5 ( To load, type 16 33 THRU                                  )
   6
   7 ( To run, type  BOOK                                        )
   8
   9 ( Initial configuration:                                    )
  10 (      15 Record maximum                                    )
  11 (      80 Character records                                 )
  12
  13 ( To reconfigure, modify the appropriate constants          )
  14
  15 ( Completed 26 February 1984                                )


SCR #17
   0 ( Part of Figure 6-15:  Declarations )
   1  13 CONSTANT EOL        ( END OF LINE CHARACTER )
   2  -1 CONSTANT NIL        ( PTR TO END OF LIST )
   3 110 CONSTANT ADDR       ( FIRST BLOCK IN ADDRESS FILE )
   4  80 CONSTANT RLEN       ( RECORD LENGTH )
   5  12 CONSTANT RPB        ( RECORDS PER BLOCK )
   6  15 CONSTANT MAXREC     ( MAX # OF RECORDS IN FILE )
   7   0 CONSTANT LNAME      ( DISPL OF LAST NAME FIELD )
   8  12 CONSTANT LNL        ( LENGTH OF LAST NAME FIELD )
   9  12 CONSTANT FNAME      ( DISPL OF FIRST NAME FIELD )
  10  12 CONSTANT FNL        ( LENGTH OF FIRST NAME FIELD )
  11  24 CONSTANT STREET     ( DISPL OF STREET ADDR FIELD )
  12  20 CONSTANT STRL       ( LENGTH OF STREET ADDR FIELD )
  13  44 CONSTANT CITY       ( DISPL OF CITY FIELD )
  14  12 CONSTANT CITL       ( LENGTH OF CITY FIELD )
  15  56 CONSTANT STATE      ( DISPL OF STATE FIELD )


SCR #18
   0 ( Part of Figure 6-15:  Declarations )
   1   2 CONSTANT STAL       ( LENGTH OF STATE FIELD )
   2  58 CONSTANT ZIP        ( DISPL OF ZIP CODE FIELD )
   3   6 CONSTANT ZIPL       ( LENGTH OF ZIP CODE FIELD )
```

Fig. 6-15. The Address Book program in Forth. (Continued on page 151.)

```
   4  64 CONSTANT PHONE      ( DISPL OF PHONE NR FIELD )
   5  14 CONSTANT PHOL       ( LENGTH OF PHONE NR FIELD )
   6  78 CONSTANT LINK       ( DISPL OF LINK FIELD )
   7 1000 CONSTANT FRP       ( DISPL OF FIRST REC PTR )
   8 1002 CONSTANT FFP       ( DISPL OF FIRST FREE REC PTR )
   9 VARIABLE OPEN?          ( FILE OPEN INDICATOR )
  10 VARIABLE FIRST          ( PTR TO FIRST RECORD IN FILE )
  11 VARIABLE FREE           ( PTR TO FIRST FREE RECORD )
  12 VARIABLE FLAG           ( GENERAL PURPOSE FLAG VAR )
  13 VARIABLE P              ( TEMPORARY POINTER )
  14 VARIABLE Q              ( " " )
  15 VARIABLE R              ( " " )

SCR #19
   0 ( Part of Figure 6-15:  Word Definitions )
   1 : RECORD             ( RECORD.NR --- ADDR )
   2    RPB  /MOD
   3    ADDR + BLOCK    ( COMPUTE BLOCK NR )
   4    SWAP RLEN * + ;  ( ADDR OF RECORD )
   5
   6 : INIT              ( INITIALIZE FILE )
   7    MAXREC 0 DO
   8      I RECORD DUP RLEN BLANK    ( BLANK FILL REC I )
   9      LINK +                     ( ADDR OF LINK FIELD )
  10      I 1+ SWAP ! UPDATE         ( PTR TO NEXT FREE REC )
  11    LOOP
  12    MAXREC 1- RECORD LINK +     ( LAST LINK )
  13    NIL SWAP ! UPDATE           ( PTR TO END OF LIST )
  14    NIL FIRST !  0 FREE !       ( INITIALIZE PTRS )
  15    1 OPEN? ! ;                 ( MARK FILE OPEN )


SCR #20
   0 ( Part of Figure 6-15:  Word Definitions )
   1
   2 : OPEN              ( OPEN FILES )
   3    ADDR BLOCK DUP
   4    FRP + @ FIRST !     ( READ PTRS FROM FILE )
   5    FFP + @ FREE !      ( AND STORE AS VARIABLES )
   6    1 OPEN? ! ;         ( MARK FILE OPEN )
   7
   8 : CLOSE             ( CLOSE FILE & SAVE PTRS )
   9    ADDR BLOCK DUP
```

```
10      FRP + FIRST @ SWAP !
11      FFP + FREE @ SWAP !
12      UPDATE
13      SAVE-BUFFERS
14      0 OPEN? ! ;         ( MARK FILE CLOSED )
15


SCR #21
  0 ( Part of Figure 6-15:  Word Definitions )
  1
  2 : CLEARSCREEN          ( FOR APPLE/SMARTERM II )
  3     12 EMIT ;
  4
  5 : GOTOXY               ( FOR APPLE/SMARTERM II )
  6     30 EMIT            ( X Y -- )
  7     SWAP 32 + EMIT
  8     32 + EMIT ;
  9
 10 : GETNUM               ( READ INTEGER & LEAVE ON STACK )
 11     QUERY
 12     BL WORD NUMBER
 13     DROP ;             ( CONVERT TO SINGLE PRECISION )
 14
 15

SCR #22
  0 ( Part of Figure 6-15:  Word Definitions )
  1
  2 : MENU                 ( DISPLAY MENU; LEAVE CHOICE ON STACK )
  3     CLEARSCREEN
  4     5 5 2DUP           ( INITIAL SCREEN COORDINATES )
  5     GOTOXY ." 1)  Initialize new file"
  6     2+ 2DUP GOTOXY ." 2)  Open existing file"
  7     2+ 2DUP GOTOXY ." 3)  Add to file"
  8     2+ 2DUP GOTOXY ." 4)  Review file on screen"
  9     2+ 2DUP GOTOXY ." 5)  List file on screen or printer"
 10     2+ 2DUP GOTOXY ." 6)  Dump file and pointers on printer"
 11     2+ 2DUP GOTOXY ." 7)  Close file"
 12     2+      GOTOXY ." 8)  Quit"
 13     CR CR
 14     ." Select 1, 2, 3, 4, 5, 6, 7, or 8:  "
 15     GETNUM ;
```

Fig. 6-15. The Address Book program in Forth. (Continued on page 153.)

```
SCR #23
  0 ( Part of Figure 6-15:  Word Definitions )
  1
  2 : WARN
  3     CR ." Warning!!!  File is full!" CR
  4     CR ." Press <SPACE> to continue..."
  5     KEY DROP ;
  6
  7 : MARKOFF                 ( COL ROW N -- )
  8     )R GOTOXY ." :"
  9     R) SPACES ." :" ;
 10
 11 : GETFREE                 ( RETURNS FIRST FREE REC NR )
 12     FREE @ DUP
 13     NIL = IF
 14        WARN DROP NIL
 15     THEN ;


SCR #24
  0 ( Part of Figure 6-15:  Word Definitions )
  1
  2 : PAINTSCREEN
  3     CLEARSCREEN
  4     1 5 2DUP GOTOXY ." Last Name:"  14 OVER LNL  MARKOFF
  5     2+  2DUP GOTOXY ." First Name:" 14 OVER FNL  MARKOFF
  6     2+  2DUP GOTOXY ." Address:"    14 OVER STRL MARKOFF
  7     2+  2DUP GOTOXY ." City:"       14 OVER CITL MARKOFF
  8     2+  2DUP GOTOXY ." State:"      14 OVER STAL MARKOFF
  9     2+  2DUP GOTOXY ." Zip:"        14 OVER ZIPL MARKOFF
 10     2+  2DUP GOTOXY ." Phone:"      14 OVER PHOL MARKOFF
 11     2DROP
 12 ;
 13
 14
 15


SCR #25
  0 ( Part of Figure 6-15:  Word Definitions )
  1
  2 : READSCREEN              ( R -- R )
  3     DUP RECORD DUP )R RLEN 2 - BLANK
  4     15 5 2DUP GOTOXY R) DUP LNAME + DUP LNL EXPECT C@
```

```
 5        0= IF DROP 2DROP DROP NIL ELSE >R
 6           R@ LINK + @ P !
 7           2+ 2DUP GOTOXY R@ FNAME  + FNL  EXPECT
 8           2+ 2DUP GOTOXY R@ STREET + STRL EXPECT
 9           2+ 2DUP GOTOXY R@ CITY   + CITL EXPECT
10           2+ 2DUP GOTOXY R@ STATE  + STAL EXPECT
11           2+ 2DUP GOTOXY R@ ZIP    + ZIPL EXPECT
12           2+       GOTOXY R@ PHONE  + PHOL EXPECT
13           P @ R> LINK + !
14           UPDATE
15       THEN ;
```

```
SCR #26
 0 ( Part of Figure 6-15:  Word Definitions )
 1
 2 : GREATER                        ( R1 R2 -- FLAG )
 3     ( FLAG =T 1 IF REC 1 ) REC 2, OTHERWISE 0 )
 4     DUP 0< IF 1 FLAG ! ELSE 0 FLAG !
 5       RECORD SWAP RECORD SWAP    ( GET BUFFER ADDRESSES )
 6       LNL FNL + 0 DO
 7           2DUP
 8           I + C@ SWAP I + C@ SWAP  ( GET CHARS TO COMPARE )
 9           2DUP
10           > IF 1 FLAG ! LEAVE  THEN
11           < IF 0 FLAG ! LEAVE  THEN
12       LOOP
13     THEN
14     2DROP
15     FLAG @ ;
```

```
SCR #27
 0 ( Part of Figure 6-15:  Word Definitions )
 1
 2 : INSERT                 ( R -- )
 3     ( INSERT REC R IN LINKED LIST )
 4     DUP R !
 5     RECORD LINK + @ FREE !     ( REMOVE FROM FREE LIST )
 6     FIRST @ P !   NIL Q !
 7     BEGIN P @ NIL = NOT  R @ P @ GREATER AND WHILE
 8         P @ Q !    P @ RECORD LINK + @ P ! UPDATE
 9     REPEAT
10     P @ R @ RECORD LINK + ! UPDATE
```

Fig. 6-15. The Address Book program in Forth. (Continued on page 155.)

```
11      Q @ NIL = IF
12          R @ FIRST !
13      ELSE
14          R @ Q @ RECORD LINK + ! UPDATE
15      THEN ;


SCR #28
  0 ( Part of Figure 6-15:  Word Definitions )
  1
  2 : APPEND                ( ADD RECORDS TO FILE )
  3      MAXREC 0 DO
  4          GETFREE DUP NIL = IF
  5              DROP LEAVE
  6          ELSE
  7              PAINTSCREEN
  8              READSCREEN
  9              DUP NIL = IF
 10                  DROP LEAVE
 11              ELSE
 12                  INSERT
 13              THEN
 14          THEN
 15      LOOP ;


SCR #29
  0 ( Part of Figure 6-15:  Word Definitions )
  1
  2 : PUTFREE               ( R -- )
  3      FREE @  OVER RECORD LINK + !
  4      FREE ! UPDATE ;
  5
  6 : PRINTREC              ( R -- )
  7      CR RECORD
  8      DUP FNAME + FNL -TRAILING TYPE SPACE
  9      DUP LNAME + LNL TYPE CR
 10      DUP STREET + STRL TYPE CR
 11      DUP CITY + CITL -TRAILING TYPE ." , "
 12      DUP STATE + STAL TYPE SPACE
 13      DUP ZIP + ZIPL TYPE CR
 14      PHONE + PHOL TYPE CR
 15      CR 10 EMIT ;
```

```
SCR #30
  0 ( Part of Figure 6-15:  Word Definitions )
  1
  2 : PRINTER   1 PR#
  3             9 EMIT ." 80N"
  4             30 EMIT ;
  5 : OFF       3 PR# ;
  6 : LISTFILE
  7     CLEARSCREEN
  8     ." List to S)creen or P)rinter?  "
  9     KEY DUP 80 = SWAP 112 = OR IF PRINTER THEN
 10     10 EMIT
 11     FIRST @ P !
 12     MAXREC 0 DO
 13        P @ DUP DUP NIL = IF DROP DROP LEAVE
 14          ELSE PRINTREC RECORD LINK + @ P ! THEN
 15     LOOP OFF ;


SCR #31
  0 ( Part of Figure 6-15:  Word Definitions )
  1
  2 : REVIEW
  3     CLEARSCREEN
  4     FIRST @ NIL = NOT IF
  5        FIRST @ R !      NIL Q !
  6        BEGIN R @ PRINTREC
  7          ." G)et next record, D)elete this record, or Q)uit? "
  8          KEY SPACE CR DUP DUP DUP 68 = SWAP 100 = OR IF
  9             Q @ NIL = IF
 10                R @ RECORD LINK + @ FIRST !
 11                R @ PUTFREE     FIRST @ R !
 12             ELSE  R @ RECORD LINK + @ Q @ RECORD LINK + !
 13                R @ PUTFREE     Q @ RECORD LINK + @ R !   THEN
 14          ELSE R @ Q !   R @ RECORD LINK + @ R ! THEN
 15          81 = SWAP 113 = OR R @ NIL = OR UNTIL THEN ;


SCR #32
  0 ( Part of Figure 6-15:  Word Definitions )
  1
  2 : DUMPFILE
```

Fig. 6-15. The Address Book program in Forth. (Continued on page 157.)

```
      3      PRINTER
      4      MAXREC 0 DO
      5        ." RECORD " I .
      6        ." LINK " I RECORD LINK + ?
      7        I PRINTREC
      8      LOOP
      9      OFF ;
     10
     11
     12
     13
     14
     15


SCR #33
  0 ( Part of Figure 6-15:  Main Program )
  1
  2 : BOOK                  ( THIS IS THE MAIN PROGRAM )
  3     0 OPEN? !           ( MARK FILE CLOSED )
  4     BEGIN  MENU DUP 8 = NOT WHILE
  5         DUP 1 = IF INIT ELSE
  6         DUP 2 = OPEN? @ NOT AND IF OPEN ELSE
  7         DUP 3 = OPEN? @ AND IF APPEND ELSE
  8         DUP 4 = OPEN? @ AND IF REVIEW ELSE
  9         DUP 5 = OPEN? @ AND IF LISTFILE ELSE
 10         DUP 6 = OPEN? @ AND IF DUMPFILE ELSE
 11         DUP 7 = OPEN? @ AND IF CLOSE
 12         THEN THEN THEN THEN THEN THEN THEN CR CR
 13         ." PRESS <SPACE> TO CONTINUE..." KEY DROP DROP
 14     REPEAT DROP CR CR ;
 15
```

157

```
              BOOK
                 MENU
                    GETNUM
                 OPEN
                 APPEND
                    GETFREE
                       WARN
                    PAINTSCREEN
                       MARKOFF
                    READSCREEN
                    INSERT
                       GREATER
                 REVIEW
                    PRINTREC
                    PUTFREE
                 LISTFILE
                    PRINTREC
                 DUMPFILE
                    PRINTREC
                 CLOSE

              Common-use subroutines:

              PRINTER         RECORD
              OFF             GOTOXY
              CLEARSCREEN
```

Fig. 6-16. The structure chart for the Address Book program.

scenarios, the operation of the program can be more easily understood.

The program is modular in nature, with no one module exceeding 16 lines in length. Some of the modules, such as PAINTSCREEN, are simple and straightforward in nature. Others, such as REVIEW, are complex and difficult to read, but the underlying concepts have already been presented, and there is not enough room here to discuss the operation of each module in detail.

ADVANTAGES AND DISADVANTAGES OF FORTH

Perhaps the most striking advantage of Forth is its extensibility. Forth comes with a basic library of operations in its dictionary, but if additional operations are needed, they can be easily added.

Forth encourages modular programming; that is, it encourages the decomposition of a complex task into a series of simpler tasks. This modularity makes the process of program development go much faster.

Another feature that makes the process of programming go faster is the interactive nature of Forth. Individual Forth words can easily be tested interactively and independently before they are incorporated into a larger program.

Forth programs produce code that is very fast and very compact, sometimes even more compact than the equivalent assembly-language code. This can be important in many applications.

Forth provides low-level control at the bit and byte level. This is important for many machine-control applications.

Forth has been implemented on many different microcomputers. Forth programs can be programmed on one microcomputer and executed on another, sometimes much smaller microcomputer, such as a computer built into a robot.

On the negative side, Forth programming is at a very low level for a high-level language. The programmer must be concerned with many low-level details such as the contents of the stack and the physical location of files on a disk. Most other high-level languages insulate the programmer from such details. It has been said by detractors of Forth that the Forth compiler leaves many of the details of compilation to the programmer.

Forth requires the programmer to think in terms of postfix or Reverse Polish Notation. Most people find this somewhat awkward. It is certainly a workable notation, but it requires the programmer to adapt to the language rather than vice versa.

Forth programs tend to be dense and hard to read. Understanding a Forth program written by someone else often requires a great deal of tedious effort to track stack effects and so on. Some would call Forth a "write only" language.

Because of the complexity of Forth, many people find it more difficult to learn than languages such as BASIC, Pascal, and Logo.

Because Forth is its own operating system, it is difficult to pass data files between Forth and non-Forth programs. If a text editor were written in Forth, for example, it would be difficult to pass files created by that editor to, say, a Pascal compiler running under the CP/M operating system.

The editor that comes with many versions of

Forth is rather primitive and inflexible. It works with "screens" of 1024 characters each, and it is inconvenient to write Forth words that span more than one screen using this editor.

Because Forth is so different than most other computer languages, it is difficult to switch between programming in Forth and programming in other languages. Forth is probably not a good choice if you intend to program in more than one language.

AVAILABILITY

Forth is available in version of many different kinds of microcomputers, large and small. The language itselfis in the public domain. Implementations of Forth are available through the Forth Interest Group (FIG) of San Carlos, California; FORTH, Inc., of Hermosa Beach, California; and Mountain View Press (MVP) of Mountain View, California. Current addresses for these and other Forth suppliers can be found in magazines specializing in microcomputers.

SUMMARY

Forth is a compact but powerful language. It is a very flexible language that can be adapted to a wide variety of applications, including machine control. Forth is a controversial language; it has many advantages and many disadvantages. Both its supporters and opponents are quite vocal.

Programs written in Forth run quite fast, usually much faster than programs written in BASIC. In addition, programs written in Forth tend to be very compact.

Forth tends to require more programming effort than other high-level languages because it requires the programmer to keep track of many low-level details. This is partially offset by the ease with which program modules can be interactively tested in Forth.

Forth is especially popular among programmers who enjoy dealing with the low-level details of microcomputers. Many Forth programmers are former assembly-language programmers.

Forth was designed to provide fast, compact code with both high-level and low-level features. It is best suited for applications in which speed, compactness, and low-level features are needed. Forth is an excellent alternative to assembly language for such applications.

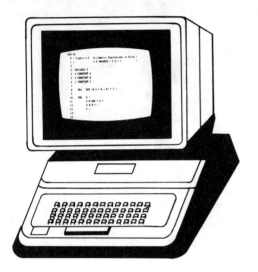

Chapter 7

FORTRAN

The FORTRAN language has been in widespread use longer than any other computer language. It was produced by a team headed by John W. Backus during the period 1954 to 1957. Backus and his team were tasked to develop a compiler for the IBM 704 computer. The IBM 704 computer is long-since obsolete, but the FORTRAN language endures.

The name FORTRAN is an acronym standing for FORmula TRANslator. FORTRAN is the language of choice of the scientific and engineering community, just as COBOL is the language of choice of the business community. As the name suggests, FORTRAN is particularly suited to the manipulation of formulas and to the performing of various mathematical calculations.

Although there are other languages today which have similar capabilities and add other features besides, FORTRAN remains firmly entrenched among nonbusiness users of large computers. Part of the reason is tradition; since the late 1950's, most scientific computing has been done in

FORTRAN. Because it is widely used, it is widely taught in universities. And because it is widely taught in universities, it is widely used.

There is a wide body of scientific software that has been created in FORTRAN and which is widely available in computer subroutine libraries in universities and in industry. These subroutines are easily incorporated into FORTRAN programs; so doing can save much programming effort.

There are two versions of FORTRAN in wide use today, FORTRAN IV and FORTRAN 77. FORTRAN IV is the name usually used to refer to the version adopted by the American National Standards Institute (ANSI) in 1966. FORTRAN 77 is the 1977 ANSI standard. The main enhancements added with the 1977 standard are improved character handling and the IF-THEN-ELSE control structure. FORTRAN 77 has not completely displaced FORTRAN IV, probably because its additional features do not provide a significantly greater capability than that of FORTRAN IV.

FORTRAN has not been widely accepted by microcomputer users. In the microcomputer world, BASIC has been available longer than FORTRAN. BASIC is therefore more popular on microcomputers than FORTRAN for much the same reasons as those that make FORTRAN so popular on large computers. Also, BASIC is often furnished at no extra cost with a microcomputer, whereas FORTRAN invariably costs extra.

FORTRAN has several advantages over BASIC, however, as will be seen below. Because it is almost always implemented as a compiled language rather than as an interpreted language, FORTRAN programs usually run much faster than BASIC programs. FORTRAN has a reputation for speed.

FORTRAN also has its limitations, as will also be seen below. Nevertheless, a language with such a long history of successful use deserves a close look.

The programming examples in this chapter were written and tested with the Nevada FORTRAN compiler by Ellis Computing.

PROGRAM STRUCTURE

A FORTRAN program is a sequence of FORTRAN statements. The usual rule is one statement per line. In earlier days, a line was synonymous with a card, and the usual rule was stated as "one statement per card." Today you will still hear FORTRAN (and COBOL) programmers talk about cards and card columns even when their programs are created and stored electronically. The tendency is to think of a line as a *card image*.

Each FORTRAN statement must follow a prescribed structure, which is described in terms of placement within columns. The statement itself can be anywhere between columns 7 and 72, inclusive. A "C" in column 1 means that the rest of the line will be treated as a comment or remark.

Statement numbers, when present, may be anywhere between columns 1 and 5. Statement numbers are needed only in certain circumstances, such as to mark the target of a GO TO statement. When they appear, statement numbers do not need to be in any particular order as long as each is unique.

Column 6 is reserved for a continuation indicator. Normally this column is left blank. Any character (except 0 or blank) in column 6 means that the line is to be considered as a continuation of the previous line. Otherwise a statement is assumed to end at the end of a line. No punctuation is needed to terminate or separate statements.

Columns 73-80 are ignored by the compiler. This dates back to the days of cards, when sequence numbers were often punched in these columns. This facilitated the reassembling of a card deck after it had been dropped on the floor. Those of you who missed the days of punched cards and keypunch machines are fortunate.

A simple FORTRAN program is shown in Fig. 7-1. This program simply prints out the message, "This is a test." The first two lines are comments, as indicated by the letter "C" in column 1. The printing is done by the WRITE statement. The (1,*) in the WRITE statement sends the output to the screen in a standardized format; it will be explained in more detail in the section on input and output.

The STOP statement causes the program to stop executing and to transfer control back to the operating system. It is usually near the last statement of the program, but can technically be anywhere in the program. The END statement tells the

```
C        FIGURE 7.1:  Minimal FORTRAN program.
C
         WRITE (1,*) 'This is a test.'
         STOP
         END
```

Fig. 7-1. A minimal FORTRAN program.

compiler that it has come to the end of the program; it must be the last statement of the program. In short, the difference between the two statements is that the STOP statement does its job at run time (when the program is run) and the END statement does its job at compile time (when the program is compiled).

DATA REPRESENTATION

The basic data types in FORTRAN are *real, double precision, complex, integer,* and *logical.* Double precision numbers are floating-point numbers with twice the storage allocation of real numbers and are sometimes needed for scientific calculations. A complex number is stored as an ordered pair of REAL numbers. (If you have to ask what a complex number is, you don't need to know! They are used by mathematicians, physicists, and engineers.)

FORTRAN 77 also includes the character data type, but FORTRAN IV does not. Character strings exist in FORTRAN IV, but must be stored in integer type arrays. How this is done will be described in the section on arrays.

Nevada FORTRAN supports the real, integer, and logical data types. Double precision data is permitted, but it is treated exactly like real data.

Constants

Numerical constants in FORTRAN follow the usual conventions, as described in Chapter 2. Literal constants can be handled in one of two ways. The simplest is to enclose the literal within single quotation marks, as in

'Literal'.

The older and less convenient way is to write

7HLiteral.

This is called a *Hollerith constant*, after the inventor of the character encoding system used on punched cards. The 7H means that the 7 characters following the letter H are to be taken as a literal constant. This is awkward and seldom used any

more because it requires the programmer to count characters.

The LOGICAL constants are .TRUE. and .FALSE. . The periods preceding and following the words are part of the constant.

FORTRAN does not support named constants, as do Pascal and C.

Variables

Variable names in FORTRAN may consist of 1 to 6 letters or digits. The first character must be a letter. Standard FORTRAN does not permit lowercase letters to be used in variable names or FORTRAN key words. Some implementations do permit lowercase letters, however. For the sake of standardization, the examples in this chapter will use lowercase letters only in literal constants.

FORTRAN permits real and integer variables to be declared by default. If a variable is not explicitly declared, it is assumed to be an integer variable if the first letter of its name is I, J, K, L, M, or N. Otherwise, it is assumed to be real. It is good programming practice, however, to declare all variables.

Figure 7-2 shows the declaration of three real variables called PI, AREA, and RADIUS. It also shows the declaration of an integer variable called I, even though it is not used later in the program.

Figure 7-2 also shows how a variable can be initialized using the DATA statement. In this case PI is initialized to the value 3.14159.

The program in Fig. 7-2 simply computes and prints the area of a circle with radius 5.

```
C FIGURE 7.2:   AREA OF A CIRCLE
  REAL PI, AREA, RADIUS
  INTEGER I
C DATA PI/3.14159/
  RADIUS = 5.0
  AREA   = PI * RADIUS**2
  WRITE (1,*) 'RADIUS = ',RADIUS
  WRITE (1,*) 'AREA   = ',AREA
  STOP
  END
```

Fig. 7-2. The area of a circle in FORTRAN.

THE ASSIGNMENT STATEMENT

FORTRAN uses the equals sign (''='') for the assignment operator. The example of Fig. 7-2 shows two examples of its use.

ARITHMETIC EXPRESSIONS

FORTRAN uses conventional infix notation (see Chapter 2) for its arithmetic expressions. It uses the usual arithmetic operators, as shown in the following table:

Operator	Meaning
+	Addition
−	Subtraction
*	Multiplication
/	Division
**	Exponentiation

The statement in the program of Fig. 7-2 that calculates the area of a circle has an arithmetic expression on the right-hand side of the assignment operator.

Parentheses should be used feeely in the construction of arithmetic expressions to eliminate any possible ambiguity.

LOGICAL EXPRESSIONS

Logical expressions evaluate to .TRUE. or .FALSE.. They are constructed with the relational and logical operators shown below:

Operator	Meaning
.GT.	Greater than
.GE.	Greater than or equal to
.EQ.	Equal to
.NE.	Not equal to
LE.	Less than or equal to
.LT.	Less than
.AND.	Logical AND
.OR.	Logical OR
.NOT.	Logical NOT

The periods are integral parts of the operator names and cannot be omitted. The meanings of these operators are as discussed in Chapter 2.

Parentheses should be used freely in the construction of logical expressions to reduce the probability that an expression could be misinterpreted.

INPUT AND OUTPUT

Figures 7-1 and 7-2 contain examples of the use of the WRITE statement in FORTRAN. A more general form of the WRITE statement is as follows:

WRITE (N1, N2) ⟨OUTPUT LIST⟩

Here N1 refers to the unit number to which the output should be directed. In Nevada FORTRAN, unit number 1 means the system console or video screen. Thus in Fig. 7-1,

WRITE (1,*) 'This is a test.

wrote the message to the video screen.

Unit number 0 is reserved for console input. Other unit numbers can be assigned as needed for a printer and disk files. An example of how to redirect output to a printer is given in Fig. 7-3. The technique of establishing the linkage to the external device may vary from compiler to compiler, but the principle of using a different unit number will stay the same.

The N2 above can be an asterisk (*) or the statement number of a FORMAT statement. Use of the asterisk invokes what is called *format-free* output. In format-free output, the compiler decides what the output should look like. If you have been running the example programs, you may have noticed that the numbers printed out by the program in Fig. 7-2 were printed in scientific notation. Often times, however, the user wishes to control the format of the output, as with the PRINT USING statement of BASIC. This is accomplished in FORTRAN by using the FORMAT statement.

Figure 7-4 shows two examples of formatted output. The program does exactly the same as the program in Fig. 7-2; only the form of the output is different.

Two FORMAT statements are used in this

163

```
C          Figure 7.3:   Demonstrate Printer Output
C
           CALL OPEN (2, 'LST:')
C
C          Note:  'LST:' is the CP/M list device (printer)
C
           WRITE (1,*) 'This goes to the video screen.'
C
           WRITE (2,*) 'This goes to the printer.'
C
           STOP
           END
```

Fig. 7-3. Printer output in FORTRAN.

example—one for each WRITE statement. The first WRITE statement in Fig. 7-4 references FORMAT statement number 200, and the second references FORMAT statement 210.

The purpose of a FORMAT statement is to describe the appearance of the output. The F10.5 in statements 200 and 210 is called a field descriptor. The F stands for *fixed point* and means a number with decimal point but no exponent. The 10 means that field is to be 10 spaces wide (counting the decimal point and the sign, if any), and the 5 means that there are to be 5 digits to the right of the decimal point.

A list of some of the more common field de-

scriptors follows. The letter w stands for the width of the field; the letter d, the number of decimal places; and the letter n the number of times the field is to be repeated.

Descriptor	Definition
nIw	Integer
nFw.d	Fixed point
nEw.d	Floating point (scientific notation)
nAw	Alphanumeric (character) data
nLw	Logical (prints T or F)
nGw.d	General
nX	Blank spaces
Tw	Tab to column w

```
C          FIGURE 7.4:   AREA OF A CIRCLE
C                        ILLUSTRATE FORMATTED OUTPUT
C
           REAL PI, AREA, RADIUS
           INTEGER I
           DATA PI/3.14159/
C
           RADIUS = 5.0
           AREA   = PI * RADIUS**2
           WRITE (1,200) RADIUS
           WRITE (1,210) AREA
           STOP
200 FORMAT (' RADIUS = ', F10.5)
210 FORMAT (' AREA   = ', F10.5)
           END
```

Fig. 7-4. Formatted output in FORTRAN.

164

Most of these are relatively self-explanatory. The A format will be discussed in more detail in a later section and the G format in the following paragraphs.

Field descriptors are matched with items in the output list by position, except for X and T descriptors, which may be interspersed between other descriptors without a corresponding item in the output list. Additionally, literal constants (such as ' RADIUS = ') may be inserted between field descriptors. In the example in Fig. 7-4, the variable RADIUS is associated with the field descriptor F10.5 by position. The variable is the first item in the output list, and the field descriptor is the first in the FORMAT statement, not counting the literal constant.

Field descriptors and literals are separated by a comma or a slash ("/"). When descriptors are separated by a slash, a new output line is started.

Data elements (variables or constants) in the output list must agree with the corresponding field descriptor in type. An F or E descriptor expects a data element that is either real or double precision. An I descriptor expects an **integer** data element; an L descriptor expects a **logical** data element; and an A descriptor expects an alphanumeric literal. The exception is the G descriptor, which can handle an integer or a real data element. In the case of an integer, Gw.d acts the same as Iw. In the case of a real element, how it acts depends on the value of the number. If the number will fit, Fw.d is used. If the number is too large or too small for Fw.d, Ew.d is used.

Technically a FORMAT statement can be almost anywhere in a FORTRAN program; the connection between the WRITE statement and the FORMAT statement is established by the statement number. In fact, two or more WRITE statements can reference the same FORMAT statement. A convenient place to group all FORMAT statements is between the STOP and END statements. This removes formatting details from the main flow of processing. Some programmers prefer to place each FORMAT statement immediately after the appropriate WRITE statement. Which way is better is a matter of individual preference.

The FORMAT statement provides the programmer with a great deal of flexibility in formatting output. It does require some effort to use, however. More examples of FORMAT statements will be found in the remaining programs in this chapter.

Input is handled by the READ statement. The general format for the READ statement is as follows:

READ (N1, N2) ⟨INPUT LIST⟩

N1 is the unit number and N2 is an asterisk or a statement number. Nevada FORTRAN has reserved unit number 0 for console input. If N2 is an asterisk, no FORMAT statement is needed. FORMAT statements are not usually needed for console input. The field descriptors described above are applicable, except that the d describing the number of places to the right of the decimal is overridden when an actual decimal point is entered.

The program in Fig. 7-4 is relatively useless, as it can compute the area of only one size circle. The program in Fig. 7-5 adds a READ statement to get the radius of the circle from the console. The program can then be used to compute the area of a circle with another radius.

If the radius is so large that the area of the circle no longer fits in an F10.5 format, 10 asterisks will be printed instead. That is FORTRAN's way of telling you that you need a wider field descriptor.

CONTROL STRUCTURES

FORTRAN has fewer control structures than more recent languages such as Pascal. Traditionally, FORTRAN programmers have relied heavily on the GO TO statement in a rather unstructured way. There is no reason, however, why well-structured programs cannot be written in FORTRAN.

Simple Selection: IF-THEN-ELSE

The IF-THEN-ELSE statement is found in all FORTRAN 77 implementations and in some ANSI 1966 FORTRAN IV implementations. In versions

```
C       FIGURE 7.5:   AREA OF A CIRCLE
C                     ILLUSTRATE READ STATEMENT
C

        REAL PI, AREA, RADIUS
        INTEGER I
        DATA PI/3.14159/
C

        WRITE (1,*)  'COMPUTE THE AREA OF A CIRCLE.'
        WRITE (1,*)
        WRITE (1,*)  'ENTER RADIUS: '
        READ  (0,*) RADIUS
        AREA   = PI * RADIUS**2
        WRITE (1,200) RADIUS
        WRITE (1,210) AREA
        STOP
200 FORMAT (' RADIUS = ', F10.5)
210 FORMAT (' AREA   = ', F10.5)
        END
```

Fig. 7-5. The READ statement in FORTRAN.

of FORTRAN that lack the IF-THEN-ELSE construct, the logical IF can be used. The logical IF is described below.

The ELSE part of the IF-THEN-ELSE statement is optional. Here is a simple example with the ELSE part omitted:

```
MONTH = MONTH + 1
IF (MONTH .GT. 12) THEN
     MONTH = 1
     YEAR = YEAR + 1
ENDIF
```

There can be as many statements as desired between the THEN and the ENDIF. Those statements should be indented as shown to visually indicate the scope of the statement. This makes programs much easier to read. The parentheses surrounding the conditional expression (MONTH.GT. 12) are mandatory.

The same task can be accomplished in another way using an else part:

```
IF (MONTH .LT. 12) THEN
     MONTH = MONTH + 1
```

```
ELSE
     MONTH = 1
     YEAR = YEAR + 1
ENDIF
```

Again note the pattern of indentation.

The GO TO Statement

A GO TO statement requires a label as a destination. A label in FORTRAN is a statement number. Statement numbers must be between columns 1 and 5 of a statement. Figure 7-6 shows a common use of a GO TO statement to implement a simple conditional loop. The program does exactly the same computations as the program in Fig. 7-5, except that it allows multiple computations within a single run.

The Logical IF Statement

When there is no ELSE part, and when there is only one statement to be conditionally executed, the Logical IF statement may be used. Suppose, for example, that a number must be set to 0 if it is negative.

166

$$IF (X .LT. 0) X = 0$$

will do the job. The single statement may be a GO TO statement.

In some versions of FORTRAN (prior to FORTRAN 77), the IF-THEN-ELSE statement is not available. In these cases, the Logical IF can be used to emulate the IF-THEN-ELSE. The example of the previous section can be emulated as follows:

```
    IF (MONTH .LT. 12) GO TO 20
        MONTH = 1
        YEAR = YEAR + 1
        GO TO 30
20  CONTINUE
        MONTH = MONTH + 1
30  CONTINUE
```

The structure of the construct is made obvious by proper indentation.

The CONTINUE statement in the example above is merely a place holder, a convenient place to attach a label.

The program in Fig. 7-6 contains an example of a Logical IF statement with a GO TO used to implement a conditional loop. The Logical IF statement with a GO TO is a combination encountered so often that it deserves a name of its own; the *Conditional GO TO* statement is an appropriate name.

The Arithmetic IF

FORTRAN provides another form of IF statement called the *Arithmetic IF statement*. Its format is as follows:

$$IF (\langle integer\ expression \rangle)\ n1,\ n2,\ n3$$

The ⟨integer expression⟩ is evaluated. If its value is negative, control is transferred to statement number n1. If its value is zero, control is transferred to statement n2. If it is positive, control is transferred to statement n3.

The Arithmetic IF is an idea whose time has come and gone. Its use can lead to confusing programs. Its use is therefore not recommended.

Multiple Selection

The IF-THEN-ELSE statement is fine when

```
C       FIGURE 7.6:    AREA OF A CIRCLE
C                      THE GO TO STATEMENT
C
        REAL PI, AREA, RADIUS
        INTEGER I
        DATA PI/3.14159/
C
        WRITE (1,*)  'COMPUTE THE AREA OF A CIRCLE.'
10      WRITE (1,*)
        WRITE (1,*)  'ENTER RADIUS:  (0 TO QUIT)'
        READ  (0,*) RADIUS
        IF (RADIUS .EQ. 0.0) GO TO 99
        AREA   = PI * RADIUS**2
        WRITE (1,200) RADIUS
        WRITE (1,210) AREA
        GO TO 10
99      STOP
200     FORMAT (' RADIUS = ', F10.5)
210     FORMAT (' AREA   = ', F10.5)
        END
```

Fig. 7-6. The GO TO statement in FORTRAN.

```
C       FIGURE 7.7:  Multiple Selection with Nested IF;
C                    Compute Weekly Pay
C
        REAL HOURS, PAY, RATE
        DATA RATE/10.00/
C
        WRITE (1,*) 'COMPUTE PAY:'
   10   WRITE (1,*)
        WRITE (1,*) 'ENTER NUMBER OF HOURS WORKED (0 TO HALT):'
        READ  (0,*) HOURS
        IF (HOURS .LE. 0.0) GO TO 99
        IF (HOURS .LE. 40.0) THEN
            PAY = HOURS * RATE
        ELSE
            IF (HOURS .LE. 50.0) THEN
                PAY = 40.0*RATE + (HOURS-40.0)*1.5*RATE
            ELSE
                PAY = 40.0*RATE + 10.0*RATE*1.5 + (HOURS-50.0)*2.0*RATE
            ENDIF
        ENDIF
        WRITE (1,200) HOURS
        WRITE (1,210) RATE
        WRITE (1,220) PAY
        GO TO 10
   99   STOP
  200   FORMAT ('HOURS WORKED:   ', F10.2)
  210   FORMAT ('NORMAL RATE:    ', F10.2)
  220   FORMAT ('GROSS PAY:      ', F10.2)
        END
```

Fig. 7-7. The computation of weekly pay in FORTRAN.

there are precisely two alternatives. If there are more than two possible alternative actions, IF statements can be nested. A simple example, which shows the computation of a weekly payroll, is shown in Fig. 7-7.

The example shows that pay for up to 40 hours is paid at the normal rate; pay for work between 40 and 50 hours is paid at one-and-one-half times the normal rate; pay for work in excess of 50 hours is paid at twice the normal rate.

FORTRAN does not have a CASE statement, as discussed in Chapter 2. The CASE statement can be emulated using a computed GO TO statement. An example is shown in Fig. 7-8.

The example program reads in an integer be-
tween 1 and 12 and then prints out the number of days in the corresponding month. The Computed GO TO statement sends control to one of the statement numbers contained within the parentheses, depending on the value of the integer MONTH. If MONTH is 1, the destination is the first-listed statement number, which is 101. If MONTH is 2, the destination is statement number 102, and so on. The numerical value of the statement number is not significant; it is the relative position of the statement number within the parentheses that matters.

Note that Conditional GO TO statements preceding the Computed GO TO keep the value of MONTH from straying beyond the proper bounds.

```fortran
C       FIGURE 7.8:  Days in a Month;
C                    The Computed GO TO Statement
C
        INTEGER MONTH, DAYS, YEAR
C
     10 WRITE (1,*)
        WRITE (1,*) 'ENTER THE MONTH (1..12):  (0 TO HALT)'
        READ  (0,*) MONTH
        IF (MONTH .LE. 0)  GO TO 999
        IF (MONTH .GT. 12) GO TO 10
C       EMULATE CASE STATEMENT
        GO TO (101,102,103,104,105,106,107,108,109,110,111,112), MONTH
C           31-DAY MONTHS
    101     CONTINUE
    103     CONTINUE
    105     CONTINUE
    107     CONTINUE
    108     CONTINUE
    110     CONTINUE
    112     CONTINUE
              DAYS = 31
              GO TO 120
C           30-DAY MONTHS
    104     CONTINUE
    106     CONTINUE
    109     CONTINUE
    111     CONTINUE
              DAYS = 30
              GO TO 120
C           FEBRUARY
    102     CONTINUE
              WRITE (1,*) 'ENTER THE YEAR:'
              READ  (0,*) YEAR
              IF (MOD(YEAR,4) .EQ. 0) THEN
                    DAYS = 29
              ELSE
                    DAYS = 28
              ENDIF
              GO TO 120
C     END CASE
    120 CONTINUE
        WRITE (1,*)
        WRITE (1,200) MONTH, DAYS
        GO TO 10
    999 STOP
    200 FORMAT (' MONTH ', I2, ' HAS ', I2, ' DAYS.')
        END
```

Fig. 7-8. FORTRAN Calendar program, Version 1.

Recall that a CONTINUE statement does nothing but hold a place. A GO TO 101 will therefore have the same result as a GO TO 112—which is to set DAYS to 31. The GO TO 120 is needed to ensure that only the appropriate case is chosen.

In the case of February, additional action is requred to determine whether or not the desired year is a leap year. The MOD function computes the modulus, or the remainder after integer division.

Loops

FORTRAN provides only one kind of loop, the DO loop. The DO loop is a counted loop. Conditional loops must be emulated using the GO TO statement.

Counted Loops: The DO Statement. The DO statement, commonly called the DO loop, is a workhorse in FORTRAN programs. The basic format of a DO loop is as follows:

```
DO 10 I = N1, N2, N3
<statements>

10  CONTINUE
```

The 10 immediately following the word DO is the statement number of the last statement in the loop. The last statement of the loop can be any statement, but it is best to make it a CONTINUE statement. The I following the 10 is the loop counter. At the beginning of the loop, I is initialized to N1. After the first iteration of the loop, N3 is added to N1. If the result is less than or equal to N2, another iteration is performed. If not, control is transferred to the statement following number 10.

If N3 is omitted, the loop counter is incremented by 1 at each iteration. A FORTRAN DO loop always performs at least one iteration, regardless of the relative values of N1 and N2. That is because the testing (of the value of N1 versus N2) is done after, rather than before, each iteration.

N1, N2, and N3 may be integers or integer variables. In either case, their value must be 1 or greater. Zero and negative values are not permitted.

The value of I is technically undefined after the loop has completed. In most versions of FORTRAN it will have the value N2 + 1, but the programmer should not rely on its value once the loop has terminated.

Chapter 2 contained a simple example in BASIC of a program that printed out the integers from 1 to 10. Figure 7-9 contains a FORTRAN program that does the same thing. Notice that the body of the loop is indented. This makes it easy to see at a glance the extent of the loop.

The Implied DO loop. The implied DO loop is another form of the DO loop. It can be used only in READ and WRITE statements. The DO loop in Fig. 7-9 could be programmed as one line using an implied DO loop as follows:

$$\text{WRITE } (1,*) \ (I, I = 1,10)$$

The I = 1,10 follows the same rules as the corresponding part of an ordinary DO loop. Implied DO loops are also useful for handling arrays and will be illustrated further following the discussion of arrays.

Conditional Loops. FORTRAN does not provide conditional loops such as the WHILE or REPEAT-UNTIL of Pascal. When the situation calls for such a loop, it must be emulated using the Logical IF and GO TO statements.

As you recall, a WHILE loop repeats as long as a condition is true, and the test is performed at the top of the loop. Because the test is at the top, the body of the loop may be executed zero times if the condition is initially false. The program in Fig. 7-10 shows how a WHILE loop can be emulated in FORTRAN. Comments are used to show what is being emulated.

```
C        FIGURE 7.9:  The DO Loop
C
         INTEGER I
C
         DO 10 I = 1,10
             WRITE (1,*) I
     10  CONTINUE
         STOP
         END
```

Fig. 7-9. The FORTRAN DO loop.

```
C       FIGURE 7.10:   The WHILE
        Loop Emulated
C
        INTEGER I
C
        I = 1
C       WHILE (I .LE. 10) DO
    10  IF (I .GT. 10) GO TO 20
            WRITE (1,*) I
            I = I + 1
            GO TO 10
    20  CONTINUE
C       END WHILE
        STOP
        END
```

Fig. 7-10. Emulation of a while loop in FORTRAN.

This program does exactly the same thing as the program in Fig. 7-9. In this particular case the DO loop of Fig. 7-9 is more appropriate. The DO loop takes care of initializing and incrementing the loop counter I.

There are other situations, however, in which the WHILE loop is more appropriate. Consider the case in which a program needs to read numbers from the console until their sum exceeds 100. The program needs to report the actual sum and a count of how many numbers were included in the sum. A DO loop would not be appropriate, because a DO loop executes a predetermined number of times. A WHILE loop is better suited to situations when the number of iterations is not known in advance.

Figure 7-11 shows the program described above. The emulated WHILE loop is labeled with comment lines. Note again that the body of the loop is indented to make it easy to see the scope of the loop at a glance.

Another type of conditional loop is the REPEAT-UNTIL loop with the test at the bottom of the loop. This type of loop is repeated until a certain condition becomes true. Figure 7-12 shows how the

```
C       FIGURE 7.11:   Program SUMUP1
C                      Another WHILE emulation
C
        INTEGER NUM, COUNT, SUM
C
        COUNT = 0
        SUM   = 0
        WRITE (1,*) 'ENTER A SERIES OF INTEGERS:'
        READ (0,*) NUM
C       WHILE ((SUM + NUM) .LE. 100) DO
    10  IF ((SUM + NUM) .GT. 100) GO TO 20
            COUNT = COUNT + 1
            SUM   = SUM + NUM
            READ (0,*) NUM
            GO TO 10
    20  CONTINUE
C       END WHILE
        WRITE (1,*)
        WRITE (1,*) COUNT, ' NUMBERS WERE READ.'
        WRITE (1,*) 'THEIR SUM IS ', SUM
        WRITE (1,*) 'THE NUMBER ', NUM, ' WAS NOT COUNTED.'
        STOP
        END
```

Fig. 7-11. Another while-loop emulation in FORTRAN.

171

```
C       FIGURE 7.12:   Program SUMUP2
C                      A REPEAT-UNTIL emulation
C
        INTEGER NUM, COUNT, SUM
C
        COUNT = -1
        SUM   = 0
        NUM   = 0
        WRITE (1,*) 'ENTER A SERIES OF INTEGERS:'
C       REPEAT
     10 CONTINUE
            COUNT = COUNT + 1
            SUM   = SUM + NUM
            READ (0,*) NUM
        IF ((SUM + NUM) .LE. 100) GO TO 10
C       UNTIL ((SUM + NUM) .GT. 100)
        WRITE (1,*)
        WRITE (1,*) COUNT, ' NUMBERS WERE READ.'
        WRITE (1,*) 'THEIR SUM IS ', SUM
        WRITE (1,*) 'THE NUMBER ', NUM, ' WAS NOT COUNTED.'
        STOP
        END
```

Fig. 7-12. A repeat-until emulation in FORTRAN.

previous problem could be programmed using the REPEAT-UNTIL structure. The emulated structure is described with comment lines.

In this example the variable COUNT was initiated to -1 so that it will be incremented to zero on the first pass through the loop. This is slightly unnatural. The WHILE loop would probably be the better choice in this situation.

Subroutines

A subprogram is a self-contained module that can be referenced from a program or from another subprogram. Subroutines and functions are the two types of subprograms available in FORTRAN. Subprograms in FORTRAN are defined after the END statement in the main program. Many versions of FORTRAN also allow subprograms to be defined in separate files.

As discussed in Chapter 2, subroutines have several advantages. Most importantly, they facilitate the breakup of large, unwieldy programs into modules of manageable size. Other potential benefits include the elimination of duplicate coding.

A sample program that contains two subroutines is shown in Fig. 7-13. One subroutine simply prints out the value of two variables, suitably labeled. The second subroutine exchanges the value of two variables. The program prints two variables, exchanges them, and then prints them again. The process is repeated with different variables to show the ability of FORTRAN subroutines to handle different variables. The first time the subroutine SWAP is invoked, it exchanges the values of P and Q; the second time, it exchanges the values of X and Y. This is a capability not found in BASIC.

Note that a subroutine in FORTRAN is invoked using the CALL statement. Following the word CALL is the name of the subroutine and a list of arguments to be passed to the subroutine in parentheses.

A subroutine is defined by writing the word

SUBROUTINE followed by the name of the subroutine and a list of parameters in parentheses. These parameters, plus any other variables to be used in the subroutine should be declared within the subroutine. Any variables used in the subroutine, except the parameters, are strictly local to the subroutine and are independent of all other variables in other parts of the program, whether or not they have the same name.

Parameters in FORTRAN are passed by reference. The result is that any changes made to a parameter within the subroutine are also made to

```
C      FIGURE 7.13:  Demonstrate SUBROUTINE usage
C                    Exchange two variables
C
       REAL P, Q, X, Y
C
       P = 1.0
       Q = 2.0
       CALL PRINT2 (P, Q)
       CALL SWAP   (P, Q)
       CALL PRINT2 (P, Q)
C
       X = 3.14159
       Y = 2.71828
       CALL PRINT2 (X, Y)
       CALL SWAP   (X, Y)
       CALL PRINT2 (X, Y)
C
       STOP
       END
C
       SUBROUTINE PRINT2 (U, V)
C          PRINT THE VALUE OF U, V
           REAL U, V
           WRITE (1,200) U, V
           RETURN
   200     FORMAT (/'FIRST  VARIABLE:  ', F15.5 /
      1               'SECOND VARIABLE:  ', F15.5)
       END
C
       SUBROUTINE SWAP (U, V)
C          EXCHANGE THE VALUES OF U AND V
           REAL U, V, TEMP
           TEMP = U
           U    = V
           V    = TEMP
           RETURN
       END
```

Fig. 7-13. FORTRAN subroutines: the Swap program.

the corresponding argument in the CALL statement in the calling program or subprogram. This is how data is passed back to the main program. Care must be exercised, however, to avoid unintentionally altering the value of a variable in the main program.

Control is passed from the subroutine back to the calling program or subprogram by the RETURN statement. The RETURN statement in the subroutine takes the place of the STOP statement of the main program. Each subroutine also requires an END statement.

Note that the body of each subroutine is indented. This makes it clear at a glance where a subroutine begins and ends.

In this example the advantage gained by using subroutines is marginal. The purpose of the example was to illustrate the mechanics of defining and using subroutines. In the comprehensive sample program at the end of the chapter, subroutines are used to much better advantage. In fact, it is typical for large, well-written programs to consist mainly of subroutines and to have a very short main program.

A subroutine in FORTRAN may CALL another subroutine, but it may not call itself, either directly or indirectly. In other words, if subroutine A calls subroutine B, subroutine B may not call subroutine A.

Functions

A function is another form of subprogram. Like a subroutine, a function is a stand-alone module that can be invoked from the main program or from another subprogram. The primary differences between a subroutine and a function lie in how each is defined and invoked, and in how each returns data to the calling program or subprogram.

FORTRAN has numerous built-in functions; you have already seen one such function, the MOD function in Fig. 7-8. Other common built-in FORTRAN functions include functions to calculate square roots, sines, and cosines, and other numerical and trigonometric functions.

User-defined functions are defined following the END statement of the main program along with the subroutines. Subroutines and functions may be defined in any order. The heading of a function contains the word FUNCTION, preceded by the type of value to be returned (for example, REAL) and followed by the function name and argument list. An example of a function definition is shown in Fig. 7-14.

The function, called MAX3, returns the largest of its three arguments. A function is invoked by writing its name in an expression (as in BIG = MAX3 (X, Y, Z)). The value returned is attached to the name of the function. In fact, the name of the function is treated as if it were a variable within the body of the function. It must be given a value somewhere within the body of the function.

In this case the value to be returned is a real number. Therefore the function is declared to be REAL, both in its heading and in the main program. If the programmer neglected to declare MAX3 as REAL in the main program, the main program would assume the result to be an integer because the default type for variables beginning with the letter M is integer.

In other ways a function is like a subroutine. They both require a RETURN and an END statement. Neither can invoke itself recursively, directly or indirectly. The parameters and arguments of each are treated the same way. Also, the body of the function has been indented in the example to show clearly the beginning and end of the function.

Recursion

As mentioned above, the FORTRAN language does not support recursive subroutine or function calls.

DATA STRUCTURES

So far, the FORTRAN programs in the examples have used only integer and real variables. More advanced data structures such as arrays, records, and linked lists are introduced in this section. In addition, how to handle character strings using integer variables and arrays is described.

Arrays

The subscripts in FORTRAN arrays are enclosed within parentheses. The lower bound for

```
      C       FIGURE 7.14:   Demonstrate a Function
      C                      Find the largest of three numbers
      C
              REAL X, Y, Z, MAX3, BIG
      C
              WRITE (1,*) 'ENTER THREE NUMBERS:'
              WRITE (1,*) 'FIRST  NUMBER:'
              READ  (0,*) X
              WRITE (1,*) 'SECOND NUMBER:'
              READ  (0,*) Y
              WRITE (1,*) 'THIRD  NUMBER:'
              READ  (0,*) Z
              BIG = MAX3 (X, Y, Z)
              WRITE (1,200) BIG
              STOP
          200 FORMAT (F10.5, ' IS THE LARGEST OF THE THREE')
              END
      C
              REAL FUNCTION MAX3 (X, Y, Z)
      C         RETURN THE LARGEST OF THE THREE ARGUMENTS
                REAL X, Y, Z
                MAX3 = X
                IF (Y .GT. MAX3) MAX3 = Y
                IF (Z .GT. MAX3) MAX3 = Z
                RETURN
              END
```

Fig. 7-14. FORTRAN function usage.

FORTRAN array subscripts is always 1. The upper bound is specified in a Dimension statement. The following shows the declaration of a real array with 100 elements:

REAL X
DIMENSION X(100)

The same result could be obtained by the following abbreviated declaration:

REAL X(100)

The usage of arrays in FORTRAN is much like that in other languages. An example is given in Fig. 7-15, which will be discussed in the section on character strings.

Character Strings

Until FORTRAN 77, there was no explicit provision in FORTRAN for character strings. Because not all versions of FORTRAN available today have the character-handling facilities of FORTRAN 77, an explanation is included here of how to handle character strings in FORTRAN using integer variables and arrays.

Integer variables in various implementations of FORTRAN are stored in two, four, six, or some other number of bytes. Nevada FORTRAN uses six bytes. You may recall that a character will fit in one byte. An integer variable in Nevada FORTRAN will therefore hold from one to six characters. Character strings longer than six characters may be stored in integer arrays.

If individual characters in a character string need to be accessed or manipulated, it is best to store the character string in an array with one character per array element. Although this is wasteful (up to six characters could go in each element), it is sometimes the only convenient way to operate.

There are three ways that a variable can receive a character value. It can receive a character value via a READ statement using an A format; it can receive a character value initially from a DATA statement; or it can receive a character value by assignment from another variable. A variable cannot receive a character value by assignment from an alphanumeric literal. In other words,

A = 'HELLO'

is illegal in FORTRAN.

Figure 7-8 contained a program that computed the number of days in a given month using the Computed GO TO statement. The program in Fig. 6-15 shows how to accomplish the same task using numeric and character arrays.

```
C        FIGURE 7.15:   Demonstrate Arrays
C                       Compute the number of days in a month.
C
         INTEGER MONTH, NUMBER, YEAR, DAYS(12), NAME(12), PROMPT(6)
         DATA DAYS/31,28,31,30,31,30,31,31,30,31,30,31/
         DATA NAME/'JAN','FEB','MAR','APR','MAY','JUN',
       1           'JUL','AUG','SEP','OCT','NOV','DEC'/
         DATA PROMPT/'ENTER THE MONTH (1-12), 0 TO QUIT:  '/
C
      10 CONTINUE
         WRITE (1,*)
         WRITE (1,200) PROMPT
         READ  (0,*) MONTH
         IF (MONTH .LE. 0)  GO TO 999
         IF (MONTH .GT. 12) GO TO 10
         NUMBER = DAYS(MONTH)
C        CHECK FOR LEAP YEAR IF MONTH IS FEBRUARY
         IF (MONTH .EQ. 2) THEN
             WRITE (1,*) 'ENTER THE YEAR:'
             READ  (0,*) YEAR
             IF (MOD(YEAR,4) .EQ. 0) THEN
                 NUMBER = NUMBER + 1
             ENDIF
         ENDIF
         WRITE (1,210) NUMBER, NAME(MONTH)
         GO TO 10
     999 STOP
     200 FORMAT (6A6)
     210 FORMAT ('THERE ARE ', I2, ' DAYS IN ', A3, '.')
         END
```

Fig. 7-15. FORTRAN Calendar program, Version 2.

Three integer arrays are declared in the program in Fig. 7-15, and each is used in a different way. The array DAYS is used in the conventional way and is initialized to contain the number of days in each month using a DATA statement.

The array PROMPT is used to store a single character string. It is also initialized using a data statement. The characters are stored six characters per array element. The WRITE statement that prints out the string simply refers to it by name, without any subscripts.

The array NAME is used to store the names of the months. Because each array element can store at most six characters, only the first three letters of each month name are used. The array is initialized with a DATA statement.

The program itself is very simple. The month is read as an integer between 1 and 12; then the number of days in that month and the name of that month are determined by consulting the arrays DAYS and NAMES respectively. Additional processing is required for February to check for leap year.

Records

In Chapter 2 I discussed the need to have a record containing the name of each student and his or her scores on up to 20 tests. There are 30 students in the class. FORTRAN does not support records directly, but they can be simulated using the concept of *parallel arrays*. Using this concept, the corresponding elements of several arrays together comprise a record. The correspondence is by subscript; thus the third record consists of the elements with subscript 3 from the arrays which make up the record.

Here is how the arrays comprising the record for the example of Chapter 2 would be declared in FORTRAN:

```
INTEGER NAME(30,5)
REAL SCORE(30,20)
```

The first subscript of each array corresponds to the student number (recall there are 30 students in the class). The second subscript of the integer array NAME is 5. This array will be used to hold the

student names, and with 6 characters per array element, there will be room for up to 30 characters in each student's name.

Suppose you wish to write the name of the fourth student and his or her score on the first test. Reading or writing a student's name presents an interesting problem. The solution is to use an implied DO loop. The required information is written as follows:

```
    WRITE (1,200) (NAME(4,J), J = 1,5),
  1    SCORE(4,1)
200 FORMAT (5A6, F6.2)
```

This will write the desired information all on one line.

Initializing a two-dimensional array such as NAME with a DATA statement should not be attempted. FORTRAN stores its arrays by columns, so the DATA statement would have to first list the first 6 characters of the first name, the first 6 characters of the second name, and so on. The array is best initialized with a READ statement.

The last two programs of this chapter contain actual examples of the usage of records in FORTRAN programs.

Linked Lists

The concept of linked lists was discussed extensively in Chapter 2. This section discusses how linked lists can be implemented in FORTRAN using parallel arrays. The implementation is nearly the same as described in Chapter 2, except that a two-dimensional array is needed to hold the names. This array is manipulated as discussed in the preceding section.

The FORTRAN declarations to set up the linked list are as follows:

```
    INTEGER EOL, NAME(5,3), FIRST, FREE,
  1    LINK(5)
    DATA EOL/0/
```

This allows for five names in the list. EOL stands for "End Of List" and is used to indicate that no more records follow in the list.

The comprehensive example program at the end of the chapter illustrates the use of linked lists in an actual FORTRAN program and shows the details of how elements are added to and deleted from a linked list.

FILE HANDLING

Microcomputer programs are frequently required to store data in files on floppy disks. FORTRAN does well in this regard, except for the difficulties of character handling, as discussed above.

Standard FORTRAN handles only sequential files, but most implementations, including Nevada FORTRAN, have provision for direct access files as well. Unfortunately these provisons vary between implementations.

A file in FORTRAN is a sequence of records. The extent of a record is determined by the FORMAT statement used to write to the file. Each record is separated by a carriage-return/line-feed pair.

Although it is possible to create binary or unformatted files in FORTRAN, most files are formatted. A formatted file is written under the control of a FORMAT statement; all numbers are converted to characters before being written to the file.

Each FORTRAN file has associated with it a unit number. Earlier you saw that unit numbers 0 and 1 are reserved for console input and output, respectively. Other unit numbers are available for printer and file output. Nevada FORTRAN supports unit numbers 0 to 7. Other versions of FORTRAN may support more unit numbers.

A unit number is associated with an external file by the OPEN subroutine. (In some versions of FORTRAN, OPEN is a FORTRAN statement, not a subroutine.) The following would open the file TEST.TXT as unit 4:

CALL OPEN (4, 'TEST.TXT')

If the user wishes to check for an error in opening the file, a third parameter is needed. Suppose IERR is an integer variable. The following,

CALL OPEN (4, 'TEST.TXT', IERR)

would be the call. Following this call, examining the value of IERR would reveal whether or not the file was opened successfully. The value 0 means a successful open, and the values 1 through 7 indicate various kinds of errors. (Such details are found in the language manual that accompanies a compiler.)

After a file has been opened and written to, the ENDFILE command is used to mark the end of the file, as in

ENDFILE 4

which puts an end-of-file mark (Control-Z in CP/M) in the unit 4 file. The file is closed by the following:

CALL CLOSE(4)

File Records

Earlier it was mentioned that a FORMAT statement determines the extent of a FORTRAN file record. Suppose that you wish to create a file consisting of the name and age of several individuals. Allow space for 24 characters in the name and 3 digits in the age. The FORMAT statement for reading and writing such a file would look as follows:

200 FORMAT (4A6, I3)

The 4A6 file descriptor allocates 24 spaces—6 for each of 4 integer variables.

The following declarations would define appropriate variables:

INTEGER NAME(4), AGE

A statement to write to the file might look like this:

WRITE (4, 200) NAME, AGE

This WRITE statement would output one record. The record length would be 29 characters: 24 for

```
C      FIGURE 7.16:  Demonstrate a Sequential File of Names and Ages
C
       INTEGER NAME(4), AGE
C
       CALL OPEN (2, 'B:AGES.TXT')
       WRITE (1,*) 'ENTER NAMES & AGES; <RETURN> TO QUIT:'
   10  WRITE (1,*)
C      GET DATA FROM KEYBOARD
       WRITE (1,*) 'NAME:'
       READ  (0,210) NAME
       IF (NAME(1) .EQ. '      ') GO TO 20
       WRITE (1,*) 'AGE:'
       READ  (0,*) AGE
C      WRITE ONE RECORD TO THE FILE
       WRITE (2,200) NAME, AGE
       GO TO 10
   20  CONTINUE
C      CLOSE FILE AND REOPEN FOR INPUT
       ENDFILE 2
       CALL CLOSE (2)
       CALL OPEN (2, 'B:AGES.TXT')
       WRITE (1,*)
       WRITE (1,*) 'HERE ARE THE NAMES AND AGES FROM THE FILE.'
       WRITE (1,*)
C      READ IN RECORDS IN SEQUENCE
   30  READ (2,200,END=40) NAME, AGE
C      DISPLAY ON SCREEN
       WRITE (1,200) NAME, AGE
       GO TO 30
   40  CONTINUE
       CALL CLOSE (2)
       STOP
  200  FORMAT (4A6, I3)
  210  FORMAT (4A6)
       END
```

Fig. 7-16. FORTRAN sequential file usage.

NAME, 3 for AGE, and 2 for the carriage-return/line-feed pair at the end.

Sequential Files

Now suppose you wish to create a sequential file consisting of the names and ages of several individuals. The file will be sequential because the records will be written in sequence, one after another, and retrieved the same way. You have already seen how each record of the file can be laid out.

The basic steps to be followed in creating the file are to open the file, write out the records, write an end-of-file mark, and close the file.

The program in Fig. 7-16 demonstrates the use of such a file. The file is created using data from the keyboard. It is then closed and reopened for input. The data is read back from the file in sequence.

In the keyboard input section, the program checks for a blank name (signifying that the user entered a carriage return when prompted for a name), and terminates keyboard input when it is found.

The loop used to read the file back in deserves closer scrutiny. In the statement numbered 30 in Fig. 7-16, the END=40 parameter causes a GO TO 40 to be executed when the program tries to read past the end of the file. It is a convenient way to implement loops for input from a file. The structure of the loop resembles that of a WHILE loop.

Direct-Access Files

Often times it is convenient to have direct access to specific records without reading the file sequentially. As mentioned earlier, standard FORTRAN does not provide for direct-access files, but most implementations of FORTRAN do. The method of handling direct-access files discussed in this chapter is that implemented in Nevada FORTRAN. Direct-access files may be handled differently in different versions of FORTRAN.

Nevada FORTRAN uses the SEEK subroutine to implement direct access. The following is a sample call to SEEK:

CALL SEEK (UNIT, DISPL)

The UNIT parameter is the unit number associated with the file when it was opened. The DISPL parameter is the relative displacement from the beginning of the file in bytes or characters. Note that this is different from the Pascal SEEK command, which computes the displacement in terms of records, not characters.

In order to use SEEK, it is necessary for the program to keep track of the position of each record in the file. Suppose that a file record is defined by the following FORMAT statement:

200 FORMAT (21A6)

The record length for this file record is 128 bytes. This is computed as $(21 * 6 = 126)$ plus an allowance for the carriage return and line feed.

Suppose DISPL, RECLEN and RECNR have been declared as integers. The following sequence will compute the displacement for record number (RECNR) 5 of the file:

RECLEN = 128
RECNR = 5
DISPL = (RECNR − 1) * RECLEN

Notice that the displacement for the first record of the file is zero.

It is convenient, though not always necessary, to allocate space for a direct-access file by writing the file initially as a sequential file, possibly with blank records. This practice is illustrated in the program in Fig. 7-17, which sets up the files for the comprehensive example program a little later in the chapter.

The direct-access file to be set up is called B:ADDRESS.TXT. The other file created by this program will be discussed later.

The use of a direct-access file in an actual program is illustrated in the comprehensive example program that follows.

GRAPHICS

FORTRAN does not support graphics.

COMPREHENSIVE SAMPLE PROGRAM

The example programs thus far in this chapter have been relatively short. Each has been intended to illustrate a particular idea, such as how to use a counted loop in FORTRAN. Short programs are well-suited for that purpose; in fact short programs are all that are found in many programming texts. Unfortunately short programs do not adequately cover the flavor of real FORTRAN programs.

Real FORTRAN programs, that is FORTRAN programs written for other than instructional pur-

```
C      FIGURE 7.17:  INITIALIZE FILE FOR DIRECT ACCESS
C                    SET UP FOR ADDRESS BOOK
C
       INTEGER NREC, C, I, EOL
       DATA EOL/0/
C
       WRITE (1,*) 'WARNING:  THIS PROGRAM INITIALIZES B:ADDRESS.TXT.'
       WRITE (1,*) 'IT WILL DESTROY AN EXISTING B:ADDRESS.TXT.'
       WRITE (1,*)
       WRITE (1,*) 'DO YOU WISH TO CONTINUE? (Y/N)'
       READ  (0,100) C
       IF ((C .NE. 'Y     ') .AND. (C .NE. 'y     ')) GO TO 999
       WRITE (1,*) 'HOW MANY RECORDS SHOULD BE ALLOCATED?'
       READ  (0,*) NREC
       CALL OPEN (2, 'B:ADDRESS.TXT')
       DO 10 I = 1, NREC
C          OUTPUT A DUMMY RECORD
           WRITE (2,200)
    10 CONTINUE
       ENDFILE 2
       CALL CLOSE (2)
C      NOW CREATE THE INDEX FILE
       CALL OPEN (3, 'B:INDEX.TXT')
C      WRITE INDEX OF FIRST ACTIVE RECORD (EOL = END OF LIST)
       WRITE (3,210) EOL
C      WRITE INDEX OF FIRST RECORD IN FREE LIST
       I = 1
       WRITE (3,210) I
C      BUILD THE CHAIN OF FREE RECORDS (FREE LIST)
       DO 20 I = 2, NREC
           WRITE (3,210) I
    20 CONTINUE
C      MARK THE END OF THE FREE LIST
       WRITE (3,210) EOL
C      MARK THE END OF THE INDEX FILE
       ENDFILE 3
       CALL CLOSE (3)
   999 STOP
   100 FORMAT (A1)
   200 FORMAT (102X)
   210 FORMAT (I4)
       END
```

Fig. 7-17. FORTRAN Address Book Setup program.

```
C       FIGURE 7.18:   COMPREHENSIVE EXAMPLE PROGRAM
CCCCCCCCCCCCCCCCCCCCCCCCCCCCCCCCCCCCCCCCCCCCCCCCCCCCCCCCCCCCCCCCC
C                                                               C
C PROGRAM:   ADDRESS BOOK                                       C
C                                                               C
C     Maintains an ordered file of names and addresses.  The program C
C     in Figure 7.17 must be run to initialize the files before this C
C     program is run for the first time.                        C
C                                                               C
C     File size is now set to 0010 records.  To expand, you must  C
C     modify the value of MAXREC and the dimension of the array   C
C     LINK.                                                     C
C                                                               C
CCCCCCCCCCCCCCCCCCCCCCCCCCCCCCCCCCCCCCCCCCCCCCCCCCCCCCCCCCCCCCCCC
C
        INTEGER MAXREC, RECLEN, LINK(10), FIRST, FREE, EOL, RECNR,
     1     C, I, P, Q, R, F1(3), F2(3), IER
        DATA MAXREC /10/, EOL /0/, F1 /'B:ADDRESS.TXT     '/,
     1     F2 /'B:INDEX.TXT       '/, RECLEN /104/
C
        CALL CLEAR
        WRITE (1,*) 'WELCOME TO YOUR ADDRESS BOOK.'
        WRITE (1,*)
        WRITE (1,*) 'INITIALIZING...'
C       OPEN FILES AND INITIALIZE PRINTER
        CALL OPEN (2, F1)
        CALL OPEN (4, 'LST:')
C       OPEN AND READ IN INDEX FILE
        CALL GETINX (LINK, MAXREC, FIRST, FREE, F2)
C       MAIN LOOP
C       REPEAT
      5 CONTINUE
          CALL MENU (C)
          IF ((C .LT. 1) .OR. (C .GT. 6)) GO TO 5
C         EMULATE CASE STATEMENT
          GO TO (10, 20, 30, 40, 50, 60), C
     10     CONTINUE
            CALL APPEND (FIRST, FREE, RECLEN, LINK, MAXREC, EOL)
            GO TO 70
     20     CONTINUE
            CALL REVIEW (FIRST, EOL, MAXREC, LINK, RECLEN, FREE)
            GO TO 70
     30     CONTINUE
            CALL LIST (FIRST, EOL, MAXREC, LINK, RECLEN)
            GO TO 70
```

Fig. 7-18. FORTRAN Address Book. (Continued on page 183.)

```
      40    CONTINUE
            CALL REORG (FIRST, FREE, EOL, MAXREC, LINK, RECLEN, F2)
            GO TO 70
      50    CONTINUE
            CALL DUMP (FIRST, FREE, MAXREC, LINK, RECLEN)
            GO TO 70
      60    CONTINUE
            WRITE (1,*) 'CLOSING FILES....'
      70    CONTINUE
C     END CASE
      IF (C .NE. 6) GO TO 5
C     UNTIL (C .EQ. 6)
C     CLEAN UP
      CALL CLOSE (2)
C     SAVE AND CLOSE INDEX FILE
      CALL SAVINX (LINK, MAXREC, FIRST, FREE, F2)
      STOP
      END
C
      SUBROUTINE GETINX (LINK, N, FIRST, FREE, FN)
C         READ INDEX FILE
          INTEGER N, LINK(N), FIRST, FREE, FN(3), I
          CALL OPEN (3, FN)
          READ (3, 200) FIRST
          READ (3, 200) FREE
C         NOW READ IN THE ARRAY LINK
          I = 1
      10    READ (3, 200, END=99) LINK(I)
                I = I + 1
                IF (I .GT. (N + 1)) THEN
                    WRITE (1,*) 'WARNING... INDEX FILE TOO BIG.'
                    GO TO 99
                END IF
                GO TO 10
      99    CONTINUE
          CALL CLOSE (3)
          RETURN
     200    FORMAT (I4)
      END
C
      SUBROUTINE SAVINX (LINK, N, FIRST, FREE, FN)
C         SAVE INDEX FILE
          INTEGER N, LINK(N), FIRST, FREE, FN(3), I
```

```
            CALL OPEN (3, FN)
            WRITE (3, 200) FIRST
            WRITE (3, 200) FREE
            DO 10 I = 1, N
                 WRITE (3, 200) LINK(I)
   10       CONTINUE
            ENDFILE 3
            CALL CLOSE (3)
            RETURN
  200       FORMAT (I4)
        END
C
      SUBROUTINE MENU (C)
C           DISPLAY MENU AND RETURN CHOICE
            INTEGER C, ROW, COL
            CALL CLEAR
            ROW = 5
            COL = 5
            CALL GOTOXY (COL, ROW)
            WRITE (1,*) '1)  ADD TO FILE'
            ROW = ROW + 2
            CALL GOTOXY (COL, ROW)
            WRITE (1,*) '2)  REVIEW FILE ON SCREEN'
            ROW = ROW + 2
            CALL GOTOXY (COL, ROW)
            WRITE (1,*) '3)  LIST FILE TO SCREEN OR PRINTER'
            ROW = ROW + 2
            CALL GOTOXY (COL, ROW)
            WRITE (1,*) '4)  REORGANIZE FILE'
            ROW = ROW + 2
            CALL GOTOXY (COL, ROW)
            WRITE (1,*) '5)  DUMP FILE TO PRINTER'
            ROW = ROW + 2
            CALL GOTOXY (COL, ROW)
            WRITE (1,*) '6)  QUIT'
            ROW = ROW + 2
            COL = 1
   10       CALL GOTOXY (COL, ROW)
            WRITE (1,*) 'SELECT 1, 2, 3, 4, 5, OR 6:'
            READ  (0,*) C
            IF ((C .LT. 1) .OR. (C .GT. 6)) GO TO 10
            RETURN
        END
```

Fig. 7-18. FORTRAN Address Book. (Continued on page 185.)

```
C
      SUBROUTINE APPEND (FIRST, FREE, RECLEN, LINK, N, EOL)
C         ADD RECORDS TO THE FILE IN THE PROPER ORDER
          INTEGER LNAME(2), FNAME(2), ADDR(4), CITY(3), STATE,
     1          ZIP(2), PHONE(3), FIRST, FREE, N, LINK(N), EOL,
     2          ROW, COL, RECNR, RECLEN
   10     CALL CLEAR
          IF (FREE .EQ. EOL) THEN
                WRITE (1,*) 'NO ROOM REMAINING IN THE FILE....'
                CALL WAIT
                GO TO 99
          ENDIF
C     DISPLAY SKELETONIZED FORM ON SCREEN
          ROW = 5
          COL = 1
          CALL GOTOXY (COL, ROW)
          WRITE (1,*) 'LAST NAME      :                :'
          ROW = ROW + 2
          CALL GOTOXY (COL, ROW)
          WRITE (1,*) 'FIRST NAME     :                :'
          ROW = ROW + 2
          CALL GOTOXY (COL, ROW)
          WRITE (1,*) 'ADDRESS        :                      :'
          ROW = ROW + 2
          CALL GOTOXY (COL, ROW)
          WRITE (1,*) 'CITY           :                    :'
          ROW = ROW + 2
          CALL GOTOXY (COL, ROW)
          WRITE (1,*) 'STATE          :  :'
          ROW = ROW + 2
          CALL GOTOXY (COL, ROW)
          WRITE (1,*) 'ZIP CODE       :            :'
          ROW = ROW + 2
          CALL GOTOXY (COL, ROW)
          WRITE (1,*) 'PHONE NR       :               :'
C     READ DATA FROM SCREEN
          ROW = 5
          COL = 15
          CALL GOTOXY (COL, ROW)
          READ (0,200) LNAME
          IF (LNAME(1) .EQ. '       ') GO TO 99
          ROW = ROW + 2
          CALL GOTOXY (COL, ROW)
```

```
                   READ (0,200) FNAME
                   ROW = ROW + 2
                   CALL GOTOXY (COL, ROW)
                   READ (0,200) ADDR
                   ROW = ROW + 2
                   CALL GOTOXY (COL, ROW)
                   READ (0,200) CITY
                   ROW = ROW + 2
                   CALL GOTOXY (COL, ROW)
                   READ (0,200) STATE
                   ROW = ROW + 2
                   CALL GOTOXY (COL, ROW)
                   READ (0,200) ZIP
                   ROW = ROW + 2
                   CALL GOTOXY (COL, ROW)
                   READ (0,200) PHONE
C        FIND FREE RECORD AND WRITE TO DISK
                   CALL GETFRE (RECNR, FREE, LINK, N)
                   CALL PUTREC (RECNR, RECLEN, LNAME, FNAME, ADDR, CITY,
      1                STATE, ZIP, PHONE)
C        INSERT IN INDEX
                   CALL INSERT (LNAME, FNAME, RECNR, RECLEN, N, LINK,
      1                EOL, FIRST)
                   GO TO 10
    99             RETURN
   200             FORMAT (4A6)
      END
C
      SUBROUTINE GETFRE(RECNR, FREE, LINK, N)
C        FIND NEXT FREE RECORD AND REMOVE FROM FREE LIST
                   INTEGER RECNR, FREE, N, LINK(N)
                   RECNR = FREE
                   FREE = LINK (FREE)
                   RETURN
      END
C
      SUBROUTINE INSERT (LNAME, FNAME, RECNR, RECLEN, N, LINK,
      1            EOL, FIRST)
C        INSERT RECNR IN INDEX IN PROPER ORDER
                   INTEGER LNAME(2), FNAME(2), RECNR, N, LINK(N), EOL, FIRST,
      1            LNB(2), FNB(2), DA(4), DC(3), DS, DZ(2), DP(3), I,
      2            P, Q, RECB, RECLEN
```

Fig. 7-18. FORTRAN Address Book. (Continued on page 187.)

```
          LOGICAL FLAG
C         LNB, FNB ARE BUFFERS FOR TEMPORARILY STORING LNAME, FNAME
C         DA, DC, ETC. ARE DUMMY VARIABLES FOR HOLDING ADDR, CITY, ETC.
C
C         MOVE NAMES TO BUFFERS
          DO 10 I = 1, 2
                LNB(I) = LNAME(I)
                FNB(I) = FNAME(I)
   10     CONTINUE
          RECB = RECNR
C         FIND PROPER PLACE IN LIST AND ADJUST LINKS
          IF (FIRST .EQ. EOL) THEN
C               LIST WAS PREVIOUSLY EMPTY
                LINK(RECB) = EOL
                FIRST      = RECB
                GO TO 99
          ELSE
                P = FIRST
                Q = EOL
          ENDIF
   20     CALL GETREC (P, RECLEN, LNAME, FNAME, DA, DC, DS, DZ, DP)
          CALL COMPAR (LNAME, FNAME, LNB, FNB, FLAG)
C         RETURNS .TRUE. IF LNAME,FNAME .LT. LNB, FNB
          IF (FLAG) THEN
                Q = P
                P = LINK(P)
                IF (P .NE. EOL) THEN
                        GO TO 20
                ENDIF
          ENDIF
C         AT THIS POINT, Q POINTS TO PREDECESSOR OF BUFFER NAME
C               AND P POINTS TO ITS SUCCESSOR
          LINK(RECB) = P
          IF (Q .EQ. EOL) THEN
                FIRST = RECB
          ELSE
                LINK(Q) = RECB
          ENDIF
   99     RETURN
       END
C
       SUBROUTINE COMPAR (LNAME, FNAME, LNB, FNB, FLAG)
C         RETURN .TRUE. IF NAME .LT. BUFFER NAME.
```

```
C           USES SYSTEM-SUPPLIED SUBROUTINE COMP, WHICH
C           RETURNS -1, 0, 1 DEPENDING ON WHETHER FIRST
C           STRING IS .LT., .EQ., OR .GT. SECOND STRING.
            INTEGER LNAME(2), FNAME(2), LNB(2), FNB(2), RESULT
            LOGICAL FLAG
C
            RESULT = COMP (LNAME, LNB, 12)
            IF (RESULT .EQ. 1) THEN
              FLAG = .FALSE.
            ELSE
              IF (RESULT .EQ. -1) THEN
                FLAG = .TRUE.
              ELSE
                RESULT = COMP (FNAME, FNB, 12)
                IF (RESULT .EQ. 1) THEN
                  FLAG = .FALSE.
                ELSE
                  FLAG = .TRUE.
                ENDIF
              ENDIF
            ENDIF
            RETURN
        END
C
      SUBROUTINE REVIEW (FIRST, EOL, N, LINK, RECLEN, FREE)
C           REVIEW RECORDS ON THE SCREEN, 1 AT A TIME.
            INTEGER FIRST, EOL, R, Q, UNIT, C, N, LINK(N), RECLEN,
     1          FREE
            CALL CLEAR
            WRITE (1,*) 'REVIEWING FILE...'
            WRITE (1,*)
            IF (FIRST .EQ. EOL) THEN
                WRITE (1,*) 'NO RECORDS TO REVIEW...'
                GO TO 99
            ENDIF
            UNIT = 1
C           UNIT 1 IS THE SCREEN
            R = FIRST
            Q = EOL
C           REPEAT
     10     CONTINUE
                CALL PRTREC (UNIT, R, RECLEN)
                WRITE (UNIT,*)
```

Fig. 7-18. FORTRAN Address Book. (Continued on page 189.)

```
                    WRITE (UNIT,*) 'SELECT'
                    WRITE (UNIT,*) '    1) GET NEXT RECORD'
                    WRITE (UNIT,*) '    2) DELETE THIS RECORD'
                    WRITE (UNIT,*) '    3) QUIT'
                    READ  (0,*) C
                    IF (C .EQ. 1) THEN
C                           GET NEXT RECORD
                            Q = R
                            R = LINK (R)
                    ELSE
                        IF (C .EQ. 2) THEN
C                               DELETE THIS RECORD
                                IF (Q .EQ. EOL) THEN
                                        FIRST = LINK(R)
                                        CALL PUTFRE (R,LINK,N,FREE)
                                        R = FIRST
                                ELSE
                                        LINK(Q) = LINK(R)
                                        CALL PUTFRE (R,LINK,N,FREE)
                                        R = LINK(Q)
                                ENDIF
                        ENDIF
                    ENDIF
            IF ((R .NE. EOL) .AND. (C .NE. 3)) GO TO 10
C           UNTIL ((R .EQ. EOL) .OR. (C .EQ. 3))
   99       CALL WAIT
            RETURN
      END
C
      SUBROUTINE PUTFRE (R, LINK, N, FREE)
C     PUT RECORD BACK IN THE FREE LIST.
C     THIS SUBROUTINE DISABLED BECAUSE OF A BUG IN THE
C     NEVADA FORTRAN COMPILER WHICH DOES NOT ALLOW REUSE
C     OF DELETED RECORDS IN THE MIDDLE OF THE FILE.
C
C     INTEGER R, N, LINK(N), FREE
C     LINK(R) = FREE
C     FREE    = R
      RETURN
      END
C
      SUBROUTINE LIST (FIRST, EOL, N, LINK, RECLEN)
      INTEGER FIRST, EOL, C, UNIT, N, LINK(N), RECLEN
```

```
C              LIST ALL RECORDS TO THE SCREEN OR PRINTER
               CALL CLEAR
               IF (FIRST .EQ. EOL) THEN
                    WRITE (1,*) 'NO RECORDS IN FILE TO LIST...'
                    GO TO 99
               ENDIF
    10         WRITE (1,*) 'LIST FILE TO 1) SCREEN OR 2) PRINTER?'
               READ (0,*) C
               IF ((C .LT. 1) .OR. (C .GT. 2)) GO TO 10
               IF (C .EQ. 2) THEN
                    UNIT = 4
C                   PRINTER
               ELSE
                    UNIT = 1
C                   SCREEN
               ENDIF
               R = FIRST
C              REPEAT
    20         CONTINUE
                    WRITE (UNIT, *)
                    CALL PRTREC (UNIT, R, RECLEN)
                    R = LINK (R)
               IF (R .NE. EOL) GO TO 20
C              UNTIL (R .EQ. EOL)
               WRITE (UNIT, *)
    99         CALL WAIT
               RETURN
          END
C
      SUBROUTINE REORG (FIRST, FREE, EOL, MAXREC, LINK, RECLEN, F2)
C          REORGANIZE FILES TO ELIMINATE DELETED RECORDS.
C          REORG USES IMPLEMENTATION-SPECIFIC SUBROUTINES.
               INTEGER FIRST, FREE, EOL, MAXREC, LINK(MAXREC), N,
     1              F2(3), R, RECLEN, DISPL, I, LNAME(2),
     2              FNAME(2), ADDR(4), CITY(3), STATE, ZIP(2), PHONE(3)
C          COPY FILE IN SEQUENCE TO A SCRATCH FILE, THEN BACK TO ITSELF
               CALL OPEN (5, 'SCRATCH.TXT')
               R = FIRST
    10         IF (R .EQ. EOL) GO TO 20
                    DISPL = (R - 1)*RECLEN
                    CALL SEEK (2, DISPL)
                    READ  (2,100,END=20) LNAME,FNAME,ADDR,CITY,STATE,ZIP,
     1                     PHONE
                    WRITE (5,100) LNAME,FNAME,ADDR,CITY,STATE,ZIP,PHONE
```

Fig. 7-18. FORTRAN Address Book. (Continued on page 191.)

```
                            R = LINK(R)
                            GO TO 10
      20        CONTINUE
                ENDFILE 5
C         REINITIALIZE LINKS
                FREE = 1
                FIRST = EOL
                N = MAXREC - 1
                DO 30 I = 1, N
                            LINK(I) = I + 1
      30        CONTINUE
                LINK(MAXREC) = EOL
C         COPY BACK TO THE ORIGINAL FILE & RE-INSERT IN INDEX
                REWIND 5
      40        READ (5,100,END=50) LNAME,FNAME,ADDR,CITY,STATE,ZIP,PHONE
                            CALL GETFRE (R, FREE, LINK, MAXREC)
                            CALL PUTREC (R, RECLEN, LNAME, FNAME, ADDR, CITY,
     1                          STATE, ZIP, PHONE)
                            CALL INSERT (LNAME, FNAME, R, RECLEN, MAXREC, LINK,
     1                          EOL, FIRST)
                            GO TO 40
      50        CONTINUE
                CALL CLOSE (5)
                CALL DELETE ('SCRATCH.TXT')
C       SAVE INDEX
                CALL SAVINX (LINK, MAXREC, FIRST, FREE, F2)
                RETURN
     100        FORMAT (2A6, 2A6, 4A6, 3A6, A6, 2A6, 3A6)
          END
C
          SUBROUTINE DUMP (FIRST, FREE, N, LINK, RECLEN)
                INTEGER LNAME(2), FNAME(2), ADDR(4), CITY(3), STATE,
     1              ZIP(2), PHONE(3), FIRST, FREE, N, LINK(N),
     2              RECLEN, I
                CALL CLEAR
                WRITE (1,*) 'DUMPING FILE TO PRINTER...'
                WRITE (4,200) FIRST, FREE
                WRITE (4,*)
                DO 10 I = 1, N
                            WRITE (4,210) I
                            CALL PRTREC(4, I, RECLEN)
                            WRITE (4,220) LINK(I)
                            WRITE (4,*)
      10        CONTINUE
```

```
            RETURN
  200       FORMAT ('FIRST ACTIVE RECORD:   ', I4,
     1              ' FIRST FREE RECORD:    ', I4)
  210       FORMAT ('RECORD NUMBER:  ', I4)
  220       FORMAT ('LINK:  ', I4)
      END
C
      SUBROUTINE PRTREC (UNIT, RECNR, RECLEN)
C         PRINT RECORD RECNR TO CONSOLE OR PRINTER, DEPENDING ON
C         THE VALUE OF "UNIT".  GETS THE RECORD FROM DISK.
          INTEGER UNIT, RECNR, LNAME(2), FNAME(2), ADDR(4), CITY(3),
     1            STATE, ZIP(2), PHONE(3), RECLEN
          CALL GETREC(RECNR, RECLEN, LNAME, FNAME, ADDR, CITY,
     1            STATE, ZIP, PHONE)
          WRITE (UNIT, 200) FNAME, LNAME, ADDR, CITY, STATE,
     1            ZIP, PHONE
  200     FORMAT (2A6, 1X, 2A6 / 4A6 / 3A6, 1X, A2, 1X 2A6 /
     1            3A6)
          RETURN
      END
C
      SUBROUTINE GETREC (RECNR, RECLEN, LNAME, FNAME, ADDR,
     1     CITY, STATE, ZIP, PHONE)
C         READS RECORD NUMBER RECNR FROM FILE
          INTEGER RECNR, RECLEN, LNAME(2), FNAME(2), ADDR(4),
     1            CITY(3), STATE, ZIP(2), PHONE(3), IER, DISPL
          DISPL = (RECNR - 1)*RECLEN
          CALL SEEK (2, DISPL, IER)
          IF (IER .NE. 0) THEN
              WRITE (1,*) 'WARNING:  SEEK ERROR IN GETREC.'
              WRITE (1,*) 'IER   = ', IER
              WRITE (1,*) 'RECNR = ', RECNR
              STOP
          ENDIF
          READ (2,200) LNAME, FNAME, ADDR, CITY, STATE, ZIP, PHONE
          RETURN
  200     FORMAT (2A6, 2A6, 4A6, 3A6, A6, 2A6, 3A6)
C         SAME AS FORMAT (17A6)
      END
C
      SUBROUTINE PUTREC (RECNR, RECLEN, LNAME, FNAME, ADDR,
     1     CITY, STATE, ZIP, PHONE)
C         WRITES RECORD NUMBER RECNR TO FILE
          INTEGER RECNR, RECLEN, LNAME(2), FNAME(2), ADDR(4),
```

Fig. 7-18. FORTRAN Address Book. (Continued on page 193.)

```
     1              CITY(3), STATE, ZIP(2), PHONE(3), IER, DISPL
        DISPL = (RECNR - 1)*RECLEN
        CALL SEEK (2, DISPL, IER)
        IF (IER .NE. 0) THEN
                WRITE (1,*) 'WARNING: SEEK ERROR IN PUTREC.'
                WRITE (1,*) 'IER   = ', IER
                WRITE (1,*) 'RECNR = ', RECNR
                STOP
        ENDIF
        WRITE (2,200) LNAME, FNAME, ADDR, CITY, STATE, ZIP, PHONE
        RETURN
  200   FORMAT (2A6, 2A6, 4A6, 3A6, A6, 2A6, 3A6)
     END
C
     SUBROUTINE CLEAR
C        CLEAR THE SCREEN (MACHINE-DEPENDENT)
C        PUT OUTPUTS A CHARACTER TO THE SCREEN GIVEN ITS ASCII VALUE
C        THIS SEQUENCE IS (ESC) "*"
        CALL PUT (27)
        CALL PUT (42)
        RETURN
     END
C
     SUBROUTINE GOTOXY (COL, ROW)
C        POSITION CURSOR AT NAMED COL & ROW (MACHINE-DEPENDENT)
C        THE LEAD-IN CHARACTERS ARE (ESC) "="
        INTEGER COL, ROW, X, Y
        CALL PUT (27)
        CALL PUT (61)
        Y = 31 + ROW
        X = 31 + COL
        CALL PUT (Y)
        CALL PUT (X)
        RETURN
     END
C
     SUBROUTINE WAIT
C      WAIT FOR (RETURN) FROM KEYBOARD
        INTEGER C
        WRITE (1,*) 'PRESS (RETURN) TO CONTINUE...'
        READ (0,200) C
        RETURN
  200   FORMAT (A1)
     END
```

poses, tend to be longer than those seen so far in this chapter, and they tend to contain numerous subroutines. Since the primary purpose of this chapter is to illustrate the flavor of the FORTRAN language, a longer programming example is appropriate.

This longer example program maintains an ordered file of names and addresses on disk. It functions as an electronic address book, providing the ability to add, display, and delete names. Names may be displayed on the video screen or listed on a printer.

This program is perhaps not the best choice to demonstrate the strengths of FORTRAN, as it involves string manipulation and not much numerical computation. It does, however, provide an excellent example of the construction of a long, complex application from a series of relatively short subroutines. In addition, it provides a good means for comparing FORTRAN to other languages, as a similar program is included in most of the other language chapters.

The basic data structure used to maintain the names in alphabetical order is the linked list. This data structure was described extensively in Chapter 2. The program uses a direct-access file to store the names and addresses and a sequential file to store the links.

A separate program, shown in Fig. 7-17, is used to initialize these files. The address file itself is initialized to blank records, while the index file is initialized to contain the appropriate pointers for an empty list. Note that the address file is initialized using sequential access, even though it will be used as a direct-access file later.

When the setup program is run for the first time, the user should respond with a 10 when asked how many records to allocate. This will match the initial configuration of the comprehensive example program, as discussed below.

The comprehensive example program itself is shown in Fig. 7-18. A structure chart that shows the hierarchical organization of the program is given in Fig. 7-19. In this chart the subroutines called by the main program are listed below the main program at the first level of indentation. A subroutine called by

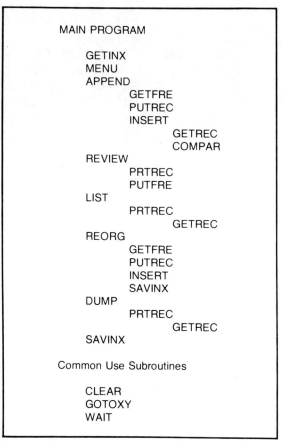

Fig. 7-19. The structure chart for the Address Book program.

another subroutine is indented another level and listed below the calling subroutine.

Notice that the main program is relatively short. Its primary function is to call the subroutines in the proper sequence. It uses system subroutines to open the files, then it reads the index file into memory. The main loop calls the menu subroutine and then passes control to the appropriate subroutine, depending on the menu item selected. When the user chooses the QUIT option, the address file is closed, and the index file is saved to disk and closed.

As described in Chapter 2, active records in the file are maintained in order using a linked list called the *active list*, and inactive records are maintained in a linked list called the *free list*. As mentioned earlier, the links are read into and maintained in main memory while the program is running. When the program terminates, the links are written back to a sequential file. The names and addresses themselves are maintained in the direct-access file, not in main memory. This makes possible the maintenance of a much longer file than would be possible if the names and addresses were all maintained in main memory.

The free list is maintained using a method that is slightly different than the one discussed in Chapter 2 and implemented in the other chapters. Records deleted from the file are not automatically returned to the free list. The subroutine PUTFRE, which would ordinarily perform this function, has been modified to do nothing by making most of its statements into comments (C in column 1). The reason for this is that a bug in the Nevada FORTRAN compiler causes damage to the file during direct-access writes to other than the last active record of the file.

To permit the eventual reutilization of deleted records, a subroutine called REORG has been added to the list of options in the program menu. This subroutine reorganizes the file so that all active records are contiguous and in the proper order at the beginning of the file and so that all remaining records are in the free list. This is accomplished by first copying the active records in order (using the links) to a scratch file and then copying them back, using the appropriate subroutines to recreate the links. If you are using a different version of FORTRAN or a corrected version of Nevada FORTRAN, the reorganization option will not be necessary provided that you remove the C in column 1 of the appropriate lines of the subroutine PUTFRE.

The subroutine COMPAR requires some comment. Because ANS 1966 FORTRAN does not support character strings directly, the results of comparisons between character strings cannot always be predicted. It depends on the particular implementation. Accordingly, the designers of Nevada FORTRAN have provided a built-in function called COMP, which compares a specified number of characters of two character strings and returns −1, 0, or 1, depending on whether the first string is less than, equal to, or greater than the

second string. Users of other versions of FORTRAN should check their documentation, as other versions may provide different solutions to this problem.

The program as written will only support a file of 10 records. This limitation was imposed in order to keep the output from the DUMP option to a reasonable length. The dump option has been provided in order to make it easy for the user to see the effects of adding and deleting records. If the user then wishes to expand the capacity of the file, it is necessary to do three things:

1. Run the program in Fig. 7-17 again to allocate more file space.
2. Change the dimension of the array LINK at the beginning of the main program in Fig. 7-18.
3. Change the value of the variable MAXREC in the DATA statement near the beginning of the main program.

Once these three things have been done, the program may be used to maintain an actual file of addresses.

ADVANTAGES AND DISADVANTAGES OF FORTRAN

The major strength of FORTRAN is the facility with which it handles numerical computations. It is particularly well-suited for scientific and engineering programs.

FORTRAN has a reputation for speed. While the speed may vary from implementation to implementation, a compiled FORTRAN program is virtually guaranteed to run much faster than the equivalent interpreted BASIC program.

FORTRAN is widely-taught in colleges and universities. Persons who have learned FORTRAN on large computers will find the transition to FORTRAN on microcomputers relatively simple.

A large volume of mathematical software has been written in FORTRAN and is available in the form of subroutine libraries in many large computer centers.

Modular programming is easy in FORTRAN because of the presence of subroutines and functions. It is easy to break large FORTRAN programs down into smaller pieces.

On the negative side, versions of FORTRAN prior to FORTRAN 77 lack direct support for character strings. Although character strings can be handled using integer variables, as seen in the example programs, it is awkward to do so.

Some versions of FORTRAN lack the IF-THEN-ELSE construct. This construct was offcially added effective with FORTRAN 77.

FORTRAN is notably weak in the area of control structures. It lacks a WHILE statement (conditional loop with test at the top), a REPEAT-UNTIL statement (conditional loop with test at the bottom), and a CASE statement. Although each of these constructs can be simulated using other FORTRAN statements, their absence is a disadvantage.

FORTRAN also lacks the ability to handle recursive subroutines and functions.

AVAILABILITY

Several versions of FORTRAN are available for microcomputers that use the CP/M operating system, including versions by Ellis Computing (Nevada FORTRAN), Microsoft, and Supersoft. Versions are also available for the IBM Personal Computer and other computers that use the MS-DOS operating system. In addition, a version of FORTRAN 77 is available under the UCSD "P" System.

SUMMARY

FORTRAN is the oldest of the high-level languages in wide use today. Its use is largely confined to minicomputers and mainframes, however. The reasons for this include the earlier availability of BASIC on microcomputers and the wide availability of more modern languages such as Pascal and C. There are a large number of applications, however, in which FORTRAN can be used to good advantage. These include applications involving intensive numerical computations, particularly when fast execution is required.

FORTRAN is similar enough in form to BASIC to make it easy for BASIC programmers to learn FORTRAN as a second language.

The fact that FORTRAN has been used by so many for so long is reason enough for it to warrant consideration for use on microcomputers.

Chapter 8

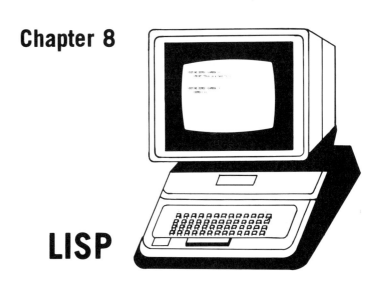

LISP

The LISP language was developed about 1960 by a group headed by Professor John McCarthy at the Massachusetts Institute of Technology. LISP is about the same age as COBOL; of the languages in general use today, only FORTRAN is older than LISP and COBOL. That these languages have survived for so long is a tribute to the farsightedness of their progenitors.

Some interesting details about the original design of LISP can be found in an important paper describing LISP (Recursive Functions of Symbolic Expressions) published by Professor McCarthy in the April 1960 issue of the *Communications of the Association for Computing Machinery* (ACM). In that article we learn that LISP (like FORTRAN) was originally designed for the IBM 704 computer and that (again like FORTRAN) certain of its characteristics can be traced to the hardware details of the IBM 704 computer. For example, two of the most commonly-used LISP functions are called CAR and CDR. CAR stands for Contents of the

Address part of the Register. CDR stands for Contents of the Decrement part of the Register. What these functions do will be described in detail in the appropriate section of this chapter; it is by no means obvious outside the context of the IBM 704.

The name LISP is an acronym that stands for LISt Processor. LISP was developed for use in research in the area of artificial intelligence, and it is still the principle language of choice in that field. Professor McCarthy has since moved to Stanford University. It is no coincidence that two of the world's most advanced centers for research in artificial intelligence are at Stanford and MIT.

The field of artificial intelligence is beyond the scope of this book. This chapter will attempt to portray the nature of LISP in other contexts.

LISP tends to divide people into two groups—insiders and outsiders. To the insiders, LISP is the greatest language ever conceived. To the outsiders, it is mysterious at best. Some of the aura of mystery stems from the unusual vocabulary of LISP which, as you have seen, includes some historical anachronisms. LISP is also very different from the more conventional languages such as FORTRAN, BASIC, and Pascal. Once you get beyond appearances, however, LISP is really a very simple and consistent language. Once a few basic concepts are mastered, the language is easy to learn.

LISP is at its best in applications that require the manipulation of symbols, whether they be words, numbers, sentences, or whatever. It supports data structures of arbitrary complexity, facilitating the organization of information for easy retrieval. It also has the capability of performing numerical computations, but it is clearly not the language of choice for such applications.

LISP was originally designed as a batch language. LISP programs were to be entered into the computer via punched cards and the output received via printout. The design of the language, however, is much better suited to today's interactive environment. LISP functions can be entered directly via the keyboard and results received via the video screen.

LISP is usually implemented as an interpreted language. The language is easily extended and modified. As a result, several dialects of LISP have grown up and come into common use. The programs in this chapter were tested on an Apple II Plus microcomputer (with Z80 Softcard) using the MuLISP interpreter distributed by Microsoft, Incorporated. Several of the keywords were modified so as to more closely resemble "standard" LISP.

LISP PROGRAMS AND FUNCTIONS

The basic building blocks of LISP are data, expressions, and functions. The subject of data will be covered in detail in a later section.

LISP uses functions instead of procedures or subroutines. All functions return a value, whether it is needed or not. If it is not needed by the calling function, the returned value can simply be ignored.

There is no clear distinction between LISP programs and LISP functions. Any LISP function can stand alone and be invoked from the keyboard, or it can be invoked by another function. A program can be thought of as a collection of one or more functions that exist simultaneously in the computer's memory in an area that I will call a *workspace*. Subject to space limitations, any number of functions can exist in a workspace at a given time. The workspace can also contain any data needed by the functions.

In the MuLISP environment, a workspace can be saved to and retrieved from disk. LISP functions can also be created using a separate text editor and read into a workspace.

LISP recognizes both upper and lowercase, but it distinguishes between them. Because the built-in functions and commands were defined in uppercase, they cannot be invoked in lowercase. It is therefore good practice to do LISP programming in all capital letters except when lowercase letters are needed in text.

Two simple LISP functions are shown in Fig. 8-1. The first one, called DEMO1, prints a simple message on the screen. To execute this function, the following is typed:

(DEMO1)

Note the parentheses. LISP uses lots of parentheses. In fact all commands you type must be enclosed in parentheses, together with any arguments. Some dialects of LISP would have you type "DEMO1 ()" instead. In either case, the system displays the following in response:

This is a test.
This is a test.

Why is the message printed twice? The first copy comes from the PRINT function. The second copy of the message is the value returned by the function DEMO1. DEMO1 must return something, and that something is the value of the last expression evaluated, which is the print function. When a function such as DEMO1 returns a value and the user doesn't say what to do with that value, LISP simply prints it out.

Let us now look at the form of the function DEMO1. Notice that the function definition begins with the word DEFINE and the name of the function, and that the whole definition is enclosed in parentheses. Next comes the word LAMBDA followed by empty parentheses. The LAMBDA function is used by LISP to define the parameters of a function. In this case there are no parameters, which is why the parentheses are empty. The word LAMBDA was borrowed from a book entitled *The Calculi of Lambda-Conversion,* by A. Church (Princeton University Press, Princeton, NJ, 1941)—another unfortunate anachronism.

LISP function parameters bound by LAMBDA are passed according to the "call by value" scheme discussed in Chapter 2. In other words, the actual arguments are evaluated and their values passed to the function. LISP also permits "call by name" in which the names of the arguments themselves are passed for use within the function. This is invoked by using the word NLAMBDA instead of LAMBDA. Fortunately this use of names is rarely needed in LISP except by those who write languages and such.

Some dialects of LISP make the use of the word LAMBDA optional. Unfortunately MuLISP is not among them.

Once the name of the function and the parameters are defined, the body of the function can follow. The body of the function consists of a series of expressions. In this case there is only one, the PRINT function. Following the last function, all that remains is to close all open parentheses.

The use of parentheses in function definitions is something that must be learned. The entire definition is enclosed by one set, and the part that begins with LAMBDA by another set. Each expression in the body of the function must also be enclosed by parentheses.

The function DEMO2 is included in Fig. 8-1 to show that a function can be invoked from another function. DEMO2 simply invokes DEMO1 and produces exactly the same results.

DATA TYPES

A data element in LISP can be an *atom* or a *list*. Each of these kinds of data is discussed in detail in the following paragraphs.

```
(DEFINE DEMO1 (LAMBDA ()
     (PRINT "This is a test.") ))


(DEFINE DEMO2 (LAMBDA ()
     (DEMO1) ))
```

Fig. 8-1. Minimal LISP functions.

Atoms

An atom is another of those unfortunate names used in LISP. An atom can perhaps best be thought of simply as a basic data element. These data elements are of two principle subtypes, numeric and nonnumeric.

Numeric atoms can be either integer or floating point. MuLISP does not support floating point numbers, however, but integers can be of almost infinite precision (would you believe 256 raised to the 256th power?).

Nonnumeric atoms are more interesting. Each has a name, a value, and a property list. To illustrate, consider the following session at the console. The "$" is the MuLISP prompt.

$	JOHN	(user)
	JOHN	(LISP)

When the user types an atom name, LISP responds with its value. Here LISP hasn't been given any other value, so it responds with the name.

$ (SETQ JOHN OLD)	(user)
OLD	(LISP)

The SETQ function, to be discussed in more detail later, gives the atom JOHN a value, which is echoed by LISP.

$	JOHN	(user)
OLD		(LISP)

Now when the user types the name of the atom, LISP responds with its new value.

```
$   (QUOTE JOHN)              (user)
JOHN                          (LISP)
```

The name of the atom is still accessible using the QUOTE function.

```
$   (PUT JOHN AGE 72)         (user)
72                            (LISP)
```

Here the user has started to create a property list for JOHN. The function PUT (called PUTPROP in some dialects of LISP) establishes a property called AGE for JOHN and sets its value to 72. If the property AGE had already existed, its previous value would have been overwritten.

```
$   (PUT JOHN                 (user)
HEALTH GOOD)
GOOD                          (LISP)
```

Here another property is established. The properties can be retrieved from the property list using the GET function, which you see below.

```
$   (GET JOHN AGE)            (user)
72                            (LISP)
$   (GET JOHN HEALTH)         (user)
GOOD                          (LISP)
```

Lists

A list is a sequence of elements, each of which may be an atom or another list. Each list element is separated by a blank. The list is enclosed in parentheses. Here is a simple example of a list:

```
(THIS IS A LIST)
```

Here is an example of a list that contains another list:

```
((A LIST) IN A LIST)
```

Lists can also include numeric atoms, as in the following:

```
(1 2 3 4 5)
```

A special case of a list is the empty list, which can be written as () or as NIL. You will see examples of its use later in the chapter.

Lists can be used to implement more complex data structures. This is discussed in more detail in the section on data structures.

List Manipulation

LISP provides a number of functions for the manipulation of lists. These functions provide for access to individual elements of a list. They also allow lists to be constructed.

Functions that allow access to individual elements of lists are called *selector* functions. The two principle selector functions are called CAR and CDR. (How these functions got their names was discussed earlier in the chapter.) CAR returns the first element of a list. CDR returns everything but the first element. Here are a few examples:

```
$   (CAR (THIS IS A LIST))    (user)
THIS                          (LISP)
$   (CDR (THIS IS A LIST))    (user)
(IS A LIST)                   (LISP)
$   (CAR ((A LIST))           (user)
IN A LIST))
(A LIST)                      (LISP)
```

Elements other than the first element of a list can be retrieved by repeated application of CAR and CDR. For example, the second element of a list could be retrieved by the following:

```
$   (CAR (CDR (THIS IS        (user)
A LIST)))
IS                            (LISP)
```

Because this is such a common occurrence, LISP provides a shortcut:

```
$   (CADR (THIS IS A LIST))   (user)
IS                            (LISP)
```

As a matter of fact, LISP provides a whole family of shortcuts of the form CxxR and CxxxR, where any of the x's can be either A or D. Where there is an A, a CAR is done, and where there is a D, a CDR is done. How this works is easier to show by example than to explain in words. You have already seen how CADR works. The following example shows how to retrieve the third elements of a list using this notation:

```
$  (CADDR (THIS IS A LIST))  (user)
A                            (LISP)
```

This is equivalent to the following:

```
$  (CAR (CDR (CDR (THIS    (user)
IS A LIST))))
A                          (LISP)
```

Here is another example:

```
$  (CDAR ((A LIST) IN A    (user)
LIST))
(LIST)                     (LISP)
```

This example was a little trickier. In stages, here is what it did:

```
$  (CAR ((A LIST) IN A LIST)) (user)
(A LIST)                      (LISP)
$  (CDR (A LIST))             (user)
(LIST)                        (LISP)
```

Functions that are used to construct lists are called constructor functions. The principle constructor functions are CONS, APPEND, LIST, and REVERSE.

CONS takes two arguments. The first argument may be a list or an atom, but the second argument must be a list. (CONS X Y) returns a list in which X has been inserted as the first element of list Y. Here are some simple examples:

```
$  (CONS A (B C D))    (user)
(A B C D)              (LISP)
$  (CONS A ())         (user)
(A)                    (LISP)
$  (CONS (A B) (C D))  (user)
((A B) C D)            (LISP)
```

APPEND takes two arguments, both of which must be lists. It returns a list that combines the two original lists. Here is a simple example:

```
$  (APPEND (A B) (C D))    (user)
(A B C D)                  (LISP)
```

The effect of LIST is a little more complicated. It can take any number of arguments and produces a list. Each argument may be an atom or a list. LIST evaluates each argument before adding it to the list. What gets added to the list is not the name of the argument, but its value. This is illustrated by the following examples:

```
$  (LIST A B C D)          (user)
(A B C D)                  (LISP)
$  (LIST JOHN MAN RIVER)   (user)
(JOHN MAN RIVER)           (LISP)
$  (SETQ JOHN (QUOTE       (user)
OLD))
OLD                        (LISP)
$  (LIST JOHN MAN RIVER)   (user)
(OLD MAN RIVER)            (LISP)
```

When first used, an atom such as JOHN evaluates to itself. Thus LIST produced no surprises until JOHN was given a different value. Then LIST caused JOHN to be evaluated to OLD before adding it to the list. This evaluation can be stopped by the QUOTE function, as illustrated below:

```
$  (LIST (QUOTE JOHN)      (user)
MAN RIVER)
(JOHN MAN RIVER)           (LISP)
```

It takes practice to become comfortable with the distinction between CONS, APPEND, and LIST. Here is an illustration showing how each of the three functions deals with the same arguments:

```
$  (CONS (A B) (C))        (user)
((A B) C)                  (LISP)
$  (APPEND (A B) (C))      (user)
(A B C)                    (LISP)
$  (LIST (A B) (C))        (user)
((A B) (C))                (LISP)
```

The REVERSE function is straightforward. It produces a list which consists of the same elements but in reverse order. Here is a simple example:

```
$  (REVERSE (JOHN MAN      (user)
RIVER))
(RIVER MAN JOHN)          (LISP)
```

One use of REVERSE is to aid in the selection of the last element of a list. The following example shows how this can be done easily:

```
$  (CAR (REVERSE (THIS     (user)
IS A LIST)))
LIST                       (LISP)
```

REVERSE caused the list to be reversed, and CAR extracted the first element of the reversed list.

Now suppose you need all but the last element of a list. REVERSE is needed twice in this case:

```
$  (REVERSE (CDR (REVERSE (THIS
    IS A LIST))))
(THIS IS A)
```

Without the additional REVERSE, the result would have been (A IS THIS).

If you anticipate needing these two operations frequently enough, you could define them as LISP functions, perhaps called LAST and BUTLAST.

Character Manipulation

Although the atom is supposedly the smallest component of matter and of LISP data, both physics and LISP recognize the existence of subatomic particles. In LISP these are characters.

LISP does not provide functions for dealing directly with characters, but it does provide functions for expanding the characters of an atom into a list and for compressing a list into an atom. Here are some examples:

```
$  (EXPLODE BOMB)          (user)
(B O M B)                  (LISP)
$  (EXPLODE 123)           (user)
(1 2 3)                    (LISP)
```

```
$  (COMPRESS (A I R))      (user)
AIR                        (LISP)
$  (COMPRESS (12 34 56)    (user)
123456                     (LISP)
```

In some dialects of LISP, the EXPLODE and COMPRESS functions are called UNPACK and PACK, respectively.

Variables

As you have already seen, an atom can have a value. This value can be an atom (numeric or non-numeric), or it can be a list. The value of a numeric atom is the number itself. Technically you can give a numeric atom a different value, but such action is strongly discouraged.

When an atom is typed at the keyboard, its value is returned. As you have seen, evaluation of an atom can be suppressed with the QUOTE function. Here are some simple examples which assume that the value of A has previously been assigned the value 10, and the value of B is the list (1 2 3):

```
$  A                       (user)
10                         (LISP)
$  (QUOTE  A)              (user)
A                          (LISP)
$  B                       (user)
(1 2 3)                    (LISP)
```

The EVAL function, on the other hand, causes evaluation to be carried one step further. Consider the following sequence of operations:

```
$  (SETQ JOHN (QUOTE       (user)
OLD))
OLD                        (LISP)
$  (SETQ OLD 80)           (user)
80                         (LISP)
$  JOHN                    (user)
OLD                        (LISP)
$  (EVAL JOHN)             (user)
80                         (LISP)
```

When the EVAL function is applied to JOHN, JOHN

is evaluated to OLD, and OLD is in turn evaluated to 80.

Variables in LISP may be *bound* or *free*. A bound variable is a variable that is listed as a parameter of a function. It is local to that function. Any action taken upon that variable or its name within the function does not affect any variable outside of that function. (This of course assumes the usual call by value, as discussed above.) When the function terminates, so does the existence of the bound variable.

A free variable, on the other hand, is not listed as a parameter of a function. It is something like a global variable in other languages. It may be used within a function or outside of a function (for example in an expression typed at the keyboard). If the value of a free variable is changed within a function, the new value outlives that function and is available to other functions. Free variables have an existence separate from any functions. If a workspace is saved to disk, all of the free variables within the workspace are saved with it.

The Equivalence of Programs and Data

A striking feature of LISP is that programs and data are equivalent in form. A program can be manipulated as data, and data can be executed as a program. This is possible because programs, functions, and expressions are stored as lists. That is why you have to use so many parentheses when entering expressions.

As a simple example, consider the expression used above:

(EVAL JOHN)

You can treat this expression as data, as in the following:

```
$  (CAR (EVAL JOHN))      (user)
EVAL                      (LISP)
```

Here the list (EVAL JOHN) is treated first as an expression and then as data.

Now consider going the other direction, treating data as an expression. The following illustrates this:

```
$  (SETQ Q (QUOTE (EVAL    (user)
JOHN)))
(EVAL JOHN)                (LISP)
$  Q                       (user)
(EVAL JOHN)                (LISP)
$  (EVAL Q)                (user)
80                         (LISP)
```

Here you have seen the list (EVAL JOHN) treated first as data (a character string) and then as an expression.

THE ASSIGNMENT FUNCTION: SETQ

You have already seen several examples of the use of the assignment function SETQ. The name SETQ is actually an abbreviation for SET QUOTE. The following two assignment functions are equivalent:

(SETQ X 12)
(SET (QUOTE X) 12)

You want the value 12 to be assigned to the name of the atom X, so you need the QUOTE function. With SETQ, the QUOTE function is understood. SETQ is used much more often than SET.

SET can have unexpected results if it is not used properly. Consider the following sequence:

```
$  (SETQ X (QUOTE Y))      (user)
Y                          (LISP)
$  (SET X 12)              (user)
12                         (LISP)
$  X                       (user)
Y                          (LISP)
$  Y                       (user)
12                         (LISP)
```

Here you can see that when you typed (SET X 12), X was evaluated to Y before the assignment took place. The QUOTE is needed to prevent the evaluation of X. Of course when SETQ is used, the QUOTE is understood and need not be repeated.

Care must also be taken to use the QUOTE

function with the second argument of the SET or SETQ function if its name and not its value is desired. It is easy to become careless in this area because the initial value of an atom is the name of the atom. Unless care is taken, the value of an expression can depend unnecessarily on the order of execution. Consider the following sequence:

```
$   (SETQ X Y)              (user)
Y                          (LISP)
$   (SETQ Y 15)            (user)
15                         (LISP)
$   X                      (user)
Y                          (LISP)
$   Y                      (user)
15                         (LISP)
```

No surprises there. Now suppose the order of the assignments is reversed:

```
$   (SETQ Y 15)            (user)
15                         (LISP)
$   (SETQ X Y)             (user)
15                         (LISP)
$   X                      (user)
15                         (LISP)
$   Y                      (user)
15                         (LISP)
```

In the expression (SETQ X Y), Y was evaluated before the assignment took place, so X was assigned the value 15 rather than the value Y. You can assume that it was the user's intention for X to have the character value Y. The use of (SETQ X (QUOTE Y)) would have prevented the mixup.

Variables that are created using an assignment function at the keyboard are free variables. (See above for a discussion of the meaning of the term "free variable.")

ARITHMETIC EXPRESSIONS

Arithmetic expressions in LISP use a form of prefix notation called Cambridge Polish Notation. (See Chapter 2 for a discussion of the various types of notation.) In other words, the arithmetic operator comes before the operands. To add 2 and 3,

for example, you would type the following:

```
$   (PLUS 2 3)             (user)
5                          (LISP)
```

The sequence for multiplying these numbers would be as follows:

```
$   (TIMES 2 3)            (user)
6                          (LISP)
```

Prefix notation takes some getting used to, but it is perfectly consistent. Most of us are used to a mixture of infix and prefix notation, as in the following BASIC expressions:

```
2 + 3                      (infix)
SQR (9)                    (prefix)
```

The following arithmetic functions are normally available in LISP:

(MINUS X)	Unary minus: returns $-X$
(PLUS X Y)	Returns $X + Y$
(DIFFERENCE X Y)	Returns $X - Y$
(TIMES X Y)	Returns $X * Y$
(QUOTIENT X Y)	Returns X / Y (integer division)
(REMAINDER X Y)	The remainder after integer division (the modulus function)
(DIVIDE X Y)	Returns X / Y (real division, or in MuLISP, returns the integer quotient and remainder.)
(ADD1 X)	Returns $X + 1$
(SUB1 X)	Returns $X - 1$
(ABS X)	Returns absolute value of X

Various dialects of LISP may include additional arithmetic functions.

LISP was not designed for applications that

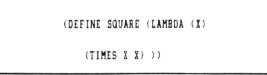

```
(DEFINE SQUARE (LAMBDA (X)

(TIMES X X) ))
```

Fig. 8-2. The square of a number in LISP.

require extensive numerical computations. It can easily handle the basics, however.

A simple LISP program that computes the area of a square, or, equivalently, the square of a number, is shown in Fig. 8-2.

LOGICAL EXPRESSIONS (PREDICATES)

Logical expressions in LISP are called *predicates*. A predicate tests an expression and returns T for true or NIL for false. (ZEROP N) is a simple logical expression that will return T if N is equal to zero; otherwise it will return NIL.

The names of most LISP predicates end in the letter P, but there are exceptions. Here is a list of some of the common LISP predicates and the conditions under which each returns T. Each one returns NIL under all other conditions.

(ATOM X)	T if X is an atom
(NUMBERP X)	T if X is a number
(NAME X)	T if X is a name
(NULL X)	T if X is an empty list
(MINUSP X)	T if X is negative
(PLUSP X)	T if X is positive
(EVEN X)	T if X is an even number
(ZEROP X)	T if X is zero
(EQ X Y)	T if X and Y are identically equal. This expression is used for name and numbers.
(EQUAL X Y)	T if X and Y are equal. This expression is used for more complicated objects.
(MEMBER X Y)	T if X is an element of the list Y.
(GREATERP X Y)	T if X and Y are numbers and X > Y.
(LESSP X Y)	T if X and Y are numbers and X < Y.
(NOT X)	T if X has the value NIL
(AND X Y Z . . .)	T if all the arguments are T
(OR X Y Z . . .)	T if any of the arguments are T
(FLAGP X Y)	T if the attribute Y is on the property list of object X

Note that the AND and OR predicates can have any number of arguments. For these two functions, any value other than NIL is considered the same as a T value.

As indicated, all predicates use prefix notations. As with all other LISP expressions, the entire expression, including the operator, must be enclosed within parentheses. The use of predicates will be illustrated by an example later in this chapter.

INPUT AND OUTPUT

Input and output operations in LISP are simple. There are functions to print and functions to read. There are ways to select input from either the keyboard or a disk file, and to direct output to the video screen, a disk file, or a printer.

The READ function reads a list. Its use can be illustrated by this simple session:

```
$   (READ)                    (user)
(Hello"," how are you?)       (user)
(Hello, how are you?)         (LISP)
```

Notice that the input to READ had to be typed as a list (with parentheses) and was returned as a list. The quotation marks are needed for special characters such as commas and periods.

The concept that READ is a function and returns a value is illustrated by the following:

```
$   (SETQ L (READ))           (user)
(Hello"," how are you?)       (user)
(Hello, how are you?)         (LISP)
```

```
$  L                          (user)
(Hello, how are you?)         (LISP)
```

The value of the list was assigned to the atom L.

The function RATOM reads an atom instead of a list. Here are a few examples:

```
$  (RATOM)                    (user)
Hello                         (user)
Hello                         (LISP)
$  (RATOM)                    (user)
"Hello, how are you?"         (user)
Hello, how are you?           (LISP)
```

Notice that a single word can be read without quotations, but to read more than one word and store it as an atom rather than a list, LISP requires quotation marks.

The PRINT function prints the value of an expression. For example,

(PRINT X)

prints the value of X and also returns the value of X. You saw how this worked in Fig. 8-1. PRIN1 works the same way, except that it does not output a carriage return and line feed after printing, as does PRINT. Note that the value of X can be an atom (numeric or nonnumeric) or a list.

To output only a carriage return and line feed, you can use the function TERPRI. The SPACES function outputs a specified number of blank spaces.

In addition to the basic input and output functions, there are additional functions for modifying the effects of the input and output functions. For example the WRS (WRite Select) function can be used to redirect output between the screen and a disk file. The command

(WRS X Y Z)

redirects output to file Z:X.Y; that is, file X.Y on drive Z.

There is a control variable called LPRINTER which controls printer output. If LPRINTER has any value other than NIL, the output also goes to a printer in addition to its regular destination (the video screen or a disk file). An example of how this is done is shown in Fig. 8-3. The program in Fig. 8-3 writes a message to the printer and then to the screen.

The RDS (ReaD Select) function can be used to select input from the keyboard or from a disk file. Disk file input and output are discussed in more detail later.

```
(DEFINE PRINTER (LAMEDA ()
    (SETQ LPRINTER T)
    (PRINT (THIS GOES TO THE PRINTER))
    (SETQ LPRINTER NIL)
    (PRINT (THIS GOES TO THE SCREEN)) ))
```

Fig. 8-3. A Printer demonstration in LISP.

CONTROL STRUCTURES

LISP has relatively few control structures compared to other languages. The most widely-used control structures are the conditional statement COND and recursion. LISP is so flexible, however, that additional control structures can be added to the language when needed.

Simple and Multiple Selection: COND

The COND function can handle both simple and multiple selection. Its format is as follows, where L1, L2, and L3 are lists.

(COND L1 L2 . . . L3)

The COND function consists of the word COND followed by a sequence of one or more lists. The CAR of each list is evaluated until one is found with a non-NIL value. The CDR of that list is executed. Suppose L2 is the first list in which a non-NIL CAR is found. COND would then execute the CDR of L2 and return the last value obtained. COND returns as soon as one list is found with a non-NIL CAR and the CDR of that list is executed. If the CDR of a list is empty, the value of the CAR is returned.

206

The operation of COND is best explained by example. Consider the following IF statement in BASIC:

IF X < 0 THEN X = 0

The LISP version of this statement would be as follows:

(COND ((MINUSP X) (SETQ X 0)))

The list following COND is the following:

((MINUSP X) (SETQ X 0))

The CAR of this list is the predicate (MINUSP X), which returns T if X is less than 0. If this is the case, then the CDR of the list, (SETQ X 0) is executed. This sets X to zero and returns the value zero.

Now consider the following IF-THEN-ELSE statement in FORTRAN:

```
IF (MONTH .EQ. 12) THEN
    MONTH = 1
    YEAR = YEAR + 1
ELSE
    MONTH = MONTH + 1
ENDIF
```

The equivalent statement in LISP would be as follows:

```
(COND
    ((EQ MONTH 12) (SETQ MONTH 1)
     (SETQ YEAR (ADD1 YEAR)) )
    (T   (SETQ MONTH (ADD1 MONTH)))
)
```

Notice that the second list begins with T. This is how LISP handles the ELSE part. If MONTH is equal to 12, the COND function returns after the remainder of that list is executed. If MONTH is not equal to 12, you want to add 1 to MONTH, so you guarantee that the CDR of the next list will be executed by starting that list off with T.

To illustrate multiple selection using COND,

consider the problem of finding the number of days in a month. A LISP solution of this problem is shown in Fig. 8-4. Here is a sample session showing this function in action:

$	(CALENDAR JANUARY)	(user)
31		(LISP)
$	(CALENDAR FEBRUARY)	(user)
(ENTER THE YEAR)		(LISP)
1984		(user)
29		(LISP)
$	(CALENDAR TUESDAY)	(user)
NIL		(LISP)

Notice that if the argument is not the name of a month, CALENDAR returns NIL. If the month is February, a special function is called to query the user for the year. If the year is evenly divisible by 4 (i.e., if (REMAINDER YR 4) is zero). FEB returns 29; otherwise it returns 28. The COND function of

```
(DEFINE CALENDAR (LAMBDA (M)
 (COND
   ((EQ M (QUOTE JANUARY)) 31)
   ((EQ M (QUOTE FEBRUARY) (FEB) )
   ((EQ M (QUOTE MARCH)) 31)
   ((EQ M (QUOTE APRIL)) 30)
   ((EQ M (QUOTE MAY)) 31)
   ((EQ M (QUOTE JUNE)) 30)
   ((EQ M (QUOTE JULY)) 31)
   ((EQ M (QUOTE AUGUST)) 31)
   ((EQ M (QUOTE SEPTEMBER)) 30)
   ((EQ M (QUOTE OCTOBER)) 31)
   ((EQ M (QUOTE NOVEMBER)) 30)
   ((EQ M (QUOTE DECEMBER)) 31) ) ))


(DEFINE FEB (LAMBDA ()
 (PRINT (ENTER THE YEAR))
 (SETQ YR (RATOM))
 (COND
   ((EQ (REMAINDER YR 4) 0) 29)
   (T 28) ) ))
```

Fig. 8-4. The Calendar program, Version 1.

FEB is a good example of a simple if-then-else statement in LISP.

Later in the chapter you will see two more versions of the calendar program.

Functions

Because of the lack of a clear distinction between functions and programs, functions have already been discussed in this chapter. A few more comments on functions are in order at this point.

Functions provide an important means of controlling the flow of execution. A good example of this was shown in Fig. 8-4. When the function CALENDAR was given FEBRUARY as an argument, it invoked the function FEB to interrogate the user for the year and to do the necessary calculations.

Note also that the arguments of a function can be atoms or lists. A function can return one atom or one list. If multiple atoms need to be returned, they can always be put in a list and returned that way.

Recursion

Recursion is the primary means of implementing repetitive actions in LISP. As discussed in Chapter 2, a function is said to be recursive if it invokes itself. Recursion is very useful in processing lists, and much programming in LISP consists of largely of processing lists.

The classic example of recursion is the factorial function. The factorial of a positive integer N is defined to be N times the factorial of N − 1. The factorial of 0 is defined to be 1. Thus the factorial function is defined in terms of itself. A version of the factorial function is shown in Fig. 8-5.

The first thing the function FACTORIAL does is to check its argument to be sure it isn't being erroneously asked to compute the factorial of a negative number. If it is, it returns NIL. It next checks to see whether N is zero. If it is, it returns the value 1. Otherwise, it applies the rule that the factorial of N is N times the factorial of N − 1. To compute the factorial of N − 1, the function FACTORIAL calls itself recursively.

This is like saying, for example, "I could compute the value of 2 factorial if only I knew what the value of 1 factorial is." The function would then call FACTORIAL with argument 1. That is like saying, "I could compute the value of 1 factorial if only I knew what the value of 0 factorial is." The function calls FACTORIAL with argument 0 to find out what 0 factorial is. This time, the function knows that 0 factorial is 1, so it returns that value. Once 0 factorial is known, 1 factorial can be computed. Once 1 factorial is known, 2 factorial can be computed. The process is then complete.

A nonnumeric example of recursion is the word triangle program. This program takes a word as input and then prints it repeatedly, dropping the first letter each time until there are no more letters. The LISP version of this program is shown in Fig. 8-6.

The function TRIANGLE operates by printing its argument (WORD) and then calling itself with an argument one character shorter. The function removes the first character of its argument by using the function EXPLODE to convert WORD to a list, CDR to drop the first element, and COMPRESS to compress the list back into an atom. The COND function is used to check for the termination condition, which occurs when there are no more letters left in WORD.

Here is a sample interchange with the function TRIANGLE:

```
$   (TRIANGLE HELLO)        (user)
HELLO                       (LISP)
ELLO                        (LISP)
LLO                         (LISP)
LO                          (LISP)
O                           (LISP)
```

The word "HELLO" can be read horizontally or vertically.

```
(DEFINE FACTORIAL (LAMBDA (N)
(COND
  ((MINUSP N) NIL)
  ((ZEROP N) 1)
  (T (TIMES N (FACTORIAL (SUB1 N)))) ) ))
```

Fig. 8-5. The recursive factorial function in LISP.

```
(DEFINE TRIANGLE (LAMBDA (WORD)
  (PRINT WORD)
  (COND
    ((NULL (CDR (EXPLODE WORD))) (TERPRI) )
    (T (TRIANGLE (COMPRESS (CDR (EXPLODE WORD)))))) ) ))
```

Fig. 8-6. The Word Triangle program in LISP.

Another example of a program that uses recursion is the second version of the calendar program, shown in Fig. 8-7. This program operates in a very different manner than the first version of the calendar program, shown in Fig. 8-4, does. It uses a list called MLIST to store the number of days in each month except February. (February is handled by a separate function called FEB, which was also used in Fig. 8-4.) To compute the number of days in a month, say March, the function CALENDAR does a table lookup.

CALENDAR uses two arguments, the name of the month for which the number of days is to be found and the list MLIST. It operates by comparing the name in the argument to the first name in the list. If there is a match, it returns the number of days from the list. If there is no match, CALENDAR calls itself using the same month name but with the CDR of MLIST. If the month is not found, CALENDAR returns NIL. February is of course handled as a special case.

Here is a sample session with this program:

$ (INIT)	(user)
$ (CALENDAR APRIL MLIST)	(user)
30	(LISP)
$ (CALENDAR JULIUS MLIST)	(user)
NIL	(LISP)

The function INIT is used to initialize MLIST. When CALENDAR was called with the erroneous name JULIUS, CALENDAR correctly returned NIL.

Three short mathematical functions are shown in Fig. 8-8. The function SUM adds up to the num-

bers in a list. The function COUNT counts the elements in a list (numbers or otherwise). The function AVERAGE uses SUM and COUNT to compute the average of the numbers in a list.

SUM works as follows: If the list L is empty

```
(DEFINE CALENDAR (LAMBDA (M MLIST)
  (COND
    ((EQ M (QUOTE FEBRUARY)) (FEB) )
    ((NULL MLIST) NIL)
    ((EQ M (CAAR MLIST)) (CADAR MLIST) )
    (T (CALENDAR M (CDR MLIST))) ) ))


(DEFINE INIT (LAMBDA ()
  (SETQ MLIST ((JANUARY 31)
               (MARCH 31)
               (APRIL 30)
               (MAY 31)
               (JUNE 30)
               (JULY 31)
               (AUGUST 31)
               (SEPTEMBER 30)
               (OCTOBER 31)
               (NOVEMBER 30)
               (DECEMBER 31))) ))


(DEFINE FEB (LAMBDA ()
  (PRINT (ENTER THE YEAR))
  (SETQ YR (RATOM))
  (COND
    ((EQ (REMAINDER YR 4) 0) 29)
    (T 28) ) ))
```

Fig. 8-7. The Calendar program, Version 2.

```
(DEFINE SUM (LAMBDA (L)
  (COND
    ((NULL L) 0)
    (T (PLUS (CAR L) (SUM (CDR L)))) ) ))


(DEFINE COUNT (LAMBDA (L)
  (COND
    ((NULL L) 0)
    (T (PLUS 1 (COUNT (CDR L)))) ) ))



(DEFINE AVERAGE (LAMBDA (L)
  (DIVIDE (SUM L) (COUNT L)) ))
```

Fig. 8-8. The SUM, COUNT, and AVERAGE functions.

(NULL), it returns 0. If the list is not empty, it returns the first element of the list plus the sum of the remaining elements. Eventually the recursion reaches the empty list, so the recursion terminates and the sum is calculated.

The function COUNT works similarly. If the list L is empty (NULL), it returns 0. If the list is not empty, it returns 1 plus the number of elements in the CDR of the list. Because each recursive call involves the CDR of the list, eventually the empty list is returned and the recursion terminates. The elements in the list L need not be numbers in order for COUNT to work. Note that COUNT counts only top-level entries. (COUNT (1 (2 3))) would return 2, as there are only two top-level entries in the list, the atom 1 and the list (2 3).

The function AVERAGE shows again how LISP functions such as SUM and COUNT can be easily used as building blocks for more complex functions.

Here are a few examples of the use of these functions:

```
$   (SUM (2 6 4))          (user)
12                         (LISP)
$   (COUNT (2 6 4))        (user)
3                          (LISP)
```

```
$   (AVERAGE (2 6 4))      (user)
(4 . 0)                    (LISP)
```

MuLISP does not support noninteger arithmetic, so the output of the DIVIDE function in AVERAGE is the integer quotient (4) and the remainder (0), which just happens to be the same as 4.0.

The GO Statement

MuLISP does not support the GO statement, but most other versions of LISP do. The GO statement is implemented in conjunction with the PROG function, which defines subprograms with local variables. I will not go into much detail about this facility, but here is how the function COUNT in Fig. 8-8 might look using the GO statement:

```
(DEFINE COUNT2 (LAMBDA (L)
  (PROG (N)
        (SETQ N 0)
  LOOP
        (COND ((NULL L) RETURN
N)))
        (SETQ N (ADD1 N))
        (SETQ L (CDR L))
        (GO LOOP)) ))
```

In this example, N is a local variable used to keep a tally of the number of elements of the list as they are processed. The value of N is returned when there is no more elements to count.

The GO function is not really necessary. Almost always there is a way to accomplish the task using recursion, as in the case of the COUNT function. Why then have a GO function? The answer is efficiency. Recursion has a certain amount of overhead associated with it. With each recursive call, LISP must keep track of the status of the function and its variables. When the recursion is deep, the overhead in extra storage requirements and processing time can be appreciable. Iterative loops using the GO function require much less overhead and can be processed faster. For simple functions such as are illustrated in this book, however, the difference is not significant.

Loops

LISP does not provide directly for any kind of looping other than recursive looping and looping using the GO statement. MuLISP, however, does provide a powerful looping construct to compensate for the lack of the GO function. This function is called LOOP and is a very general and very powerful form of conditional loop.

The MuLISP function consists of the word LOOP followed by a series of lists. Each list is called a task. At least one of these tasks must begin with a predicate (conditional expression). A task is said to begin with a predicate if the CAR of the CAR of the task is an atom. The tasks within the body of the loop are evaluated consecutively until a task with a non-NIL predicate is found, as in a COND function. The difference is that if all the predicates evaluate to NIL, execution starts again with the first task in the LOOP function.

An example of the LOOP function is shown in Fig. 8-9. The COUNT3 function counts the number of top-level elements in a list, just as the function COUNT of Fig. 8-8 and the function COUNT2 shown above do. Note that COUNT3 has an extra argument (N) following LAMBDA. This is the way MuLISP provides for local variables within a function. The local variable N is initialized to zero at the beginning of the function.

The LOOP function in COUNT3 contains only one predicate, which checks to see whether or not the list L is empty. If it is, that is, if (NULL L) has the value T, LOOP returns the current value of N. If it is not, one is added to the value of N, and L is set to its CDR. Eventually L will be empty; this will occur just as the last element of L has been counted.

The natural question to ask at this point is,

"When should I use recursion and when should I use iteration?" If efficiency is not an issue, you should use whichever seems easier. If efficiency is important for an application, and if all that you need to do is to step through the elements of a list one at a time, iteration should be used.

DATA STRUCTURES

The building blocks for data structures in LISP are atoms, lists, and property lists. From these data structures of arbitrary complexity can be constructed. Advanced data structures such as queues and trees are easily implemented using lists. The use of advanced data structures is, however, beyond the scope of this book.

Arrays

LISP does not directly support arrays. An array can be readily emulated in LISP, however, using a list. You have already seen that CAR retrieves the first element of a list, CADR the second element, and CADDR the third element. A function can easily be written to retrieve the Ith element of a list. The function RETRIEVE shown in Fig. 8-10 is such a function. RETRIEVE retrieves the Ith element of the list A. I therefore corresponds to the subscript of the array.

Association Lists

It is not terribly useful to emulate arrays in LISP. There is usually another data structure that can do the job as well or better. One such data structure is the *association list*.

In an array, the value of an element is associated with a subscript. If X(1) has the value 13,

```
(DEFINE COUNT3 (LAMBDA (L N)
  (SETQ N 0)
  (LOOP
    ((NULL L) N)
    (SETQ N (ADD1 N))
    (SETQ L (CDR L)) ) ))
```

Fig. 8-9. The MuLISP LOOP function.

```
(DEFINE RETRIEVE (LAMBDA (I A)
  (COND
    ((EQ I 1)
     (CAR A) )
    (T (RETRIEVE (SUB1 I) (CDR A))) ) ))
```

Fig. 8-10. A function to retrieve the Ith item from a list.

you are associating the value 13 with the subscript 1. It is often simpler to associate a value with a name, which I will call a *key value*. In this case suppose X(1) represents the age of a person named Nat. You can associate the name Nat and the value 13 together in a list, such as (NAT 13). You could also add some other value, such as a gender indicator (M or F). Suppose there is another person named Heather, who is 9 years old. You can now form an association list as follows:

((NAT 13 M) (HEATHER 9 F))

LISP provides the built-in function ASSOC to retrieve data from association lists. Suppose the above list is called ALIST. ASSOC can be used to retrieve the sublist that has the key value NAT. Here is how:

$ (ASSOC NAT ALIST)   (user)
(NAT 13 M)   (LISP)

The key value is always the CAR of a sublist. In this case, Nat's age can be retrieved with CADR, and his gender with CADDR. If there were more elements in the sublist, the function RETRIEVE in Fig. 8-10 could be used.

When necessary, association lists can also be used within each sublist. Here is an example:

((NAT (AGE 13) (SEX M)) (HEATHER (AGE 9) (SEX F)))

If this list were called BLIST, you could retrieve Nat's age by typing the following:

$ (ASSOC AGE   (user)
   (ASSOC NAT BLIST))
(AGE 13)   (LISP)

Again, CADR could be used to extract the age itself.

The second version of the calendar program, shown in Fig. 8-7, is a good example of the use of recursion in LISP, but it would have been easier to use the function ASSOC. The list MLIST in Fig. 8-7

is organized as an association list. The month name is the key value and the number of days in the month is the associated value.

Once MLIST is in existence (recall it was created by the function INIT), values can be retrieved from it as follows:

$ (ASSOC SEPTEMBER   (user)
MLIST)
(SEPTEMBER 30)   (LISP)
$ (CADR (ASSOC JULY   (user)
MLIST))
31   (LISP)

```
(DEFINE CALENDAR (LAMBDA (M)
  (COND
    ((EQ M (QUOTE FEBRUARY))
     (FEB) )
    ((NULL MLIST) NIL)
    ((CADR (ASSOC M MLIST))) ) ))


(DEFINE FEB (LAMBDA ()
  (PRINT (ENTER THE YEAR))
  (SETQ YR (RATOM))
  (COND
    ((EQ (REMAINDER YR 4) 0) 29)
    (T 28) ) ))


(DEFINE INIT (LAMBDA ()
  (SETQ MLIST ((JANUARY 31)
               (MARCH 31)
               (APRIL 30)
               (MAY 31)
               (JUNE 30)
               (JULY 31)
               (AUGUST 31)
               (SEPTEMBER 30)
               (OCTOBER 31)
               (NOVEMBER 30)
               (DECEMBER 31))) ))
```

Fig. 8-11. The Calendar program, Version 3.

212

ASSOC returned the first sublist of MLIST whose CAR was the name of the month. To extract the number of days in that month, the CADR function was used.

Figure 8-11 shows still another version of the calendar program, this time using the ASSOC function. Note that this version of the calendar program is nonrecursive. Also note that only one argument is needed, as in the following:

```
$   (CALENDAR JULY)          (user)
31                           (LISP)
```

Property Lists

Earlier in this chapter we discussed property lists in LISP. You may be wondering why the things that were done in the previous section using association lists couldn't have been done with property lists. The answer is that you could easily have used property lists.

Consider the example of the age and gender of an individual. You could type the following to establish these values:

```
(PUT NAT AGE 13)
(PUT NAT GENDER M)
```

The following could then be used to retrieve these values:

```
$   (GET NAT AGE)            (user)
13                           (LISP)
$   (GET NAT GENDER)         (user)
M                            (LISP)
```

You have thus seen that some functions can be served by either a property list or an association list. Which to use is largely a matter of preference.

Records

In Chapter 2 we discussed the concept of a record. A record contains related information, such as the name and age of an individual or the name of a month and the number of days in that month. You have thus already seen examples of the use of records in LISP. Lists provide a convenient means of grouping related information into records.

Chapter 2 discussed an example of the structure of a group of records, each containing the name of a student and that student's scores on a series of tests. Conventional languages such as BASIC or Pascal require that such structures be defined rigidly in advance. The number of records and the number of test scores must be specified. In LISP this is not necessary; lists are flexible building blocks for more complex data structures.

The following LISP expression creates a structure containing the names and test scores of two students:

```
(SETQ CLASS (((JOHN DOE) (95 87 100
93))
    ((MARY SMITH) (98 85 95 88))))
```

The various elements of this structure can be retrieved in an ad hoc fashion as in the following examples:

```
$   (CAR CLASS)              (user)
((JOHN DOE) (98 87 100       (LISP)
93))
$   (CADR CLASS)             (user)
((MARY SMITH) (98 85 95      (LISP)
88))
$   (CAAR CLASS)             (user)
JOHN DOE)                    (LISP)
$   (CDAAR CLASS)            (user)
(DOE)                        (LISP)
$   (CAR (REVERSE (CAAR      (user)
CLASS)))
DOE                          (LISP)
$   (CAR (CADAR CLASS))      (user)
95                           (LISP)
```

This last example is the first test score of the first student.

While the above examples are certainly illustrative, retrieving information in that manner would get tedious rather quickly. Imagine what you would

```
(DEFINE ROSTER (LAMBDA (CLASS)
 (PRINT (CAAR CLASS))
 (COND
   ((NOT (NULL (CDR CLASS)))
    (ROSTER (CDR CLASS)) ) ) ))


(DEFINE CLASSBOOK (LAMBDA (CLASS)
 (COND
   ((NULL CLASS) NIL)
   (T (PRINT (CAR CLASS)) (CLASSBOOK (CDR CLASS))) ) ))


(DEFINE SCORES (LAMBDA (N)
 (CADR (RETRIEVE N CLASS)) ))


(DEFINE TEST (LAMBDA (I N)
 (RETRIEVE I (SCORES N)) ))
```

Fig. 8-12. The Classbook program.

have to write to get the fourth test score of the fourteenth student in a larger class. A better way is needed.

A better way is to write LISP functions to do the work. A set of basic functions would include the following:

1. A function to print out a class roster.
2. A function to print out a classbook, including names and test scores.
3. A function to retrieve the Ith record of the list.
4. A function to retrieve the record that matches a given student name.
5. A function to retrieve the test scores of the Nth student.
6. A function to retrieve the Ith test score of the Nth student.

The function RETRIEVE in Fig. 8-10 will take care of requirement number 3. The built-in function ASSOC will take care of requirement number 4. Functions to take care of requirements 1, 2, 5, and 6 are shown in Fig. 8-12.

To obtain a roster of the class, type the following:

(ROSTER CLASS)

The function will print out the names in order, followed by NIL, which signifies the end of the list. To obtain a classbook type the following:

(CLASSBOOK CLASS)

The following sequence illustrates the use of the functions to satisfy requirements 5 and 6:

```
$  (SCORES 1)          (user)
(95 87 100 93)         (LISP)
$  (TEST 2 1)          (user)
87                     (LISP)
```

The first example retrieves the scores of the first student. The second example retrieves the score on test number 2 of student number 1.

214

Ordered Lists

Chapter 2 showed how ordered lists could be implemented using arrays in a language such as BASIC, which does not directly support linked lists. Because the list is an integral feature of LISP, it is not necessary to emulate linked lists. Neither is it necessary to worry about the links between list elements nor any special end-of-list indicator; these functions are handled by LISP without direct involvement by the user.

The list illustrated in Chapter 2 consisted of first names. Initially the list contained the names Bob, Ernie, and Jim. The following expression would create such a list in LISP:

(SETQ L (BOB ERNIE JIM))

Recall that the list is to be maintained in alphabetical order. Functions are needed to insert and delete names from the list. These functions are shown in Fig. 8-13.

The basis for ordering the names in the list is

```
(DEFINE INSERT (LAMBDA (NAME L)
  (COND
    ((NULL L)
      (LIST NAME) )
    ((LTEQ NAME (CAR L))
      (CONS NAME L) )
    (T (CONS (CAR L) (INSERT NAME (CDR L)))) ) ))



(DEFINE DELETE (LAMBDA (NAME L)
  (COND
    ((NOT (MEMBER NAME L)) L)
    ((EQ NAME (CAR L))
      (CDR L) )
    (T (CONS (CAR L) (DELETE NAME (CDR L)))) ) ))



(DEFINE LTEQ (LAMBDA (A B)
  (COND
    ((LESSP (ASCII A) (ASCII B)) T)
    ((GREATERP (ASCII A) (ASCII B)) NIL)
    ((AND
        (EQ (ASCII A) (ASCII B))
        (AND
          (EQ 1 (LENGTH A))
          (EQ 1 (LENGTH B)) ) ) T)
    (T (LTEQ (DROP1 A) (DROP1 B))) ) ))



(DEFINE DROP1 (LAMBDA (WORD)
  (COMPRESS (CDR (EXPLODE WORD))) ))
```

Fig. 8-13. Insertion and deletion with an ordered list.

the ability to determine whether one name comes before another alphabetically. The LISP functions LESSP and GREATERP cannot be used directly, because they must have numeric arguments. The ASCII function must be used to convert a name to a number so that LESSP and GREATERP can be used. ASCII returns the numeric code that corresponds to the first letter in a name.

The process of comparing two names for alphabetic precedence is more difficult than it might seem. The function LTEQ in Fig. 8-13 provides this capability. It returns T if its first argument is Less Than or EQual to its second argument, and NIL otherwise. If the first letters of each word are different, the process is easy. If they are the same, you must first check to see if they are the only letters in each word. If they are, the words are equal, and T is returned. Otherwise, the function drops the first letter of each word and calls itself recursively.

The process of dropping a letter from a word is accomplished by the separate function DROP1, also shown in Fig. 8-13.

With these preliminaries out of the way, we can discuss the functions INSERT and DELETE, which are also shown in Fig. 8-13. INSERT inserts the name given as its first argument into the list given as its second argument. There are three possible cases for INSERT. In the first case, the list is empty, so INSERT returns the name in the form of a list. In the second case, the name comes before the first name of the list, so CONS is used to put the name first in the list. In the third case, CONS is used to combine the CAR of the list with the results of recursively applying INSERT to the CDR of the list.

DELETE is quite similar. If the name to be deleted is not a member of the list, the list is returned intact. (Note: MEMBER is a primitive LISP function.) This line also covers the case in which the list is empty. If the name is equal to the CAR of the list, the CDR of the list is returned. Otherwise, CONS is used to combine the CAR of the list with the results of recursively applying DELETE to the CDR of the list.

Here are a few examples of the use of these functions. You should note that the list must be created with SETQ before anything is inserted to or deleted from it. Setting it to NIL is sufficient.

$ L	(user)
(BOB ERNIE JIM)	(LISP)
$ (INSERT JERRY L)	(user)
(BOB ERNIE JERRY JIM)	(LISP)
$ L	(user)
(BOB ERNIE JIM)	(LISP)
$ (SETQ L (INSERT JERRY L))	(user)
(BOB ERNIE JERRY JIM)	(LISP)
$ L	(user)
(BOB ERNIE JERRY JIM)	(LISP)
$ (SETQ L (DELETE ERNIE L))	(user)
(BOB JERRY JIM)	(LISP)

Notice that a LAMBDA (call by value) function does not change its arguments. To make the insertion "permanent," you had to use SETQ.

FILE HANDLING

MuLISP allows the reading and writing of sequential text files and system files. There is no provision for direct-access disk files.

Sequential disk files are created by using the WRS (WRite Select) function to divert text that would ordinarily go to the screen to the disk. These files can be read in by using the RDS (ReaD Select) function to take input from a disk file rather than from the keyboard. A file that is to be read in from disk should have (RDS) as the last record of the file. Without this the system will attempt to continue to read from the disk file rather than from the keyboard.

The following causes a file to be read in from disk:

```
(RDS X Y A)
```

Data that is read in from disk is evaluated as if it were being typed from the keyboard. It is therefore easy to read in function definitions, but it is difficult to read in data and associate the data with a variable. Advanced LISP programmers could write a special evaluation function for this purpose. Another way to store and retrieve data would be to store it as a function which, when evaluated, assigns the value of the data to the appropriate variable name. Both of these methods are beyond the scope of this book.

MuLISP uses the concept of a *workspace*. All the functions that are created or are read in during an interactive session reside in the system memory in an area called a workspace. Free variables (such as the list L in the preceding example) also reside in the workspace. Anything that resides in the workspace is accessible to an interactive user.

A workspace can be saved intact as a system file using the SAVE function. It can be reloaded intact using the LOAD function. The workspace includes functions and free variables. The MuLISP user therefore does not need to read or write text files, as both programs and data can be stored as system files. The classbook program in Fig. 8-12 could be used to maintain records, and the records could be saved as part of the workspace at the end of each session.

GRAPHICS

LISP has no inherent graphics capabilities. The Apple version of MuLISP provides access to the Apple's low-resolution graphics, but not its high-resolution graphics. In keeping with the intention of this book to avoid machine-dependent functions as much as possible, this topic will not be pursued further.

COMPREHENSIVE SAMPLE PROGRAM

The sample programs shown thus far in this chapter have been rather short. While they convey how individual features of LISP are used, they do not adequately convey how larger, more complex LISP programs are put together. For that reason, a comprehensive sample program is included in the chapter.

The comprehensive sample program maintains a list of names and addresses in alphabetical order by name. It functions as sort of an electronic address book. The program permits records to be added to the list, deleted from the list, reviewed on the screen, and listed to a printer. The program is shown in Fig. 8-14.

The data for this program is not stored in a separate file, as in the corresponding programs in most of the other languages presented in this book. The data is instead stored in a free variable called ALIST. The data is saved on disk as part of the workspace by the function SAVE. It is reloaded as part of the workspace by the function LOAD. The user must therefore remember to save the workspace at the end of each interactive session. A disadvantage of this method is that the amount of data that can be handled by the program is limited by the amount of computer memory available.

This program does not include a DUMP function. The DUMP function was included in the corresponding programs in some of the other languages in order to permit the user to see and examine the linkages between records. This is unnecessary in LISP for two reasons. First, there are no visible linkages in LISP data structures because LISP takes care of such details out of sight of the user. Second, because the data resides in the workspace, the user can interactively print the data out for inspection without the assistance of a program.

You may have noticed that this program is much shorter than the corresponding program in BASIC, Pascal, and most of the other languages covered in this book. This is due largely to the fact that the basic data structure of the program is the list, and LISP was designed for processing lists. The language takes care of most of the housekeeping details that must be taken care of by the programmer when other languages are used.

Earlier I pointed out as a disadvantage of LISP the fact that the user has to remember to save the workspace at the end of a session in which the data is updated. A compensating advantage of LISP is that the programmer does not have to specify the length of each data field in advance. In Pascal, for example, the programmer would have to specify that the street address field could not exceed 20 characters in length. If a particular street address required more than 20 characters, the user would have to abbreviate names or be out of luck. Not so

```
(DEFINE BOOK (LAMBDA ()
  (COND
    ((ATOM AB)
      (SETQ AB NIL) ) )
  (SETQ BLANK " ")
  (SETQ C (MENU))
  (COND
    ((EQ C 1)
      (ADDREC) )
    ((EQ C 2)
      (REVIEW AB) )
    ((EQ C 3)
      (LISTFILE AB) ) )
  (COND
    ((EQ C 4) EXIT)
    (T (BOOK)) ) ))


(DEFINE MENU (LAMBDA ()
  (CLEARSCREEN)
  (PRINT "1)  ADD TO FILE")
  (TERPRI 1)
  (PRINT "2)  REVIEW FILE ON SCREEN")
  (TERPRI 1)
  (PRINT "3)  LIST FILE TO SCREEN OR PRINTER")
  (TERPRI 1)
  (PRINT "4)  QUIT")
  (TERPRI 2)
  (PRIN1 "SELECT 1, 2, 3, OR 4: ")
  (SETQ C (RATOM))
  (COND
    ((NOT (NUMBERP C))
      (MENU) )
    ((LESSP C 1)
      (MENU) )
    ((GREATERP C 4)
      (MENU) )
    (T C) ) ))


(DEFINE ADDREC (LAMBDA ()
  (CLEARSCREEN)
  (WLIST (ADD RECORDS TO THE FILE))
```

Fig. 8-14. LISP Address Book. (Continued on page 219.)

```
      (TERPRI 1)
      (WAIT)
      (GETRECS) ))


(DEFINE GETRECS (LAMBDA (R)
  (SETQ R (GETENTRY))
  (COND
    ((NOT (NULL R))

      (SETQ AB (INSERT R AB))
      (GETRECS) ) ) ))


(DEFINE INSERT (LAMBDA (R AB)
  (COND
    ((NULL AB)
      (LIST R) )
    ((LTEQ (CONCATKEY R) (CONCATKEY (CAR AB)))
      (CONS R AB) )
    (T (CONS (CAR AB) (INSERT R (CDR AB)))) ) ))


(DEFINE GETENTRY (LAMBDA ()
  (CLEARSCREEN)
  (WLIST (FOLLOW EACH ENTRY WITH """/""" (RETURN)))
  (WLIST ("""/""" AT THE BEGINNING OF ANY ENTRY TERMINATES INPUT))
  (SETQ COL 1)
  (SETQ ROW 5)
  (GOTOXY COL ROW)
  (PROMPT ((LAST NAME:) (FIRST NAME:) (ADDRESS:) (CITY:) (STATE:) (ZIP:)
      (PHONE:)))
  (SETQ COL 15)
  (SETQ INCR 2)
  (READLIST L 7 COL ROW INCR) ))


(DEFINE PROMPT (LAMBDA (L)
  (COND
    ((NULL L) NIL)
    (T (WLIST (CAR L)) (TERPRI 1) (PROMPT (CDR L))) ) ))


(DEFINE READLIST (LAMBDA (L N COL ROW INCR TL)
  (COND
```

```
                    ((ZEROP N) L)
                    (T (GOTOXY COL ROW)
                       (SETQ TL (RLIST TL))
                       (COND
                          ((NULL TL) NIL)
                          (T (READLIST (REVERSE (CONS TL (REVERSE L)))
                             (SUB1 N) COL (PLUS ROW INCR) INCR)))))
                    ) ))


            (DEFINE LTEQ (LAMBDA (A B)
              (COND
                ((LESSP (ASCII A) (ASCII B)) T)
                ((GREATERP (ASCII A) (ASCII B)) NIL)
                ((AND
                    (EQ (ASCII A) (ASCII B))
                    (AND
                      (EQ 1 (LENGTH A))
                      (EQ 1 (LENGTH B)) ) ) T)
                (T (LTEQ (DROP1 A) (DROP1 B))) ) ))
            (DEFINE CONCAT (LAMBDA (N1 N2)
              (COMPRESS ((CAR N1) BLANK (CAR N2))) ))


            (DEFINE CONCATKEY (LAMBDA (R)
              (CONCAT (RETRIEVE 1 R) (RETRIEVE 2 R)) ))


            (DEFINE REVIEW (LAMBDA (L)
              (COND
                ((NULL L)
                  (WAIT) )
                (T (TERPRI 1)
                   (LISTREC (CAR L))
                   (TERPRI 2)
                   (PRINT ("1:" GET NEXT RECORD))
                   (PRINT ("2:" DELETE THIS RECORD))
                   (PRINT ("3:" QUIT))
                   (TERPRI 1)
                   (PRIN1 (SELECT 1 2 OR "3:"))
                   (SETQ C (RATOM))
                   (COND
                      ((EQ C 1)
```

Fig. 8-14. LISP Address Book. (Continued on page 221.)

```
                              (REVIEW (CDR L)))
                   ((EQ C 2)
                      (SETQ AB (DELREC (CAR L) AB)) (REVIEW (CDR L)))
                   ((EQ C 3) NIL)
                   (T (REVIEW L))))
       ) ))


(DEFINE LISTREC (LAMBDA (R)
   (TERPRI 1)
   (WLIST (LIST (CAADR R) (CAAR R)))
   (WLIST (RETRIEVE 3 R))
   (WLIST1 (RETRIEVE 4 R))
   (WLIST ((CAR (RETRIEVE 5 R)) BLANK (CAR (RETRIEVE 6 R))))
   (WLIST (RETRIEVE 7 R)) ))


(DEFINE LISTFILE (LAMBDA (F)
   (SETUP)
   (LISTF F)
   (SETQ LPRINTER NIL)
   (TERPRI 1)
   (WAIT) ))


(DEFINE LISTF (LAMBDA (F)
   (COND
      ((NULL F) NIL)
      (T (LISTREC (CAR F)) (LISTF (CDR F))) ) ))
 (DEFINE SETUP (LAMBDA ()
    (CLEARSCREEN)
    (PRINT (SEND OUTPUT TO SCREEN OR PRINTER?))
    (PRIN1 (TYPE """S""" FOR SCREEN OR """P""" FOR PRINTER:))
    (SETQ C (RATOM))
    (COND
       ((EQ C P)
         (SETQ LPRINTER T) )
       (T (COND ((NOT (EQ C S)) (SETUP)))) ) ))


(DEFINE DELREC (LAMBDA (R L)
   (COND
      ((NULL L) L)
```

```
        ((EQUAL R (CAR L))
          (CDR L) )
        (T (CONS (CAR L) (DELREC R (CDR L)))) ) ))


(DEFINE RLIST (LAMBDA (L W)
  (SETQ W (RATOM))
  (COND
    ((EQ W (QUOTE /)) L)
    (T (RLIST (REVERSE (CONS W (REVERSE L))))) ) ))


(DEFINE WLIST (LAMBDA (L)
  (COND
    ((ATOM (CAR L))
      (PRIN1 (CAR L))
      (SPACES 1) )
    (T (WLIST (CAR L))) )
  (COND
    ((NULL (CDR L))
      (TERPRI)
      BLANK )
    (T (WLIST (CDR L))) ) ))


(DEFINE WLIST1 (LAMBDA (L)
  (COND
    ((NULL L) BLANK)
    (T (PRIN1 (CAR L)) (SPACES 1) (WLIST1 (CDR L))) ) ))


(DEFINE CLEARSCREEN (LAMBDA ()
  (PRIN1 (ASCII 27))
  (PRIN1 (ASCII 42))
  BLANK ))


(DEFINE GOTOXY (LAMBDA (COL ROW)
  (PRIN1 (ASCII 27))
  (PRIN1 (ASCII 61))
  (PRIN1 (ASCII (PLUS 31 ROW)))
  (PRIN1 (ASCII (PLUS 31 COL)) BLANK) ))
```

Fig. 8-14. LISP Address Book. (Continued on page 223.)

```
(DEFINE PUTXY (LAMBDA (MSG COL ROW)
 (GOTOXY COL ROW)
 (PRIN1 MSG)
 BLANK ))


(DEFINE DROP1 (LAMBDA (WORD)
 (COMPRESS (CDR (EXPLODE WORD))) ))


(DEFINE RETRIEVE (LAMBDA (I A)
 (COND
  ((EQ I 1)
   (CAR A) )
  (T (RETRIEVE (SUB1 I) (CDR A))) ) ))


(DEFINE WAIT (LAMBDA ()
 (PRIN1 (PRESS ANY LETTER AND (RETURN) TO CONTINUE))
 (RATOM) ))
```

with LISP. Because each data field is a list, it can be as long or as short as needed.

There are a couple of limitations in the way that MuLISP handles input and output that limit the usefulness of this example program. First, MuLISP requires that list read in from the keyboard be delimited with parentheses. Because this is inconvenient for the user who must type the data into the program, an alternate solution is desirable. One solution is to read in individual words as atoms and assemble them into a list. Because the input functions do not recognize carriage returns at the end of an input line, some sort of delimiter is still needed. My solution was to write the function RLIST, which requires that each line of text be terminated with the / character.

The second limitation is that leading zeros in numeric atoms are suppressed. A zip code such as 01234 is printed as 1234. A telephone number such as 123-0987 is printed as 123-987.

The hierarchical structure of the address book program is shown in the structure chart in Fig. 8-15. The main program is the function called BOOK. The functions called by BOOK are MENU, ADDREC, REVIEW, and LISTFILE, as indicated by the fact that the names of the functions are indented one level from BOOK. Functions called by these functions are indicated by further indentation.

Several common-use utility functions are listed at the bottom of the chart. These include the functions CLEARSCREEN and GOTOXY, which handle machine-specific screen manipulation; WAIT, which holds the display in place until the user responds; and several list utilities. RETRIEVE returns the Ith element of a list. RLIST reads in a list terminated by a /. WLIST writes out a list without the parentheses. It can handle nested lists, printing each on a separate line, and is perhaps the most complex function shown in this chapter. WLIST1 is a simpler version of WLIST that does not output a carriage return after printing the list.

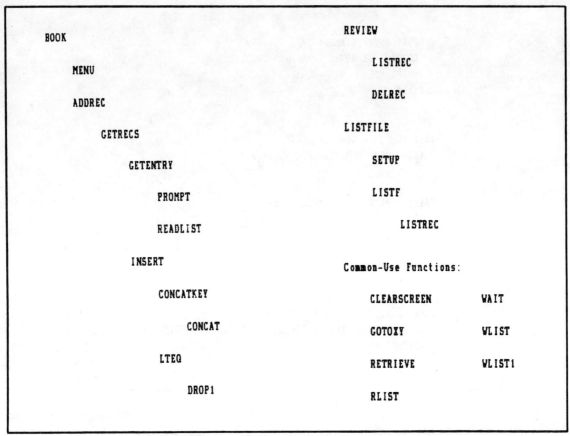

Fig. 8-15. The structure chart for the LISP address Book program.

The function BOOK is rather simple. If the data list AB is an atom (because it has not yet been established as a list) it is initialized as the empty list. The constant BLANK is initialized. The function MENU is called to prompt the user to select the desired function. A COND function is used to invoke the selection function. Another COND is used to determine whether or not the QUIT option was selected. If it was, BOOK returns the word EXIT; otherwise it invokes itself recursively.

The MENU function is straightforward. Note that it validates its input so that it cannot return an invalid menu selection.

The ADDREC function takes care of adding records to the file by calling the function GET-RECS. GETRECS in turn calls GETENTRY to read in a record and then calls INSERT to place that record in its proper place in the list.

The function GETENTRY is responsible for creating the user input screen and reading in the input. This rather tedious task is simplified considerably by the functions PROMPT and READLIST.

PROMPT merely prints a series of list elements on the screen in a column. These form the user prompts. READLIST reads a specified number of user inputs into a list. These two functions are coordinated to work together in presenting a unified input screen. This is a good illustration of how programs can be made simpler by properly breaking down tasks into simpler subtasks.

INSERT relies on the functions CONCATKEY and LTEQ to compare names in order to determine the proper place for a record in a list. CONCAT-KEY concatenates (joins together) last and first names, separated by a blank. To do this, it uses the subfunction CONCAT. The concatenated names are passed to LTEQ, which determines whether or not its first argument is alphabetically Less Than or EQual to its second argument. LTEQ requires the subfunction DROP1, which returns the name of an atom, less its first letter. (Note: LTEQ was previously used in Fig. 8-13.)

The function REVIEW permits the data file to be reviewed on the video screen a record at a time. After each record is displayed, the user is given the choice of going to the next record, deleting the current record, or returning to the main menu. If the user chooses to delete the record, the function DELREC is called. (The function DELREC is similar in operation to the function DELETE in Fig. 8-13.)

Individual records are displayed by REVIEW, which calls the function LISTREC. LISTREC accomplishes such mundane tasks as printing the first name before the last name and putting city, state, and zip code all on the same line. The functions WLIST and RETRIEVE are used to accomplish this.

LISTFILE allows the file to be listed in its entirety to either the video screen or to an attached line printer. The function SETUP prompts the user for a selection of output devices. If the printer is selected, the variable LPRINTER is set to T. LISTFILE sets it back to NIL to deselect the printer before exiting.

LISTFILE calls LISTF to take care of the actual listing of the file. LISTF uses LISTREC to print individual records and then calls itself recursively until there are no more records left to list.

Notice that each function that makes up the address book program is quite short. The interactive nature of LISP allows these functions to be developed and tested independently. When a program is intelligently divided into subfunctions, the ability to use these sections independently can greatly facilitate program development.

ADVANTAGES AND DISADVANTAGES OF LISP

Before looking at the advantages and disadvantages of LISP, you need to consider that LISP was developed for a specific purpose: research in the area of artificial intelligence. It was not intended to serve as a general-purpose language. Some of the disadvantages listed below relate to its limitations as a general-purpose language, which is perhaps unfair. It is, however, in keeping with the purpose of this book to point out limitations where they exist.

The principle strength of LISP is the ease with which it handles complex data structures. You have seen how LISP handles lists, association lists, and property lists; LISP also supports trees, queues, and other advanced data structures. This ability to easily handle complex data structures is important in many applications, including those applications that require the organization of large of amounts knowledge. Such applications are often called *expert systems*.

Another strength of LISP is its suitability for interaction. Commands can be executed interactively from the keyboard outside of a program. Program modules can be developed and tested independently and then easily linked together as a system. Programs developed in this manner are relatively easy to maintain and modify.

On the negative side, LISP has relatively primitive facilities for input and output. A list that is to be read from a file or from the keyboard requires delimiters. LISP cannot easily handle the input of data from a sequential file (unless the data is embedded within LISP functions). LISP has no facilities for handling direct-access files. (Note: some implementations of LISP may have extensions which correct these deficiencies.)

Although LISP can handle simple calculations, numeric computation is not among its strengths. Its use of prefix notation is an annoyance to many.

Because LISP functions are stored as lists, LISP is rife with parentheses. The difficulty of matching so many parentheses is another minor annoyance.

LISP provides no built-in features for the formatting of output, such as the PRINT USING statement of BASIC or the FORMAT statement of FORTRAN.

LISP is an interpreted language and as such can be expected to produce programs that execute more slowly than equivalent programs written in a compiled language.

AVAILABILITY

Several versions of LISP are available for microcomputers that run the CP/M operating system, including MuLISP from Microsoft and an inexpensive starter version from the Software Toolworks. A version called P-LISP is available for the Apple microcomputer from Gnosis of Philadelphia, PA. By the time this book is published there will likely be a version of LISP available for the IBM Personal Computer as well.

SUMMARY

LISP is a very powerful language, intended primarily for use in artificial intelligence research. It is also useful for applications that require extensive symbol manipulation (such as symbolic differential calculus) or the organization and application of knowledge (expert systems).

Although LISP is very different from conventional programming languages, it has a simple syntax and is remarkably consistent. Programming in LISP requires the understanding of a few basic concepts such as prefix notation, recursion, and list manipulation. Once these concepts are mastered, programming in LISP is very simple.

Not all applications are suitable for programming in LISP. For appropriate applications, however, a LISP program will probably be much simpler to write than a program in a more conventional language such as BASIC or Pascal. LISP deserves a place in a programmer's bag of tricks.

Chapter 9

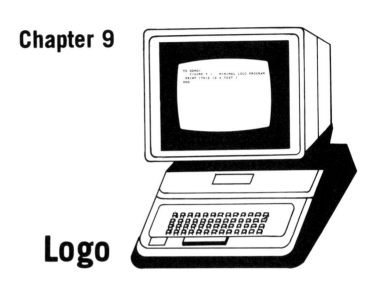

Logo

The Logo language was developed in 1968 by a group of people (W. Feurzeig, S. Papert, M. Bloom, R. Grant, and C. Solomon) working at Bolt, Beranek and Newman, Inc., in Cambridge, Massachusetts, under the sponsorship of the National Science Foundation. Further work on Logo has been done at the Massachusetts Institute of Technology in the Artificial Intelligence Laboratory and in the Division for Study and Research in Education.

The name "Logo" is not an acronym; it was coined by Feureig and is derived from the Greek word meaning "word" or "thought". Because it is not a acronym, it is not written in all capital letters like the names of some other computer languages.

Logo is based on the earlier language LISP (see Chapter 8 for a discussion of the LISP language). In fact Logo is considered by some to be a dialect of LISP.

LISP was created for use in artificial intelligence research. Logo was created for use in intro-ducing young children to computers and computer programming. The intent was to create a programming environment that would encourage learning.

The creators of Logo have succeeded admirably in designing a language suitable for children. Much effort has gone into the user interface, into making the language "friendly" and easy to use. An innovative graphics package with the engaging name Turtle Graphics has been included. An entire programming environment has been developed to support Logo.

The success Logo has achieved with children has led many to believe that it is a toy language, not suitable for use by adults. Nothing could be further from the truth! Underneath the friendly user interface lies the power of LISP, which is very much a serious language. Logo has many serious applications, as I will attempt to illustrate in this chapter. Besides, we adults can use a little friendliness now and then. A language needn't be difficult to use to be powerful.

Because Logo is so different in form from more conventional languages such as BASIC and Pascal, the topics in this chapter are presented in a somewhat different order than in most of the other chapters in this book.

The examples in this chapter have been tested on an Apple II Plus using the Logo implementation by Terrapin, Inc., of Cambridge, Massachusetts.

LOGO PROGRAMS AND PROCEDURES

Logo commands can be executed directly, outside of any program. For example, typing

PRINT [HELLO]

at the keyboard will cause the system to print HELLO on the screen. In this way Logo resembles BASIC.

Logo statements can also be combined into Logo *procedures*. Logo procedures are modules that can stand alone or be invoked by another procedure. A Logo procedure is invoked by typing its name followed by any required arguments.

These procedures can be thought of as building blocks from which larger units can be built. What is different about Logo is that these procedures exist more or less independently in what is called a *workspace*. A workspace consists of whatever procedures and variables have been defined during a session. It is saved to disk as a unit and read back in from disk as a unit. Subject to space limitations, any number of Logo procedures can be in a workspace, whether or not they are related.

The distinction between a Logo program and a Logo procedure is not clear. The same module can serve both as an independent program and as a subprocedure of another program. For purposes of discussion, I could say that a program is a module that is invoked by the user, whereas a procedure is a module invoked by a program or another procedure. It is impossible to distinguish between the two, however, except by context. The term procedure will therefore be used in this chapter to refer to both Logo programs and Logo procedures.

All Logo commands, procedures, and so forth must be written in uppercase. Logo does not support lowercase, even in character strings.

A simple Logo procedure (program) is shown in Fig. 9-1. All this procedure does is print THIS IS A TEST. on the screen. The first line, TO DEMO1 is the procedure heading. Conceptually it can be thought of as saying, "To execute the procedure called DEMO1, do the following." The next line, which begins with a semicolon (;), is a comment line and serves only to document the procedure. The last line (END) serves to terminate the procedure. The body of the procedure in this case consists only of the PRINT statement.

This procedure is executed by simply typing its name, DEMO1, at the console. A procedure can also be executed from within another procedure, as shown in Fig. 9-2. This procedure invokes the procedure in Fig. 9-1.

DATA TYPES

The basic data elements in Logo are numbers, words, and lists. Each is discussed in detail in the paragraphs which follow.

Numbers

Logo numbers can be integers or floating point numbers. Integers can range between approximately plus 2 billion and minus 2 billion. Floating point numbers can range in magnitude from approximately ten to the minus 38th power to ten to the plus 38th power. Floating point numbers are accurate to about 7 digits.

```
TO DEMO1
; FIGURE 9.1:  MINIMAL LOGO PROGRAM
PRINT [THIS IS A TEST.]
END
```

Fig. 9-1. A minimal Logo program.

228

```
TO DEMO2
    ; FIGURE 9.2:   THIS PROCEDURE CALLS DEMO1
    DEMO1
    END
```

Fig. 9-2. A Logo procedure demonstration.

Floating point constants can be written with or without an exponent. Here are several examples:

3.14159
−2.3E2
2.5N1

The first two numbers are written in the same manner as they are in most other languages. The E in the second number indicates a positive power of 10; that number could also be written as

−230.

The N in the third number indicates a negative power of 10; that number could also be written as

0.25.

Logo numbers are *weakly typed*. In other words, there is no strong distinction between integers and floating point numbers. They may be used more or less intercheably within the appropriate ranges. Logo converts freely between integer and floating point numbers as necessary in arithmetic expressions.

Words

A *word* in Logo is a string of characters. A word is written with a leading quotation mark, for example

"HELLO

is a word. A word is terminated by a space or a square bracket; no final quotation mark is required. In fact, the statement

PRINT "HELLO"

will produce

HELLO"

on the screen.

It is possible to have embedded spaces in a word, but it is not common, as the same effect can be achieved using a list.

Here is an example, however, of a word with embedded spaces:

'"THIS IS A WORD WITH EMBEDDED SPACES'

The single quotation mark serve as delimiters.

Logo has commands that allow the individual characters of a word to be manipulated. They are FIRST, BUTFIRST, LAST, and BUTLAST. FIRST produces the first character of a word. Thus,

PRINT FIRST "LOGO

will print the letter L. BUTFIRST produces the word consisting of all but the first character of the word. The statement

PRINT BUTFIRST "LOGO

will print "OGO".

Similarly, LAST produces the last character, and BUTLAST the word consisting of all but the last character. Thus,

PRINT LAST "LOGO
PRINT BUTLAST "LOGO

will produce O and LOG, respectively.

Access to the interior letters of a word is gained indirectly. Procedures for doing so will be discussed later in the chapter.

So far I have discussed numbers and words. There is a relationship between the two: a number is a word, but a word is not necessarily a number. Anywhere a word can appear, so can a number. The commands that are used to manipulate words will also manipulate numbers in the same way. Not surprisingly, however, arithmetic operations cannot be performed with words that are not numbers.

The words "TRUE and "FALSE have special meaning, as will be discussed in the section on logical expressions.

The empty word is indicated by a quotation mark alone, so

PRINT "

will print nothing.

Lists

The remaining type of data element is the list. A list is a sequence of words, separated by blanks. It is delimited by square brackets, as in the following example:

[TODAY IS SUNDAY]

One difference between a word and a list is that while a word is manipulated character-by-character, a list is manipulated word-by-word. Quotation marks are not needed for the words in a list. A list may include numbers.

There is only one space between the words in a list; if you try to put multiple spaces between the words in a list, the system will eliminate them. Multiple spaces must be embedded within a word, as discussed in the section on words.

A list may also contain another list, as in

[[A LIST] IN A LIST]

In this example, the list contains four elements, one of which is a list and three of which are words. The innermost list contains two words. This is a powerful concept which can be used to build more complex data structures. It is discussed in more detail in the section on data structures.

Individual elements in a list can be manipulated by the FIRST, BUTFIRST, LAST, and BUTLAST commands. When used with lists, these commands operate on the elements of the list, which are usually words. Thus,

PRINT FIRST [TODAY IS SUNDAY]

produces TODAY, and

PRINT FIRST [[A LIST] IN A LIST]

produces A LIST. Similarly,

PRINT LAST [TODAY IS SUNDAY]

produces SUNDAY, and

PRINT BUTLAST [[A LIST] IN A LIST]

produces [A LIST] in A.

The empty list is written as "[]".

Procedures for manipulating lists to get at interior elements are discussed in later sections of this chapter.

Other Word and List Operations

I have already examined the operation of the FIRST, BUTFIRST, LAST, and BUTLAST commands. In this section I will examine the operation of the WORD, LIST, SENTENCE, FPUT, and LPUT commands.

The WORD command takes two or more words as inputs and combines them into a single word. Here is an example with two inputs:

PRINT WORD "ONE "TWO

produces

ONETWO

on the screen. Parentheses must be used with more than two inputs. The parentheses must contain the command as well as its arguments. Here is an example with three inputs:

PRINT (WORD "ONE 2 "THREE)

produces

ONE2THREE

on the screen. This example emphasizes that a number is also a word and that a quoted word must be followed by a space before a parenthesis.

The LIST command also deals with two or more inputs, but each input may be a word or a list. The result is a single list. If an input is a list, that list will remain intact as an element of the new list. Here is a simple example:

PRINT (LIST "ONE [TWO THREE] 4)

produces

ONE [TWO THREE] 4

on the screen.

The SENTENCE operation is similar to LIST, but it strips one level of brackets off arguments that are lists. Thus

PRINT (SENTENCE "ONE [TWO THREE] 4)

will produce

ONE TWO THREE 4

on the screen. Applying the same logic to an example with nested lists,

PRINT (SENTENCE [THIS] [IS] [[ALIST] IN A LIST])

will produce

THIS IS [A LIST] IN A LIST

on the display screen.

FPUT and LPUT each require exactly two inputs. The first input of each may be a word or a list, but the second must be a list. The result is a list with the first input inserted into the second input (which was a list to begin with). With FPUT, the first input is inserted at the beginning of the list, and with LPUT, it is inserted at the end.

Distinguishing between the actions of LIST, SENTENCE, and FPUT can be confusing at first. The following table attempts to illustrate the distinctions by example:

COMMAND	RESULT
LIST [A B] [C]	[[A B] [C]]
SENTENCE [A B] [C]	[A B C]
FPUT [A B] [C]	[[A B] C]
LIST [A B] "C	[[A B] C]
SENTENCE [A B]"C	[A B C]
FPUT [A B] "C	*
LIST [[A]] [B]	[[[A]] [B]]
SENTENCE [[A]] [B]	[[A] B]
FPUT [[A]] [B]	[[[A]]B]

The asterisk indicates that an error would result because the second input of FPUT must be a list, not a word.

Mastering these operations is not difficult, but it takes practice.

Variables

Variables in Logo can have values that are numbers, words, or lists. Variables do not need to be explicitly declared.

A variable name can be any legitimate Logo word. To refer to the name of a variable, the leading quotation mark is used. The value of a variable can be obtained in two different ways. Suppose the variable "X has the value 2. The Logo function THING can be used to get at this value. Thus,

PRINT THING "X

will print out 2. Because this is such a common

operation, there is another, abbreviated, way to accomplish the same thing:

    PRINT :X

The colon is usually called *dots* in Logo.

The following would print out the variable name itself:

    PRINT "X

This of course is the same as printing the word "X, emphasizing that the variable name is a word.

THE ASSIGNMENT STATEMENT: MAKE

The MAKE command is used in Logo to assign a value to a variable. When you assign a value to a variable, you are really associating the variable name and a value. Accordingly, the two arguments required by MAKE are a variable name and a value. Here are several examples of assignment statements in Logo:

    MAKE "X 2
    MAKE "Y "HELLO
    MAKE "Z [TODAY IS SUNDAY]
    MAKE "W :X

These examples illustrate several points. The first argument of MAKE is the variable name, written with leading quotation mark. The second argument is the value to be assigned. That value may be a number, a word, a list, or the value of another variable. Recall that to obtain the value of that other variable, you must precede its name with "dots."

To print out the value of these four variables, we could write

    PRINT :X
    PRINT :Y
    PRINT :Z
    PRINT :W

The results would be, respectively,

    2
    HELLO
    TODAY IS SUNDAY
    2

Logo variables may be local to a particular procedure, or they may be global. Global variables in Logo are called *free variables*. A free variable has an existence of its own in a workspace and is accessible from within any Logo procedure in that work space. A free variable keeps its value from one execution of a procedure to the next. When a workspace is saved, the values of all free variables are saved with it.

Typing

    MAKE "X 2

outside of a procedure in Logo creates X as a free variable.

ARITHMETIC EXPRESSIONS

Most arithmetic expressions in Logo use conventional infix notation. The arithmetic operators provided are +, −, *, and /. An example illustrating an arithmetic expression is shown in Fig. 9-3. This example also illustrates the use of an assignment statement in an actual program.

The procedure in Fig. 9-3 is called AREA. It calculates and prints the area of a circle. Notice that the procedure heading includes an argument (:RADIUS). This permits the procedure to be used to compute the areas of circles of differing radii. Typing

    AREA 5

would result in the printing of the area of a circle of radius 5, while

    AREA 10

would result in the printing of the area of a circle of radius 10.

The division operator (/) produces real results, that is

```
TO AREA :RADIUS
  ; FIGURE 9.3:    CALCULATE AREA OF A CIRCLE
  ;                ILLUSTRATE ASSIGNMENT AND ARITHMETIC
  EXPRESSIONS
  MAKE "PI 3.14159
  MAKE "A :PI * :RADIUS * :RADIUS
  PRINT :A
END
```

Fig. 9-3. Logo numerical computations.

PRINT 5/2

will print 2.5. When integer division is desired, the operator QUOTIENT is available. This operator uses *prefix* notation. Thus, to find the integer quotient of 5 and 2, you would write

PRINT QUOTIENT 5 2

and the result would be 2. Similarly, the remainder can be found by typing

PRINT REMAINDER 5 2

and this result would be 1.

Another operator provided by Logo is RANDOM.

PRINT RANDOM 5

will print a random integer between 0 and 4. If desired, the random number generator can be reinitialized using the RANDOMIZE command.

LOGICAL EXPRESSIONS (PREDICATES)

Logical expressions in Logo are called *predicates*. The result of a predicate in Logo is either "TRUE or "FALSE. Thus,

PRINT 2 > 1

would print TRUE, and

PRINT 2 < 1

would print FALSE.

The basic logical operators in Logo are $<$, $>$, and $=$, which have the usual meanings. The operator NOT also has the usual meaning.

Other logical operators provided by Logo include the following:

ALLOF
ANYOF
NUMBER?
WORD?
LIST?
THING?

Each of these uses prefix notation. ALLOF corresponds to a logical AND, while ANYOF corresponds to a logical OR. Each has a default number of two arguments, as in

ALLOF (2 > 1) (:X > :Y)

and

ANYOF (2 > 1) (2 > 3)

If either operator is to have more than two arguments, the entire expression including the operator is enclosed in parentheses. For example,

PRINT (ALLOF (2 > 1) (3 > 2) (4 > 3))

would print TRUE. Note carefully the placement of parentheses.

The operator NUMBER? returns "TRUE if its argument is a number. Similarly, WORD? and LIST? return "TRUE if their arguments are words or lists, respectively. The operator THING? outputs "TRUE if its argument is a variable that has some value associated with it.

INPUT AND OUTPUT

Input and output operations in Logo are rather simple. You have already seen examples of the PRINT statement. PRINT usually takes one argument, whether it be a number, word, or list. It can take multiple arguments when the command and its arguments are enclosed by parentheses. The following two PRINT statements will produce identical results:

```
PRINT [THIS IS A TEST]
(PRINT "THIS "IS "A "TEST )
```

Note that in the former statement, PRINT has but one argument, which is a list. In the latter statement, PRINT has four arguments, each of which is a word. Note carefully the placement of parentheses. Note that the last parenthesis is separated from the preceding word by a space; otherwise Logo would think that the word was TEST) and wouldn't be able to find the closing parentheses.

The PRINT statement always causes a carriage return and line feed to be output after its arguments. If this is not desired, the PRINT1 statement can be used. Otherwise, the two statements are identical. The PRINT1 statement is useful for labeling output, as in the following example:

```
PRINT1 [THE ANSWER IS]
PRINT :X
```

In this example, THE ANSWER IS and the value of X will both appear on the same line of the display.

A procedure may also cause a result to be output using the OUTPUT statement. Here is a simple example:

```
TO DOUBLE :X
    OUTPUT 2 * :X
END
```

If the user types DOUBLE 2, Logo will respond RESULT: 4. The OUTPUT statement also causes an immediate exit from the procedure, regardless of its position within the procedure.

In a later section you will see how the OUTPUT statement can be used to pass data from a procedure to the procedure that called it.

Output can be redirected from the screen to a printer. Unfortunately, the technique for doing so is implementation-dependent. For Terrapin Logo running on an Apple, the command that redirects output is called OUTDEV. For an Apple with a printer interface card in slot number 1, the command

```
OUTDEV 1
```

turns printer output on and

```
OUTDEV 0
```

turns printer output off. When printer output is on, the output of a PRINT statement appears on the printer and on the screen. When printer output is off, the output of a PRINT statement appears only on the screen. An example program is shown in Fig. 9-4.

Logo provides two commands for input from the keyboard. REQUEST reads an input line and returns the result as a list, and READCHARACTER reads a single character and returns it as a word. A common error in Logo is to fail to recognize the form of the input. If a number is desired as an input, a list must be read and the number extracted from the list. This process is illustrated in the program in Fig. 9-5.

This program is a rewrite of the program in Fig. 9-3. It also calculates the area of a circle, but it prompts the user to input the radius from the keyboard. The command REQUEST returns a list

```
TO OUTDEMO
  ; FIGURE 9.4:  DEMONSTRATE OUTPUT TO SCREEN AND PRINTER
  PRINT [THIS GOES TO THE SCREEN]
  OUTDEV 1
  PRINT [THIS GOES TO THE PRINTER]
  OUTDEV 0
END
```

Fig. 9-4. Logo printer output.

from the keyboard, and FIRST REQUEST extracts the first word from that list, which happens to be a number. The MAKE command assigns the value of this number to the variable RADIUS. This form of input takes some getting used to by programmers with experience in more conventional languages such as BASIC or Pascal.

An example of the use of READCHARACTER is illustrated in a later section. It is used much less frequently than REQUEST by most Logo programmers.

CONTROL STRUCTURES

Logo has relatively few control structures when compared to some other languages such as Pascal. Other than simple selection (the IF statement), the most widely-used control structure in Logo is recursion. The counted loop (REPEAT) is primitive, and there is no conditional (while) loop nor case statement.

The absence of these structures can be misleading. It does not mean that Logo is less powerful than languages with these structures. First, the need for more advanced looping structures can be replaced by recursion. Second, the power of Logo is such that if a new control structure (such as a while loop or a more powerful counted loop) is needed, it can be created using the Logo RUN command.

Simple Selection: IF-THEN-ELSE and TEST

The format for the IF-THEN-ELSE statement is as follows:

IF predicate THEN s1 ELSE s2

Recall that a predicate in Logo is equivalent to a

```
TO CIRCLE
  ; FIGURE 9.5:  ILLUSTRATE INPUT USING REQUEST
  PRINT []
  PRINT1 "'ENTER RADIUS '
  MAKE "RADIUS FIRST REQUEST
  MAKE "A 3.14159 * :RADIUS * :RADIUS
  PRINT []
  PRINT [THE AREA OF A CIRCLE]
  ( PRINT1 "'WITH RADIUS ' :RADIUS "' IS ' :A )
  PRINT []
  PRINT []
END
```

Fig. 9-5. Logo console input.

conditional or logical expression in other languages. The symbols s1 and s2 each stand for one or more statements. If the predicate is true, the statements(s) marked s1 are executed; if the predicate is false, the statement(s) marked s2 are executed.

Here is a simple example of an IF-THEN-ELSE statement in Logo:

```
IF :MONTH = 12 THEN MAKE "MONTH 1
MAKE "YEAR
:YEAR + 1 ELSE MAKE "MONTH
:MONTH + 1
```

The major problem with this structure is that the entire IF-THEN-ELSE construct must be typed as one line, as in most versions of BASIC. (It may wrap around to the next line; here it was typed as four lines.) This restriction tends to make the structure hard to read, especially compared to the equivalent statements in Pascal or C.

Because of this problem, Logo offers another way to achieve the same result. Here is the same example using the TEST, IFTRUE, and IFFALSE statements:

```
TEST :MONTH = 12
IFTRUE MAKE "MONTH 1 MAKE "YEAR
:YEAR + 1
IFFALSE MAKE "MONTH :MONTH + 1
```

It should be obvious what this sequence of statements does.

By this time, the reader should be getting accustomed to the quotes and dots of Logo. Recall that preceding a name by quotes indicates that you are referring to the name of the variable, while preceding a name by dots indicates that you are referring to the value of the variable.

Loops: The REPEAT Statement

The only type of loop built in to Logo is the REPEAT statement. The form of this statement is as follows:

```
REPEAT :N [statement(s)]
```

The :N may be either a variable or a constant. The statement or statements within the square brackets are repeated the appropriate number of times. There is no automatic incrementing of a counter variable as in the FOR statement of BASIC or Pascal, nor is there any conditional testing as in a while statement.

A simple example of a REPEAT statement is given in the program in Fig. 9-6. The program prints the integers from 1 to 10 on the screen.

Procedures and Functions

Procedures were discussed in an earlier section because of their similarity to Logo programs. One point that needs to be discussed in more detail, however, is the manner of passing data to procedures.

A Logo procedure, like a procedure in most languages, has a list of arguments. Most languages, however, enclose the list of arguments in parentheses. Logo does not. The arguments are simply written after the name of the procedure, separated by blanks. Arguments of Logo procedures may be numbers, words, or lists.

Logo does not make a clear distinction between functions and procedures. A procedure that contains the OUTPUT statement behaves the same way as a function behaves in other languages and will be called a function in this chapter. The OUTPUT statement was discussed above in the section on input and output.

```
TO COUNT
  ; FIGURE 9.6:   COUNT TO 10
  MAKE "I 1
  REPEAT 10 [PRINT :I MAKE "I :I + 1]
END
```

Fig. 9-6. A Logo counted loop demonstration.

```
TO TYPE
   ; FIGURE 9.7:    EMULATE A TYPEWRITER
   ;                REQUIRES A PRINTER
   MAKE "C READCHARACTER
   OUTDEV 1
   PRINT1  :C
   OUTDEV 0
   TYPE
END
```

Fig. 9-7. Logo Electronic Typewriter, Version 1.

Logo provides the usual built-in functions such as SQRT. To find the square root of 25, you would type

SQRT 25

If the square root of 25 were to be assigned to the variable X, you would type

MAKE "X SQRT 25

The point is that the value returned by the function SQRT can be used in an arithmetic operation.

Suppose you wanted a simple function to divide a number by two. It could be defined as follows:

```
TO HALVE :X
   OUTPUT :X / 2
END
```

This function could then be used in exactly the same way as the built-in function SQRT.

Recursion

As mentioned in Chapter 2, a procedure or function is recursive if it calls or invokes itself. The use of recursion is very common in Logo. Recursion is a powerful technique for the processing of lists and can also be used for looping.

An example of a recursive procedure is shown in Fig. 9-7. The procedure permits a computer with a printer to be used as an electronic typewriter.

Because Logo does not support lowercase, neither does this electronic typewriter. Also, depending on the printer, it may not output anything until a carriage return is typed; then it will print the whole line.

The program reads a character from the keyboard, turns the printer on, prints the character, turns the printer back off, and then calls itself. When the procedure calls itself, the process starts over, repeating the same actions.

There are several features about this procedure that deserve comment. For one thing, it is much shorter than the corresponding program in other chapters. For another thing, it has no provision for stopping itself. Logo programs can be stopped from the keyboard, usually by typing Control-G. It is therefore common to deliberately include infinite loops in Logo programs; it makes the program simpler.

A recursive procedure can also be used in much the same way as a conditional loop would be in another language. Consider, for example, a procedure to count backwards from a given number to zero. Such a program is given in Fig. 9-8.

Notice that the first line of the program (after the comment) is a test for termination. This is not an infinite loop; it terminates as soon as the termination condition is met.

Next, consider a recursive function. The factorial of a positive integer is a mathematical function that is defined recursively. The factorial of zero is defined as one. The factorial of a positive integer N is defined as N times the factorial of N-1. This

237

```
TO COUNTDOWN :N
; FIGURE 9.8:  A RECURSIVE PROCEDURE
;                TO COUNT IN REVERSE
IF :N < 0 THEN STOP
PRINT :N
COUNTDOWN :N - 1
END
```

Fig. 9-8. Recursion in Logo: Count Down.

definition is recursive because it is defined in terms of itself. A recursive implementation of the factorial function is shown in the program in Fig. 9-9.

Recursive functions can also be used to advantage to process words and lists. Figure 9-10 contains a program called TRIANGLE. It accepts a word as an argument and then prints the word repeatedly, dropping the first letter of the word after each iteration. When there are no more letters remaining, the procedure stops. The result looks something like a word triangle that can be read horizontally and vertically.

Consider the problem of summing a list of numbers when it is not known in advance how many numbers there are in the list. The numbers may have been read in from the keyboard or put in the list by another procedure. This process is easy to handle in Logo. A recursive procedure that sums the numbers in the list is shown in Fig. 9-11.

To sum a list of numbers using this procedure, you could type the following:

SUM [5 2 1 7 9 6]

Logo would print out the result, which is 30.

Getting accustomed to using recursion as a matter of routine often takes some time for programmers who first learned to program with a nonrecursive language such as BASIC. Most find, however, that it is well worth the effort.

The GO Statement

The GO statement of Logo corresponds to the GO TO statement of most other languages. It is not often needed, but occasionally can be used to advantage.

Consider again the electronic typewriter program in Fig. 9-7. The program in Fig. 9-12 is a rewrite of this program, this time using a GO statement rather than recursion for looping.

DATA STRUCTURES

The basic Logo data types of numbers, words, and lists support the construction of some very sophisticated data structures. The key to this flexibility is that a list can include other lists as members.

Arrays

One data structure that Logo does not support is the array. Its place is taken by the list. It is quite

```
TO FACTORIAL :N
; FIGURE 9.9:  COMPUTE N FACTORIAL
IF :N = 0 THEN OUTPUT 1
OUTPUT :N * FACTORIAL :N - 1
END
```

Fig. 9-9. Recursion in Logo: Factorial.

238

```
TO TRIANGLE :W
  ; FIGURE 9.10:    PRINT A WORD TRIANGLE
  PRINT :W
  IF NOT BUTFIRST :W = " TRIANGLE BUTFIRST :W
END
```

Fig. 9-10. Recursion in Logo: Word Triangle.

simple to write a procedure to retrieve a particular element from a list (say the third element) as if that list were an array. Here is such a procedure, called GET:

```
TO GET :I :A
IF :I = 1 THEN OUTPUT FIRST :A
OUTPUT GET (:I − 1) BUTFIRST :A
END
```

The first parameter of the function, :I, is equivalent to the subscript of the array. The second parameter, :A, is the list itself.

Records

Chapter 2 discussed the need for records. The example given was that of a record containing the name of a student and his or her scores on up to 20 tests. You can represent the name of the student by a list, and the test scores by another list. These two lists form the first and second elements of another list, which corresponds to the record. Because you are using lists instead of arrays, you need not specify in advance how many test scores there might be.

Because Logo does not require the advance declaration of data structures, this structure is illustrated by example. The following creates a structure containing the records of two students:

MAKE "CLASS [[[JOHN DOE] [95 87 100 93]] [[MARY SMITH] [98 85 95 88]]]

(This must be entered as one line.)

The following illustrates the organization of this data structure: If you type

FIRST :CLASS

the result is

[[JOHN DOE] [95 87 100 93]]

This is the first record of the data structure. If you type

LAST :CLASS

the result is

[[MARY SMITH] [98 85 95 88]]

This is the last record of the data structure. Each record consists, as expected, of a name and several test scores.

Now suppose you wish to extract the name from the first record. This can be accomplished by typing

```
TO SUM :L
  ; FIGURE 9.11:    SUM THE NUMBERS IN A LIST
  IF BUTFIRST :L = [] THEN OUTPUT FIRST :L
  OUTPUT ( FIRST :L ) + SUM BUTFIRST :L
END
```

Fig. 9-11. Recursion in Logo: Sum-Up.

```
TO TYPEGO
  ; FIGURE 9.12:  ELECTRONIC TYPEWRITER WITH GO STATEMENT
  PRINT [WELCOME TO YOUR ELECTRONIC TYPEWRITER.]
  PRINT []
  PRINT [ENTER YOUR TEXT,]
  PRINT [FOLLOWED BY <CONTROL-C>]
  PRINT []
  OUTDEV 1
  LOOP: MAKE "C READCHARACTER
  IF :C = CHAR 3 THEN PRINT [] OUTDEV 0 STOP
  PRINT1 :C
  GO "LOOP
END
```

Fig. 9-12. Logo Electronic Typewriter, Version 2.

PRINT FIRST FIRST :CLASS

The following will extract the last name of the first student:

PRINT LAST FIRST FIRST :CLASS

Similarly, the first test score for this student can be retrieved by the following command:

PRINT FIRST LAST FIRST :CLASS

As you may have noticed, this can get a bit tedious, even if you fully understand what is going on. Imagine what you would have to write in order to print the third test score of the seventeenth student in a larger class. There must be a better way.

As a matter of fact, there is a better way. Logo procedures can be written to take care of all the busy work involved in retrieving records and elements of records from the data structure. Figure 9-13 shows several such procedures, including procedures to do the following:

1. Print out all the student names
2. Retrieve the Ith record in the list
3. Retrieve the record that matches a given student name

4. Retrieve the scores from a given record (as a list)
5. Retrieve the Ith test score from a list of scores

These procedures can be used singly or in combination to handle most requirements for record retrieval. Another set of procedures could be written to handle update requirements. Notice that each procedure is quite short.

To print out all the names, that is, a class roster, type

ROSTER :CLASS

To print out the name and scores of the second student, type

PRINT GET 2 :CLASS

To print out the record of John Doe, type

PRINT GETNAME [JOHN DOE] :CLASS

The scores are separated from the rest of the record using GETSCORES. Individual test scores are retrieved from a list of scores using GETTEST. For example, to print the score received by John Doe on the third test, type

240

```
TO ROSTER :CLASS
 PRINT FIRST FIRST :CLASS
 IF NOT BUTFIRST :CLASS = [] THEN ROSTER BUTFIRST :CLASS
END



TO GET :I :A
 IF :I = 1 THEN OUTPUT FIRST :A
 OUTPUT GET ( :I - 1 ) BUTFIRST :A
END



TO GETNAME :NAME :CLASS
 ; RETURN THE RECORD OF :NAME
 IF :CLASS = [] THEN PRINT [NOT FOUND] OUTPUT [] STOP
 IF :NAME = FIRST FIRST :CLASS THEN OUTPUT FIRST :CLASS
 OUTPUT GETNAME :NAME BUTFIRST :CLASS
END



TO GETSCORES :NAME :CLASS
 IF :CLASS = [] THEN PRINT [NOT FOUND] OUTPUT [] STOP
 IF :NAME = FIRST FIRST :CLASS THEN OUTPUT FIRST BUTFIRST
    FIRST :CLASS
    OUTPUT GETSCORES :NAME BUTFIRST :CLASS
  END



TO GETTEST :I :RECORD
 ; RETRIEVE THE ITH TEST SCORE
 IF :I = 1 THEN OUTPUT FIRST :RECORD
 IF BUTFIRST :RECORD = [] PRINT [THERE AREN'T THAT MANY
 TESTS] OUTPUT [] STOP
 OUTPUT GETTEST ( :I - 1 ) BUTFIRST :RECORD
END



TO CLASSBOOK :CLASS
 PRINT FIRST :CLASS
 IF NOT BUTFIRST :CLASS = [] THEN CLASSBOOK BUTFIRST :CLASS
END
```

Fig. 9-13. Logo Gradebook program.

PRINT GETTEST 3 GETNAME [JOHN DOE] :CLASS

This illustrates how Logo procedures can be combined, with the output of one procedure becoming the input to another procedure.

Linked Lists

Chapter 2 showed how linked lists could be implemented using arrays in a language such as BASIC, which does not directly support linked lists. Because the list is supported directly in Logo, it is not necessary to emulate linked lists. Neither is it necessary to deal directly with the links or an end-of-list indicator, as these are taken care of by the language, safely out of sight of the user.

The list illustrated in Chapter 2 consisted of first names. Initially the list consisted of the names Bob, Ernie, and Jim. The list could be created in Logo as follows:

MAKE "L [BOB ERNIE JIM]

Procedures for adding and deleting names from this list are shown in Fig. 9-14. Using the INSERT procedure you could add Jerry to the list as follows:

MAKE "L INSERT "JERRY :L

Ernie could be deleted from the list by typing the following:

MAKE "L DELETE "ERNIE :L

Logo does not provide directly for the comparison of characters or words. The < and > operators work only with numbers. (The = works with numbers and words.) The INSERT procedure requires word comparison so that the name can be inserted into its proper position alphabetically. A new procedure had to be written to carry out this comparison.

The procedure LTEQ compares its two inputs and determines whether or not its first input is less than or equal to its second input (alphabetically). The comparison is done a letter at a time and uses the ASCII function to convert the letter to its numeric representation. The procedure first attempts to make the comparison based on the first letters of each word. If the first letters are equal, it first checks to see whether one of the words has no more letters. (This would distinguish B from BE, for example.) If not, the procedure is called recursively to deal with the remaining letters of each word.

The logic of the INSERT and DELETE procedures may take some study to understand. Neither is very long, however. Short procedures such as this can be used as building blocks for longer, more complicated procedures.

FILE HANDLING

Logo does not provide facilities for the reading and writing of disk files from within programs. Logo relies instead on the concept of a workspace, as discussed above.

If a Logo program needs to maintain a set of data from one session to the next, it does not need to create a separate disk file. It can instead store the data in free variables within the workspace. Then when the workspace is saved, the free variables are saved along with any procedures that happen to be in the workspace.

You have already seen an example of maintaining data in a free variable in the preceding section on linked lists. The list L is a free variable and can be saved from session to session by saving the workspace along with the procedures INSERT, LTEQ and DELETE.

The command to save a workspace in Terrapin Logo is as follows:

SAVE "WSNAME

where WSNAME is the desired name for the workspace. The workspace can be read back in by typing the following:

READ "WSNAME

GRAPHICS

In the beginning of this chapter I stated that

242

```
TO INSERT :NAME :L
  ; INSERT A NAME IN A LIST
  IF :L = [] THEN OUTPUT SENTENCE :NAME :L
  IF LTEQ :NAME FIRST :L THEN OUTPUT FPUT :NAME :L
  OUTPUT ( SENTENCE FIRST :L INSERT :NAME BUTFIRST :L )
END




TO LTEQ :A :B
  ; DETERMINE WHETHER :A IS LESS THAN OR EQUAL TO :B
  IF ASCII FIRST :A < ASCII FIRST :B THEN OUTPUT "TRUE
  IF ASCII FIRST :A > ASCII FIRST :B THEN OUTPUT "FALSE
  IF BUTFIRST :A = " THEN OUTPUT "TRUE
  IF BUTFIRST :B = " THEN OUTPUT "FALSE
  OUTPUT LTEQ BUTFIRST :A BUTFIRST :B
END




TO DELETE :NAME :L
  ; DELETE A NAME FROM A LIST
  IF :L = [] THEN OUTPUT :L
  IF :NAME = FIRST :L THEN OUTPUT BUTFIRST :L
  OUTPUT SENTENCE FIRST :L DELETE :NAME BUTFIRST :L
END
```

Fig. 9-14. List insertion and deletion in Logo.

Logo was designed for children and has been used extensively by them. At this point you may be wondering why children find list insertion and deletion so fascinating. The fact is, they don't. What attracts children to Logo is the graphics. What keeps their interest is the friendly, interactive environment. Lists and recursion and the other features of Logo are simply means to an end.

The graphics package provided with Logo is called Turtle Graphics. It is very similar to the graphics package of the same name provided as part of the Apple implementation of UCSD Pascal. The main difference is that in Logo, unlike UCSD Pascal, graphics commands can be executed directly from the keyboard.

The central metaphor of Turtle Graphics is the turtle. The turtle is an imaginary creature that can be moved about the screen. He carries with him a pen, which can be "down" so that it leaves a trail, or "up" so that it does not leave a trail. The pen can write with different colors of ink, depending on the capabilities of the computer and video monitor.

Because a turtle has a head, he is always heading in a single direction. The turtle can be moved forward or backward a given number of steps, or he can be turned to the right or left a specified number of degrees. Using combinations of these movements, the turtle can be made to trace out any shape.

The details of turtle graphics may vary slightly from implementation to implementation. The discussion in this section is based on the Terrapin implementation of Logo on the Apple microcomputer.

The graphics mode is entered with the command DRAW. This command clears the screen and displays the turtle as a small triangle in the center of the screen. With the turtle thus displayed, its position and heading are readily observed. The turtle can be hidden from view if desired with the command HIDETURTLE.

The main commands for moving the turtle and changing its direction are FORWARD, BACKWARD, RIGHT, and LEFT. Each command is followed by a number. In the case of FORWARD and BACKWARD, the number represents the number of steps to be taken in the specified direction. In the case of RIGHT and LEFT, the number represents the number of degrees to turn.

Some interesting designs can be made using just these simple commands. Figure 9-15 contains three short Logo procedures that were used to create the patterns shown in Fig. 9-16.

The procedure SETUP in Fig. 9-15 is used to clear the screen and initialize the turtle. The procedure TRI draws a single equilateral triangle. The procedure PATTERN creates a pattern consisting of multiple equilateral triangles.

PATTERN calls TRI to draw a triangle, turns the turtle to the right, then calls itself recursively. The only way to stop the procedure is by typing Control-G. The parameter : N of PATTERN is used to determine how many triangles to draw in one complete revolution. The first design in Fig. 9-16 was created with the following commands:

```
SETUP
PATTERN 6
```

Following the drawing of each triangle, the turtle was turned 360/6 = 60 degrees to the right. There are therefore 6 triangles visible in the pattern.

The second design in Fig. 9-16 was created with the following commands:

```
SET UP
PATTERN 12
```

In this case the turtle turned 360/12 = 30 degrees between triangles. The third design in Fig. 9-16 was created with the following:

```
TO PATTERN :N
 TRI
 RIGHT 360 / :N
 PATTERN :N
END




 TO TRI
 REPEAT 3 [FORWARD 80 RIGHT 120]
END




 TO SETUP
 DRAW
 LEFT 30
 HIDETURTLE
END
```

Fig. 9-15. Logo Turtle Graphics Program.

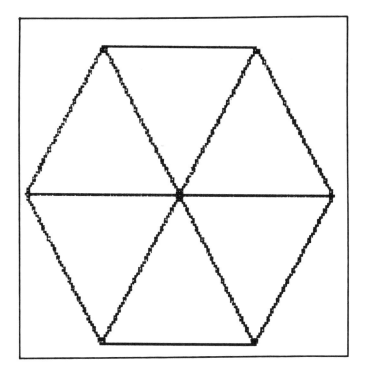

Fig. 9-16 (a). Sample Turtle Graphics output.

Fig. 9-16 (b). Sample Turtle Graphics output.

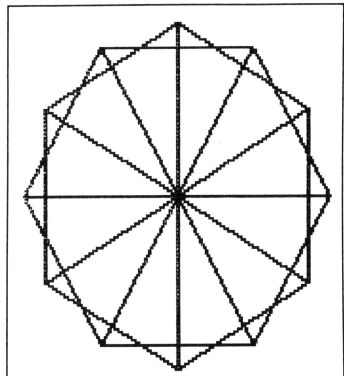

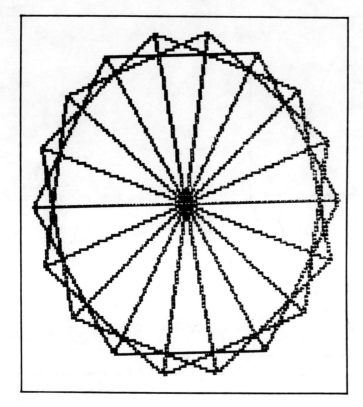

Fig. 9-16 (c). Sample Turtle Graphics output.

SETUP
PATTERN 18

In this case the turtle turned 20 degrees between triangles.

One of the fascinating things about turtle graphics in Logo is that a few short procedures can be used to create such a variety of designs. Given a few short procedures, a child (or even an adult!) can create variation upon variation on the basic theme.

Turtle graphics procedures are easy to write in Logo. It would be a simple matter to write a procedure to create a square instead of a triangle and then to substitute it for TRI in the PATTERN procedure. This would permit the creation of a whole new family of designs. From there, a short procedure could be written to create any regular polygon (triangle, square, pentagon, hexagon) for incorporation into the PATTERN procedure.

I have only touched on the power of turtle graphics in Logo. My intent has been to convey a little of their flavor and a hint at their potential. More extensive coverage of graphics in Logo may be found in almost any of the available books on Logo. A particularly excellent book on Logo is *Logo For the Apple II* by Harold Abelson (Byte/McGraw-Hill, Peterborough, NH, 1982).

COMPREHENSIVE SAMPLE PROGRAM

The example programs shown so far in this chapter have been rather short. One can gain a better appreciation for Logo by examining a longer example, one that does something useful.

The comprehensive example program of this chapter maintains a list of names and addresses in alphabetical order by name. The program permits records to be added to the list, deleted from the list, reviewed on the screen, and listed to a printer. The program is shown in Fig. 9-17.

The list itself is stored in a free variable called AB. The list is not stored in a separate disk file as it is in the corresponding programs in other chapters.

It is instead saved as part of the workspace along with the Logo procedures that comprise the program. The user must therefore remember to save the workspace at the end of a session in which records have been added or deleted. (A Logo user should consult the documentation that came with his or her system for procedures to save and retrieve workspaces.) The disadvantage of this technique is that the size of the address list is limited by the amount of computer memory available.

One feature that this program lacks that is found in the corresponding programs in other chapters is the dump feature. It is not necessary in the Logo version because all the links are hidden from the user. A user who wants to examine the structure of the list can do so interactively.

The most striking feature of this program is that it is only about one third the length of the corresponding programs in most of the other chapters. This is attributable to the fact that Logo directly supports the list as a data structure, making the emulation of a list using arrays and pointers unnecessary. The system takes care of all the housekeeping functions that are taken care of by the program in languages such as BASIC and Pascal.

An advantage of the Logo program over most of the other versions of this program is that the lengths of the individual fields do not have to be specified in advance. This is because each field is a list, and lists can be of any length. In languages such as Pascal and C, the programmer has to specify in advance the length of each field (for example 12 characters for a last name) and reserve the appropriate amount of space. Space allocation is handled by the system in Logo.

The structure of the program is illustrated by the structure chart in Fig. 9-18. The main program is called BOOK. It consists of a control loop that calls the appropriate procedure depending on the option selected interactively. BOOK uses a primitive emulation of a case statement to handle the choices.

The procedure APPEND uses the procedure GETENTRY to read a name and address record from the console and the procedure INSERT to add the record to the list in the proper position. The logic used in the INSERT procedure is similar to that used in the insert procedure of Fig. 9-14. Before doing alphabetic comparisons of names, the first names are concatenated to the end of the last names using the Logo primitive WORD.

Both the REVIEW and the LISTFILE procedures use the procedure LISTREC to print a single record. LISTREC in turn relies on the procedure GET to extract individual elements of the record. GET was first seen in Fig. 9-13.

The REVIEW procedure provides the option of deleting a record by calling the DELETE procedure. The logic for deletion is similar to that seen in Fig. 9-14.

The LISTFILE procedure provides the option of sending the names to a printer as well as seeing them on the screen. This is accomplished by the subprocedure SETUP.

Each of the procedures in this program is quite short. The longest is GETENTRY; this procedure is not involved—only tedious. Its length is governed by the amount of data to be read in from the console and by the need to format the input screen. The substantive procedures such as INSERT and DELETE are only a few lines long.

ADVANTAGES AND DISADVANTAGES OF LOGO

One of the main advantages of Logo is its ease of use. Even young children can learn to program in Logo, almost as soon as they can learn to read. Logo is designed for interactive uses with the user seated at the keyboard. Most other languages (including FORTRAN, COBOL, Pascal, and even BASIC) were designed for batch use with the user interacting by means of keypunch, card reader, and printer.

Logo easily supports data structures of many kinds, including lists, queues, and trees. These data structures are well-suited for the organization of knowledge. The available control structures are well-suited for manipulating these data structures. The result is a language that can accommodate the development of programs that rely upon accumulated knowledge and upon decision making based on that knowledge. In other words, Logo is well-suited

```
TO BOOK
  ; FIGURE 9.17:   ADDRESS BOOK
  ;                MAINTAIN A LIST OF NAMES AND ADDRESSES
  ;                IN ALPHABETICAL ORDER BY NAME
  ;                THE LIST IS THE FREE VARIABLE "AB
  ; []
  IF NOT THING? "AB THEN MAKE "AB []
  LOOP: MAKE "CASE MENU
  IF :CASE < 1 THEN GO "LOOP
  IF :CASE > 4 THEN GO "LOOP
  IF :CASE = 1 THEN APPEND GO "LOOP
  IF :CASE = 2 THEN REVIEW :AB GO "LOOP
  IF :CASE = 3 THEN LISTFILE GO "LOOP
  IF :CASE = 4 THEN STOP
END



TO MENU
  ; DISPLAY MENU AND RETURN 1, 2, OR 3
  CLEARTEXT
  PRINT [1) ADD TO FILE]
  PRINT []
  PRINT [2) REVIEW FILE ON SCREEN]
  PRINT []
  PRINT [3) LIST FILE TO SCREEN OR PRINTER]
  PRINT []
  PRINT [4) QUIT]
  PRINT []
  PRINT []
  PRINT1 [SELECT 1, 2, 3, OR 4: '   ']
  OUTPUT FIRST REQUEST
END



TO APPEND
  ; ADD RECORDS TO THE FILE
  CLEARTEXT
  PRINT [ADD RECORDS TO THE FILE]
  PRINT []
  WAIT
  LOOP: MAKE "E GETENTRY
```

Fig. 9-17. Logo Address Book. (Continued on page 249.)

```
  IF :E = [] THEN STOP
  MAKE "AB INSERT :E :AB
  GO "LOOP
END



TO GETENTRY
  ; PROMPT USER AND RETURN A RECORD
  CLEARTEXT
  MAKE "ROW 5
  MAKE "COL 1
  CURSOR :COL :ROW
  PRINT1 [LAST NAME:]
  MAKE "ROW :ROW + 2
  CURSOR :COL :ROW
  PRINT1 [FIRST NAME:]
  MAKE "ROW :ROW + 2
  CURSOR :COL :ROW
  PRINT1 [ADDRESS:]
  MAKE "ROW :ROW + 2
  CURSOR :COL :ROW
  PRINT1 [CITY:]
  MAKE "ROW :ROW + 2
  CURSOR :COL :ROW
  PRINT1 [STATE:]
  MAKE "ROW :ROW + 2
  CURSOR :COL :ROW
  PRINT1 [ZIP CODE:]
  MAKE "ROW :ROW + 2
  CURSOR :COL :ROW
  PRINT1 [PHONE:]
  MAKE "ROW 5
  MAKE "COL 15
  CURSOR :COL :ROW
  MAKE "E []
  MAKE "E FPUT REQUEST :E
  IF FIRST :E = [] THEN OUTPUT []
  REPEAT 6 [MAKE "ROW :ROW + 2 CURSOR :COL :ROW MAKE "E LP
  UT REQUEST :E]
  OUTPUT :E
END
```

```
TO INSERT :ENTRY :AB
 ; INSERT AN ENTRY IN THE ADDRESS BOOK
 ; IN ALPHABETICAL ORDER
 IF :AB = [] THEN OUTPUT FPUT :ENTRY :AB
 IF BEFORE ( WORD ( FIRST FIRST :ENTRY ) ( FIRST FIRST BUT
FIRST :ENTRY ) ) ( WORD
FIRST FIRST FIRST :AB ) ( FIRST FIRST BUTFIRST FIRST :
AB ) ) THEN OUTPUT FPUT :ENTRY :AB
  OUTPUT FPUT FIRST :AB INSERT :ENTRY BUTFIRST :AB
END




TO BEFORE :A :B
 ; DETERMINE WHETHER :A COMES BEFORE :B ALPHABETICALLY
 IF ASCII FIRST :A < ASCII FIRST :B THEN OUTPUT "TRUE
 IF ASCII FIRST :A > ASCII FIRST :B THEN OUTPUT "FALSE
 IF BUTFIRST :A = " THEN OUTPUT "TRUE
 IF BUTFIRST :B = " THEN OUTPUT "FALSE
  OUTPUT BEFORE BUTFIRST :A BUTFIRST :B
END




TO REVIEW :L
 ; PRINT RECORDS TO SCREEN 1 AT A TIME
 ; ALLOWS DELETION OF CURRENT RECORD
 IF :L = [] THEN PR [] WAIT STOP
 PR []
 LISTREC FIRST :L
 L1: PR []
 PR []
 PRINT [1) GET NEXT RECORD]
 PRINT [2) DELETE THIS RECORD]
 PRINT [3) QUIT]
 PR []
 PRINT1 [SELECT 1, 2, OR 3: '   ']
 MAKE "C FIRST REQUEST
 IF ANYOF ( :C < 1 ) ( :C > 3 ) THEN GO "L1
 IF :C = 1 THEN REVIEW BUTFIRST :L
 IF :C = 2 THEN MAKE "AB DELETE FIRST :L :AB REVIEW BUTFIR
ST :L
END
```

Fig. 9-17. Logo Address Book. (Continued on page 251.)

```
TO LISTREC :ENTRY
 ; DISPLAY A SINGLE RECORD
 PRINT []
 ; FIRST THE NAME
 PRINT1 GET 2 :ENTRY
 PRINT1 "' '
 PRINT GET 1 :ENTRY
 ; NOW THE ADDRESS
 PRINT GET 3 :ENTRY
 ; NOW THE CITY, STATE, AND ZIP CODE
 PRINT1 GET 4 :ENTRY
 PRINT1 "', '
 PRINT1 GET 5 :ENTRY
 PRINT1 "' '
 PRINT GET 6 :ENTRY
 ; NOW THE PHONE NUMBER
 PRINT GET 7 :ENTRY
END




TO DELETE :E :L
 ; DELETES ELEMENT :E FROM LIST :L
 IF :L = [] THEN OUTPUT :L
 IF MATCH :E FIRST :L THEN OUTPUT BUTFIRST :L
 OUTPUT FPUT FIRST :L DELETE :E BUTFIRST :L
END




TO MATCH :A :B
 ; COMPARES TWO LIST ELEMENTS
 OUTPUT ALLOF ( ( GET 1 :A ) = ( GET 1 :B ) ) ( ( GET 2 :
A ) = ( GET 2 :B )
END




TO LISTFILE
 ; LIST FILE TO SCREEN OR PRINTER
 SETUP
 LISTF :AB
 OUTDEV 0
```

```
  PR []
  WAIT
END



TO SETUP


  CLEARTEXT
  L1: PRINT1 [LIST FILE TO S)CREEN OR P)RINTER?]
  MAKE "C FIRST REQUEST
  IF :C = "P THEN OUTDEV 1 ELSE IF NOT :C = "S THEN GO "L1
END



TO LISTF :F
  IF :F = [] STOP
  LISTREC FIRST :F
  LISTF BUTFIRST :F
END



TO WAIT
  PRINT1 [PRESS <RETURN> TO CONTINUE...]
  MAKE "C REQUEST
END



TO GET :I :A
  ; RETRIEVE ITH RECORD OF :A
  IF :I = 1 THEN OUTPUT FIRST :A
  OUTPUT GET ( :I - 1 ) BUTFIRST :A
END
```

Fig. 9-17. Logo Address Book. (Continued from page 251.)

for programs in the field of artificial intelligence.

Logo can handle symbols as well as numbers. It is excellent for those sorts of problems that require the manipulation of words, characters, and other symbols. One such potential application would be symbolic differential calculus.

Another of Logo's principal strengths is in the area of graphics. Complex graphic images are easily created in Logo using Turtle Graphics.

Another plus is the way that Logo procedures can be developed and defined separately, and then can be used together. This means that when a single

```
BOOK
        MENU
        APPEND
                GETENTRY
                INSERT
                        BEFORE
        REVIEW
                LISTREC
                DELETE
                        MATCH
        LISTFILE
                SETUP
                LISTF
                    LISTREC


Common-Use Procedures:


                WAIT
                GET
```

Fig. 9-18. The structure chart for the Address Book program.

procedure is modified, the other procedures in the program do not have to be redefined. This greatly speeds the development of complex programs such as the program in Fig. 9-17.

On the negative side, Logo does not directly support the reading and writing of data files from within programs. Because Logo is an interpretive language, Logo programs are relatively slow in execution.

Although Logo can handle simple calculations, numeric computation is not its main strength. It lacks an exponentiation function, although one can easily be defined.

AVAILABILITY

Versions of Logo are available for several popular microcomputers including the Apple II series, the IBM Personal Computer, the Radio Shack Color Computer, the Commodore 64, and the Texas Instrument TI 99/4A.

SUMMARY

Logo is a very powerful and easy-to-use language. It is well-suited for many applications including graphics, symbol manipulation, artificial intelligence, and general programming.

Logo is easy to learn. Programming in Logo tends to be somewhat different than programming in BASIC, Pascal, or one of the other common languages. This is largely due to the prevalence of recursion as a control structure and to Logo's ability to handle data in lists.

Logo is an excellent choice for both children and adults. It deserves to be much more widely-used than it is at present.

Chapter 10

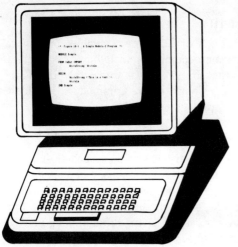

Modula-2

Modula-2 is the newest of the languages presented in this book. It was developed by Niklaus Wirth of the Eidgenossische Technische Hochschule (Federal Institute of Technology), Zurich, Switzerland, and first implemented in 1979. It was first made available to the public in 1981.

Niklaus Wirth is perhaps better known as the creator of the Pascal language. After creating Pascal, Wirth developed an experimental language called Modula. Modula has some interesting features, but it was never intended for widespread use. Modula-2 is the direct descendant of both Pascal and Modula. It could as easily have been called Pascal-2, but Wirth chose Modula-2 because its syntax more closely resembles that of Modula. In any event, programmers who are familiar with Pascal will find many similarities between Pascal and Modula-2.

Modula-2 also has roots in the language Mesa, which Wirth encountered while on sabbatical leave in 1976 at the Xerox Palo Alto Research Center, Palo Alto, California.

The name Modula is an acronym standing for MODUlar LAnguage. The name is customarily written as *Modula-2* rather than *MODULA-2*, so that custom will be followed in this book. Modula-2 is often referred to simply as *Modula*.

Modula-2 is a general-purpose language; it is suitable for most programming applications, including scientific applications, business applications, and systems programming applications. It is particularly well-suited for large, complex applications.

The sample programs of this chapter were tested on an Apple II microcomputer using the Modula-2 implementation by Volition Systems, Del Mar, California. This implementation runs under the UCSD Pascal operating system.

PROGRAM STRUCTURE: THE MODULE CONCEPT

The feature that most distinguishes Modula-2 from other languages is the *module*. The structure of a Modula-2 program is defined in terms of modules. The outermost module corresponds to the main program of other languages. Other modules can be defined within the outermost module. A module usually consists of a group of related procedures (subroutines). Thus the module provides a level of organization that is between the main program and the procedure.

A module can be thought of as a fence around a segment of a program. This fence allows selected variables and procedures to be isolated from the remainder of the program. This reduces the chance of different parts of the program interfering with each other. Data and access to procedures can be passed explicitly from one module to another using the IMPORT and EXPORT statements. These will be described shortly.

A major feature of Modula-2 is that modules can be stored in different files and compiled separately. This greatly facilitates the development and testing of large programs. Once a module has been compiled and tested successfully, it need not be recompiled, no matter how many times the main program is recompiled. With languages that lack this feature, all parts of the program must be recompiled whenever any part of the program is changed. This feature will be illustrated later in the chapter.

A simple example of a Modula-2 program is shown in Fig. 10-1. This program simply prints "This is a test." on the video screen. The first line of the program is a comment, enclosed between the symbols (* and *). It serves to identify the program. The program itself begins with the heading "MODULE Simple;".

An illustration of the modular structure of Modula-2 is found in the next line. The basic input and output routines are implemented as procedures in a separately compiled module called InOut. This module resides in the system library. (With most languages, such routines are embedded within the compiler. The Modula-2 approach improves the portability of the language and keeps the size of the compiler to a minimum. This program needs the procedures WriteString and WriteLn, so it must IMPORT these procedures from the module InOut, as illustrated.

The main body of the program is contained between "BEGIN" and "END Simple." Note that the name of the module follows the END, and that

```
(*  Figure 10-1:  A Simple Modula-2 Program  *)

MODULE Simple;

FROM InOut IMPORT
        WriteString, WriteLn;

BEGIN
        WriteString ('This is a test.');
        WriteLn;
END Simple.
```

Fig. 10-1. A simple Modula-2 program.

both are followed by a period, because this is the last END of the program.

The main body of the program is quite simple, consisting of only two statements. There are several points to note, however. First, Modula-2 is case-sensitive. In other words, "WriteString" is not the same as "Writestring." They differ because the letter s is capitalized in one instance and lowercase in the other. All Modula-2 keywords, such as BEGIN and FROM, must be written with all capital letters. Procedure and variable names can be upper or lowercase, or mixed upper and lowercase.

Second, WriteString can print out exactly one character string. It cannot handle any other data type. It does not even output a carriage return and line feed at the end; WriteLn is needed for that. Similarly, as we shall see, separate output procedures are needed for each data type. There is no generic output statement or procedure such as the PRINT statement of BASIC or the WRITELN statement of Pascal.

More details about the structure of Modula-2 programs will be discussed as they are illustrated in subsequent example programs.

The Volition Systems version of Modula-2 is implemented as an intermediate-code compiler. A Modula-2 source program is compiled to intermediate code (P-code). This intermediate code resembles the assembly language of a hypothetical computer which may or may not exist anywhere. The intermediate code is interpreted at run time. The advantage of this scheme is that the compiler can be easily transported from one computer to another; only the intermediate code interpreter need be rewritten. The disadvantage is that the resulting compiled program may not run as fast as it would if it had been compiled completely into native machine code.

Another implementation of Modula-2 is available from Logitech, Inc., of Redwood City, California. It produces native machine code. Still another version is available from Modula Research Institute of Provo, Utah. It produces intermediate code. Reviews of these three implementations can be found in the issue of *PC Magazine* dated April 3, 1984.

DATA REPRESENTATION

The basic data types in Modula-2 are real, integer, cardinal, char (character), and Boolean (logical). The character strings can be represented as arrays of the CHAR type.

The cardinal type consists of zero and the positive integers. Many situations call for non-negative integers; the cardinal type allows Modula-2 to verify that no negative integers are used in these situations. The smallest number of the cardinal type is 0. The largest number of the cardinal type depends on the system. In most implementations it is 65535. This compares to the usual range for variables of the integer type, which is -32768 to $+32767$.

Like Pascal, Modula-2 includes a provision for defining new data types. For example, there is usually a library module that makes the string type available. Electrical engineers might need a type called COMPLEX; such a type could be easily added in a library module.

Constants

Integer and cardinal constants are represented in the usual way. The Boolean constants are TRUE and FALSE. Real constants include a decimal point and an optional exponent. The following are examples of real constants:

    1.0
    −9.1
    3.2E4

The last example is read, "Three point two times

ten to the fourth power." Modula-2 requires that the E be in the uppercase; a lowercase e is unacceptable.

String constants may be enclosed between either single or double quotation marks. If double quotation marks are used, apostrophes can be used freely within. Similarly, if single quotation marks are used, double quotation marks can be used freely within the string. Here are two examples:

    "Don't give up."
    'He said, "Hello." '

Symbolic constants can be declared and given values. One advantage of this is that programs can be made easier to read when constants are used. For example, a program that computes sales tax could contain the following constant:

    CONST rate = 0.06;

Throughout the program the symbol "rate" could be used wherever the tax rate is needed. Not only does this make the program easier to understand, it also makes the program easier to change when the tax rate changes.

A program that uses a symbolic constant is shown in Fig. 10-2. It simply prints out the value of

```
(* Figure 10-2: Illustrate Constant
    Declaration *)
MODULE Trig;

FROM InOut IMPORT WriteString, WriteLn;

FROM RealInOut IMPORT WriteReal;

CONST  PI = 3.14159;

BEGIN

        WriteString ('PI = ');
        WriteReal   (PI, 12);
        WriteLn;

END Trig.
```

Fig. 10-2. An Illustration of constant declarations.

the constant PI, which is used in geometry and trigonometry. The program imports WriteString and WriteLn from the module InOut, as did the previous program. Because PI is of type REAL, this program must import the procedure WriteReal from the module RealInOut.

The constant declaration follows the import lists. The only other new item in this program is the WriteReal procedure. It requires two arguments; the first is the value to be printed, and the second is the width of the field in which to print it. The number is printed in scientific notation, as follows:

3.1415901E+00

The extra fraction at the end resulted from the inability of the computer to store decimal fractions exactly in its internal binary format.

Variables

All variables must be declared in Modula-2. Variables may be declared at the beginning of a module or at the beginning of a procedure. (Remember that the main program is a module.) Variables are only "visible" within the module or procedure in which they are declared, unless they are specifically exported to another module.

A program illustrating the declaration and use of several variables is shown in Fig. 10-3. This program computes and prints the area of a circle with a radius of 5. Two variables of the real type are declared—**area** and **radius**. A variable of the integer type (i) is declared for illustration purposes, but it is not used in the program.

This program imports its output procedures from the modules Texts and Reals rather than InOut and RealInOut. The output procedures from these modules require an extra argument to specify the destination of the output, which in this case is the console, or video screen. This version of WriteReal also permits real numbers to be written in fixed-point notation, with a specified number of decimal places. In this case the numbers **radius** and **area** are written with four decimal places in fields that are ten characters in width.

```
(* Figure 10-3: Illustrate Variable
   Declarations *)

MODULE Circle;

FROM Texts IMPORT WriteString, WriteLn, console;

FROM Reals IMPORT WriteReal;

CONST PI = 3.14159;

VAR
      area, radius:   REAL;
      i:              INTEGER;   (* Not used *)

BEGIN

      radius := 5.0;
      area   := PI * radius * radius;
      WriteString (console, 'Radius: ');
      WriteReal   (console, radius, 10, 4);
      WriteLn     (console);
      WriteString (console, 'Area:    ');
      WriteReal   (console, area,   10, 4);
      WriteLn     (console);

END Circle.
```

Fig. 10-3. An Illustration of variable declarations.

THE ASSIGNMENT STATEMENT

The assignment operator in Modula-2 is a colon followed by an equals sign (:=). An example is shown in the program in Fig. 10-3, where the variable **radius** is assigned the value 5.0. The statement that immediately follows is also an assignment statement.

A variable name always appears on the left side of an assignment statement. On the right there can be another variable, a constant, or an arithmetic expression. (Arithmetic expressions are discussed in the following section.)

Whatever appears on the right side of an assignment statement must be compatible in type with the variable on the left. In other words, a real value cannot be assigned to an integer variable. In those instances where this must be done, Modula-2 provides the TRUNC function to convert a real value to an integer, and FLOAT to convert an integer to a real value.

ARITHMETIC EXPRESSIONS

Arithmetic expressions use conventional infix notation (see Chapter 2). Modula-2 supports the usual arithmetic operators (+, −, *, and /). The operator / works only for the division of real numbers. The division of integer and cardinal numbers is handled with the DIV operator. The MOD operator is available to compute the modulus of two integer or cardinal numbers (the remainder after integer division).

The INC and DEC operators can be used to increment or decrement, respectively, variables of the integer type. The following examples are illustrative:

Modula-2 Expression	Equivalent Expression
INC(n)	n := n + 1
INC(n, 3)	n := n + 3
DEC(n)	n := n − 1
DEC(n, 2)	n := n − 2

These operators are quite handy in practice. Of the other languages presented in this book, only C has a similar facility.

Like Pascal, Modula-2 lacks an exponentiation operator. Wirth apparently feels that exponentiation should be performed by repeated multiplication in the case of integers or with logarithms in the case of real numbers. A Modula-2 user who needs to perform exponentiation regularly can easily create a library function to handle the task.

A simple example of an arithmetic expression is shown in the statement that computes the value of the variable **area** in Fig. 10-3.

BOOLEAN EXPRESSIONS

In Chapter 2 logical expressions were discussed. These are called *Boolean expressions* in Modula-2. Modula-2 supports the usual relational and logical operators, such as > (greater than) and OR, that are listed in Chapter 2.

Modula-2 permits the use of the symbol # as a synonym for <>, meaning not equal to. The symbol & is a synonym for the logical operator AND.

An advantage of Modula-2 over most other languages is that Boolean expressions are evaluated only far enough to determine the truth or falsity of the expression. For example, suppose M and N are of type INTEGER. The expression

$$(N > 0) \text{ AND } ((M \text{ DIV } N) > 5)$$

would produce an error in Pascal if N had the value 0 because the subexpression (M DIV N) would be undefined. In Modula-2 the falsity of the entire expression would be determined as soon as the sub-expression (N > 0) was found to be false; the remainder of the expression would not be evaluated.

INPUT AND OUTPUT

The first three sample programs contained examples of the WriteString, WriteReal, and WriteLn procedures. The module InOut also includes the procedures WriteInt and WriteCard, which print variables of the integer and cardinal types respectively.

If the variable I is of the integer type, and the variable C is of the cardinal type, they could be printed using the following statements:

```
WriteInt (I, 5);
WriteCard (C, 5);
WriteLn;
```

These statements would write the values of the two variables on the same line, each in a field with a width of 5. The WriteLn procedure outputs are carriage return and line feed.

The Texts module also contains versions of these procedures. The Texts versions require that the destination of the write statement be given explicitly, as in the following:

```
WriteInt (console, I, 5);
WriteCard (console, C, 5);
WriteLn (console);
```

The above statements do exactly the same thing as

the preceding statements. Why then is it necessary to specify console? The answer is that if you can specify the console, you can also specify some other output device, such as the printer.

It would be convenient if there were a module in the standard library that provided for printer output. Unfortunately the method of handling printer output varies from operating system to operating system and from computer to computer. A standard module is therefore not practical. One of the beauties of Modula-2, however, is that the user can easily create such a library module, which can be imported to any program that requires it.

For the moment, assume that such a module exists and is called PrinterIO. The program in Fig. 10-4 shows how this module can be used to direct output to the printer. How PrinterIO works and is implemented will be explained in the section on separate compilation.

The program in Fig. 10-4 imports the variable **printer** and the procedures PrinterOn and PrinterOff. The variable **printer** is used in lieu of **console** as the destination of the WriteString and WriteLn procedures, which are imported from the Texts module. As might be expected, PrinterOn in-

itializes the printer, and PrinterOff turns the printer off. (Strictly speaking, it is not always necessary to turn the printer off, but it doesn't hurt.)

The most common input procedures are listed below together with the module or modules in which they reside:

Procedure	Module
Read	InOut, Texts
ReadInt	InOut, Texts
ReadCard	InOut, Texts
ReadString	InOut
ReadLn	Texts
ReadReal	RealInOut, Reals

The procedures in InOut and RealInOut require only the name of the variable into which the data is to be read. As an argument the procedures in Texts and Reals require the name of the source of the information, such as console as an argument in addition to the name of the variable.

ReadInt, ReadCard, and ReadReal all read in numbers to variables of the appropriate type. Each ignores leading blanks and control characters and

```
(* Figure 10-4: Test Printer Output *)
MODULE TestPrint;

FROM Texts IMPORT
        console, WriteString, WriteLn;

FROM PrinterIO IMPORT
        printer, PrinterOn, PrinterOff;

BEGIN
        WriteString (console, 'This goes to the screen.');
        WriteLn (console);

        PrinterOn;
        WriteString (printer, 'This goes to the printer.');
        WriteLn (printer);
        PrinterOff;

END TestPrint.
```

Fig. 10-4. Test printer output.

terminates when it encounters a trailing blank or a control character. (A carriage return is a good example of a control character.)

ReadString reads in a character string, skipping leading blanks and terminating on a blank or control character. ReadLn, on the other hand, reads until it comes to the end of a line of text. Each reads into a character string.

The procedure Read reads in a single character at a time, including blanks and control characters.

When using procedures from the modules InOut and RealInOut, you can tell when you have come to the end of a text stream by checking the value of the Boolean variable **Done**. If **Done** is True, the end of the text stream has been encountered. When using procedures from Texts, the Boolean functions EOL and EOT return True when an end-of-line or end-of-text, respectively, is encountered.

Like the output procedures, input procedures in Modula-2 can only handle one data element at a time, and can only handle data elements of a particular type. Examples of the use of the Read and ReadLn procedures are shown in Fig. 10-5 and 10-6.

The programs in Figs. 10-5 and 10-6 each em-

```
(*  Figure 10-5:  Electronic Typewriter, Version 1  *)

MODULE Typewriter1;

FROM Texts IMPORT console, ReadLn, EOT, WriteString, WriteLn;

FROM PrinterIO IMPORT printer, PrinterOn, PrinterOff;

FROM Strings IMPORT STRING;

FROM Screen  IMPORT ClearScreen;

VAR S:  STRING;

BEGIN
        PrinterOn;
        ClearScreen;
        WriteString (console, 'Welcome to your Electronic Typewriter.');
        WriteLn (console);
        WriteLn (console);
        WriteString (console, 'Enter your text, followed by "Control-C".');
        WriteLn (console);
        WriteLn (console);
        LOOP
                ReadLn (console, S);
                IF EOT(console) THEN EXIT END;
                WriteString (printer, S);
                WriteLn (printer);
        END;
        WriteLn (printer);
        PrinterOff;
    END Typewriter1.
```

Fig. 10-5. Electronic Typewriter, Version 1.

```
(* Figure 10-6: Electronic Typewriter, Version 2  *)
MODULE Typewriter2;

   (*  Emulate a typewriter using character input & output  *)

FROM Texts IMPORT console, Read, EOL, EOT, Write, WriteString, WriteLn;

FROM PrinterIO IMPORT printer, PrinterOn, PrinterOff;

FROM Screen IMPORT ClearScreen;

VAR C:  CHAR;

BEGIN
        PrinterOn;
        ClearScreen;
        WriteString (console, 'Welcome to your Electronic Typewriter.');
        WriteLn (console);
        WriteLn (console);
        WriteString (console, 'Enter your text, followed by "Control-C".');
        WriteLn (console);
        WriteLn (console);
        LOOP
                Read (console, C);
                IF EOT(console) THEN EXIT END;
                IF EOL(console) THEN WriteLn (printer) END;
                Write (printer, C);
        END;
        WriteLn (printer);
        PrinterOff;
    END Typewriter2.
```

Fig. 10-6. Electronic Typewriter, Version 2.

ulate an electronic typewriter: what is typed at the console is echoed on the printer. The major difference between the two is that the program in Fig. 10-5 uses string input (ReadLn) and output (WriteString), whereas the program in Fig. 10-6 uses character input (Read) and output (Write).

Notice that each program imports a number of procedures from various library modules, including EOT, EOL, and ClearScreen. As mentioned previously, EOT is a Boolean function which returns True if the end of a text stream is encountered. Under the UCSD operating system, the end of a

text stream is marked by a Control-C character.

EOL is a Boolean function which returns True if the end of a line of text is encountered. The function of ClearScreen is obvious from its name.

The program in Fig. 10-5 also imports the type STRING.

As mentioned above, the program in Fig. 10-5 handles text as character strings, a line at a time. This has the advantage that the text can be edited as it is entered; that is, you can backspace over mistakes before they are printed on the printer. The program in Fig. 10-6 handles data a character at a time. The implication is that once an error is typed, it is sent to the printer; there is no chance to correct it beforehand.

Each program contains a loop; the first loops for every line, and the second for every character. The LOOP statement will be discussed in more detail in a later section. Simply put, the loop repeats until an EXIT statement is encountered. In both cases, the EXIT statement is executed when the end of text condition is encountered.

LIBRARY MODULES: SEPARATE COMPILATION

The preceding programs assumed the existence of a library module called PrinterIO. This module was not furnished with the system; it was created and compiled separately. This section will show how this was done.

There are several advantages to having separately compiled modules. One advantage is that commonly-used routines such as PrinterIO can be made available to any number of other programs. With separate compilation it is not necessary to compile the module into every program that uses it.

Another advantage is that during the development cycle of a large program with many modules, once a module is compiled correctly and tested, it need not be recompiled. Without separate compilation, every module would have to be recompiled every time any module was recompiled.

To add a module to the library requires the creation and compilation of a *definition* module and an *implementation* module. The definition module establishes the interfaces between modules. It contains declarations and procedure headings for all data, types, and procedures that are to be exported. Viewed another way, a definition module contains all the information that a programmer needs to know to call the module from another module. The definition module for PrinterIO is shown in Fig. 10-7.

The implementation module contains the actual bodies of the procedures to be exported. It also may contain local variables and procedures, and may import data, types, or procedures from another source. The implementation module for PrinterIO is shown in Fig. 10-8.

```
(* Figure 10-7: Definition Module for
   PrinterIO *)
DEFINITION MODULE PrinterIO;   (* $SEG:=10 *)

FROM Texts IMPORT TEXT;

EXPORT QUALIFIED printer,PrinterOn,PrinterOff;

VAR printer:  TEXT;

PROCEDURE PrinterOn;

PROCEDURE PrinterOff;

END PrinterIO.
```

Fig. 10-7. A definition module for PrinterIO.

The form of the definition module is relatively straightforward. Note that the heading begins with the words DEFINITION MODULE. Note also the assignment of a segment number in the following comment. This is called a *compiler directive*. It is an implementation-specific requirement and tells Modula-2 where in the library to put the module. The segment number can range from 8 to 47.

The rest of the definition module consists of import and export lists, a variable declaration, and procedure headings.

The implementation module in Fig. 10-8 is straightforward in form, but the definitions of the procedures IOError, PrinterOn, and PrinterOff require some explanation.

The printer is treated as a file in Modula-2. Note that the type FILE is imported from the module Files, and that a variable called pfile is declared to be of type FILE. The Open procedure, also imported from the module Files, is used to open the printer file and associate it with the variable pfile. This is done in the PrinterOn procedure.

The Open procedure is actually a function and returns a value. An IF statement is used to determine whether or not Open returns an appropriate value. If it does not, the IOError procedure is called to print an error message and halt the program.

Once the printer "file" is open, it must be connected to a text stream in the form of a variable of type TEXT. The variable printer is such a vari-

```
(* Figure 10-8: Implementation Module for PrinterIO *)
IMPLEMENTATION MODULE PrinterIO;

FROM Files IMPORT FILE, FileState, Open, Close;

FROM Texts IMPORT TEXT, TextState, console,
        WriteString, Connect, Disconnect;

VAR  pfile:    FILE;

PROCEDURE IOError;
BEGIN
        WriteString (console, "I/O Error");
        HALT;
END IOError;

PROCEDURE PrinterOn;
BEGIN
        IF Open (pfile, 'PRINTER:') () FileOK THEN IOError END;
        IF Connect (printer, pfile) () TextOK THEN IOError END;
END PrinterOn;

PROCEDURE PrinterOff;
BEGIN
        IF Disconnect (printer) () TextOK THEN IOError END;
        IF Close (pfile)        () FileOK THEN IOError END;
END PrinterOff;

END PrinterIO.
```

Fig. 10-8. An implementation module for Printer IO.

able. Note that **printer** was declared in the definition module. It need not, in fact cannot, be redeclared in the implementation module. The text variable **printer** is connected to the file variable **pfile** by the Connect procedure.

The Connect procedure is also a function and returns a value. That value is checked by an IF statement. If it does not have an acceptable value, IOError is called.

Note that the values **FileOK** and **TextOK** are not declared anywhere within sight. **FileOK** is an instance of the type FileState, which is imported from Files. The value comes along with the type. Similarly, the type TextState is imported from the module Texts.

The operation of the PrinterOn procedure has been discussed. The operation of the PrinterOff procedure is analogous.

The modules that comprise the main programs in the earlier examples are called *program modules*. Another way to refer to the module that imports another module is to call it the *host* module. There are thus three kinds of modules that you need to be concerned with: host modules, definition modules, and implementation modules. You have seen examples of each.

The order of compilation of these three kinds of modules is important. The definition module must be compiled first. This defines the interface between the host module and the implementation module. Once this is done, the other two modules can be compiled in any order.

Modula-2 maintains version control between modules. Once a definition module is compiled, it is assigned a unique version number. That version number is noted by both the host and the implementation modules. When a host module is executed, it checks to make sure that the implementation module it imports has the same version number as the definition module with which the host module was compiled. If it does not, the host module will abort.

This procedure has several implications. First, if the definition module and implementation module are recompiled, possibly altering the interface, the host module must also be recompiled. This provides protection against unwanted interactions caused by changes to library modules.

The second implication is that if the definition module is not recompiled, the host module and the implementation module can be recompiled at will. This means that different parts of a complex program can be modified independently so long as the interfaces are not disturbed.

In short, separate compilation of modules makes the development of large, complex programs simpler. The way in which Modula-2 implements separate compilation provides protection against unwanted interactions between different modules.

CONTROL STRUCTURES

Modula-2 supports a wide variety of control structures, more than enough for any occasion. The one control statement it lacks is a GO TO statement. The other control statements provided make a GO TO statement unnecessary.

The control structures facilitate the modern concept of structured programming. The scope of each control structure is well-defined and delimited by key words. With one exception (REPEAT . . . UNTIL), all Modula-2 control structures are terminated by the keyword END. (Pascal programmers should note that the keyword BEGIN is used only at the beginning of a Modula-2 module or procedure and not in control structures.)

Simple Selection: The IF Statement

The basic form of the IF statement in Modula-2 is as follows:

```
IF condition THEN
    statement(s)
END;
```

The condition can be any Boolean expression as defined earlier. There may be one or many statements between the THEN and the END; the END is required no matter how many or few statements there are in the body of the statement.

Suppose that you have two variables called **month** and **year** and that you wish to increment **month**. Here is one way to do this using a simple IF statement:

```
INC (month);
IF month > 12 THEN
    month := 1;
    INC (year)
END;
```

The standard procedure INC can be used to increment an integer or cardinal variable. What this IF statement does is to determine whether or not **month** has been incremented too far; if it has been, **month** is set back to 1 and **year** is incremented.

An IF statement may also have an ELSE part; the format is as follows:

```
IF condition THEN
    statement(s)
ELSE
    statement(s)
END;
```

An IF statement with ELSE can be used to accomplish the same task as in the previous example:

```
If month < 12 THEN
    INC (month)
ELSE
```

```
       month := 1;
       INC (year)
END
```

Modula-2 provides for nested IF statements through the use of the ELSIF clause of an IF statement. For example, consider the computation of a weekly payroll. If the hours worked do not exceed 40, payment is made at the standard rate. If more than 40 but less than 50 hours are worked, the hours in excess of 40 are paid at 1.5 times the standard rate. All hours worked in excess of 50 hours per week are paid at 2 times the standard rate. This computation could be programmed as follows in Modula-2:

```
IF hours <= 40.0 THEN
       pay := hours*rate
ELSIF hours <= 50.0 THEN
       pay := 40.0*rate +
              (hours—40.0)*rate*1.5
ELSE
       pay := 40.0*rate +
              10.0*rate*1.5 +
              (hours—50.0)*rate*2.0
END;
```

Notice that the statement following ELSE is continued to the next line. None of the statements within the body of the construct above end with a ; because the semicolon is a statement separator in Modula-2, not a statement terminator. No harm would be done, however, by including the semicolons. (Note that in Pascal the extra semicolons would not be allowed.)

Multiple Selection: The CASE Statement

The IF statement provides selection between two alternatives. Nested IF statements can provide selection between more than two alternatives. Another way of providing selection between multiple alternatives (when those alternatives can be enumerated) is the CASE statement.

An example of a CASE statement is shown in Fig. 10-9. This program reads a month number from the keyboard; then it prints the name of the corre-

sponding month. If the month number is not one of the numbers 1 through 12, it prints out an appropriate error message. This is accomplished by the ELSE clause. Note that the various cases are separated by the | symbol (vertical line).

Loops

Modula-2 supports four different kinds of loop: the FOR statement, the WHILE statement, the REPEAT . . . UNTIL statement, and the generalized LOOP statement. Each of these is described in the sections that follow.

Counted Loops: The FOR Statement. Chapter 2 included a simple sample program in BASIC that prints out the integers from 1 to 10. Figure 10-10 contains a Modula-2 program that accomplishes the same thing.

In this program, the variable i serves as the loop counter. It happens to be of the cardinal type, but it could also be of the integer type. (Recall that cardinal numbers cannot be negative.)

The FOR statement initializes i to 1; then it checks to see whether or not i exceeds 10 (the upper limit). If it does, control passes to the statement following END; if it does not, the statements between the DO and END delimiters are executed. Following execution of the body of the loop, the counter i is incremented. If i does not exceed 10, the process is repeated.

Note that the FOR statement performs its test for termination *before* the body of the loop is ever executed. Thus the body of the loop may never be executed. The following is a simple example of this possibility:

```
FOR i := 1 TO 0 DO
       WriteString ('Never happen . . . ')
END;
```

In this case the WriteString statement will never be executed, because the initial value of i exceeds the limiting value, which is 0.

Conditional Loops. A counted loop repeats a specified number of times. A conditional loop executes as long as a certain condition is true or until a certain condition becomes true. Modula-2 includes

```
(*  Figure 10-9:  The Calendar Program, Version 1  *)
MODULE Calendar1;
FROM InOut IMPORT ReadCard, Read, WriteCard, WriteString, WriteLn;
VAR month, days, year:  CARDINAL;
    reply:  CHAR;
BEGIN
  REPEAT
        WriteLn;
        WriteString ('Enter the Month (1..12):  ');
        ReadCard (month);
        CASE month OF

            1, 3, 5, 7,
            8, 10, 12:    days := 31 |

            4, 6, 9, 11:  days := 30 |

            2:            WriteString ('Enter the Year:  ');
                          ReadCard (year);
                          IF (year MOD 4 = 0) THEN
                             days := 29
                          ELSE
                             days := 28
                          END
            ELSE
                          WriteLn;
                          WriteString ('Sorry, month must be 1..12.');
                          WriteLn;
                          days := 0

          END;
        WriteString ('Month');
        WriteCard   (month, 3);
        WriteString (' has');
        WriteCard   (days, 3);
        WriteString (' days.');
        WriteLn;
        WriteLn;
        WriteString ('Again?  (y/n)');
        Read (reply);
        WriteLn
    UNTIL reply <> 'y';
    END D Calendar1.
```

Fig. 10-9. The Calendar program, Version 1.

two kinds of conditional loop, the WHILE statement and the REPEAT . . . UNTIL statement.

The WHILE statement repeats as long as the stated condition is true. The test is performed at the top of the loop, so the body of the loop may never be executed if the condition is initially false. The body of the loop must contain some logic that will eventually cause the condition to become false; otherwise the loop would try to continue infinitely.

The program in Fig. 10-11 is a rewrite of the program in Fig. 10-10 using the WHILE statement instead of the FOR statement. The program prints the numbers from 1 to 10 on the screen. Note that in Fig. 10-11, the counter variable i must be initialized and incremented explicitly; in Fig. 10-10 these functions were taken care of by the FOR statement.

The function of these two programs is identical. In this case the FOR statement is probably more appropriate. There are other cases, however, in which a conditional loop is more appropriate. Such a case is shown in the program in Fig. 10-12.

This program reads in a series of numbers from the console, stopping when the sum of the numbers exceeds 100. It then prints out a count of the numbers entered, their sum, and the number that would have caused the sum to go over 100.

Notice that this program repeats the statement

ReadInt (num)

```
(* Figure 10-10: Counted Loops: The FOR
Statement *)
MODULE ForDemo;

FROM InOut IMPORT WriteCard, WriteLn;

VAR i: CARDINAL;

BEGIN

    FOR i := 1 TO 10 DO
        WriteCard (i, 3);
        WriteLn
    END;

END ForDemo.
```

Fig. 10-10. Counted Loops: the FOR statement.

```
(* Figure 10-11: Conditional Loops: The
WHILE Statement *)
MODULE WhileDemo;

FROM InOut IMPORT WriteCard, WriteLn;

VAR i: CARDINAL;

BEGIN

    i := 1;
    WHILE i <= 10 DO
        WriteCard (i, 2);
        WriteLn;
        INC (i)
    END;

END WhileDemo
```

Fig. 10-11. Conditional Loops: the WHILE statement.

both before the WHILE loop and at the bottom of the WHILE loop. This is necessary so that the condition can be checked both on the first pass and on subsequent passes through the loop. (Later you will see how to avoid this duplication using a generalized loop.)

Notice also that there are two forms of the INC statement within the body of the loop. The statement

INC (count)

simply increments count by 1. The statement

INC (sum, num)

is equivalent to the following statement:

sum := sum + num

The remainder of the program is straightforward.

The other form of conditional loop is the RE-PEAT . . . UNTIL statement. This statement repeats until the specified condition becomes true. An example of this construct was seen in the program in Fig. 10-9. In that program the body of the loop was repeated until the user replied something other

```
(* Figure 10-12: Another WHILE Statement Demonstration *)
MODULE SumUp1;

FROM InOut IMPORT ReadInt, WriteInt, WriteString, WriteLn;

VAR num, count, sum: INTEGER;

BEGIN

    count := 0;
    sum   := 0;
    WriteLn;
    WriteString ('Enter a series of numbers:');
    WriteLn;  WriteLn;

    ReadInt (num);
    WHILE (sum + num) <= 100 DO
        INC (count);
        INC (sum, num);
        ReadInt (num)
    END;

    WriteLn;
    WriteInt (count, 3);
    WriteString (' numbers were read.');
    WriteLn;

    WriteString ('They sum to ');
    WriteInt (sum, 5);
    WriteString ('.');
    WriteLn;

    WriteString ('The number ');
    WriteInt (num, 5);
    WriteString (' was not counted.');
    WriteLn;

END SumUp1.
```

Fig. 10-12. Another WHILE statement demonstration.

than y when asked if he or she would like to repeat the process again.

The Generalized Loop. Modula-2 provides a more general form of loop. Its format is as follows:

LOOP

   . . .

IF condition THEN EXIT END;

   . . .

END;

The LOOP . . . END construct by itself is an infinite

loop. The EXIT statement within the IF statement provides a means of exiting the loop. The EXIT statement can appear anywhere within the loop. In fact, there may be some rare occasions where no EXIT is desired. An example might be a program to continuously monitor the thermometers in an office building.

If the conditional EXIT statement is the first statement within the body of the loop, the construct is equivalent to a WHILE statement with the test at the top. If the conditional EXIT statement is the last statement within the body of the loop, the construct is equivalent to a REPEAT . . . UNTIL statement. The real usefulness of the LOOP and EXIT combination is that the conditional EXIT may be anywhere within the body of the loop. An example of this was presented in the program in Fig. 10-5.

Another example of the generalized loop construct is shown in the program in Fig. 10-13. This program is a rewrite of the program in Fig. 10-12 using a LOOP statement instead of a WHILE statement. The primary difference between the two is that the second version requires only one ReadInt statement.

It is the presence of the generalized loop construct with EXIT, together with the HALT procedure, which can terminate execution of a program, that makes a GO TO statement unnecessary in Modula-2.

Procedures

Chapter 2 discussed subroutines. Subroutines are called *procedures* in Modula-2.

A procedure is a more-or-less self-contained unit of a program that performs a particular function. It is defined at the beginning of a module, either within a program module or within a separately-compiled module. Once defined, a procedure can be invoked (almost) anywhere within a program. Procedures can be exported from and imported into modules.

Together with the use of modules, the use of procedures makes it easier to divide a large, complex program into smaller, simpler components. This makes the program much easier to write and maintain.

One purpose of a procedure is reduce the amount of duplicative coding in a program. Consider, for example, a program that must exchange the values of two real numbers in several parts of the program. A procedure can be written to perform the swap. The procedure can be called from wherever in the program it is needed. Such a program is shown in Fig. 10-14.

The program initializes two variables, prints them, exchanges their values, and then prints them again. The process is repeated with two other variables. The point is that a procedure can be invoked in different parts of the program with different inputs.

The procedure that exchanges the variables is called Swap. The program also contains a procedure called Print2, which prints two variables with appropriate labels. Note the placement of the procedure declarations; they are after the declaration of variables for the main program and before the BEGIN of the main program. Next, note the heading of each procedure. The parameters of each procedure are listed in parentheses following the procedure name.

The parameters of Swap are u and v. When Swap is invoked in the main program, its arguments are p and q the first time, and x and y the second time. The first time Swap is involed, the values of p and q are exchanged; the second time Swap is invoked, the values of x and y are exchanged.

Notice that Swap has a local variable called temp, declared between the heading and body of the procedure. The scope of temp is restricted to that procedure. In other words, the variable temp is not accessible from anywhere else in the program.

The procedure Print2 also has two parameters, u and v. When Print2 is called using, for example, p and q as arguments, the values of p and q are printed.

Notice that the procedure heading of Swap contains the word VAR and that the procedure heading of Print2 does not. This affects how the arguments are passed to the procedures. In the case of Print2 (no VAR), only the values of the arguments are passed. In the case of Swap (with Var),

```
(* Figure 10-13:  The Generalized Loop  *)
MODULE SumUp2;

FROM InOut IMPORT ReadInt, WriteInt, WriteString, WriteLn;

VAR num, count, sum:  INTEGER;

BEGIN

    count := 0;
    sum   := 0;
    WriteLn;
    WriteString ('Enter a series of numbers:');
    WriteLn;  WriteLn;

    LOOP
        ReadInt (num);
        IF (sum + num) > 100 THEN EXIT END;
        INC (count);
        INC (sum, num)
    END;

    WriteLn;
    WriteInt (count, 3);
    WriteString (' numbers were read.');
    WriteLn;

    WriteString ('They sum to ');
    WriteInt (sum, 5);
    WriteString ('.');
    WriteLn;

    WriteString ('The number ');
    WriteInt (num, 5);
    WriteString (' was not counted.');
    WriteLn;

END SumUp2.
```

Fig. 10-13. The generalized loop.

the arguments themselves are passed to the procedure. This permits Swap to exchange the values of these two variables. Without the VAR, swap would have no effect on the arguments in the main program (p, q, x, and y). If you have access to a Modula-2 compiler, try running this program with

and without the VAR in the heading of Swap.

Because Print2 returns no values to the main program, there is no need for VAR in its heading.

A procedure can be called from the main program or from another procedure as long as the procedure being called is in the same module or is

```
(*  Figure 10-14:   Use of Procedures  *)
MODULE ProcDemo;

    FROM InOut IMPORT WriteString, WriteLn;

    FROM RealInOut IMPORT WriteReal;

    VAR p, q, x, y.  REAL;

    PROCEDURE Swap (VAR u, v:  REAL);
       (* Exchange the values of two real variables *)
       VAR  temp:  REAL;
       BEGIN
          temp := u;
          u    := v;
          v    := temp;
       END Swap,

    PROCEDURE Print2 (u, v:  REAL);
       (* Print and label two real variables *)
       BEGIN
          WriteLn,
          WriteString ('First  Variable:  ');
          WriteReal   (u, 15);
          WriteLn;
          WriteString ('Second Variable:  ');
          WriteReal   (v, 15);
          WriteLn;
       END Print2;

BEGIN

    p := 1.0;   q := 2.0;
    Print2 (p,q);
    Swap (p,q);
    Print2 (p,q);

    x := 3.14159;   y := 2.71828;
    Print2 (x,y);
    Swap (x,y);
    Print2 (x,y);

END ProcDemo.
```

Fig. 10-14. The use of procedures.

imported from another module. A procedure can also call itself in Modula-2. This is called *recursion* and will be discussed in more detail below.

Functions

A function is similar to a procedure. The difference is that a function has a value attached to its name. A function is invoked by writing its name in an expression, as in the following example:

x := ABS(y)

Here ABS is a standard function supplied with the language; it produces the absolute value of its argument. That value, in effect, takes the place of the function name in the expression.

A procedure call, on the other hand, stands alone; it is not used in an expression. For example,

INC(n)

is a call to a procedure that increments the variable n.

Because a function name returns a value, the function must be given a type (for example, integer). This is done in the heading of the function. Suppose, for example, that you need a function to return the value of its argument divided by two. Here is how such a function could be defined:

```
PROCEDURE Half (x: REAL): REAL;
  BEGIN
    RETURN x/2.0;
  END Half;
```

Note that the heading of a function definition in Modula-2 uses the word PROCEDURE rather than FUNCTION. Modula-2 differs from Pascal in this regard. The : REAL following the parenthesized parameter list gives the function a type. The presence of such a type declaration is the easiest way to distinguish a function from a procedure in Modula-2.

A function must have at least one RETURN statement. In this case, the value that is returned is x/2.0. That value is then used in the expression in which the function name appears in the invoking program or procedure. For example, the following could appear in a program:

x := Half(y)

A simple example showing the use of a function in an actual program is given in Fig. 10-15. This program includes a function that returns the largest of its three integer arguments. The function uses a local variable called **max** and a nested IF statement to compute the maximum of the three values, and then a RETURN statement to return that value to the main program.

Recursion

Another way to control the flow of execution in a program is through the use of recursive procedures and functions. As discussed in Chapter 2, a recursive procedure or function is one which calls itself. Obviously the process must be finite, so the procedure or function must have some provision for terminating the recursion.

Many programming problems can be solved equally well with or without recursion. As an example, consider the program in Fig. 10-16. This program prints a character string, drops the first character, and then repeats the process until there are no more characters to print. A typical output from this program would appear as follows:

```
HELLO
ELLO
LLO
LO
O
```

Notice the call to PrintAndDrop within the procedure itself. This is the recursive call. The IF statement within the procedure allows the recursion to be continued only as long as there are more characters in the string. The Delete procedure, imported from the Strings module, is used to drop the first character (character 0) from the string after the string has been printed.

There are some problems, however, which

```
                    (*  Figure 10-15:  Function Demonstration  *)
            MODULE GetMax;

                FROM InOut IMPORT WriteString, WriteInt, WriteLn,
                                   Read, ReadInt;

                VAR   i, j, k:  INTEGER;
                      c:  CHAR;
                PROCEDURE Max3 (x, y, z:  INTEGER):  INTEGER;
                    (*  Returns the largest of the 3 inputs  *)
                    VAR max:  INTEGER;
                    BEGIN
                        IF (x )= y) AND (x )= z) THEN
                            max := x
                        ELSIF (y )= x) AND (y )= z) THEN
                            max := y
                        ELSE
                            max := z
                        END;
                        RETURN max;
                    END Max3;
            BEGIN
                REPEAT
                    WriteLn;  WriteLn;
                    WriteString ('You will be asked to enter three integers.');
                    WriteLn;
                    WriteString ('The program will then print the largest one.');
                    WriteLn;  WriteLn;

                    WriteString ('Enter an integer:  ');
                    ReadInt (i);
                    WriteString ('Enter an integer:  ');
                    ReadInt (j);
                    WriteString ('Enter an integer:  ');
                    ReadInt (k);
                    WriteLn;

                    WriteInt (Max3 (i,j,k), 5);
                    WriteString (' is the largest of the three.');
                    WriteLn;  WriteLn;

                    WriteString ('Again? (y/n):  ');
                    Read (c)
                UNTIL (c <> 'y') AND (c <> 'Y');

            END GetMax.
```

Fig. 10-15. A function demonstration.

```
(* Figure 10-16: Demonstrate Recursive Procedure *)
MODULE Recurse;

    FROM InOut   IMPORT WriteString, WriteLn, Read, ReadString;
    FROM Strings IMPORT STRING, Delete, Length;

    VAR s:  STRING;
        c:  CHAR;

    PROCEDURE PrintAndDrop (s:  STRING);
        (* Print a string, drop first character, repeat *)
        BEGIN
            IF Length(s) > 0 THEN
                WriteString(s);
                WriteLn;
                Delete(s,0,1);
                PrintAndDrop(s)
            END;
        END PrintAndDrop;

BEGIN

    REPEAT

        WriteLn;  WriteLn;
        WriteString('Type a string:  ');
        ReadString(s);
        WriteLn;
        PrintAndDrop(s);
        WriteLn;  WriteLn;

        WriteString('Again?  (y/n):  ');
        Read(c);

    UNTIL (c <> 'y') AND (c <> 'Y');

END Recurse.
```

Fig. 10-16. A sample recursive procedure.

naturally lend themselves to recursive solution. Here is an example from mathematics: The factorial of zero is defined as one. The factorial of a positive integer N is defined as N times the factorial of N-1. The definition of the function is itself recursive; in other words, the function is defined in terms of itself.

The program in Fig. 10-17 contains a recursive function to compute the factorial of an integer between 0 and 34. The lower limit is required because the factorial function is not defined for negative numbers. The upper limit is required because the factorial of 35 is on the order of 10 raised to the 40th power, which is too large to be accommodated by

```
              (*  Figure 10-17:  Demonstrate Recursive Function  *)
         MODULE RecursiveFunction;

             FROM InOut IMPORT WriteString, WriteLn, Read, ReadCard;
             FROM Reals IMPORT WriteReal;
             FROM Texts IMPORT console;

             VAR x:  CARDINAL;
                 n:  REAL;
                 c:  CHAR;
             PROCEDURE Factorial (n:  REAL):  REAL;
                 (*  Compute the Factorial of a non-negative integer  *)
                 (*  Floating Point Error for n )= 35  *)
                 VAR f:  REAL;
                 BEGIN
                     IF (n < 0.0) OR (n )= 35.0)  THEN
                         WriteLn;
                         WriteString('Sorry, n must be between 0 and 34.');
                         WriteLn;
                         f := 0.0
                     ELSIF n = 0.0 THEN
                         f := 1.0
                     ELSE
                         f := n * Factorial(n-1.0)
                     END;
                     RETURN f;
                 END Factorial;

         BEGIN
             REPEAT
                 WriteLn;  WriteLn;
                 WriteString('Enter an integer between 0 and 34:  ');
                 ReadCard(x);
                 n := FLOAT(x);
                 WriteReal(console, n, 1, 0);
                 WriteString(' Factorial is ');
                 WriteReal(console, Factorial(n), 1, 0);
                 WriteLn;  WriteLn;

                 WriteString('Again?  (y/n):  ');
                 Read(c)

             UNTIL (c <> 'y') AND (c <> 'Y');

         END RecursiveFunction.
```

Fig. 10-17. A sample recursive function.

most implementations of microcomputer languages.

The Factorial function is invoked by writing its name in a WriteReal statement in the main program. Each recursive call computes the factorial of a smaller number; eventually the number reaches zero and the recursion terminates.

The details of the console input and output of this program require comment. First, the number is read as a cardinal number. This prevents negative and fractional numbers from being read. It also allows the user to omit typing a decimal point, as he would have to if a real number were being read. The cardinal number is converted to a real number by the built-in function FLOAT.

Second, the WriteReal procedure from the module Reals is used rather than the one from RealInOut, because this version permits real numbers to be written in fixed-point format (without an exponent). A field width of 1 with 0 decimal places is specified. The field width should be interpreted as the minimum field width; it is expanded as necessary.

DATA STRUCTURES

Modula-2 supports a wide variety of data structures, including arrays and records. Further, Modula-2 records and pointer variables can be used to construct more complicated data structures such as linked lists and trees.

Arrays

Modula-2 uses square brackets to delimit the subscripts of arrays. As in most languages, arrays must be declared before use.

Chapter 2 included an illustration of an array called POINTS. In Modula-2 this array could be declared as follows:

```
VAR Points: ARRAY
[1 . . 10, 1 . . 20] OF INTEGER;
```

This notation means that the first subscript can range from 1 to 10, and the second subscript from 1 to 20. The OF INTEGER means that each element of the array is to be of the integer type.

An example of the use of arrays in Modula-2 is shown in the program in Fig. 10-18. This program is a calendar program similar to that in Fig. 10-9, except that it uses arrays rather than a CASE statement to do the work.

The program uses an array called DaysIn to store the number of days in each month and an array called NameOf to store the name of each month. The subscript of each array corresponds to the number of the month. Each array is declared in and initialized in a subordinate module called Initialize. Initialize exports the arrays to the main module. The important point to note here is that the body of the Initialize module is executed before the body of the main module, Calendar2, so that it can be used to initialize variables and arrays. Also note that a module, unlike a procedure, is not "called" by the main program.

Other than the initialization, the program is straightforward. Note that the value of the variable month is validated before being used as an array subscript.

Records

Chapter 2 discussed the need to have a record containing the name of a student and his or her scores on up to 20 tests. Suppose there may be up to 30 students in the class. An array of records will do the job. The following declarations would establish such a data structure:

```
CONST NrOfStudents = 30;
      NrOfTests    = 20;
TYPE Entry =
  RECORD
      Name: ARRAY [0 . . 25] OF
      CHAR;
      Score: ARRAY [1 . . NrOfTests]
      OF REAL;
  END;
VAR Student: ARRAY [1 . . NrOf Students]
    OF ENTRY;
```

A new type called Entry is declared. Once a type is declared, as many variables as desired can be declared to be of that type. In this case that type is a record. The variable **Student** therefore ends up being an array of records, as desired.

Up until now you have stored all character strings in variables of the string type. TYPE STRING is equivalent to the following:

ARRAY [0 . . 80] OF CHAR;

In this record such a long string was not needed and would have used too much memory, so a smaller ARRAY OF CHAR was declared.

Suppose that you need to write out the name of the fourth student and the score that student received on the first test. The following statements would print these items.

WriteString(Student[4]. Name);
WriteReal (console, Student
[4]. Score [1], 4, 1);

The period or dot (.) is used to refer to individual record elements.

Examples of the use of records is actual programs will be presented in later sections of this chapter.

Linked Lists

Chapter 2 explained the concept of linked lists and showed how they could be implemented using arrays. Modula-2 also provides a more advanced means of handling linked lists using pointers and dynamic allocation of storage space. These advanced topics are, however, not necessary for the understanding of linked lists and so are omitted.

This section explains how linked lists can be implemented using arrays of records. The methodology is essentially the same as that described in Chapter 2, except that an array of records is used instead of parallel arrays. Also, the value -1 is used to mark the end of a list.

The following declarations will establish the necessary array of records to support the example given in Chapter 2:

CONST EndList = −1;
    MaxSize = 5;

VAR First, FirstFree: INTEGER;
    List: ARRAY
    [1 . . MaxSize] OF
        RECORD
            name: ARRAY
            [0 . . 15] OF CHAR;
            link: INTEGER;
        END;

The name part of the third record of the structure could be printed by the following:

WriteString (List[3]. name);

The subscript of the next record in the list can then be found in this element:

List[3]. link

The comprehensive sample program at the end of the chapter illustrates the use of linked lists in an actual program. That example shows the details of how linked lists can be manipulated and how records can be added to and deleted from a linked list.

FILE HANDLING

For a microcomputer to process data, that data must be input to the program in some way. One way is via the keyboard. If an application requires the same data day after day, it would become rather tedious to reenter the data every day using the keyboard. A better solution is to key the data in once and save it in a disk file.

There are two principle types of files in Modula-2. First is the text file. A text file is a sequence of characters. It is accessed sequentially. The printer and console can be thought of as text files, as the organization is the same (except, of course, you cannot read from a printer). The implementation module of PrinterIO in Fig. 10-8 showed how a file of the text type can be interfaced with. The standard library module Texts includes procedures for handling files of the text type.

The other type of file in Modula-2 is a sequence of records. Each record may be as simple as an integer or as complex as needed. The record

```
(* Figure 10-18:  The Calendar Program, Version 2  *)
MODULE Calendar2;

    FROM InOut IMPORT ReadCard, Read, WriteCard, WriteString, WriteLn;
    FROM Strings IMPORT STRING;

    VAR month, days, year:  CARDINAL;
        reply:  CHAR;

    MODULE Initialize;
        IMPORT STRING;
        EXPORT DaysIn, NameOf;
        VAR DaysIn:  ARRAY [1..12] OF CARDINAL;
            NameOf:  ARRAY [1..12] OF STRING;
        BEGIN
            DaysIn[1]  := 31;  NameOf[1]  := 'January';
            DaysIn[2]  := 28;  NameOf[2]  := 'February';
            DaysIn[3]  := 31;  NameOf[3]  := 'March';
            DaysIn[4]  := 30;  NameOf[4]  := 'April';
            DaysIn[5]  := 31;  NameOf[5]  := 'May';
            DaysIn[6]  := 30;  NameOf[6]  := 'June';
            DaysIn[7]  := 31;  NameOf[7]  := 'July';
            DaysIn[8]  := 31;  NameOf[8]  := 'August';
            DaysIn[9]  := 30;  NameOf[9]  := 'September';
            DaysIn[10] := 31;  NameOf[10] := 'October';
            DaysIn[11] := 30;  NameOf[11] := 'November';
            DaysIn[12] := 31;  NameOf[12] := 'December';
        END Initialize;

BEGIN

    REPEAT
        WriteLn;
        WriteString ('Enter the Month (1..12):  ');
        ReadCard (month);
        IF (month > 0) AND (month <= 12) THEN
            days := DaysIn[month];
            IF month = 2 THEN
                WriteString ('Enter the Year:  ');
                ReadCard (year);
                IF (year MOD 4 = 0) THEN
                    INC(days);
                END;
            END;
```

Fig. 10-18. The Calendar program, Version 2. (Continued on page 279.)

```
                    WriteString (NameOf[month]);
                    WriteString (' has');
                    WriteCard   (days, 3);
                    WriteString (' days.');
                    WriteLn;
                ELSE
                    WriteString('Month must be in the interval 1..12.');
                    WriteLn;
                END;

                WriteLn;
                WriteString ('Again?  (y/n):   ');
                Read (reply);
                WriteLn

            UNTIL (reply () 'y') AND (reply () 'Y');

        END Calendar2.
```

facility described earlier is useful for defining file records. A file of records can be accessed using either sequential access or direct access methods. This kind of file is classified as being of the *file* type.

The standard procedures for creating, opening, and closing files are found in the Files module. A file can be created using the Create procedure. Files that previously existed can be accessed using the Open procedure. With each file is associated a variable of the file type, called the *file variable*. Both Create and Open establish the connection between the file variable and the name of the external file. The Close procedure terminates access to a file.

With each text file is associated a variable of the text type. This variable must be connected to a file using the standard procedure Connect. The standard procedure Disconnect terminates the connection. Examples of the use of these procedures are given in Fig. 10-8.

The versions of the standard procedures Write, WriteString, WriteLn, WriteInt, Read, ReadLn, ReadInt, and so on found in the Texts module are used to write data to and read data from a text file. The standard procedures WriteRec and ReadRec from the Files module are used to write data to and read data from other files.

Sequential Files

The distinguishing characteristic of a sequential file is that it is accessed from beginning to end, one record at a time. It is impossible, for example, to access the second record of the file without having first accessed the first record.

The program in Fig. 10-19 stores a file of records; each record consists of a name and an age. The records are read from the keyboard and stored sequentially in the file. After the last record has been written to the disk, the file is closed. It is then reopened and read in from the disk. Each record is written to the console as it is read from the disk.

The records are written to the file using the standard procedure WriteRec, and read from the file using the standard procedure ReadRec. Note that each transfers the contents of the entire record in one operation.

Notice that the procedures Create, Open, and Close are function procedures. If they return the value FileOK, the operation was successful. Because they are function procedures, it is necessary to use the value returned in an expression of some

```
(* Figure 10-19:  Sequential File Demonstration  *)

MODULE Sequential;  (* Stores a file of names and ages *)

    FROM Texts IMPORT ReadLn, ReadCard, WriteString, WriteLn,
        WriteCard, console;
    FROM Files IMPORT FILE, FileState, Create, Open, Close,
        ReadRec, WriteRec;

    TYPE ENTRY =
        RECORD
            name:   ARRAY[0..20] OF CHAR;
            age:    CARDINAL;
        END;

    VAR R:   ENTRY;
        f:   FILE;

BEGIN

    IF Create (f, 'AGES.TEXT') <> FileOK THEN
        WriteString (console, 'Unable to Create file...');
        HALT;
    END;
    (* First read from keyboard and write to disk *)
    WriteLn (console);  WriteLn (console);
    WriteString (console, 'Enter Names and Ages; Age 0 to quit.');
    WriteLn (console);
    REPEAT
        WriteLn (console);
        WriteString (console, 'Name:   ');
        ReadLn (console, R.name);
        WriteString (console, 'Age:    ');
        ReadCard (console, R.age);
        WriteRec (f, R)
    UNTIL R.age = 0;
    IF Close (f) <> FileOK THEN
        WriteString (console, 'Unable to Close File...');
        HALT;
    END;

    (* Now read the file back and display on the screen *)
    IF Open (f, 'AGES.TEXT') <> FileOK THEN
        WriteString (console, 'Unable to Open file...');
        HALT;
    END;
```

Fig. 10-19. A sequential file demonstration. (Continued on page 281.)

```
        WriteLn (console);  WriteLn (console);
        WriteString (console, 'Here are the contents of the file:');
        WriteLn (console);  WriteLn (console);
        LOOP
            ReadRec (f, R);
            IF R.age = 0 THEN EXIT END;
            WriteString (console, 'Name:    ');
            WriteString (console, R.name);
            WriteLn (console);
            WriteString (console, 'Age:     ');
            WriteCard (console, R.age, 1);
            WriteLn (console);  WriteLn (console);
        END;
        IF Close (f) <> FileOK THEN
            WriteString (console, 'Unable to Close file...');
            HALT;
        END;
        WriteString (console, 'All done...');

END Sequential.
```

sort, usually in an IF statement as shown.

Note that the necessary standard procedures plus the types FILE and FileState are imported from the File module.

Direct-Access Files

There are many applications for which sequential access is inadequate. It is often necessary to access a particular record directly, without first accessing the previous records. An example would be a bank program that is designed to lookup the balance of a customer's account. It is certainly desirable to be able to go to that customer's account record without first accessing the account records of many other customers.

The records in a file can be numbered, starting with 0. Each record has associated with it a file position, that is, the point in the file at which that record begins. Modula-2 provides a type called FilePos (for File Position) in the Files module. The problem is to calculate the file position corresponding to a record number and to position the file at that position.

The standard procedure CalcPos is used to calculate the starting position for a given record. As input it requires the record number and the size of the record. The size of a record can be calculated with the function procedure Size, found in the module System (because it is system-dependent).

Once the file position is calculated, the standard procedure SetPos sets the file at that position. A subsequent ReadRec or WriteRec will then access the desired record in the file.

A program illustrating the use of direct-access files is included as the comprehensive sample program later in this chapter.

GRAPHICS

The Volition implementation of Modula-2 on the Apple microcomputer provides an interface to the Apple/UCSD Pascal TURTLEGRAPHICS unit. Turtle graphics are explained in detail in the

```
MODULE AddressFile;

(* A program to create and maintain a file of names and
   addresses.  The file is maintained in alphabetical
   order using an index consisting of a linked list of
   pointers.  A linked list of vacant (free) records is
   also maintained. *)

FROM PrinterIO IMPORT
    printer, PrinterOn, PrinterOff;

FROM FileIO IMPORT
    OpenFiles, CloseFiles, GetRec, PutRec, RecType,
    InBuf, OutBuf, Index, EndList, MaxRecords;

FROM TextIO IMPORT PrintRec, GetEntry, Menu;

FROM Texts IMPORT TEXT, console, WriteString, WriteLn, WriteInt;

FROM Screen IMPORT ClearScreen;

FROM Terminal IMPORT Read;

FROM Strings IMPORT CompareStr;

VAR c:  CARDINAL;

PROCEDURE Pause;
    (* Pause until any key is pressed *)
    VAR a:  CHAR;
    BEGIN
        WriteLn (console);  WriteLn (console);
        WriteString (console, 'Press any key to continue...');
        Read (a)
    END Pause;

PROCEDURE GetFree ():  CARDINAL;
    (* Get record number of next free record and
       remove it from the free list *)
    VAR free:  CARDINAL;
    BEGIN
        free := Index[-1];          (* First free record *)
        Index[-1] := Index[free];   (* Update first free *)
        RETURN free
```

Fig. 10-20 (a). The AddressFile program. (Continued on page 283.)

```
            END GetFree;

PROCEDURE Greater (a, b:  RecType):  BOOLEAN;
    (* Return TRUE if a.name > b.name *)
    VAR i, j:  INTEGER;
    BEGIN
        i := CompareStr (a.name.last, b.name.last);
        j := CompareStr (a.name.first, b.name.first);

        IF (i = 1) OR ((i = 0) AND (j = 1)) THEN
            RETURN TRUE
        ELSE
            RETURN FALSE
        END
    END Greater,

PROCEDURE Insert (InBuf:  RecType);
    (* Insert the record r into the index and write to disk *)
    VAR p, q, free:  INTEGER;
        TempBuf:  RecType;
    BEGIN
        free := GetFree ();
        PutRec (free, InBuf);
        p := Index[0];              (* First record in use *)
        q := 0;
        IF p <> EndList THEN
            GetRec (p, TempBuf);
            WHILE (p <> EndList) AND (Greater (InBuf, TempBuf)) DO
                q := p;
                p := Index[p];
                GetRec (p, TempBuf)
            END,
        END;
        Index[free] := p;          (* Insert into linked list *)
        Index[q] := free;
    END Insert;

PROCEDURE Append;
    (* Add records to the file *)
    VAR finished:  BOOLEAN;
    BEGIN
        IF Index[-1] = EndList THEN
            WriteString (console, 'No room left in the file...');
            Pause;
```

```
                RETURN
            END;
        LOOP
            GetEntry (InBuf, finished);
            IF finished THEN EXIT END;
            Insert (InBuf)
        END
    END Append;


PROCEDURE Review;
    (* Review records 1 at a time on screen;
       has option to delete a record *)
    VAR q, r: [0..MaxRecords];
        c: CHAR;
        Buf: RecType;


    PROCEDURE PutFree (r: INTEGER);
        (* Put record r in the free-list *)
        BEGIN

        Index[r] := Index[-1];
        Index[-1] := r
    END PutFree;


BEGIN
    ClearScreen;
    r := Index[0];      (* First record in linked list *)
    q := 0;
    LOOP
        IF r = EndList THEN EXIT END;
        WriteLn (console);
        PrintRec (console, r);
        WriteLn (console);
        WriteString (console,
            'G)et next record, D)elete this record, or Q)uit?');
        Read (c);
        WriteLn (console);
        CASE c OF
            'G', 'g': q := r;           (* Get Next *)
                      r := Index[r] ;
            'D', 'd': Index[q] := Index[r];
                      PutFree (r);      (* Delete *)
                      r := Index[q] ;
            'Q', 'q': EXIT
```

Fig. 10-20 (a). The AddressFile program. (Continued on page 285.)

```
                        END     (* Case *)
                END         (* Loop *)
        END Review;

    PROCEDURE List (VAR f:  TEXT);
        (* List all active records to f in alphabetical order *)
        VAR i:  [-1..MaxRecords];
        BEGIN
            i := Index[0];              (* first record *)
            WHILE i <> EndList DO
                WriteLn (f);
                PrintRec (f, i);
                i := Index[i]
            END
        END List;

    PROCEDURE ListFile;
        (* Find out whether to lis to screen or printer,
           then call List *)
        VAR a:  CHAR;
        BEGIN
            ClearScreen;
            WriteString (console, 'List to S)creen or P)rinter?  ');
            Read (a);
            WriteLn (console);
            CASE a OF
                'S', 's':  List (console) |
                'P', 'p':  List (printer)
            ELSE
                ListFile                (* Recursive call *)

            END;
            Pause
        END ListFile;

    PROCEDURE Dump;
        (* List file and pointers to printer for analysis *)
        VAR i:  CARDINAL;
        BEGIN
            WriteString (printer, 'First Free Record:  ');
            WriteInt (printer, Index[-1], 1);
            WriteLn (printer);
            WriteString (printer, 'First Record in Use:  ');
            WriteInt (printer, Index[0], 1);
```

```
                         WriteLn (printer);
                         FOR i := 1 TO MaxRecords DO
                              WriteLn (printer);
                              WriteString (printer, 'Record ');
                              WriteInt (printer, i, 1);
                              WriteLn (printer);
                              PrintRec (printer, i);
                              WriteString (printer, 'Next Record:  ');
                              WriteInt (printer, Index[i], 1);
                              WriteLn (printer)
                         END
                    END Dump;


          BEGIN                          (* Main Program *)
               OpenFiles;
               PrinterOn;
               LOOP
                    Menu (c);
                    CASE c OF
                         1:  Append ;
                         2:  Review ;
                         3:  ListFile ;
                         4:  Dump ;
                         5:  EXIT            (* Quit *)
                    END      (* Case *)
               END;         (* Loop *)
               PrinterOff;
               CloseFiles
          END AddressFile.
```

Fig. 10-20 (a). The Address File program. (Continued from page 285.)

Logo chapter. Because the use of graphics in Modula-2 is implementation dependent, the topic will not be pursued further in this book.

COMPREHENSIVE SAMPLE PROGRAM

All of the sample programs so far in this chapter have been relatively short. Each has had the purpose of illustrating a particular concept. Unfortunately not all "real" programs are short. In order to illustrate what a real Modula-2 program that performs a nontrivial function looks like, a comprehensive sample program is included.

The program is called AddressFile and main-

tains a file of names, addresses, and phone numbers in alphabetical order on disk. It also maintains an index file to keep track of the order of the records and of any unused records. This program illustrates the use of a direct-access file and is shown in Fig. 10-20a through 10-20e.

The organization of the program is illustrated in the structure chart in Fig. 10-21. Each name shown in the figure is the name of a procedure. The hierarchical structure of the program is indicated by indentation. A procedure is called by a given procedure if it is listed below it and one level of indentation to the right. For example, the GetFree proce-

```
DEFINITION MODULE FileIO;        (* $SEG:=12 *)

    FROM Files IMPORT FILE;

    EXPORT QUALIFIED
        OpenFiles, CloseFiles, GetRec, PutRec,
        RecType, InBuf, OutBuf, Index, EndList, MaxRecords;

    CONST
        MaxRecords = 10;
        EndList    = 0;
        FName      = 'ADDRESS.FILE';
        IName      = 'INDEX.FILE';

    TYPE
        NameType =
            RECORD
                last, first: ARRAY[0..12] OF CHAR;
            END;
        RecType =
            RECORD
                name:    NameType;
                address: ARRAY[0..20] OF CHAR;
                city:    ARRAY[0..12] OF CHAR;
                state:   ARRAY[0..2]  OF CHAR;
                zip:     ARRAY[0..5]  OF CHAR;
                phone:   ARRAY[0..14] OF CHAR;
            END;

    VAR
        InBuf, OutBuf: RecType;
        AddrFile, IndexFile: FILE;
        Index: ARRAY[-1..MaxRecords] OF INTEGER;
        (* Note:
            Index[-1] is subscript of first free record
            Index[0]  is subscript of first record in use *)

    PROCEDURE OpenFiles;
        (* Opens Address and Index files; reads Index file *)
    PROCEDURE CloseFiles;
        (* Saves Index and closes AddrFile and IndexFile *)
    PROCEDURE GetRec (i: CARDINAL; VAR InBuf: RecType);
        (* Reads Record i of AddrFile into InBuf *)
    PROCEDURE PutRec (i: CARDINAL; OutBuf: RecType);
        (* Writes OutBuf to file position i of AddrFile *)
END FileIO.
```

Fig. 10-20 (b). The FileIO definition module for AddressFile.

```
IMPLEMENTATION MODULE FileIO;

FROM Files IMPORT
    Open, Close, Create, FILE, FileStatus, FileState,
    ReadRec, WriteRec, CalcPos, FilePos, SetPos;

FROM SYSTEM IMPORT SIZE;

FROM Terminal IMPORT WriteString, WriteLn;

VAR IndexBuf: [0..MaxRecords];

PROCEDURE CloseIt (VAR f:  FILE);
    (* Close a file *)
    BEGIN
        IF Close (f) () FileOK THEN
            WriteString ('Error closing file...');
            HALT
        END;
    END CloseIt;

PROCEDURE InitFiles;
    (* Establish AddrFile and IndexFile.  Initializes
       AddrFile by filling it with blank records.
       Initializes IndexFile as a linked list of free
       records.  *)
    CONST blank = ' ';
    VAR i: [0..MaxRecords];
    BEGIN
        IF Create (AddrFile, FName) () FileOK THEN
            WriteString ('Unable to Create Address File...');
            HALT
        END;
        WITH OutBuf DO
            name.last   := blank;
            name.first  := blank;
            address     := blank;
            city        := blank;
            state       := blank;
            zip         := blank;
            phone       := blank
        END;
        FOR i := 0 TO MaxRecords DO
            WriteRec (AddrFile, OutBuf)
```

Fig. 10-20 (c). The FileIO implementation module for Address File. (Continued on page 289.)

```
            END;
            CloseIt (AddrFile);
            (* Now initialise Index File *)
            IF Create (IndexFile, IName) <> FileOK THEN
                WriteString ('Unable to Create Index File...');
                HALT
            END;
            IndexBuf := 1;                (* First Free Record *)

            WriteRec (IndexFile, IndexBuf);
            IndexBuf := EndList;          (* No Records in Use *)
            WriteRec (IndexFile, IndexBuf);
            (* Complete Free List *)
            FOR i := 1 TO MaxRecords-1 DO
                IndexBuf := i + 1;
                WriteRec (IndexFile, IndexBuf)
            END;
            IndexBuf := EndList;
            WriteRec (IndexFile, IndexBuf);
            CloseIt (IndexFile);
        END InitFiles;


    PROCEDURE OpenFiles;
        (* Open the Address and Index file; read Index File *)
        VAR i:  [-1..MaxRecords];
            flag:  FileState;
        BEGIN
            flag := Open (AddrFile, FName);
            IF flag = NameError THEN
                InitFiles;
                flag := Open (AddrFile, FName)
            END;
            IF flag <> FileOK THEN
                WriteString ('Unable to open Address File...');
                HALT
            END;
            IF Open (IndexFile, IName) <> FileOK THEN
                WriteString ('Unable to opne Index File...');
                HALT
            END;
            FOR i := -1 TO MaxRecords DO
                ReadRec (IndexFile, IndexBuf);
                Index[i] := IndexBuf
            END;
        END OpenFiles;
```

```
                PROCEDURE CloseFiles;
                    (* Write Index File to disk and close both files *)
                    VAR i:  [-1..MaxRecords];
                        index :  CARDINAL;
                        newpos:  FilePos;
                    BEGIN
                        (* Find beginning of IndexFile *)
                        index := 0;
                        CalcPos (index, SIZE (IndexBuf), newpos);
                        SetPos (IndexFile, newpos);
                        FOR i := -1 TO MaxRecords DO
                            IndexBuf := Index[i];
                            WriteRec (IndexFile, IndexBuf)
                        END;
                        CloseIt (IndexFile);
                        CloseIt (AddrFile);
                    END CloseFiles;

                PROCEDURE Seek (i:  CARDINAL; rec:  RecType);
                    (* Position file at record i of AddrFile *)
                    VAR newpos:  FilePos;
                    BEGIN
                        CalcPos (i, SIZE (rec), newpos);
                        SetPos (AddrFile, newpos);
                        IF FileStatus (AddrFile) <> FileOK THEN
                            WriteString ('File seek error...');
                            HALT
                        END;
                    END Seek;


                PROCEDURE GetRec (i:  CARDINAL;  VAR InBuf:  RecType);
                    (* Reads Record i of AddrFile into Inbuf *)
                    BEGIN
                        Seek (i, InBuf);
                        ReadRec (AddrFile, InBuf)
                    END GetRec;


                PROCEDURE PutRec (i:  CARDINAL;  OutBuf: RecType);
                    (* Writes OutBuf to file position i of AddrFile *)
                    BEGIN
                        Seek (i, OutBuf);
                        WriteRec (AddrFile, OutBuf)
                    END PutRec;


        END FileIO.
```

Fig. 10-20 (c). The FileIO implementation module for Address File. (Continued from page 289.)

```
DEFINITION MODULE TextIO;                    (* $SEG:=11 *)

    FROM Texts IMPORT TEXT;

    FROM FileIO IMPORT RecType;

    EXPORT QUALIFIED PrintRec, GetEntry, Menu;

    PROCEDURE PrintRec (VAR f:  TEXT; i:  CARDINAL);
        (* Print record i on text file f *)

    PROCEDURE GetEntry (VAR r:  RecType;  VAR finished:  BOOLEAN);
        (* Read 1 record from console into record r *)

    PROCEDURE Menu (VAR c:  CARDINAL);
        (* Display the main menu and return selection *)

END TextIO.
```

Fig. 10-20 (d). The TextIO definition module for AddressFile.

dure is called by Insert, which is called by Append, which is called by the main program, AddressFile.

The program is implemented as three modules. The main program is the AddressFile module, which is shown in Fig. 10-20a. The FileIO module is shown in Fig. 10-20b (the definition module) and in Fig. 10-20c (the implementation module). The TextIO module is shown in Fig. 10-20d and 10-20e.

The details of file input and output have been restricted to the FileIO module. This module includes the procedures to initialize files, to open and close files, and to access particular records in the address file. It also includes the record and type definitions for this particular file structure.

The details of accessing a particular record in a file discussed above are illustrated in the procedures Seek, GetRec, and PutRec, found in Fig. 10-20c.

The details of screen input and output and printer output are found in the TextIO module. Notice that the interface presented to the main module by the definition module in Fig. 10-20d is very simple. All of the tedious details are in the implementation module in Fig. 10-20e.

A program that has been segmented into modules such as this is easier to understand than one that has not. To judge for yourself, compare this program with the Pascal program in Fig. 11-18. The algorithms used are the same. Separate compilation of modules also makes implementation easier. A long program takes longer to compile than a short module; the difference can be significant on a microcomputer.

Using the AddressFile program is simple. It presents a menu of options, including adding a record to the file, reviewing the file one record at a time, listing the file to the screen or printer, and dumping the file to the printer.

When you are adding a record to the file, the program presents a screen to be filled in with the appropriate data. Pressing the RETURN key at the beginning of the last name field terminates input. When the data has been entered, it is written to disk in the next available location. It is then inserted into the index in the appropriate places. The index is maintained as a linked list, much like the linked list described in Chapter 2.

The review option also allows records to be deleted. When a record is deleted, it is removed

```
IMPLEMENTATION MODULE TextIO;

    FROM FileIO   IMPORT GetRec, RecType;

    FROM Texts    IMPORT TEXT, Write, WriteString, WriteLn,
        ReadCard, console;

    FROM Screen   IMPORT ClearScreen, GotoXY;

    FROM Terminal IMPORT ReadLn;

    FROM Strings  IMPORT Length;

    PROCEDURE PrintRec (VAR f: TEXT; i:  CARDINAL);
        (* Print record i on text file f *)
        VAR r:  RecType;
        BEGIN
            GetRec (i, r);
            WITH r DO
                WriteString (f, name.first);
                WriteString (f, ' ');
                WriteString (f, name.last);
                WriteLn (f);
                WriteString (f, address);
                WriteLn (f);
                WriteString (f, city);
                WriteString (f, ', ');
                WriteString (f, state);
                WriteString (f, ' ');
                WriteString (f, zip);
                WriteLn (f);
                WriteString (f, phone);
                WriteLn (f)
            END
        END PrintRec;


    PROCEDURE NextField (VAR row, col:  CARDINAL);
        (* Position cursor 2 rows down, same column *)
        BEGIN
            INC (row,2);
            GotoXY (col, row)
        END NextField;
```

Fig. 10-20 (e). The TextIO implementation module for AddressFile. (Continued on page 293.)

```
PROCEDURE GetEntry (VAR r:  RecType; VAR finished:  BOOLEAN);
    (* Read 1 record from console into record r *)
    VAR row, col, start, i:  CARDINAL;

    PROCEDURE MarkOff (start, spaces:  CARDINAL);
        (* Mark off data input area with colons *)
        BEGIN
            GotoXY (start, row);
            Write (console, ':');
            FOR i := 1 TO spaces DO
                Write (console, ' ')
            END;
            Write (console, ':')
        END MarkOff;

    BEGIN (* Body of GetEntry *)
        ClearScreen;
        (* First display skeleton record *)
        start := 14;
        row   := 5; col   := 1;
        GotoXY (col, row);
        WriteString (console, 'Last Name:');
        MarkOff (start, 12);  NextField (row, col);
        WriteString (console, 'First Name:');
        MarkOff (start, 12);  NextField (row, col);
        WriteString (console, 'Address:');
        MarkOff (start, 20);  NextField (row, col);
        WriteString (console, 'City:');
        MarkOff (start, 12);  NextField (row, col);
        WriteString (console, 'State:');
        MarkOff (start, 2);   NextField (row, col);
        WriteString (console, 'Zip:');
        MarkOff (start, 5);   NextField (row, col);
        WriteString (console, 'Phone:');
        MarkOff (start, 14);
        (* Now read in each field *)
        row := 5;  col := 15;
        GotoXY (col, row);
        WITH r DO
            ReadLn (name.last);          :
            finished := (Length (name.last) = 0);  (* Empty String *)
            IF NOT finished THEN
                NextField (row, col);
```

```
                        ReadLn (name.first);
                        NextField (row, col);
                        ReadLn (address);
                        NextField (row, col);
                        ReadLn (city);
                        NextField (row, col);
                        ReadLn (state);
                        NextField (row, col);
                        ReadLn (zip);
                        NextField (row, col);
                        ReadLn (phone)
                    END
                END
            END GetEntry;

        PROCEDURE Menu (VAR c:  CARDINAL);
            (* Display the main menu and return selection *)
            VAR row, col:  CARDINAL;
            BEGIN
                ClearScreen;
                row:= 5;  col := 5;
                GotoXY (col, row);
                WriteString (console, '1)  Add to File');
                NextField (row, col);
                WriteString (console, '2)  Review File on Screen');
                NextField (row, col);
                WriteString (console, '3)  List File to Screen or Printer');
                NextField (row, col);
                WriteString (console, '4)  Dump File to Printer');
                NextField (row, col);
                WriteString (console, '5)  Quit');
                INC (row, 2);
                col := 1;
                REPEAT
                    GotoXY (col, row);
                    WriteString (console, 'Select 1, 2, 3, 4, or 5:  ');
                    ReadCard (console, c)
                UNTIL c IN {1..5}
            END Menu;
        END TextIO.
```

Fig. 10-20 (e). The TextIO implementation module for AddressFile. (Continued from page 293.)

from the index of active records and added to the list of free records for subsequent reuse.

The list option lists the file in alphabetical order. The user is given the choice of whether to list it on the video screen or on the printer.

The dump option is provided as a learning tool. It prints all records, active or free, in the order in which they are stored. It also prints the appropriate

```
                AddressFile
                  OpenFiles
                    InitFiles
                  PrinterOn
                  Menu
                    NextField
                  Append
                    Pause
                    GetEntry
                      MarkOff
                      NextField
                    Insert
                      GetFree
                      PutRec
                        Seek
                      GetRec
                        Seek
                      Greater
                  Review
                    PrintRec
                      GetRec
                    PutFree
                  ListFile
                    List
                        PrintRec
                    Pause
                  Dump
                      PrintRec
                  PrinterOff
                  CloseFiles
```

Fig. 10-21. The structure chart for the AddressFile program.

record pointers. A good way to learn how the file is structured is to add a few records, dump the file, delete a record, dump the file, and repeat the process.

The constant MaxRecords in the FileIO module limits the size of the file to 10 names. This conserves paper when you run the dump option. If this program is to be used to maintain an actual list of names, addresses, and phone numbers, the constant MaxRecords should be increased in value and the modules recompiled.

Notice that the FileIO module is used by both AddressFile and TextIO. This means that the

definition module of FileIO must be compiled before either AddressFile or TextIO is compiled. Because TextIO is used by AddressFile, the definition module of TextIO must be compiled before AddressFile can be compiled.

ADVANTAGES AND DISADVANTAGES OF MODULA-2

This chapter has only scratched the surface of Modula-2. It has not discussed, for example, the ability of Modula-2 to handle coprocessing, dynamic storage allocation, or open arrays. Much more space than is available in this chapter is needed to discuss these features of Modula-2. In this section, only those features that have been presented will be appraised.

As a successor to Pascal, Modula-2 is in the enviable position of having "learned" from Pascal's shortcomings. Perhaps the greatest advantage of Modula-2 over Pascal is the availability of modules and separate compilation.

The availability of the module encourages the proper structuring of programs and provides safeguards against unwanted interference between different parts of programs.

Modula-2 includes an additional control structure, the LOOP . . . END structure with EXIT. This permits increased flexibility in implementing loops.

Modula-2 includes an ELSE clause in its CASE statement. This corrects an apparent oversight in Pascal. The individual cases in Modula-2 can be subranges such as ['A' . . 'Z']. In Pascal, the equivalent case would have to enumerate each letter 'A', 'B', 'C', and so on through 'Z'.

Modula-2 terminates its control structures (except the REPEAT . . . UNTIL structure) with END. This eliminates all the extra BEGINs found in Pascal.

On the negative side, the fact that Modula-2 implements its input and output statements as procedures in library modules has some undesirable side effects. Consider the output procedures for example. Separate procedures are needed for writing a character, a string, an integer, a real number, and a carriage return. Furthermore, each procedure can handle only one data item. Thus to write a line containing two character strings, an integer, and a real number would require five separate procedure calls, two to WriteString (for the character strings), one to WriteInt (for the integer), one to WriteReal (for the real number), and one to WriteLn (for the terminating carriage return and line feed).

A related feature that I did not like was the fact that there are multiple versions of procedures such as WriteString in different libraries, and the syntax used in accessing them differs. To write a message to the screen, for example, one would write

```
WriteString ('Hello')
```

using the version of the procedure from the modules InOut or Terminal, but

```
WriteString (console, 'Hello')
```

using the version of the procedure from the Texts module. It is easy to confuse the two forms of the statement.

Like Pascal, Modula-2 lacks an exponentiation operator.

AVAILABILITY

Modula-2 is a relatively new language, having been introduced in the 1980's. To date, there are relatively few implementations available. Versions are available from Volition Systems of Del Mar, California; Logitech, Inc., of Redwood City, California; and Modula Research Institute, of Provo, Utah.

SUMMARY

Modula-2 is an extremely powerful, yet compact language. It is the newest of the languages presented in this book, and, although it is relatively little-used today, it shows promise of becoming increasingly popular in the future.

Modula-2 has features that facilitate the orderly development of large-scale programming systems. The module structure and the enforced interface standards between modules (including version control) are especially useful when a program is to be developed by a team of programmers.

Modula-2 offers facilities (not discussed herein) for low-level operations, such as minipulating bits and bytes. This makes it suitable for systems programming applications such as operating systems.

Modula-2 is similar enough to Pascal that Pascal programmers can make the transition to Modula-2 in a matter of a few hours.

Modula-2 encourages good structured programming style. It is an excellent language for general-purpose programming and for the development of large-scale programming systems.

Chapter 11

Pascal

The Pascal language was designed by Niklaus Wirth of the Eidgenossische Technische Hochschule (Federal Institute of Technology), Zurich, Switzerland. It is based largely on an earlier language known as ALGOL 60. ALGOL 60 was developed between 1957 and 1960 and as such is one of the earliest high-level computer languages. It found favor in Europe, but was little used in the United States outside of universities. Professor Wirth was associated with ALGOL in the 1960s, both at Zurich and at Stanford University in California.

The late 1960s saw the introduction of a successor to ALGOL 60 known as ALGOL 68. Professor Wirth and others objected to ALGOL 68 as being too unwieldy. The professor's response was to develop (between 1968 and 1970) a more streamlined successor to ALGOL 60, a language he called Pascal. The mathematician, Blaise Pascal, is credited with inventing the world's first digital calculating machine.

Pascal was originally designed as a language suitable for teaching computer programming to stu-

dents. It has achieved great popularity not only as a teaching language, but also as a general-purpose language. Because of its streamlined design, it is easily implemented on microcomputers. Dr. Kenneth Bowles of the University of California at San Diego (UCSD) deserves special recognition for his early implementation of Pascal on microcomputers.

ALGOL 68, the "official" successor of ALGOL 60, has faded quietly into oblivion. Pascal, on the other hand, is probably second only to BASIC in popularity among microcomputer users.

The examples in this chapter were tested using the Apple/UCSD implementation of Pascal.

PROGRAM STRUCTURE

A Pascal program consists of a heading and a block. A simple Pascal program that does nothing but print "This is a test" can be written as shown in Fig. 11-1.

The first line is the heading; it gives a name to the program and identifies any input or output files. The file OUTPUT means normal console output. (Note: some versions of Pascal make the listing of

297

```
PROGRAM TEST(OUTPUT);

   { Minimal Test Program }

BEGIN

   WRITELN('This is a test');

END.
```

Fig. 11-1. A minimal Pascal program.

input and output files in this line optional.) The second line contains a comment between the braces. Comments are inserted for clarity. The main body of the program is the block that begins with BEGIN and ends with END.

In this case the body of the program consists of a single statement, which writes a message to the console. Statements in Pascal are separated by semicolons. A semicolon need not appear just before an END, however; the last semicolon in Fig. 11-1 is optional. A period must appear after the final END in a program.

A useful feature of Pascal, inherited from ALGOL, is that wherever a statement can appear, so can a block. A block is defined as zero or more statements bracketed by BEGIN and END. Pascal for that reason is sometimes called a block-structured language. The significance of this feature will become clear in subsequent sections of this chapter.

Most implementations of Pascal on microcomputers use *native-code* compilers or *intermediate-code* compilers. Native code is another name for the machine language of a particular computer. Intermediate code (sometimes called *p-code*) resembles the assembly language of a hypothetical computer that may not exist anywhere. An intermediate code compiler translates a program from its source language (in this case Pascal) to intermediate code. The intermediate code is then interpreted. The advantage of this scheme is that the compiler need be written only once; only the intermediate-code interpreter need be rewritten to implement the system on another host computer. Of the popular

implementations of Pascal on microcomputers, UCSD Pascal, Pascal M, and JRT Pascal use intermediate-code compilers; while Pascal MT+ and Pascal Z use native-code compilers.

DATA REPRESENTATION

The basic data types in Pascal are real, integer, char (character) and Boolean (logical). Character strings are represented as arrays of characters in standard Pascal, but most versions also incorporate a string type. Some implementations also support a form of binary-coded decimal (BCD) representation called *long integer*. This form of representation is particularly useful for business applications.

An interesting feature of Pascal is that the programmer can define additional types of his/her own description. As a simple example, suppose that a program requires a nonnegative integer value. A type can be declared as follows:

TYPE NATURAL = 0..MAXINT;

MAXINT is a predefined constant that represents the largest integer that can be represented on a particular computer. The type NATURAL thus includes all integers between 0 and MAXINT.

Constants

Pascal allows constants to be named and declared in a program. A simple example is shown in Fig. 11-2. In this program, PI is declared to be a

```
PROGRAM TRIG(OUTPUT);

   CONST

      PI = 3.14159;

BEGIN

   WRITELN('PI = ', PI);

END.
```

Fig. 11-2. Pascal constant declaration.

constant and is given a value, which it retains for the duration of the program. This helps to document programs. While in this case the value of the constant PI is not likely to ever change, in some cases there are constants, such as the sales tax rate, that remain relatively constant, but may change over time. By naming and declaring such constants at the beginning of the program, the programmer makes subsequent updatings of the program much easier.

Representation of both integer and real numerical constant is conventional, as described in Chapter 2. The two Boolean constants are of course true and false.

Variables

Variables in Pascal must be declared at the beginning of the program. A simple example is given in Fig. 11-3. The program simply computes and prints out the area of a circle with a radius of 5.0. The integer variable I was not actually used; it was declared simply to display the format for declaring variables for different types.

THE ASSIGNMENT STATEMENT

The assignment operator in Pascal is a colon followed by an equals sign (:=). The above example contains two simple assignment statements immediately following BEGIN.

The assignment statement is very particular about types. For example, the statement

I := AREA

in the program in Fig. 11-3 would not compile correctly because I is an integer and AREA is a real number.

ARITHMETIC EXPRESSIONS

Pascal uses conventional infix notation (see Chapter 2) for its arithmetic expressions. It has the usual arithmetic operators (+, −, *, /) with the significant exception of an exponentiation operator. Wirth apparently reasoned that exponentiation can be performed by repeated multiplication (in the case of integer exponents) or by using logarithms,

```
PROGRAM CIRCLE(OUTPUT);

    CONST

        PI = 3.14159;

    VAR

        AREA, RADIUS:   REAL;

        I:   INTEGER;

BEGIN

    RADIUS := 5.0;

    AREA := PI * RADIUS * RADIUS;

    WRITELN('RADIUS:    ',RADIUS);

    WRITELN('AREA:       ',AREA);

END.
```

Fig. 11-3. Pascal numerical computation.

and that it is better to let the programmer decide how it should be done than to let the system decide. Absence of this operator is a minor annoyance.

BOOLEAN EXPRESSIONS

Chapter 2 discussed logical expressions. Pascal calls logical expressions *Boolean expressions*. Pascal has the usual relational and logical operators as listed in Chapter 2 (for example, > and OR.)

A minor difficulty arises when combining simple Boolean expressions to form compound Boolean expressions. Suppose that A, B, C, and D are all real variables. In most languages the expression A > B OR C > D would be perfectly acceptable. In Pascal you would have to write (A > B) OR (C > D). This latter expression is easier to read anyway.

INPUT AND OUTPUT

You have already seen examples of the

WRITELN statement in Fig. 11-2 and 11-3. These examples directed output to the system console (video screen). An alternate form of the WRITELN statement allows the output to be directed to the system printer or, as will be discussed in a later section, to a disk file.

How this is done unfortunately varies somewhat from system to system. An example will be given anyway because the topic is too often not covered properly in the individual language manuals. Figure 11-4 shows a simple program that writes to both the video screen and to the printer. The example is valid for the Apple version of UCSD Pascal; the details may vary somewhat for other Pascal implementations.

The standard output file in Pascal is called OUTPUT and refers to the video screen. The file OUTPUT does not have to be declared explicitly. Note that OUTPUT appears in parentheses following the program name. Standard Pascal requires all input and output file names to be so listed. (Some microcomputer versions omit this requirement.) This program introduces another file called PRT.

Note that PRT is also listed in parentheses following the program name. PRT, however, is not a standard file and must therefore be declared. Note that it is declared to be a text variable. TEXT is shorthand for FILE OF CHAR; printer files must be of this type.

The statement

REWRITE(PRT,'PRINTER:')

serves to open the file PRT for output and to associate the internal file name PRT with the external device called PRINTER:, which is the name UCSD Pascal gives to the system printer.

The form of a WRITELN statement allows the first item inside the parentheses to be the name of a file. If it is not, then the default output file OUTPUT is assumed. The first WRITELN in Fig. 11-4 could also have been written as

WRITELN(OUTPUT,'THIS GOES TO THE VIDEO SCREEN.').

In the following WRITELN, PRT is the first item inside the parentheses, so output is directed to the file PRT, which in this case is the printer.

A WRITELN statement always causes a carriage return at the end of the output. If the output device is the video screen, this means that the cursor automatically returns to the first column of the next line. If this is not desired, the WRITE

```
PROGRAM PRINTEST(OUTPUT,PRT);

    ( This program writes to the video screen
      and to the printer )

    VAR PRT: TEXT;

BEGIN

    REWRITE(PRT,'PRINTER:');

    WRITELN('THIS GOES TO THE VIDEO SCREEN.');

    WRITELN(PRT,'THIS GOES TO THE PRINTER.');

END.
```

Fig. 11-4. Pascal printer output.

300

statement can be used instead of the WRITELN statement. Otherwise there is no difference between the two statements.

It is often useful to be able to control the format of the output. In the case of a character string, this means the field width of the output should be controlled. Suppose the character string C has the value Hi. The statement

WRITE(C:5)

would write Hi   to the screen and the cursor would be left three spaces to the right of the letter i. Thus the total field width would be five: two columns for the character string and three for trailing blanks. Assuming the H went in column 1, anything written thereafter would begin in column 6.

As illustrated above, character strings are left-justified in the designated field. Numbers are right-justified. For example, if A has been declared an integer,

A := 1 ;
WRITE(A:5);

would write   1 to the screen, that is, a 1 preceded by four blanks.

The user can also control the number of digits to the right of the decimal point in real numbers. For example, if X has been declared real,

X := 3.1 ;
WRITE(X:5:2);

would write   3.10 to the screen. The total number of spaces occupied is five with two places to the right of the decimal point.

The READ and READLN statements are used for input. The standard input device is the terminal or keyboard and is formally called *input*. Thus INPUT needs to be mentioned in the parentheses in the PROGRAM line at the top of the program for all programs containing READ or READLN statements.

The distinction between READ and READLN needs to be studied carefully. When using READ

with a CHAR variable, READ takes a single character from the file at a time and assigns its value to the variable in the READ statement. For example, if C is a CHAR variable,

READ(C)

or

READ(INPUT,C)

would read one character from the INPUT file and assign its value to the variable C. When the end-of-line character (a carriage return, ASCII 13) is encountered, READ returns a space (ASCII 32) rather than a carriage return.

There are two Boolean variables called EOLN (End Of LiNe) and EOF (End Of File) implicit in every program. EOLN becomes true when the end-of-line character is encountered by a READ or READLN statement. EOF becomes true when the end of the INPUT file is encountered. The end-of-file character is Control-C (ETX or ASCII 3). Control-C is entered from the keyboard by holding down the Control (CTRL) key while pressing the C key. Testing for EOF is inconvenient when reading from the INPUT file.

When READ is used with a numeric variable (READ or INTEGER), it skips any spaces or end-of-line characters preceding the number and then reads the digits until it encounters a space, end-of-line, or end-of-file character. The next READ statement will start looking in the very next position in the same line (unless the previous READ was terminated by an end-of-line or end-of-file character).

READLN may be used with variables of the CHAR, STRING, INTEGER, REAL, or (when implemented) LONG REAL types. The format is

READLN(V1, V2, . . . ,VN)

or

READLN(INPUT,V1,V2, . . . , VN).

The difference between READ and READLN is

that after the last variable in the list (VN in this case) is read, the remainder of the current input line is skipped. The next READ or READLN statement will start looking on the next line.

Most of the time READ and READLN produce the same results when used with the standard INPUT file, but not always. READLN is usually preferred, as its results are usually easier to predict.

READLN is especially convenient for reading string variables from the console (INPUT). Suppose S is a string variable. The following statement reads an entire line from the console and stores it in the variable S:

READLN(S).

The program in Fig. 11-5 serves as an electronic typewriter; it reads line after line from the console, sending them successively to the printer.

```
PROGRAM TYPEWRITER1(INPUT,OUTPUT,PRT);

   (This program emulates an electronic
    typewriter using the READLN statement
    with a STRING variable.)

   VAR S:   STRING;

      PRT:  TEXT;

BEGIN

   REWRITE(PRT,'PRINTER:');

   WRITELN('Welcome to your Electronic Typewriter.');

   WRITELN;

   WRITELN('Enter your text, followed by "Control-C".');

   WRITELN;

   READLN(S);

   REPEAT

      WRITELN(PRT,S);

      READLN(S)

   UNTIL EOF;

   END.
```

Fig. 11-5. Pascal Electronic Typewriter, Version 1.

```
PROGRAM TYPEWRITER2(INPUT,OUTPUT,PRT);

    (This program emulates an electronic
     typewriter using the READ statement
     with a CHAR variable.)

    VAR C:  CHAR;

      PRT:  TEXT;

BEGIN

    REWRITE(PRT,'PRINTER:');

    WRITELN('Welcome to your Electronic Typewriter.');

    WRITELN;

    WRITELN('Enter your text, followed by "Control-C".');

    WRITELN;

    READ(C);

    REPEAT

        WRITE(PRT,C);

        IF EOLN THEN WRITELN(PRT);

        READ(C)

    UNTIL EOF;

END.
```

Fig. 11-6. Pascal Electronic Typewriter, Version 2.

(Note: the use of the REPEAT-UNTIL construct was introduced in Chapter 2 and is discussed in more detail in a later section of this chapter.)

For comparison, the program in Fig. 11-6 does essentially the same thing using READ and a character variable. The first thing you will note is that the logic is slightly more complex. If you try the two programs, you will note that the program in Fig. 11-5 is much more forgiving; it lets you backspace and correct errors. The program in Fig. 11-6 does not. That alone is sufficient reason for preferring the use of READLN and string variables over READ and character variables for console input.

CONTROL STRUCTURES

Pascal has a rich set of control structures, much richer than such languages as FORTRAN, COBOL, or BASIC have. The control structures in Pascal are highly-structured in addition to being numerous. What this means is that Pascal control structures follow the fundamental principle that there should be only one entry to and one exit from a control structure. This makes it easier to follow the logic of a program.

The format of the various control structures rely heavily on the block structure of Pascal. Recall from the discussion above that wherever the language calls for a statement, a block containing several statements can occur, delimited by BEGIN and END.

Simple Selection: IF-THEN-ELSE

The general format for this statement in Pascal is

```
IF condition THEN
    statement1
ELSE
    statement2;
```

the ELSE and statement2 are optional. The condition is understood to be any Boolean expression as defined above. Statement1 and statement2 can be single statements or blocks.

Below is a simple IF statement without an ELSE part. It is intended to prevent division by zero and signal when it would have occurred. NUM, DENOM, and QUOTIENT are real variables, and FLAG is a Boolean variable assumed to be false initially.

```
IF DENOM = 0.0 THEN
    BEGIN
        DENOM := 1.0;
        FLAG    := TRUE
    END;
QUOTIENT := NUM/DENOM;
```

In this example the two statements between BEGIN and END are treated as if they were syntactically one statement.

Now suppose in the same situation that you could not assume that FLAG was initially false. Here is a solution:

```
IF DENOM = 0.0 THEN
    BEGIN
        DENOM := 1.0;
        FLAG    := TRUE
    END
ELSE
    FLAG := FALSE;
QUOTIENT := NUM/DENOM;
```

In this case FLAG is set to false if DENOM is not zero. This example illustrates another point: there can be no semicolon after the END before the ELSE. A semicolon would cause the compiler to think that everything between IF and the semicolon was a single statement. It would then try unsuccessfully to form a new statement starting with the ELSE.

One (or both) of the statements within the IF-THEN-ELSE construct can also be an IF or IF-THEN-ELSE. Suppose that you are computing a weekly payroll; time-and-a-half is paid for all hours worked in excess of 40 but less than 50, and double-time is paid for all hours worked in excess of 50.

```
IF HOURS <= 40 THEN
    PAY := HOURS * RATE
ELSE IF HOURS <= 50 THEN
    PAY := 40 * RATE + (HOURS – 40) *
    RATE * 1.5
ELSE
    PAY := 40 * RATE + 10 * RATE * 1.5
            + (HOURS – 50) * RATE * 2;
```

This is called a nested IF. Notice that the statement following the last ELSE is continued onto the next line. Also, remember that statements in Pascal are separated by semicolons; it makes no difference that the statement spills over onto the next line.

```
PROGRAM MONTHS(INPUT,OUTPUT);

    VAR

        MONTH, YEAR, DAYS:   INTEGER;

BEGIN

    WRITE('ENTER THE MONTH (1..12):   ');

    READLN(MONTH);

    CASE MONTH OF

        1,3,5,7,

        8,10,12:   DAYS := 31;

        4,6,9,11:  DAYS := 30;

        2:             BEGIN

                        WRITE('ENTER THE YEAR :   ');

                        READLN(YEAR);

                        IF YEAR MOD 4 = 0 THEN

                            DAYS := 29

                        ELSE

                            DAYS := 28;

                    END;

    END;

    WRITELN('MONTH ',MONTH,' HAS ',DAYS,' DAYS');

END.
```

Fig. 11-7. Pascal Calendar program.

The CASE Statement

IF statements permit selection between two alternatives. Nested IF statements permit selection between a number. The CASE statement provides another form of selection between multiple alternatives. Whereas nested IF statements are generally useful, the CASE statement is often more convenient in situations in which the choice to be made depends on the value of a specific variable. The type of that variable must be integer, Boolean, character, or user-defined scalar. (Note: as mentioned earlier, user-defined types are beyond the scope of this book.)

An example of Pascal CASE statement was given in Chapter 2. For another example, suppose that a program needs to calculate the number of days in a month. You all know the old poem, "Thirty days hath September, . . . ," but most computers do not. Figure 11-7 shows a short program that handles this problem. This program reads in the month and then uses the CASE statement to decide what value to assign to the variable DAYS. Notice that there are only three cases: one case for the 31-day months, one case for the 30-day months, and one case for February. The CASE statement permits like cases to be grouped together, so this situation is easy to accommodate. In the case of February, the program must know the year so that it can determine whether or not it is a leap year. The operator MOD computes the modulus, or remainder after integer division. Thus if

$$(YEAR\ MOD\ 4 = 0),$$

the year is evenly divisible by 4 and is a leap year.

A shortcoming of the standard Pascal CASE statement is that what should happen if the case selector variable is not one of the values listed is not defined. In this case that means that there is no protection against the user asking for the number of days in the 13th month. To guard against such possibilities, the programmer should precede the CASE statement with one or more IF statements to check for such a situation. Many implementations of Pascal extend the language in the form of an "else" or "otherwise" clause in the CASE statement.

Loops

Pascal provides a variety of control structures for repetition—one kind of counted loop and two kinds of conditional loop.

Counted Loops: The FOR Statement. Chapter 2 contained a simple example in BASIC of a program that printed out the integers from 1 to 10. Figure 11-8 contains a Pascal program that accomplishes the same thing.

In this program, the variable I serves as the loop counter. The variable I is incremented from 1 to 10; during each loop the value of I is printed out on the screen using the WRITELN statement. The WRITELN statement is the body of the loop. In this case the body of the loop consists of only one statement. If there were a need for more than one statement in the body of the loop, the statements would be bracketed by BEGIN and END, forming a block.

Conditional Loops. Conditional loops repeat a sequence of statements until a certain condition is met or as long as a certain condition stays true. The two types of conditional loop in Pascal are the WHILE loop and the REPEAT-UNTIL Loop.

The WHILE loop repeats as long as the stated condition is true. The test of the condition is performed at the top of the loop, before the body of the loop is performed. Thus if the condition is initially false, the body of the loop will not be performed at all. Figure 11-9 shows how the task performed by

```
PROGRAM TESTFOR(OUTPUT);

    (AN EXAMPLE OF THE FOR LOOP)

    VAR I :   INTEGER;

BEGIN

    FOR I := 1 TO 10 DO

        WRITELN(I);

END .
```

Fig. 11-8. The Pascal counted loop (FOR Statement).

```
PROGRAM TESTWHILE(OUTPUT);

    {AN EXAMPLE OF THE WHILE LOOP}

    VAR I :   INTEGER;

BEGIN

    I := 1;

    WHILE I <= 10 DO

        BEGIN

            WRITELN(I);

            I := I + 1;

        END;

END.
```

Fig. 11-9. The Pascal conditional loop (WHILE Statement).

the program in Fig. 11-8 can be performed using a WHILE loop rather than a FOR loop.

Note that the program in Fig. 11-9 is longer than that in Fig. 11-8, even though they do exactly the same thing. Thus a FOR loop is more efficient than the WHILE loop for this particular application. Nonetheless, the program in Fig. 11-9 is useful for pointing out some of the functions performed automatically by the FOR loop. Note that the variable I must be initialized to 1 before the loop begins, and that it must be incremented at the bottom of the loop. These are functions performed automatically by the FOR loop.

There are other situations, however, in which the WHILE loop is more appropriate than the FOR loop. Suppose, for example, a program is required to read in integers from the console and add them as long as the sum does not exceed 100. The program must then print out the sum and the number of integers that were added to yield the sum. The last integer read is not to be counted or summed. Such a program is shown in Fig. 11-10.

This program is slightly more complicated than earlier programs in this chapter. One reason is that the task is more complicated. Another reason is that the program is designed to be interactive, so it contains a number of WRITELN statements intended to prompt the user for input and to explain the output.

In this example the initialization step consists of setting the variables COUNT and SUM to zero and reading in the first value of NUM. The WHILE statement checks to see whether the most recent value of NUM added to the current value of SUM is less than or equal to 100. If it is, the body of the loop is executed. The body of the loop consists of counting the number just read, adding it to SUM, and reading in the next value of NUM. The process is repeated as long as the last value of NUM would not push the sum over 100. The rest of the program merely reports the results.

The REPEAT-UNTIL loop repeats a sequence of statements until a certain condition is attained. In contrast to the WHILE statement, the REPEAT-UNTIL statement performs the test at the bottom of the loop. In some situations it is preferable to test at the bottom, and in some it is preferable to test at the top. In other situations it doesn't make any difference one way or the other.

The program in Fig. 11-11 performs the same task as that in Fig. 11-10 using a REPEAT-UNTIL loop rather than a WHILE loop. Notice that certain adjustments had to be made because the REPEAT-UNTIL loop tests at the bottom and therefore must execute at least one time. The variable COUNT had to be initialized to -1, and NUM had to be initialized to 0 so that the first iteration would not throw off the count and the total. Although this works perfectly well, it is less straightforward than the approach taken when the WHILE loop was used. In this case, then, the WHILE loop is preferable to the REPEAT-UNTIL loop. In other cases the REPEAT-UNTIL may be preferable.

Procedures

Subroutines are called procedures in Pascal. A procedure is a more-or-less self-contained module

```
PROGRAM SUMUP(INPUT,OUTPUT);

    {READ UNTIL SUM > 100}

    VAR

        NUM, COUNT, SUM:  INTEGER;

BEGIN

    COUNT := 0;

    SUM   := 0;

    WRITELN('ENTER A SERIES OF NUMBERS:');

    READLN(NUM);

    WHILE (SUM + NUM) <= 100 DO

        BEGIN

            COUNT := COUNT + 1;

            SUM   := SUM + NUM;

            READLN(NUM);

        END;

    WRITELN;

    WRITELN(COUNT,' NUMBERS WERE READ.');

    WRITELN('THEIR SUM IS ',SUM,'.');

    WRITELN('THE NUMBER ',NUM,' WAS NOT COUNTED.');

END.
```

Fig. 11-10. The Pascal Sum-Up program, Version 1.

that is defined at the beginning of a Pascal program and that can be invoked almost anywhere in a program. The use of procedures in a Pascal program usually makes the program easier to design, develop, and maintain. Program development is accomplished largely by subdividing large, complex tasks into smaller, simpler tasks. These smaller tasks are conceptually much easier to deal with.

The advantages of using procedures are discussed further in the section on subroutines in Chapter 2.

Sometimes procedures are convenient because they reduce the amount of duplicate coding in a program. Consider for example a program in which the value of two real variables must be exchanged at various places in the program. Figure 11-12 shows such a program.

```
PROGRAM SUMUP2(INPUT,OUTPUT);

    {READ UNTIL SUM > 100}

    {USING REPEAT-UNTIL  }

    VAR

        NUM, COUNT, SUM:  INTEGER;

BEGIN

    COUNT := -1;

    SUM   := 0;

    NUM   := 0;

    WRITELN('ENTER A SERIES OF NUMBERS:');

    REPEAT

        COUNT := COUNT + 1;

        SUM   := SUM + NUM;

        READLN(NUM)

    UNTIL (SUM + NUM) > 100;

    WRITELN;

    WRITELN(COUNT,' NUMBERS WERE READ.');

    WRITELN('THEIR SUM IS ',SUM,'.');

    WRITELN('THE NUMBER ',NUM,' WAS NOT COUNTED.');

END.
```

Fig. 11-11. The Pascal Sum-Up program, Version 2.

```
PROGRAM PROC(OUTPUT);

    {Demonstrate a simple procedure to swap two variables}

    VAR
      P,Q,X,Y:  REAL;

    PROCEDURE SWAP(VAR U,V:  REAL);

      VAR
        TEMP:  REAL;

      BEGIN
        TEMP := U;
        U    := V;
        V    := TEMP;
      END;  {SWAP}

    PROCEDURE PRINT(U,V:  REAL);

      {Print out two variables}

      BEGIN
        WRITELN;
        WRITELN('FIRST  VARIABLE:  ',U);
        WRITELN('SECOND VARIABLE:  ',V);
      END;  {PRINT}

  BEGIN

    P := 1.0;  Q := 2.0;
    PRINT(P,Q);
    SWAP(P,Q);
    PRINT(P,Q);

    X := 3.14159;  Y := 2.71828;
    PRINT(X,Y);
    SWAP(X,Y);
    PRINT(X,Y);

  END.  {PROGRAM}
```

Fig. 11-12. Pascal procedures: the Swap program.

This program contains two procedures, one to exchange the values of two variables and one to print out two variables with labels. Clearly this program could have been written without any procedures. With such simple tasks the benefit of using procedures is perhaps marginal. Had the procedures consisted of 30 lines each rather than 3 lines each, the savings of not having a place the code "in line" would have been more significant. In either case, however, the main program is simpler to read and understand. This is particularly true when the names of the procedures are descriptive of the tasks to be performed, as in this program.

Several details concerning the program in Fig. 11-12 need to be pointed out. First, note the placement of the procedure declarations. They are placed after the declaration of variables for the main program and before the BEGIN of the main program. Next, note the heading of each procedure. The parameters of the procedures are listed in parentheses following the name of the procedure. The parameters of SWAP are U and V. When SWAP is invoked in the main program, its arguments are first P and Q, and then X and Y. The first time SWAP is invoked, the values of P and Q are exchanged; the second time SWAP is invoked, the value of X and Y are exchanged.

Notice the presence of the word VAR in the parameter list of the SWAP procedure and its absence in the parameter list of the PRINT procedure. When VAR is present, any changes made to the parameters in the procedure are reflected in the value of their arguments in the main program. Without VAR, the values of the arguments in the main program remain unchanged no matter what happens in the procedure. To demonstrate this, try running the program as is; then remove the word VAR from the parameter list of SWAP, recompile the program and run it again.

The PRINT procedure is straightforward. Because PRINT returns no values to the main program, there is no need for VAR in its parameter list.

Procedures can invoke other procedures in Pascal and can even be recursive (self-invoking). (Recursion is discussed further later in the chapter.) Because procedures must be defined *before*

they are used (before means closer to the top of the program), Pascal programs tend to be "upside down." The main program comes last, immediately preceded by the highest-level procedures. The lowest-level procedures come first.

Functions

A function is similar to a procedure. Each is a more-or-less self-contained module that is defined at the beginning of a Pascal program and can be invoked almost anywhere in that program. As explained in Chapter 2, the primary differences between a function and a procedure are in the heading of the definition and in the manner in which the result is returned to the invoking program or procedure.

Pascal has built-in or predefined functions that perform the usual standard mathematical operations such as computing square roots, sines, cosines, and so on. The user can also define functions as necessary.

A function definition begins with the word FUNCTION, followed by the name of the function, a parameter list in parentheses, a colon, and the type of the function. A function must have a type; this determines the type of the value returned by the function to the invoking program or procedure. A simple example that finds the largest of three integers is shown in Fig. 11-13. In this example the name of the function is MAX3, and its type is IN-TEGER.

The function heading is followed by the declaration of local constants and variables (as in a procedure). In this case there are none. The body of the function follows, enclosed in a BEGIN-END block. Notice that MAX3, the name of the function, is used as a variable in the function. The value of the variable MAX3 at the end of the function will be the value returned to the invoking program or procedure.

Notice that in the example I have included a comment on the same line as the final END of the function to indicate that this END is the end of the procedure MAX3.

Recursion

As indicated above and in Chapter 2, a proce-

```
        PROGRAM GETMAX(INPUT,OUTPUT);

        {Demonstrate a simple function}

        VAR
           I,J,K:   INTEGER;

        FUNCTION MAX3(X,Y,Z:   INTEGER):   INTEGER;
           {Returns the largest of the 3 inputs}
           BEGIN
              IF (X )= Y) AND (X )= Z) THEN
                 MAX3 := X
              ELSE IF (Y )= X) AND (Y )= Z) THEN
                 MAX3 := Y
              ELSE
                 MAX3 := Z;
           END;   {MAX3}

     BEGIN
        WRITE('ENTER THREE INTEGERS SEPARATED BY SPACES:   ');
        READLN(I,J,K);
        WRITELN;
        WRITELN(MAX3(I,J,K),' IS THE LARGEST OF THE THREE.');
     END.
```

Fig. 11-13. A Pascal function demonstration.

dure or function is said to be recursive if it invokes itself. How this works in Pascal will be illustrated using two simple examples. The first is a recursive function that computes factorials; the second is a recursive procedure which demonstrates simple string manipulation.

The factorial of a positive integer is a mathematical function that is defined recursively. The factorial of zero is defined as one. The factorial of a positive number N is defined as N times the factorial of N−1. Such a recursive definition (the factorial function is defined in terms of itself) seems to cry for a recursive implementation. Such an implementation is shown in the program in Fig. 11-14.

The recursive function in this program is appropriately called FACTORIAL. It is of the REAL type rather than the INTEGER type because the largest INTEGER value in most microcomputer versions of Pascal is 32767, and the factorial of

numbers as small as 8 exceed that value. Note that there are three possibilities when the function is invoked: N can be a negative number, zero, or a positive number. If N is negative, something has gone wrong (probably a meaningless input) so an error message is printed and an impossible value (0) returned for FACTORIAL. If N is zero, FACTORIAL is set to one. In either of these cases, the function is not invoked again. In the third case, N is positive, so the recursive definition that N factorial is N times N-1 factorial is applied.

You will be better able to understand how this works through a simple example. Consider the computation of the factorial of the number 3. When FACTORIAL is called with N = 3, the function notes that 3 is positive and so decides that 3 factorial is 3 times 2 factorial. Thus FACTORIAL is invoked again with N = 2. Again, the function notes that 2 is positive and so decides that 2 factorial must be 2 times 1 factorial. FACTORIAL is invoked again with N = 1. Similarly, the function decides that 1 factorial is 1 times 0 factorial, and FACTORIAL is invoked for the fourth time, this time with N = 0. It is important to note that each of these invocations of FACTORIAL is independent and is working with a different value of N. Because N = 0 this time, the function returns the value FACTORIAL = 1. Now the third invocation of the function can compute 1 factorial as 1 times 0 factorial, which is 1. This value is then returned to the second invocation, which computes 2 factorial as 2 times 1.

The first invocation of the function FACTORIAL can now compute 3 factorial as 3 times 2 factorial, or 6.

An example of recursion that does not involve mathematics is shown in Fig. 11-15. This program illustrates how a recursive procedure can be used to manipulate a character string. The procedure takes a string of length N and prints it N times, dropping the first letter each time until there are no letters remaining. The result is sort of a triangle that can be read horizontally and vertically. The procedure uses the UCSD Pascal string intrinsics LENGTH

```
PROGRAM FACT(INPUT,OUTPUT);

        ( Demonstrate a recursive function
          to compute factorials )

        VAR
            N:  REAL;
            REPLY:  STRING;

        FUNCTION FACTORIAL(N: REAL): REAL;
            BEGIN
                IF N ( 0 THEN
                    BEGIN
                        WRITE('MEANINGLESS.  N MUST BE ) ');
                        FACTORIAL := 0
                    END
                ELSE IF N = 0 THEN FACTORIAL := 1
                ELSE FACTORIAL := N * FACTORIAL(N-1);
            END;  ( FACTORIAL )

    BEGIN
        REPEAT
            WRITE('ENTER A NON-NEGATIVE INTEGER:  ');
            READLN(N);
            WRITELN(N,' FACTORIAL IS ',FACTORIAL(N));
            WRITELN;
            WRITE('AGAIN (Y/N)?  ');
            READLN(REPLY);
            WRITELN
        UNTIL (REPLY () 'Y') AND (REPLY () 'y');
    END.
```

Fig. 11-14. Recursion in Pascal: factorials.

```
            PROGRAM RECURSE(INPUT,OUTPUT);

            (Demonstrate recursion)

            VAR S:    STRING;

            PROCEDURE PRINT_AND_DROP(S:    STRING);
                (Print a string, drop first char, then repeat)
                BEGIN
                    IF LENGTH(S) ) 0 THEN
                        BEGIN
                            WRITELN(S);
                            DELETE(S,1,1);
                            PRINT_AND_DROP(S);
                        END;
                END;   (PRINT_AND_DROP)

        BEGIN
            WRITE('TYPE A STRING:    ');
            READLN(S);
            PRINT_AND_DROP(S);
        END.
```

Fig. 11-15. Recursion in Pascal: word triangle.

and DELETE. LENGTH is a function that returns the number of characters in a string. DELETE is a procedure that deletes a character or characters from a string—in this case one character from the first position of the string.

Each time the procedure PRINT-AND-DROP is called, it checks the length of the string S. If the length of S is greater than zero, it prints the string, deletes the first character of the string, and calls itself again using the remaining part of the string as its argument. If the string has a length of zero, it does nothing and thus terminates the recursive process.

The GOTO Statement

The GOTO statement is not often needed in Pascal programs because of the rich variety of other control statements available. Occasionally, however, it is convenient to exit from a loop when a certain condition is met. There are also times when it is necessary to escape from a deeply-nested situation when an error condition is met. Thus, while many programming experts advocate keeping the number of GOTO statements in a program to a minimum, it is not always possible or desirable to eliminate GOTO statements altogether. Care must be taken, however, to avoid their indiscriminate use.

A GOTO statement requires a label as a destination, and the label must be declared. Pascal labels must be integers of up to 4 digits and must be declared before constants and variables are declared.

The situations that call for the use of a GOTO statement are difficult to illustrate in a short example. The example given in Fig. 11-16 is therefore somewhat contrived. This sample program contains an input routine that validates the input to be sure it is positive before proceeding. The same result could have been achieved using the REPEAT-UNTIL construct.

The example contains two compiler dependencies which may require clarification. First, { $G+ } or equivalently (*$G+*) is a signal to the compiler that tells it to allow GOTO statements. In its absence, the UCSD compiler will flag all GOTO statements as errors. The second dependency is the statement USES TRANSCEND. The SQRT function and other transcendental functions are located in a special library unit called TRANSCEND. The compiler must be told that fact before it can find those functions.

DATA STRUCTURES

So far the Pascal programs in the examples have used simple data structures. One of the great strengths of Pascal is its ability to handle complex data structures. In fact Pascal contains the facilities to define data structures of arbitrary complexity.

Arrays

The subscripts of arrays are delimited by square brackets.

In Chapter 2 an integer array called POINTS was used. In Pascal this array would be declared as follows:

VAR POINTS: ARRAY [1..10, 1..20] OF INTEGER;

The 1..10 indicates that the first subscript can range between 1 and 10, while the 1..20 indicates that the second subscript can range between 1 and 20. The OF INTEGER indicates that each element of the array is of the INTEGER type.

The usage of arrays in Pascal is similar to that in most other languages. Examples of the proper usage of arrays in Pascal can be found in subsequent sections of this chapter.

Records

In Chapter 2 the need for a record containing a student's name and his scores on up to 20 tests was discussed. Suppose there may be up to 30 students in the class. What is needed is an array of records. It is convenient to define what each element of the array looks like and what it is. Here is how the

```
PROGRAM SQUARE_ROOT(INPUT,OUTPUT);

        ( A program to illustrate the GOTO statement )

        ($G+)   ( Compiler toggle to permit GOTO)

        USES TRANSCEND;   ( Required in UCSD Pascal when SQRT used )

        LABEL 1;

        VAR  X, SQ:  REAL;

BEGIN
    1:  WRITE('ENTER A POSITIVE NUMBER:   ');
        READLN(X);
        IF X < 0.0 THEN GOTO 1;
        SQ := SQRT(X);
        WRITELN('THE SQUARE ROOT OF ',X,' IS ',SQ);
    END.
```

Fig. 11-16. The Pascal GO TO statement.

declaration might look:

```
CONST NR_OF_STUDENTS = 30;
TYPE ENTRY = RECORD
    NAME:   STRING[25];
    SCORE: ARRAY [1..20] OF REAL
END;
VAR STUDENT:  ARRAY [1..NR_OF
_STUDENTS] OF ENTRY;
```

Notice that a constant was used for NR_OF_STU-DENTS. This makes it easier to change the program at a later day if the number of students increases. The same thing could have been done for the number of scores recorded for each student. We also declared that the name of a student could contain up to 25 characters.

Now suppose that you want to write out the name of the fourth student and the score he or she received on the first test. Here is how it would look:

```
WRITELN(STUDENT[4].NAME, STU-
DENT[4].SCORE[1];
```

The period ('.') is used to refer to individual record elements. In the first case the record element referred to was a string (NAME), and in the second case it was an element of an array (SCORE[1]).

Examples of the usage of records in actual programs wil be found in the later sections of this chapter.

Linked Lists

Pascal contains advanced facilities for the handling of linked lists, including the dynamic allocation of space. For the beginner, however, it is probably easier to understand what linked lists are all about without going into pointer variables and dynamically allocated storage. These topics are treated in some of the better texts on Pascal and in some advanced texts on the topic of data structures.

This section discusses how linked lists can be implemented in Pascal using arrays of records. The methodology is essentially the same as that described in Chapter 2, except that an array of records is used rather than parallel arrays, and the value −1

is used to mark the end of the list.

Here are the declarations to support the appropriate data structure in Pascal:

```
CONST END_LIST = −1;
    MAX_SIZE = 5;
VAR FIRST, FIRST_FREE:  INTEGER;
    LIST: ARRAY [1..MAX_SIZE] OF
    RECORD
        NAME: STRING[15];
        LINK : INTEGER
    END;
```

To reference the fourth record of the structure following these declarations, for example, you would write

LIST[4].NAME and LIST[4].LINK.

The comprehensive example at the end of the chapter illustrates the use of linked lists in an actual program. It shows the details of how elements are added to and deleted from linked lists.

FILE HANDLING

To be useful in a variety of applications, a microcomputer programming language must provide for the storage of data on a disk (floppy disks or hard disks). Standard Pascal as defined by Wirth provides only for sequential files. Most implementations of Pascal have added provision for the handling of direct access files as well. Unfortunately, not all such extensions are compatible. Most of them follow the example set by the authors of UCSD Pascal, as described below.

A file in Pascal may be thought of as a sequence of components, each of which is of the same type. In the simplest kind of file, called a text file, each component of the file is simply a character. Each file has a file variable of the appropriate type associated with it. For text files, the appropriate type is called text. Suppose that F is the file variable of a particular text file. It would be declared as follows:

VAR F: TEXT;

A file must be opened before it is accessed. To

open an existing file for input, the RESET procedure is used. The RESET procedure associates the file variable with the external filename. How this is done varies between implementations, so the user should verify the correct procedure for his or her version of Pascal. Here is an example of how this might be done in UCSD Pascal:

RESET(F,'EXAMPLE.TEXT');

In this example, 'EXAMPLE.TEXT' is the name of the file to be read from the disk. Access to text files is gained by using the standard procedures READ, READLN, WRITE, and WRITELN. If S has been declared a variable of the STRING type, the following would read a line from the file F:

READLN(F,S);

Pascal treats the keyboard and display as special, predeclared text files called INPUT and OUTPUT, respectively. If a READ or READLN does not include the name of a file variable, it is assumed to refer to the standard file INPUT. If a WRITE or WRITELN does not include the name of a file variable, it is assumed to refer to the standard file OUTPUT.

Some versions of Pascal allow a file that was opened for input using RESET to also be used for output. To create a new file, however, the REWRITE procedure is needed. If the file 'EXAMPLE.TEXT' did not already exist, it could be created as follows:

REWRITE(F,'EXAMPLE.TEXT');

Files are closed using the CLOSE procedure. The UCSD system requires the option LOCK to be specified with the close procedure as follows:

CLOSE(F,LOCK);

If LOCK is omitted, the default option is PURGE, which results in the loss of the file.

Windows and Buffer Variables

Associated with each file variable is something called a *window*, which may be thought of as a view of a single component of the file or as a buffer that can hold a single component of that file. This window or buffer is commonly called a *buffer variable*. If F is the file variable for a particular file, then F ↑ is the buffer variable for that file. With text files you usually have no need to refer to the buffer variable, as it is sufficient to rely on the READ, READLN, WRITE, and WRITELN procedures. With other types of files, however, input and output is performed with the intrinsic procedures GET and PUT in conjunction with the buffer variable.

Recall that a text file is a sequence of characters. Buffer variables and the GET and PUT procedures become necessary when the file in question is a sequence of components other than characters. Suppose, for example, you have a file consisting of records containing the names and ages of individuals. This file could be defined as follows:

```
TYPE
    ENTRY = RECORD
        NAME: STRING[20];
        AGE:   INTEGER
    END;
VAR
    G:   FILE OF ENTRY;
```

ENTRY was defined as a type consisting of two elements: NAME, which is a string of 20 characters, and AGE, an integer. This record forms the template for one component of the file. G was defined as the file variable for this file. This automatically defines the buffer variable G↑ . The significance of the buffer variable and the use of GET and PUT are discussed in the next section.

Sequential Files

A disk file is said to be sequential if it is accessed one record at a time, from the beginning to the end. Figure 11-17 contains a program that illustrates the use of a sequential file to store a list of names and ages, and then to print them out again. The program also illustrates the use of REWRITE, RESET, PUT, and GET with a sequential file.

REWRITE opens the file for output. Once the

```
PROGRAM SEQUENTIAL(INPUT,OUTPUT,G);

        ( Illustrates the use of a sequential file to store
          a list of names & ages. )

        TYPE
            ENTRY = RECORD
                            NAME:     STRING[20];
                            AGE:      INTEGER
                        END;
        VAR
            G:   FILE OF ENTRY;

  BEGIN

        ( First read in the records from the keyboard and
          write to the sequential file G. )

        REWRITE(G,'AGES.TEXT');
        WRITELN('ENTER NAMES AND AGES;  AGE 0 TO QUIT.');
        WRITELN;
        REPEAT
                WRITE('NAME:   ');
                READLN(G↑.NAME);
                WRITE('AGE:    ');
                READLN(G↑.AGE);
                WRITELN;
                PUT(G)
        UNTIL G↑.AGE = 0;
        CLOSE(G,LOCK);

        ( Now read the file back in and display the records. )

        RESET(G,'AGES.TEXT');
        WRITELN('Here are the names and ages from the file:');
        WHILE G↑.AGE <> 0  DO
        BEGIN
                WRITELN('NAME:   ',G↑.NAME);
                WRITELN('AGE:    ',G↑.AGE);
                WRITELN;
                GET(G)
        END;
        CLOSE(G,LOCK);
        WRITELN('All done...');
  END .
```

Fig. 11-17. A Pascal sequential file demonstration.

file is open, the values to be written are stored in the buffer variable using the notation shown. G ↑ .NAME refers to the NAME component of the record (buffer) pointed to by the buffer variable. G ↑ .AGE means the AGE component of that record. When the PUT(G) procedure is executed, the contents of the buffer are written to the file, and the file window is advanced to the next record.

If REWRITE is used to open a file that already existed, the new file will replace the existing file.

This program uses AGE = 0 as a signal that it should stop reading from the keyboard. Note that this last record is written to the file to serve as a sentinel to indicate the end of the file. After AGE = 0 is encountered, the file is closed.

RESET opens an existing file for input, positions the window at the first record of that file, and reads that record into the buffer. The contents of the first record can thus be accessed without further action. (It is as if an automatic GET has been performed.) GET(G) advances the window to the next record of the file and reads that record into the buffer. The WHILE loop repeats the input process until the AGE = 0 sentinel record is encountered.

UCSD Pascal has a special file type called INTERACTIVE. For files of this type, no automatic GET is performed when the file is RESET.

Direct-Access Files

Suppose you want to access the fifth record of a file. If the file is a sequential file, the first four records must be read before the fifth record can be read. In a direct-access file the program can read the fifth record directly and ignore the first four records.

Direct-access files are not a part of standard Pascal as defined by Wirth. Most microcomputer implementations of Pascal have added this capability. Most versions, with the exception of JRT Pascal, have followed the lead of UCSD Pascal by implementing direct-access files using the SEEK procedure.

For the purposes of the SEEK procedure, the file records are assumed to be numbered beginning with 0. To access the fifth record of the file G, you would write

```
SEEK(G,4);
```

Note that 4 appears rather than 5 because numbering starts with 0. After the SEEK, a GET or PUT will access that record.

In creating a new direct-access file, care must be taken to allocate sufficient disk space to accommodate as many records as the file will ever have. For example, if a file is expected to have up to 100 records eventually, but it will have only 10 records the first time it is used, space for the 100 records should be allocated when the file is first opened. Here is a procedure that would allocate space for N records for the file in Fig. 11-17:

```
PROCEDURE ALLOCATE (N: IN-
TEGER);
    { Assumes that G is declared and
      opened in the main program }
    VAR I:  INTEGER;
BEGIN
    G↑.NAME := ' ';
    G↑.AGE   := 0;
    FOR I := 1 TO N DO PUT(G)
END;  { ALLOCATE }
```

Note that sequential access is used to establish the size of the file by writing N dummy records with the name field blank and the age field containing a zero.

The comprehensive sample program discussed below illustrates the use of direct-access files.

GRAPHICS

The Apple/UCSD implementation of Pascal supports a form of graphics called Turtle Graphics. Turtle Graphics are discussed in more detail in the chapter on Logo. Because most other implementations of Pascal do not support graphics, the topic will not be discussed further in this chapter.

COMPREHENSIVE SAMPLE PROGRAM

All the programs so far in this chapter have been relatively short and straightforward; each has illustrated a particular feature of the language. There is a need for a more comprehensive example

```
PROGRAM ADDRESS_FILE (INPUT,OUTPUT,PTR,A_FILE,I_FILE);

    { A program to create and maintain a file of names and addresses.}
    { The file is maintained in alphabetical order at all times,
      using an index of pointers.  The index is a linked list.  A
      linked list of vacant records is also maintained. }
    { 5/26/83}


    CONST
        MAX_RECORDS = 10;              {Modify as required}
        F_NAME = 'ADDRESS.FILE';   { "              " }
        I_NAME = 'INDEX.FILE';
        END_LIST = 0;

    TYPE
        A_NAME = RECORD
                LAST, FIRST: STRING[12];
             END;
        ENTRY = RECORD
                NAME:      A_NAME;
                ADDRESS:   STRING[20];
                CITY:      STRING[12];
                STATE:     STRING[2];
                ZIP:       STRING[5];
             END;

    VAR
        IN_BUFFER:  ENTRY;
        INDEX:  ARRAY[-1..MAX_RECORDS] OF INTEGER;
                { ARRAY[-1] = POINTER TO FIRST FREE RECORD
                  ARRAY[0]  = POINTER TO FIRST USED RECORD }
        A_FILE:  FILE OF ENTRY;
        I_FILE:  FILE OF INTEGER;
        PTR:      TEXT;
        FINISHED:  BOOLEAN;
        A:  CHAR;
        C:  INTEGER;

    PROCEDURE INITIALIZE_FILES;
        { Establish the address file and the index file.  Initialize
          address file by filling with blank records.  Initialize
          index as a linked list of free records. }
        VAR I:  INTEGER;
        BEGIN
```

Fig. 11-18. The Pascal Address Book program. (Continued on page 321.)

```
        REWRITE(A_FILE,F_NAME);
        WITH A_FILE^ DO
           BEGIN
              NAME.LAST   := ' ';
              NAME.FIRST  := ' ';
              ADDRESS     := ' ';
              CITY        := ' ';
              STATE       := ' ';
              ZIP         := ' ';
           END;

        FOR I := 0 TO MAX_RECORDS DO PUT(A_FILE);
        CLOSE(A_FILE,LOCK);
        REWRITE(I_FILE,I_NAME);
        { Initialize Free List }
        I_FILE^ := 1;        { First Free Record }
        PUT(I_FILE);
        { Indicate No Records in Use }
        I_FILE^ := END_LIST;
        PUT(I_FILE);
        { Now Complete Free List }
        FOR I := 1 TO MAX_RECORDS - 1  DO
           BEGIN
              I_FILE^ := I + 1;
              PUT(I_FILE);
           END;
        I_FILE^ := END_LIST;
        PUT(I_FILE);
        CLOSE(I_FILE,LOCK);
     END;  { INITIALIZE_FILES }

PROCEDURE OPEN_FILES;
   { Open the address file and the index file for random access.
     Read in the index file.  }
   VAR I:  INTEGER;
   BEGIN
      {$I-}  (Turn off I/O checking)
      RESET(A_FILE,F_NAME);
      IF IORESULT()0 THEN
         BEGIN                    (If file did not already exist.)
            INITIALIZE_FILES;
            RESET(A_FILE,F_NAME)
         END;
      {$I+}  (Restore I/O checking)
```

```
            RESET(I_FILE,I_NAME);
            FOR I := -1 TO MAX_RECORDS DO
                BEGIN
                    INDEX[I] := I_FILE^;
                    GET(I_FILE)
                END;
            REWRITE(PTR,'PRINTER:')
        END;   { OPEN_FILES }

PROCEDURE CLOSE_FILES;
    { Write index file to disk and close both files. }
    VAR I:   INTEGER;
    BEGIN
        SEEK(I_FILE,0);
        FOR I := -1 TO MAX_RECORDS DO
            BEGIN
                I_FILE^ := INDEX[I];
                PUT(I_FILE)
            END;
        CLOSE(I_FILE,LOCK);
        CLOSE(A_FILE,LOCK)
    END;   { CLOSE_FILES }

PROCEDURE PRINT_REC(VAR F:  TEXT; I:   INTEGER);
    { Print record I to file F }
    BEGIN
        SEEK(A_FILE,I);
        GET(A_FILE);
        WITH A_FILE^ DO
            BEGIN
                WRITE(F,NAME.FIRST,' ');
                WRITELN(F,NAME.LAST);
                WRITELN(F,ADDRESS);
                WRITELN(F,CITY,', ',STATE,' ',ZIP);
            END;
    END, { PRINT_REC }

PROCEDURE DUMP;
    { Dump entire file to printer, including empty records
      and index file entries.  Useful for learning how
      program works. }
    VAR I:   INTEGER;
    BEGIN
        WRITELN(PTR,'FIRST FREE RECORD:  ',INDEX[-1]);
```

Fig. 11-18. The Pascal Address Book Program. (Continued on page 323.)

```
            WRITELN(PTR,'FIRST USED RECORD:  ',INDEX[0]);
        FOR I := 1 TO MAX_RECORDS DO
            BEGIN
                WRITELN(PTR);
                WRITELN(PTR,'RECORD ',I);
                PRINT_REC(PTR,I);
                WRITELN(PTR,'NEXT RECORD:  ',INDEX[I]);
            END;
    END;  ( DUMP )

PROCEDURE LIST(VAR F:  TEXT);
    ( List all active records in alphabetical order to
      file F )
    VAR I:  INTEGER;
    BEGIN
        I := INDEX[0];     ( First record )
        WHILE I<>END_LIST DO
            BEGIN
                WRITELN(F);
                PRINT_REC(F,I);
                I := INDEX[I]
            END;
    END;  ( LIST )

FUNCTION GET_FREE:  INTEGER;
    ( Get record number of next free record
      and remove from free list )
    VAR FREE:  INTEGER;
    BEGIN
        FREE := INDEX[-1];
        INDEX[-1] := INDEX[FREE];
        GET_FREE := FREE
    END;  ( GET_FREE )

PROCEDURE PUT_FREE(I:  INTEGER);
    ( Put record I back into the free list )
    BEGIN
        INDEX[I] := INDEX[-1];
        INDEX[-1] := I
    END;  ( PUT_FREE )

PROCEDURE INCREMENT(VAR ROW, COL:  INTEGER);
    ( Position cursor 2 rows down, same column )
    BEGIN
```

```
            ROW := ROW + 2;
            GOTOXY(COL,ROW)
        END;   ( INCREMENT )


    PROCEDURE GET_ENTRY(VAR FINISHED:   BOOLEAN);
        ( Read 1 record from keyboard )
        VAR
            ROW, COL, START: INTEGER;
        PROCEDURE MARKOFF(START,SPACES:   INTEGER);
            ( Mark off data input area with colons )
            BEGIN
                GOTOXY(START,ROW);
                WRITE(':');
                WRITE(' ':SPACES);
                WRITE(':');
            END;   ( MARKOFF )
        BEGIN
            PAGE(OUTPUT);   ( Clear Screen )
            START := 14;
            ROW := 5;
            COL := 1;
            GOTOXY(COL,ROW);
            WRITE('LAST NAME:');   MARKOFF(START,12);
            INCREMENT(ROW,COL);
            WRITE('FIRST NAME:');  MARKOFF(START,12);
            INCREMENT(ROW,COL);
            WRITE('ADDRESS:');     MARKOFF(START,20);
            INCREMENT(ROW,COL);
            WRITE('CITY:');        MARKOFF(START,12);
            INCREMENT(ROW,COL);
            WRITE('STATE:');       MARKOFF(START,2);
            INCREMENT(ROW,COL);
            WRITE('ZIP CODE:');    MARKOFF(START,5);
            ROW := 5;
            COL := 15;
            GOTOXY(COL,ROW);
            WITH IN_BUFFER DO
                BEGIN
                    READLN(NAME.LAST);
                    FINISHED := (NAME.LAST = '');   ( EMPTY STRING )
                    IF NOT FINISHED THEN
                    BEGIN
                        INCREMENT(ROW,COL);
                        READLN(NAME.FIRST);
```

Fig. 11-18. The Pascal Address Book Program. (Continued on page 325.)

```
                    INCREMENT(ROW,COL);
                    READLN(ADDRESS);
                    INCREMENT(ROW,COL);
                    READLN(CITY);
                    INCREMENT(ROW,COL);
                    READLN(STATE);
                    INCREMENT(ROW,COL);
                    READLN(ZIP);
                END;
          END;
   END;  { GET_ENTRY }

FUNCTION GREATER(VAR A,B:  ENTRY):  BOOLEAN;
   { Returns TRUE if A > B, using name as the key field }
   BEGIN
      IF (A.NAME.LAST>B.NAME.LAST) OR
         ((A.NAME.LAST=B.NAME.LAST) AND
          (A.NAME.FIRST>B.NAME.FIRST)) THEN
              GREATER := TRUE
      ELSE
              GREATER := FALSE
   END;  { GREATER }

PROCEDURE INSERT;
   { Insert the record in IN_BUFFER into the INDEX and
     write it to disk }
   VAR
      P,Q,FREE:  INTEGER;
   BEGIN
      FREE := GET_FREE;
      SEEK(A_FILE,FREE);
      A_FILE^ := IN_BUFFER;
      PUT(A_FILE);
      P := INDEX[0];
      Q := 0;
      IF P<>END_LIST THEN
         BEGIN
            SEEK(A_FILE,P);
            GET(A_FILE);
            WHILE (P<>END_LIST) AND (GREATER(IN_BUFFER,A_FILE^)) DO
               BEGIN
                  Q := P;
                  P := INDEX[P];
                  SEEK(A_FILE,P);
```

```
                            GET(A_FILE)
                      END;
               END;
          { Insert into linked list }
          INDEX[FREE] := P;
          INDEX[Q]    := FREE;
     END; { INSERT }

PROCEDURE MENU(VAR C:  INTEGER);
    { Display the main menu and input selection }
    VAR ROW, COL:  INTEGER;
    BEGIN
        PAGE(OUTPUT);
        ROW := 5;
        COL := 5;
        GOTOXY(COL,ROW);
        WRITELN('1)  ADD TO FILE');
        INCREMENT(ROW,COL);
        WRITELN('2)  REVIEW FILE ON SCREEN');
        INCREMENT(ROW,COL);
        WRITELN('3)  LIST FILE TO SCREEN OR PRINTER');
        INCREMENT(ROW,COL);
        WRITELN('4)  DUMP FILE TO PRINTER');
        INCREMENT(ROW,COL);
        WRITELN('5)  QUIT');
        COL := 1;
        ROW := ROW + 2;
        REPEAT
            GOTOXY(COL,ROW);
            WRITE('SELECT 1, 2, 3, 4, OR 5:  ');
            READLN(C)
        UNTIL C IN [1..5];
    END;  { MENU }

PROCEDURE APPEND;
    {Add records to the file}
    BEGIN
        GET_ENTRY(FINISHED);
        WHILE NOT FINISHED DO
            BEGIN
                INSERT;
                GET_ENTRY(FINISHED);
            END;
    END;  { APPEND }
```

Fig. 11-18. The Pascal Address Book Program. (Continued on page 327.)

```
PROCEDURE REVIEW;
    {Step through the file, 1 record at a time.
     Allows deletion of records.}
    VAR Q,R:   INTEGER;
        C:   CHAR;
    BEGIN
       PAGE(OUTPUT);        {Clear Screen}
       R := INDEX[0];
       Q := 0;
       REPEAT
          SEEK(A_FILE,R);
          WRITELN;
          PRINT_REC(OUTPUT,R);
          WRITELN;
          REPEAT
             WRITE('G)ET NEXT RECORD, D)ELETE THIS RECORD, OR Q)UIT?');
             READLN(C)
          UNTIL C IN ['G','g','D','d','Q','q'];
          CASE C OF
             'G','g':   BEGIN                        {Get Next}
                           Q := R;
                           R := INDEX[R];
                        END;
             'D','d':   BEGIN                        {Delete}
                           INDEX[Q] := INDEX[R];
                           PUT_FREE(R);
                           R := INDEX[Q];
                        END;
             'Q','q':                                {Quit}
          END
       UNTIL (R=END_LIST) OR (C IN ['Q','q']);
    END;  { REVIEW }

PROCEDURE LIST_FILE;
    { Find out whether to list file to screen or printer,
      then call LIST. }
    BEGIN
       PAGE(OUTPUT);
       REPEAT
          WRITE('LIST TO S)CREEN OR P)RINTER? ');
          READLN(A)
       UNTIL A IN ['S','s','P','p'];
       IF (A='S') OR (A='s') THEN
```

```
                    LIST(OUTPUT)
          ELSE
              LIST(PTR);
          WRITELN;
          WRITE('PRESS (ENTER) TO CONTINUE ');
          READLN(A);
        END;  ( LIST_FILE )


  BEGIN                                      (Main Program)
        OPEN_FILES;
        REPEAT
          MENU(C);
          CASE C OF
            1:   APPEND;
            2:   REVIEW;
            3:   LIST_FILE;
            4:   DUMP;
            5:                     (Quit)
          END
        UNTIL C=5;
        CLOSE_FILES;
    END.
```

Fig. 11-18. The Pascal Address Book Program. (Continued from page 327.)

program in order to convey more completely the flavor of the language.

The sample program is shown in Fig. 11-18. The purpose of the program is to establish and maintain a file of names and addresses. The program provides the capability of adding records to the file, listing the file on the screen or on a printer, and deleting records from the file. The file is maintained in alphabetical order by name, but the file is never explicitly sorted. This is possible because the file is maintained as a linked list, and all names are inserted in the correct order as they are added to the file.

Because the program is relatively long (compared to the other programs presented in this chapter), it is difficult to see at a glance how it is organized. Figure 11-19 is a structure chart for the program in Fig. 11-18. The structure of the program is shown by indentation. A module that is subordinate to another module is listed indented

below that module. At the top of the chart is the main program. At the next level of indentation are the procedures called directly by the main program: OPEN__FILES, MENU, APPEND, REVIEW, LIST__FILE, DUMP, and CLOSE__FILES. The procedure OPEN__FILES calls the procedure INITIALIZE__FILES, and so on. Procedures marked by an asterisk (*) are called by more than one higher-level procedure.

Notice that the main program in the example is quite short. This is typical of well-written Pascal programs. Most of the work is done in procedures; the purpose of the main program is to invoke its subordinate procedures in the proper order.

Several other features of the program are worthy of note. First you should notice the way in which the file is kept in alphabetical order. A linked list is used to keep track of the disk records in use and those not in use. The discussion earlier in the chapter illustrated the use of linked lists for a simi-

```
        MAIN PROGRAM
            OPEN_FILES
                INITIALIZE_FILES
        MENU
                INCREMENT*
        APPEND
                GET_ENTRY
                    MARKOFF
                    INCREMENT*
                INSERT
                    GET_FREE
                    GREATER
        REVIEW
                PRINT_REC*
                PUT_FREE
        LIST_FILE
                LIST
        DUMP
                PRINT_REC*
        CLOSE_FILES



Structure Chart:  PROGRAM
                  ADDRESS_FILE
```

Fig. 11-19. The Structure Chart: Address Book program.

lar application. Careful study of the sample program will reveal how records are added to and deleted from a linked list. The DUMP procedure prints out all the links as well as the data elements to help you understand the techniques used.

Another feature of note is the manner in which data is input from the keyboard. The user appears to be filling out a form on the screen. Implementation of this technique requires the GOTOXY function that positions the cursor on the screen. If a particular version of Pascal does not come with this function, you must provide it.

The program as written will only accommodate 10 records. To change this, all you need to do is to change the value of the constant MAX__RECORDS at the beginning of the program. It is recommended that MAX__RECORDS be left small

until you have used the DUMP procedure to analyze how the program works.

ADVANTAGES AND DISADVANTAGES OF PASCAL

Pascal was designed as a language to be used for teaching students how to write good programs. Clarity of expression is therefore its major strength. Pascal is a compact language. It has been implemented successfully on numerous microcomputers. Some of its specific advantages are enumerated below.

Pascal has a large repertoire of control structures, including the FOR statement, the RE-PEAT-UNTIL statement, the WHILE statement, the CASE statement, and recursion. It is therefore possible to express algorithms clearly and concisely in Pascal.

Pascal has the facilities for defining a large variety of data structures. The ability to define new data structures of the user's own design makes the language extremely powerful. The power of Pascal with respect to handling data structures has only been hinted at in this book.

Some colleges have begun to teach their students Pascal as a first language, as a preparation for later courses in COBOL or FORTRAN. This is because Pascal as a language encourages good programming techniques.

Programs written in Pascal usually execute faster than those written in interpreted BASICs. How much faster depends on whether the particular version of Pascal compiles to intermediate code or machine code.

On the negative side, standard Pascal as defined by Wirth does not have several desirable features. Perhaps most serious is the fact that standard Pascal will not accommodate direct-access files. Most implementations have corrected this omission by adding a SEEK procedure.

Standard Pascal also does not support separate compilation of procedures. Most implementations of Pascal have some way of accommodating separately compiled procedures.

Standard Pascal does not have an exponentiation function. The user must solve this problem through repeated multiplication or by using logarithms and antilogarithms.

Some might consider the fact that Pascal is usually implemented as a compiled language as a disadvantage. This means that the user must go through a separate compile step before the program can be run.

AVAILABILITY

There are many implementations of Pascal available to microcomputer owners. Versions of UCSD Pascal are available for most microcomputers including Apple and the IBM Personal Computer. UCSD Pascal is compiled to an intermediate code, which is then interpreted.

Several versions of Pascal are available to users of the CP/M operating system (a product of Digital Research, Inc.). These include Pascal M+ by Digital Research and Pascal Z by Ithaca Intersystems, both of which compile to machine code, and Pascal M by Sorcim and JRT Pascal by JRT, both of which compile to intermediate code.

Owners of the IBM PC can also choose IBM Pascal, which is actually a product of Microsoft, Inc. Turbo Pascal, by Borland International, is now available in versions for the IBM PC (PC-DOS) and for the CP/M, CP/M-86, and MS-DOS operating systems.

SUMMARY

Pascal is a compact yet powerful language and is available on most brands of microcomputer. It is the second most popular language (after BASIC) among microcomputer users. It provides many advanced features not available in BASIC, and programs written in Pascal generally run faster than those written in BASIC.

Pascal is an excellent language for learning. It encourages the use of modern structured programming techniques and provides powerful facilities for handling complex data structures. It is an excellent language for the user interested in constructing complex programs.

Chapter 12

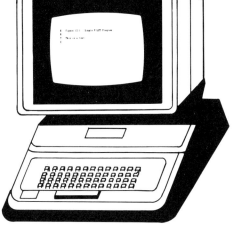

PILOT

PILOT is a special-purpose language intended for use in the area of Computer-Assisted Instruction (CAI). It was first developed by Professor John A. Starkweather of the University of California in San Francisco in the late 1960s and early 1970s. PILOT is used both for the preparation of CAI lessons by a teacher or author and for the administration of these lessons to a student. The name PILOT is an acronym which stands for Programmed Inquiry, Learning Or Teaching.

PILOT is a very simple language. It has relatively few commands, and each is simple. PILOT's commands are tailored to the needs of CAI. An example is the MATCH command, which matches a student's response to a list of possible correct answers. PILOT is a tool that can be easily used by subject-matter specialists with no prior programming experience to develop instructional materials. These instructional materials may then be used by students for independent study.

Because PILOT is very different from the other languages discussed in this book, the order of presentation in this chapter varies somewhat from that of the other chapters.

PILOT is quite suitable for implementation on a microcomputer. The PILOT programs in this chapter were tested using Nevada PILOT, written by John Starkweather and distributed by Ellis Computing.

PROGRAM STRUCTURE

A PILOT program is simply a sequence of PILOT statements. A simple PILOT program that does nothing but print "This is a test" is shown in Fig. 12-1.

The first two lines of this program are simply remarks. They serve the purpose of documenting the program, but do not affect the execution of the program. The third line of this program is a TYPE statement: it types whatever follows it on the screen. The fourth is the END statement, which marks the end of a program or subroutine. Most PILOT commands consist of one or two letters followed by a colon.

PILOT is usually implemented with an interpreter. With an interpreter, each line of the program is translated into machine code as it executes. If a particular line is executed five times, it must be translated five times. This implementation scheme is quite adequate for the kinds of programs written in PILOT because execution speed is usually unimportant.

DATA REPRESENTATION

There are two types of data in PILOT: character strings and integers. (Some versions of PILOT may also support real numbers.) Character strings are written without quotation marks. The default maximum length of a character string is 80 characters, but this may be increased or decreased as desired using the INMAX: statement.

Constants

Integers may range in magnitude from -32768 to $+32767$. The logical values true and false are represented by the integers $+1$ and 0, respectively. In logical contexts, however, any nonzero number is interpreted as true.

Variables

Variables need not be declared as to type in PILOT. In fact, there is no way to do so. Integer variable names may consist of one letter (A-Z) preceded by the "#" sign. There are thus 26 possible integer variables in a PILOT program. The following are legitimate names for integer variables in PILOT:

    #A
    #X

Until given a value, an integer variable has the value of zero. All integer variables can be reset to zero by the following command:

    VNEW:#

String variable names may consist of up to 10 characters preceded by the "$" sign. The following are legitimate names for string variables in PILOT:

```
R:  Figure 12-1:  Simple PILOT Program
R:
T:  This is a test.
E:
```

Fig. 12-1. A simple PILOT program.

    $NAME
    $AGE

If more space is needed for string variables, all previous string variables can be erased by one of the following commands:

    VNEW:$
    VNEW:

The second command shown also resets all integer variables to zero.

INPUT AND OUTPUT

In Fig. 12-1, you saw a simple example of the TYPE statement. It is frequently necessary to display a number of lines of text on the screen. These may be background reading for a series of questions or they may be multiline questions. This can be done as follows:

    T: This is a
    T: passage consisting of
    T: three lines.

A common shortcut is to eliminate the T on the second and subsequent lines, as in the following:

    T: This is a
    : passage consisting of
    : three lines.

A carriage return is automatically output at the end of a line printed using T:. If this is not desired, the TH: command can be used instead. TH: stands for TYPE HANG. It is so named because it leaves the cursor "hanging" at the end of the line. This is often useful when the user is being prompted for input. Here is a simple example:

TH: Type a number between 1 and 5:

As long as the next statement is an ACCEPT statement, the cursor will wait at the end of the line for the user to respond.

Output can be made to echo to a printer by using the TP: command. TP: stands for "TYPE on PRINTER".

A simple PILOT program that illustrates printer and screen output is shown in Fig. 12-2.

Input from the keyboard is accomplished by the ACCEPT statement. Consider the following sequence of PILOT statements:

TH: Enter a number between 1 and 5:
A:

The TH statement displays the prompt for the user, leaving the cursor at the end of the line. The A: (ACCEPT) statement waits for the user to type in a number. When the user does type the number, it is read into the *accept buffer*.

The accept buffer is a special place in memory that can hold one number or string at a time. A value in the accept buffer is available for comparison with other values, as discussed below in the section on the MATCH statement. A value stays in the accept buffer until displaced by another value.

The ACCEPT statement can also be used to read values into a variable. Here is a simple example:

TH: What is your name?
A: $NAME
T: Hello, $NAME. I am glad to meet you.

In this case the user's response is stored in the

```
R:   Figure 12-2:  Illustrate Printer Output
R:
TP:  This goes to the printer.
R:
T:   This goes to the screen.
E:
```

Fig. 12-2. PILOT printer output.

```
R:   Figure 12-3:  The TYPE, ACCEPT, and MATCH
     Statements
R:
CH:
T:   Who is buried in Grant's Tomb?

       a.   Robert E. Lee

       b.   Ulysses S. Grant

       c.   Groucho Marx

TH:  Select a, b, or c:
A:
M:   b, Grant
T:
TY:  Congratulations!  You are right!
TN:  Sorry, the answer is Grant.
E:
```

Fig. 12-3. The TYPE, ACCEPT, and MATCH statements.

variable $NAME. If the user responds, Mary, PILOT will then display, "Hello, Mary. I am glad to meet you."

THE MATCH STATEMENT

The MATCH statement compares the contents of the accept buffer with the values listed in the MATCH statement. If a match with any of its arguments is found, the MATCH statement sets the *yes flag*. If no match is found, it sets the *no flag*. Subsequent statements can then be conditioned on whether the yes flag or the no flag is set. A simple program illustrating this is shown in Fig. 12-3.

In Fig. 12-3, the first new statement is the CH: statement, which clears the screen and *homes* the cursor (that is, places the cursor in the upper left corner). After the question is typed, the A: (ACCEPT) statement reads the user's response into the accept buffer. The following statement tries to match the response to the letter b or the name Grant, either of which would be accepted as a correct response. (Note: MATCH does not distinguish between upper and lowercase.) If there is a match, the yes flag is set. If anything but "b" or "Grant" is entered, the no flag is set. The following statement, TY:, is read as TYPE YES. It is a TYPE statement that is executed only if the yes flag is set. The TN: statement is a TYPE statement that is executed only if the no flag is set.

You have just seen that the TYPE statement can have a condition between the letter T and the colon. As you shall see later, other PILOT statements can have a condition in the same place, and will behave similarly.

THE COMPUTE STATEMENT

The COMPUTE statement is used to assign a value to a variable. It is also used for all numerical computation in PILOT. For example, the following statement adds two numbers and assigns the result to the variable #X:

    C: #X = 2 + 3

A subsequent

    T: #X

will cause PILOT to show a 5 on the screen.

COMPUTE is often used in conjunction with the MATCH statement and yes and no flags to keep track of right and wrong answers. The statement

    CY: #N = #N + 1

will add 1 to the variable #N if the previous MATCH statement set the yes flag.

The arithmetic operators available for use in the COMPUTE statement are +, −, *, /, and %. The / operator stands for integer division. The % operator is the modulus function and produces the remainder after integer division. PILOT uses conventional infix notation for all arithmetic expressions. (See Chapter 2 for an explanation.)

PILOT also provides a random number generator. The function RND(N) returns a random integer between 1 and N, where N is less than or equal to 32767. The following example generates a random number between 1 and 100 and assigns it to the variable #N:

    C: #N = RND(100)

LOGICAL EXPRESSIONS

PILOT supports the usual relational operators: =, <> (not equal), <, <= (less than or equal to), >, and >= (greater than or equal to). In addition it supports the logical operators \ (not), & (and), and ! (or).

The form of PILOT logical expressions is conventional. For example, the expression

    (#X > 5)

tests whether or not the value of the variable # is greater than 5. Because anything other than zero is taken to mean true in a logical context, the expression

    (#X)

can be taken as a logical expression that is false if #X has a value of zero, and true in all other cases.

What is unusual about logical expressions in PILOT is the way that they are used. Recall that it was mentioned earlier that the TYPE statement and some other PILOT statements can have a condition just before the colon. That condition can be any PILOT logical expression. Here are two examples:

    T(#X>5):   The number is greater than 5.
    T(#X):   The number is not zero.

The first TYPE statement above is executed only if the value of the variable #X exceeds 5. The second is executed in all cases except when the value of #X is zero.

CONTROL STRUCTURES

PILOT offers only two basic ways to alter the flow of execution of a program: the JUMP statement and the USE statement. The JUMP statement is much like the GO TO statement of most other languages, with a few variations. The USE statement is a subroutine call. Nevada PILOT also supports calls to machine-language subroutines, but such calls are beyond the scope of this book.

The JUMP Statement

The destination of a JUMP (J:) statement can be a label, the previous ACCEPT statement, the next MATCH statement, or the next PR: (PRoblem) statement. Each of these possibilities is explained in the paragraphs which follow.

Any PILOT statement in a program can be preceded by a label. A PILOT label may consist of up to 10 characters preceded by an asterisk (*). A JUMP statement, like most other PILOT statements, can be modified by a condition. Examples of PILOT JUMP statements follow:

```
JY:  *NEXT
JN:  *AGAIN
J(#X=0):  *DEFAULT
```

In the above examples, *NEXT, *AGAIN, and *DEFAULT are all PILOT labels. A program illustrating a JUMP to a label is shown in Fig. 12-4. The label in Fig. 12-4 is called *START.

If a user supplies the wrong answer, it is sometimes desirable to provide another chance. This can be done with a JUMP to the previous ACCEPT statement. The form for this is as follows:

```
J:@ A
```

A JUMP to the next MATCH is sometimes convenient if you wish to provide different replies for different responses. This can be done as follows:

```
J:@ M
```

If the user gets the correct answer right away, you may wish for him to JUMP immediately to the next problem. The next problem can be marked by PR: and the following JUMP executed:

```
J:@ P
```

Illustrations of the use of these three forms of the JUMP statement can be found in the program in Fig. 12-5.

Something new in Fig. 12-5 is the AS: statement, which ACCEPTs a single character. This statement is useful for multiple choice questions such as these.

The program first asks which state is famous for growing potatoes. If the user selects b, the JY: @ P takes him or her to the next problem. If the user selects a, the program says that Iowa is famous for corn, not potatoes. The J: @ A then JUMPs to the previous ACCEPT statement to await the user's next choice. If the user had not selected a,

```
R: Figure 12-4:  JUMP to a Label
R:
CH:
TH: What is your name?
A: $NAME
T: This is a math quiz, $NAME.  I hope you have been studying.
   :
*START  T: How much is 2 plus 2?
A: #S
M: 4
T:
TN: Sorry, 2 plus 2 does not equal #S.  Try again.
JN: *START
T:
   . Congratulations!  You are absolutely correct!
E:
```

Fig. 12-4. A JUMP to a label.

```
R: Figure 12-5:   JUMPs to the Previous Accept, the Next Match,
R:                    and the Next Problem
R:
CH:
T: Which state is famous for growing potatoes?
 :
 :      a.  Iowa
 :      b.  Idaho
 :      c.  Florida
 :
TH: Enter a, b, or c:
AS:
M: b
T:
TY: Correct.  Now for another tough question.
JY: @P
M: a
JN: @M
T: No, Iowa is famous for growing corn, not potatoes.  Try another choice.
J: @A
M: c
TY: No, Florida is famous for growing oranges, not potatoes.
TY: Try another choice.
JY: @A
T: Your answer wasn't one of the choices.  Type a, b, or c.
J: @A
PR:
T:
 : Which state extends the farthest west?
 :
 :      a.  California
 :      b.  Alaska
 :      c.  Hawaii
 :
AS: Enter a, b, or c:
M: b
JN: @M
T: Correct.  Alaska's Aleutian Islands extend farther west than any other
 : state, including Hawaii.
J:*END
M: a
JN: @M
T: No, both Alaska and Hawaii extend farther west.  Try another choice:
J: @A
```

Fig. 12-5. JUMPs to the Previous Accept, the Next Match, and the Next Problem. (Continued on page 337.)

```
M: c
TY: No.  There is another state which extends farther west.
TY: Try another choice.
JY: @A
T: Sorry, you must select a, b, or c.  Enter your choice.
J: @A
*END E:
```

the JN: @M passes control to the next MATCH statement, which checks for an answer of c. If c was chosen, the user is told why Florida is not the correct answer and then given the chance to pick another answer. If none of the choices was selected, the user is informed of the error and offered another chance.

The second problem is labeled with a PR: to serve as the destination to one of the previous JUMPs. The structure of the second question is similar to that of the first.

The logic in this example could have been simplified and a few of the JUMPs eliminated. It was left as it is in order to illustrate the various kinds of JUMPs. As an exercise, you may want to restructure the program slightly to simplify the logic.

The MATCH JUMP and JUMP MATCH Statements

Two other approaches to handling multiple choice questions are the MATCH JUMP (MJ:) and JUMP MATCH (JM:) statements. The MJ: statement is equivalent to a M: statement followed by a JN: @M statement. In other words, it does a MATCH, and if no match is found, it jumps to the next MATCH statement. The use of this statement is illustrated in the first half of the program in Fig. 12-6. (Figure 12-6 is of course a modified version of Fig. 12-5.)

The second half of the program in Fig. 12-6 illustrates the JUMP MATCH (JM:) statement. This statement allows for multiple selection, and is related to the CASE statement described in Chapter 2. Here is a simple example:

```
A:
M: C1, C2, C3
JM: *CASE1, *CASE2, *CASE3
```

The JM: statement causes a JUMP to the first, second, or third label listed, depending on whether the preceding M: statement found a match for the first, second, or third item in its list. Of course, the number of possible matches and possible destinations is not limited to three.

Use of the JM: statement, as in the second half of the program in Fig. 12-6, provides an easy and clean way to handle multiple choice questions.

Subroutines: The USE and END Statement

The USE (U:) statement is used to call a subroutine. The argument of the U: statement is usually a label that marks the beginning of the subroutine. The argument of the U: statement can also be @M or @P, as with the J: statement described above.

The end of a subroutine is marked with an END (E:) statement. This functions like the RETURN statement of BASIC, causing control to return to the statement following the U: statement. If a subroutine is at the end of a program, there must be two E: statements, one for the subroutine and one for the program.

All variables in PILOT are global; in other words, there can be no variables that are purely local to a subroutine. Consequently there is no passing of arguments from a main program to a subroutine.

One possible use of a subroutine in a PILOT

program is to provide additional instructions to the user upon request. An example of this is shown in Fig. 12-7.

PILOT is not designed for recursion, but subroutines can call each other within limits. For Nevada PILOT, this limit is a depth of seven. In other words, no more than seven U: statements can be pending at a given time.

Loops

Loops are possible using the JUMP and COMPUTE statements, but there is very little occasion for their use in ordinary PILOT programs. An example of a loop is nevertheless provided in the program in Fig. 12-8. This program prints out the integers from 1 to 10.

DATA STRUCTURES

This is an easy topic to cover with respect to the PILOT language, because PILOT does not support any data structures more complicated than a simple variable and a character string. There are no arrays, lists, records, trees, or the like; nor is there any convenient way to simulate them. This is not such a bad thing; in the kind of programs for which PILOT was intended, there is no need for such advanced data structures.

FILE HANDLING

There are many instances in which it is necessary or at least convenient to save data from one session to the next. In the case of PILOT, a particular lesson may take more than one session to

```
R: Figure 12-6:  The MATCH JUMP (MJ:) and JUMP MATCH (JM:) Statements
R:
CH:
T: Which state is famous for growing potatoes?
 :
 :    a.  Iowa
 :    b.  Idaho
 :    c.  Florida
 :
TH: Enter a, b, or c:
AS:
MJ: b
T:
T: Correct.  Now for another tough question.
J: @P
MJ: a
T: No, Iowa is famous for growing corn, not potatoes.
T: Try another choice.
J: @A
M: c
TY: No, Florida is famous for growing oranges, not potatoes.
TY: Try another choice.
JY: @A
T: Your answer wasn't one of the choices.  Type a, b, or c.
J: @A
```

Fig. 12-6. The MATCH JUMP (MJ:) and JUMP MATCH (JM:) statements. (Continued on page 339.)

```
PR:
T:
 : Which state extends the farthest west?
 :
 :      a.  California
 :      b.  Alaska
 :      c.  Hawaii
 :
T: Enter a, b, or c:
AS:
M: a, b, c
JM: *CA, *AK, *HI
T: Sorry, you must select a, b, or c.  Enter your choice again.
J: @A
*AK T: Correct.  Alaska's Aleutian Islands extend farther west than any other
 : state, including Hawaii.
J: *END
*CA T: No, both Alaska and Hawaii extend farther west.
T: Try another choice.
J: @A
*HI T: No.  There is another state which extends farther west.
T: Try another choice.
J: @A
*END E:
```

complete, and it would be convenient to keep a record of the student's progress during each session on disk so that subsequent sessions can begin in the appropriate place and so that the student's overall performance can be evaluated at the end of the final session.

PILOT supports sequential files, but not direct-access files. PILOT provides commands to create a file, open a file, write to a file, read from a file, "rewind" a file, close a file, and delete a file.

Files are created by the CREATEF: command. The argument of the command is the name of the file. The following would create a file called "AGES.TXT":

CREATEF:AGES.TXT

If the file is to be created on a disk drive other than the default disk drive, the filename may be preceded by the drive designator, as in the following:

CREATEF:B:AGES.TXT

Nevada PILOT permits up to two files to be in use at a given time. Files that are in use are identified within the program by a numeric variable. That variable is associated with the external filename by the OPENF: command. Here is an example:

OPENF:AGES.TXT,F

Normally numeric variables such as "F" are

```
R: Figure 12-7:  The USE Statement
R:
CH:
T: Welcome to a Math Quiz.
 :
TH: Would you like instructions?
A:
M: n
T:
UN: *HELP
T: How much is 12 times 9?
A:
M: 108
TN: Try again.
JN: @A
T:
T: How much is 11 times 11?
A:
M: 121
TN: Try again.
JN: @A
T:
 : That wasn't so hard, was it?  Come again some time.
E:
*HELP
T:
 : You will be asked several math problems.  If you do not
 : answer correctly, you will be asked to try again until
 : you get it right.
 :
E:
```

Fig. 12-7. The USE statement.

preceded by the # sign. In many instances in PILOT, it doesn't seem to matter whether or not the # is present. Nevada PILOT is quite fussy about the form of its file-handling commands, however. The presence of the # or even of an extraneous space can cause unexpected and unwanted results.

The WRITE: and WR: commands both cause the contents of the accept buffer to be written to a file. The RW: (Remark Write) command behaves like the T: command, except that it writes to the disk instead of the screen. The RW: command can therefore be used to write the contents of a variable or any arbitrary text to a file.

When a file is opened (with the OPENF: command), it is positioned so that the first read or write will take place at the beginning of the file. If a file is closed and then reopened, a subsequent WRITE: will overlay whatever was in the file before. If you want to add something to the end of a file that has just been opened, the APPEND: command can be used to write to the file at its end.

```
R: Figure 12-8:  A Loop in PILOT
R:
CH:
T: This program prints the numbers from 1 to 10.
T:
C: #N = 1
*TOP
T: #N
C: #N = #N + 1
J(#N(=10): *TOP
E:
```

Fig. 12-8. A loop in PILOT.

If you intentionally overwrite the previous contents of a file, it is a good idea to mark the new end of the file by issuing an EOF: command. Otherwise, the old and new contents may be inadvertently mixed.

The READ: command reads a line of text into the accept buffer, and, if you wish, into a string variable.

The CLOSEF: command is used to close a file after the last record has been written. The KILLF: command can be used to delete a file from the disk.

Suppose that you want to write some data in a file and then read it back. One way is to write the file, close it, and then open it again. Another way is to use the REWIND: command to reposition the file at its beginning.

In the preceding paragraphs the CREATEF:, OPENF:, WRITE:, WR:, RW:, EOF:, APPEND:, READ:, REWIND:, CLOSEF:, and KILLF: commands have been discussed. The CREATEF: and KILLF: commands require only the filename as an argument. All of the other commands require the numeric file designator (discussed above under the OPENF: command) as an argument.

The program in Fig. 12-9 illustrates the use of most of these commands. This program reads a name and age pair from the keyboard, writes it to a sequential disk file, and repeats the process until a / is entered instead of a name. The file is then closed, reopened, and read back in from the disk. Note the use of the numeric file indicator variable F in the file-access commands.

GRAPHICS

Apple PILOT includes excellent graphics facilities. It permits pictures, charts, and diagrams to be used as part of lesson materials. It also includes facilities for producing simple musical tunes.

Nevada PILOT does not support sound or graphics. It can, however, control a video cassette recorder. This opens up a whole new dimension in the preparation of course materials.

COMPREHENSIVE SAMPLE PROGRAM

The example programs thus far in this chapter have been relatively short. Each has served to illustrate a particular feature of the language. A longer, more comprehensive example is needed to provide a better picture of what PILOT programs are like.

The comprehensive example programs for most other languages presented in this book have been programs which maintain an address book. Because PILOT is a special-purpose language intended for use in the area of computer-assisted instruction (CAI), an address book program would not fairly illustrate the nature of a typical PILOT program. Such a program would also be difficult to implement in PILOT because PILOT lacks direct-access files, arrays, and lists. For these reasons, the comprehensive example program in this chapter will not be an address book program. Instead it will be a quiz covering North American geography.

The program is shown in Fig. 12-10. The program begins by displaying user instructions. The subroutine WAIT is used to keep the instructions on the screen until the user is ready to proceed.

The remainder of the program consists of five questions on North American geography plus a section to compute the final score. This may seem like a lot of program for only five questions. Upon examination of the program, it is apparent that the bulk of the text is taken up with the questions themselves, not with the instructions that administer the quiz.

The hard part of preparing a PILOT program is in the design of the subject matter to be presented. The skills involved in his effort are subject matter

```
R: Figure 12-9:  The Name and Age File.
R:
CH:
T: You will be asked to enter a series of names and ages.
 : Type "/" to quit.
CREATEF:AGES.TXT
OPENF:AGES.TXT,F
*TOP
T:
TH: Name:
A:
WRITE: F
M: /
JY: *OUT
TH: Age :
A:
WRITE: F
J: *TOP
*OUT
CLOSEF: F
T:
 :
 : The file will now be read back from disk:
 :
OPENF:AGES.TXT,F
*LOOP
READ: F,$N
M: /
JM: *END
T: $N
READ: F,$A
T: $A
T:
J: *LOOP
*END
CLOSEF: F
E:
```

Fig. 12-9. The name and age file.

skills, not computer skills. The computer skills needed are minimal.

There is little in this program that has not been illustrated in previous examples. One new thing is the addition of the funny looking character (~) at the end of each TH: command. This character is not printed on the screen, but it ensures that the preceding blanks are printed, so that the cursor "hangs" several spaces beyond the preceding colon.

The screen is cleared (using CH:) before each question is presented, so that only one question

```
R: Figure 12-10:  North American Geography
R:
R: This program presents a series of questions concerning North
R:   American geography.  The program provides appropriate feedback
R:   when an incorrect answer is chosen and positive reinforcement
R:   when the correct answer is chosen.  The program keeps track of
R:   the number of right and wrong answers and prints the user's
R:   score at the end.
R:
R: First initialize the number Right and Wrong:
C: #R=0
C: #W=0
CH:
T: Welcome to a quiz on North American Geography.
 :
 : You will be asked a series of questions about various geographical
 : facts about North America.  You will be given an opportunity to
 : answer a question repeatedly until you get it right.  Your score
 : will be the number of correct answers divided by the total number
 : of answers.
 :
U: *WAIT
T: Which of the following is NOT a North American river?
 :
 :     a.  Mississippi
 :
 :     b.  Colorado
 :
 :     c.  Amazon
 :
 :     d.  Mackenzie
 :
TH: Select a, b, c, or d:  ˜
AS:
M: a,b,c,d
T:
JM: *Q1a, *Q1b, *Q1c, *Q1d
TH: Sorry, you must type a, b, c, or d:  ˜
J: @A
*Q1a
T: No, the Mississippi River is the queen of North American rivers.
TH: Select a river that is NOT in North America:  ˜
C: #W=#W+1
J: @A
```

Fig. 12-10. North American geography. (Continued on page 344.)

```
*Q1b
T: No, the Colorado River flows through the United States and Mexico.
TH: Select a river that is NOT in North America:  "
C: #W=#W+1
J: @A
*Q1c
T: Correct.  The Amazon River is in SOUTH America.
U: *WAIT
C: #R=#R+1
J: @P
*Q1d
T: No, the Mackenzie River flows north through Canada.
TH: Select a river that is NOT in North America:  "
C: #W=#W+1
J: @A
PR:
T: Which of the following rivers flows into the Pacific Ocean?
  :
  :      a.  Columbia
  :
  :      b.  Colorado
  :
  :      c.  Rio Grande
  :
  :      d.  Hudson
  :
TH: Select a, b, c, or d:  "
AS:
M: a, b, c, d
T:
JM: *Q2a, *Q2b, *Q2c, *Q2d
TH: Sorry, you must select a, b, c, or d:  "
J: @A
*Q2a
T: Correct.  The Columbia River flows into the Pacific Ocean.
C: #R=#R+1
U: *WAIT
J: @P
*Q2b
T: No, the Colorado River flows into the Gulf of California.
TH: Select a, b, c, or d:  "
C: #W=#W+1
J: @A
*Q2c
```

Fig. 12-10. North American geography. (Continued on page 345.)

```
T: No, the Rio Grande River flows into the Gulf of Mexico.
TH: Select a, b, c, or d:  ˝
C: #W=#W+1
J: @A
*Q2d
T: No, the Hudson River flows into the Atlantic Ocean.
TH: Select a, b, c, or d:  ˝
C: #W=#W+1
J: @A
PR:
T: Which of the following mountain ranges is located in North America?
 :
 :       a.  Andes
 :
 :       b.  Pyrenees
 :
 :       c.  Himalayas
 :
 :       d.  Sierra Madre
 :
TH: Select a, b, c, or d:  ˝
AS:
M: a, b, c, d
T:
JM: *Q3a, *Q3b, *Q3c, *Q3d
TH: Sorry, you must select a, b, c, or d:  ˝
J: @A
*Q3a
T: No, the Andes Mountains are in SOUTH America.
TH: Select a, b, c, or d:  ˝
C: #W=#W+1
J: @A
*Q3b
T: No, the Pyrenees Mountains are in Europe, between France and Spain.
TH: Select a, b, c, or d:  ˝
C: #W=#W+1
J: @A
*Q3c
T: No, the Himalaya Mountains are in Asia.
TH: Select a, b, c, or d:  ˝
C: #W=#W+1
J: @A
*Q3d
T: Correct.  The Sierra Madre Mountains are in Mexico.
```

345

```
C: #R=#R+1
U: *WAIT
J: @P
PR:
T: Which of the following deserts is located in North America?
    :
    :        a.  Sahara
    :
    :        b.  Gobi
    :
    :        c.  Mojave
    :
    :        d.  Great Sandy

TH: Select a, b, c, or d:  ~
AS:
M: a, b, c, d
T:
JM: *Q4a, *Q4b, *Q4c, *Q4d
TH: Sorry, you must select a, b, c, or d:  ~
J: @A
*Q4a
T: No, the Sahara Desert is in northern Africa.
TH: Select a, b, c, or d:  ~
C: #W=#W+1
J: @A
*Q4b
T: No, the Gobi desert is in Asia, in northern China and in Mongolia.
TH: Select a, b, c, or d:  ~
C: #W=#W+1
J: @A
*Q4c
T: Correct.  The Mojave Desert is in southern California.
C: #R=#R+1
U: *WAIT
J: @P
*Q4d
T: No, the Great Sandy Desert is in Australia.
TH: Select a, b, c, or d:  ~
C: #W=#W+1
J: @A
PR:
T: Which of the following is the tallest mountain in North America?
    :
```

Fig. 12-10. North American geography. (Continued on page 347.)

```
              :      a.   Mount Whitney
              :
              :      b.   Mount McKinley
              :
              :      c.   Mount St. Helens
              :
              :      d.   Mount Rainier
              :
TH: Select a, b, c, or d:  "
AS:
M: a, b, c, d
T:
JM: *Q5a, *Q5b, *Q5c, *Q5d
TH: Sorry, you must select a, b, c, or d:  "
J: @A
*Q5a
T: No, at 14,495 feet, Mount Whitney is the tallest mountain in
 : the 48 adjacent United States, but there is a taller mountain
 : elsewhere in North America.
TH: Select a, b, c, or d:  "
C: #W=#W+1
J: @A
*Q5b
T: Correct.  At 20,320 feet, Alaska's Mount McKinley is the highest
 : peak in North America.
C: #R=#R+1
U: *WAIT
J: @P
*Q5c
T: No.  Even before it blew its top, Mount St. Helens was only
 : 9,678 feet tall.  It is now 8,364 feet tall.
TH: Select a, b, c, or d:  "
C: #W=#W+1
J: @A
*Q5d
T: No, Washington's Mount Rainier is only 14,410 feet in elevation.
TH: Select a, b, c, or d:  "
C: #W=#W+1
J: @A
PR:
C: #T=#W+#R
T:
 : Number right:  #R     Number wrong:  #W      Total:  #T
C: #P=100*#R/#T
```

```
T:
  : Percent right:  #P
E:
*WAIT
CA: 23,1
TH: Press (RETURN) to continue...
A:
CH:
E:
```

Fig. 12-10. North American geography. (Continued from page 347.)

appears on the screen at a given time. If a user answers a question incorrectly, he or she is given a short message and then given another opportunity to answer. When the correct answer is given, the user is told that it is the correct answer; then the subroutine WAIT is called to hold the display until the user is ready to proceed.

The JM: (JUMP MATCH) command, which was discussed earlier, is used to direct the flow of control to the proper place, depending on the user's response. Erroneous responses (for example, an "x" when the choices are a, b, c, and d) are trapped and the user is given another chance. As each answer is processed, the variable #R (for number right) or the variable #W (for number wrong) is incremented as appropriate.

After all the questions have been processed, the user's score is calculated as 100 times the number right divided by the total number of responses. The factor of 100 is needed to make the percentage a number between 0 and 100, because Nevada PILOT supports only integer arithmetic.

ADVANTAGES AND DISADVANTAGES OF PILOT

Any evaluation of the merits of PILOT as a language must consider that PILOT is a special-purpose language, designed for use in the preparation of computer-assisted instruction (CAI) materials. It was never intended as a general-purpose language.

One advantage of PILOT is its terseness. Its commands are simple (such as T:, A:, M:, and so on), yet they take care of the functions most commonly needed in the preparation of CAI materials.

The MATCH (M:) instruction is a good example. It can handle one or several possible answers and can pick answers out of context. For example, if it is told to match "no," it will also match such answers as "Not really" and "Definitely not." To accomplish the same thing in any other language presented in this book would require a significant amount of programming.

PILOT is an easy language to learn and to use. Because the language is so simple, the programmer can concentrate on the subject matter instead of on the mechanics of programming.

On the negative side, PILOT does not support loops or other advanced control structures. Although the simple and conditional JUMP statements permit the emulation of structured constructs, they also permit haphazard programming.

PILOT does not support data structures other than simple numeric variables and character strings. In most cases this is not a problem, but there are instances in which arrays would be welcome.

Nevada PILOT does not support floating point arithmetic. Limiting numbers to integer values is a serious limitation when mathematical and scientific subject matter must be presented.

PILOT is not at all suited for use as a general-purpose programming language. Of course it was never intended to be used as such.

AVAILABILITY

Nevada PILOT (by Ellis Computing) is available for microcomputers that run the CP/M operating system. Apple Computer distributes

Apple Pilot and Super Pilot for Apple microcomputers. This author is not aware of any other microcomputer versions of PILOT that are widely available at this time.

SUMMARY

PILOT is a language designed for use in preparing computer-assisted instruction (CAI) materials. It is a simple, easy-to-learn language, yet it includes commands that greatly simplify the preparation of CAI materials.

PILOT is highly recommended for use in preparing CAI materials. It is not at all recommended for use as a general-purpose language.

Chapter 13

High-Level Languages Compared

Ten high-level languages have been covered in this book:

BASIC	LISP
C	Logo
COBOL	Modula-2
Forth	Pascal
FORTRAN	PILOT

A chapter has been devoted to each language, describing the features of that language. Each language has been described in isolation, independent of the other languages. This has given you the freedom to read the language chapters in any order, skipping those languages not of interest.

The purpose of this chapter is to consider the languages as a group, analyzing the strengths and weaknesses of each in relation to the others. This is intended to make it easier for you to select an appropriate language for a particular application.

Which language is most suitable for a particular application depends on the nature of that application. There is no one universal language that is best for all applications. A language that is excellent for one application might be terrible for another. As an example, PILOT is an excellent choice for the preparation of computer-assisted instruction programs, but it is a terrible choice for programs involving extensive numerical computations.

Figure 13-1 contains a chart comparing the ten languages in various performance categories. The performance categories are listed down the left side and the languages across the top of the chart.

The numerical ratings for each language in each performance category are on a scale of 1 to 5, with 1 meaning very poor and 5 meaning excellent. The rating scale is described in more detail in the figure. Within each category, the score of the top-ranking language is marked with an asterisk.

The ratings are discussed by performance category in the paragraphs which follow.

NUMERICAL COMPUTATION

This performance category refers to the ability of the language to support applications involving extensive numerical computations. The clear win-

	BASIC	C	COBOL	FORTH	FORTRAN	LISP	LOGO	MODULA-2	PASCAL	PILOT
1. Numerical Computations	4	4	2	2	5*	2	3	4	4	3
2. Character Handling	5*	5	4	3	2	5	5	4	4	3
3. Data Structures	3	5	5	2	3	4	4	5*	5*	1
4. Control Structures	3	5	3	4	3	3	5	5*	5	2
5. Console Input/Output	5*	4	2	3	4	2	4	5	4	5
6. File Input/Output	4	4	5*	3	4	2	2	5	4	2
7. Subroutine Interface	2	3	2	3	5	4	4	5*	4	2
8. Low-Level Operations	3	5*	2	5	2	2	2	5	3	1
9. User Friendliness	5	3	3	2	3	4	5*	4	4	5

Rating Scale:

    5 = Excellent

    4 = Good

    3 = Fair

    2 = Poor

    1 = Very Poor

(* Indicates best in category.)

Fig. 13-1. High-level languages compared.

ner in this area is FORTRAN. This should not be too surprising, inasmuch as FORTRAN was designed to support numerical computations; number-crunching is FORTRAN's reason for existence.

Although FORTRAN is the oldest of the languages covered in this book, it is still the overwhelming favorite of engineers and mathematicians. FORTRAN compilers usually include a large library of predefined mathematical functions for operations such as finding the secant of an angle. Most implementations also include functions for handling complex numbers. (If you aren't mathematically inclined, you may not know what secants and complex numbers are. The point is that FORTRAN is one of the few languages that directly support such mathematical operations.)

Other possible choices for applications involving numerical computations include BASIC, C, Modula-2, and Pascal. BASIC supports most of the essential operations needed for numerical operations, but it is usually rather slow in execution.

Modula-2, Pascal, and C are fast enough for numerical operations, but each lacks an operator for performing exponentiation. The structure of these languages, however, permits the creation and use of user-defined functions to perform exponentiation and other mathematical operations.

Each of the other languages supports simple arithmetic operations, but they are rated lower. COBOL is rated low because its verbosity makes numerical computations tedious. LISP is rated low because it uses prefix notation. Forth is rated low both because it uses postfix notation and because it requires the programmer to do most of the work of analyzing and evaluating arithmetic expressions.

CHARACTER HANDLING

Most of the languages covered handle characters very well. BASIC is the winner in this category based on ease of use. Logo and LISP are actually more powerful in that they offer greater flexibility in the handling of characters. C also has excellent character handling facilities.

COBOL, Modula-2, and Pascal are rated just slightly lower in this category because they require

the maximum length of a character string to be declared in advance. Forth also requires the maximum length of the string to be declared in advance, plus it requires the programmer to do more of the work, such as keeping track of how many characters there are in each character string.

Many versions of FORTRAN do not even support a character type directly, requiring that characters be stored as integer variables. This omission has been corrected with the latest version, FORTRAN 77.

Pilot supports character strings, but offers little in the way of operators to manipulate them.

DATA STRUCTURES

To earn a high rating in the data structures category, a language must support advanced structures such as records, lists, and so forth, as well as traditional data structures such as arrays. Several languages earn the top rating: C, COBOL, Modula-2, and Pascal. The distinction of best of category is shared by Modula-2 and Pascal, as they are almost identical in this area.

LISP and Logo do an excellent job of supporting advanced data structures and would have earned the top rating except that they do not support arrays.

FORTRAN and BASIC support arrays, but little else in the way of data structures. Advanced data structures in these languages must be simulated using arrays. Forth can support many data structures but, as usual, it makes the programmer do most of the work. PILOT does not support any data entities beyond simple variables and character strings.

CONTROL STRUCTURES

To earn top rating in the category of control structures, a language must support an IF-THEN-ELSE statement, a CASE statement (or its equivalent), a counted loop, one or more kinds of conditional loop, functions and/or subroutines, and recursion. Only C, Modula-2, and Pascal win the top rating.

COBOL lacks recursion and a CASE statement. Forth lacks a CASE statement. FORTRAN lacks a CASE statement, conditional loops, and recursion. BASIC lacks a CASE statement and recursion. The LISP COND statement is a very powerful variation of the IF statement, but LISP lacks loops. Logo has a counted loop, but no conditional loop.

PILOT has only simple conditional statements and jumps (similar to the IF and GO TO of other languages).

The winner in this category is Modula-2. It is rated higher than Pascal and C on the strength of the generalized LOOP statement (with EXIT) and on the presence of the ELSE clause for the CASE statement.

CONSOLE INPUT/OUTPUT

This category covers the ease of reading data from the console and writing data to the console. It includes the ability to control the appearance of the output, for example, width of the data value and the number of decimal places for real numbers. The languages covered vary widely in this category.

BASIC wins in this category. (Those versions of BASIC such as Applesoft that lack a PRINT USING statement would not be rated as high.) Modula-2 and PILOT are also rated high. Pascal is rated slightly lower because it does not permit errors to be backspaced over when you are entering real numbers.

LISP is downgraded in this category because it cannot easily distinguish the end of a character string in the input stream. COBOL is downgraded because it does not handle the input of numbers from the console well.

FILE INPUT/OUTPUT

This category covers the ease of reading data from and writing data to disk files. COBOL is the clear winner in this category. This should not be a surprise because COBOL was designed for applications that consist primarily of maintaining data files.

A high rating in this category requires the ability to handle sequential files and direct-access files, and to perform the read and write operations easily. An advantage COBOL has over all the others is the ability to easily control the format of the data being stored. For example, the number 734 could be stored by a COBOL program as a binary integer, as a binary-coded decimal number, or as ASCII characters.

Microsoft BASIC and IBM PC BASIC do very well in supporting file input and output.

Standard Pascal lacks direct-access files, but most implementations include this feature. The situation with C is similar, but the less expensive implementations do not support direct-access files.

Forth supports a unique file structure, in which the data is organized as "screens" of 1024 characters. Forth treats the disk as if it were an extension of memory. The major disadvantage of many implementations of Forth is that Forth files are not compatible with any other kind of files.

PILOT supports data files, but limits what can be written to them to what has been read in. Logo does not support the storage of data in files except as part of a workspace. LISP supports files, but to read in data, that data must have been written out in the form of a program.

SUBROUTINE INTERFACE

The covered languages vary greatly in the way in which data are passed to and from subroutines and functions. The clear winner in this category is Modula-2.

The superiority of Modula-2 in this category lies in the way in which it implements separately-compiled modules. Modula-2 controls the interface between modules, ensuring that changes made in one module do not adversely affect another module.

Most implementations of FORTRAN also support separately-compiled subroutines. Unfortunately this feature is difficult to implement on most microcomputers. LISP, Logo, and Pascal also have very good interface mechanisms between programs and subroutines.

Forth communicates with subroutines using the stack. This works well, but requires careful planning by the programmer.

The C language has an adequate interface between subroutines (functions), but it requires explicit reference to the passing of pointers for variables that are to have their values changed in the subroutine.

BASIC and PILOT support subroutines, but have no provision for the passing of data between programs and subroutines. All values are global in these languages; that is, all values are equally accessible from anywhere in the program. The disadvantage of this is that it is difficult for a subroutine to operate on more than one set of data. (In other words, a short subroutine could only sort one specific array.)

LOW-LEVEL OPERATIONS

Operations on bits and bytes are called *low-level* operations. They are often required for interfacing directly with computer hardware, such as in writing a driver routine for a serial interface to a modem.

Low-level operations have not been discussed much in this book, because this book concentrates on high-level operations. Nevertheless, for the sake of completeness, the languages are rated on their abilities to handle low-level operations.

The winner in this category is C. Evidence of its suitability for low-level operations is the fact that the UNIX operating system is written in C. (Operating systems typically require numerous low-level operations.) Modula-2 and Forth also have excellent provisions for low-level operations.

Pascal supports low-level operations, but not without resort to various programming tricks. The PEEK and POKE operations of BASIC can be used to provide direct access to the hardware, and some versions of BASIC provide some bit manipulation operators. The other high-level languages covered provide little or no support of low-level operations.

USER FRIENDLINESS

User friendliness is a much-abused term, but it generally refers to the ease of use of a software product. It includes such factors as how easy it is to compile and execute a program, how easy it is to understand the language as a whole, and how easy it is to write a program in that language.

The clear winner in this category is Logo. Logo is so user friendly that it can easily be taught to young children as soon as they can read. BASIC and PILOT are also very easy to use, partly because they do not require a separate compile step.

LISP is a remarkably consistent language. Because it is so different from most other languages, it at first appears foreboding. Once a few basic concepts are mastered, LISP is actually a very easy language to learn and use.

Modula-2 and Pascal are not quite as friendly, but because they are strongly-typed languages, they do provide good error diagnostics and excellent protection against stupid mistakes. C and Forth provide no such protection. C and Forth are powerful tools in the hands of experts, but can be frustrating to beginners.

MATCHING THE LANGUAGE AND THE APPLICATION

Life would be simple if there were one language that was best for all applications. Unfortunately life is not that simple.

Of the languages covered in this book, four best fit the description of general purpose languages: BASIC, C, Modula-2, and Pascal. In theory at least, any program can be written in any one of these languages. A programmer having a wide variety of applications and wishing to do all of his or her programming in only one language would do well to choose one of these languages.

Not all programmers, however, are faced with a wide variety of applications. For a particular set of applications, some other language may be better.

For business applications the language of choice is COBOL. COBOL rates high in support of data structures and in file handling. In addition, COBOL can perform exact arithmetic in the decimal system, as is often required for business applications. Other possible choices for business applications include the general-purpose languages (BASIC, C, Modula-2, and Pascal) and FORTRAN.

For scientific applications involving numerical applications, FORTRAN is the language of choice. As an alternative, one of the general-purpose languages could be used.

For developing computer-assisted instruction, PILOT is the language of choice. Other possible choices for this type of application are Logo and

LISP. BASIC would be a distant fourth choice.

For applications involving artificial intelligence or knowledge-based systems, the best choices are LISP or Logo.

For applications involving character manipulation, the best choices are C, BASIC, Logo, and LISP. Pascal and Modula-2 would also be acceptable choices. FORTRAN should be ruled out.

For applications involving bit and byte manipulations, the best choices are C, Modula-2, and Forth.

For teaching children to program, the first choice is clearly Logo. Logo has been successfully used with children in kindergarten, although second grade is a more common starting level. Second choice for children is BASIC. Sixth grade is probably a good time to start children with BASIC.

CONCLUSIONS

The purpose of this book has been to describe a wide variety of high-level languages available for microcomputers. Illustrative sample programs have been presented in each language. Some of the sample programs have been the same from language to language, making it easier to compare the features of each language.

Many of you will have purchased this book because you know one language and want to see what other languages are like. You may be planning to buy another language and need help in deciding which language to buy.

The one inescapable conclusion to be drawn is that, despite the availability of general-purpose languages, some things are easier to do in one language than in other languages. The clear implication is that it is an advantage for a programmer to be able to program in more than one language. It is hoped that each of you will be motivated to learn at least one more language.

Index

A

Address book program in BASIC, 36-45

Address book program in C, 72-84

Address book program in COBOL, 110-124

Address book program in Forth, 149-158

Address book program in FORTRAN, 180-195

Address book program in LISP, 217-225

Address book program in Logo, 246-251

Address book program in Modula-2, 282-295

Address book program in Pascal, 319-329

Advantages of BASIC, 45

Advantages of C, 84

Advantages of COBOL, 124

Advantages of Forth, 184

Advantages of FORTRAN, 195

Advantages of LISP, 225

Advantages of Logo, 247

Advantages of Modula-2, 295

Advantages of Pascal, 329

Advantages of PILOT, 348

Allen, Paul, 19

Applications, appropriate, 354

Arithmetic expression in Modula-2, 258

Arithmetic expressions, 7

Arithmetic expressions in C, 49

Arithmetic expressions in COBOL, 91

Arithmetic expressions in Forth, 131

Arithmetic expressions in FORTRAN, 163

Arithmetic expressions in LISP, 204

Arithmetic expressions in Logo, 232

Arithmetic expressions in Pascal, 299

Arithmetic statements in BASIC, 21

Arrays, 13

Artificial intelligence, 197

Assembler, 2

Assembly languages, 1

Assignment statement, 7

Assignment statement in BASIC, 20

Assignment statement in C, 49

Assignment statement in COBOL, 91

Assignment statement in FORTRAN, 163

Assignment statement in LISP, 203

Assignment statement in Logo, 232

Assignment statement in Modula-2, 257

Assignment statement in Pascal, 299

Availability of C, 85

Availability of COBOL, 125

Availability of Forth, 159

Availability of FORTRAN, 196

Availability of LISP, 226

Availability of Logo, 253

Availability of Modula-2, 296

Availability of Pascal, 330

Availability of PILOT, 348

B

Backus, John W., 160

BASIC, 19-45

BASIC sample program, 36-45

BCPL, 46

Bell Laboratories, 46

Binary numbers, 1

Boole, George, 6

Boolean expression in Modula-2, 258

Boolean expressions in Pascal, 299

C

Calendar program in C, 46 - 85

Cambridge notation, 8

CASE statement, 10

Central processing unit, 1

Character handling, 352

Characters, 6

COBOL, 86-125

Comparison of languages, 350-355

Compilation in Modula-2, 262
Compiler, 2
Computer-assisted instruction, 331
COMPUTE statement in PILOT, 334
Conclusions, 355
Conditional expressions in C, 50
Constant, 5
Control structures, 352
Control structures in BASIC, 24
Control structures in C, 53
Control structures in COBOL, 95-100
Control structures in Forth, 137-140
Control structures in FORTRAN, 165-174
Control structures in LISP, 206-211
Control structures in Logo, 235-238
Control structures in Modula-2, 264-276
Control structures in Pascal, 304-315
Control structures in PILOT, 334-338
Control structures, 9

D

Data representation, 4
Data representation in BASIC, 20
Data representation in C, 47
Data representation in COBOL, 89
Data representation in Forth, 129-131
Data representation in FORTRAN, 162
Data representation in Modula-2, 256
Data representation in Pascal, 298
Data representation in PILOT, 332
Data structures, 13, 325
Data structures in BASIC, 29
Data structures in C, 63
Data structures in COBOL, 100-105
Data structures in Forth, 140-146
Data structures in FORTRAN, 174-178
Data structures in LISP, 211-216
Data structures in Logo, 238-242
Data structures in Modula-2, 276
Data structures in Pascal, 315
Data structures in PILOT, 338
Data types in LISP, 199-203
Data types in Logo, 228-232
Decimal numbers, 6
Direct-access files, 17
Disadvantages of BASIC, 45
Disadvantages of C, 84
Disadvantages of COBOL, 124
Disadvantages of Forth, 158
Disadvantages of FORTRAN, 195
Disadvantages of LISP, 225
Disadvantages of Logo, 247
Disadvantages of Modula-2, 295
Disadvantages of Pascal, 329
Disadvantages of PILOT, 348

E

Exponent, 6

Expressions, arithmetic, 7
Expressions, logical, 8

F

File handling, 16
File handling in BASIC, 31
File handling in C, 66
File handling in COBOL, 105-112
File handling in Forth, 146-149
File handling in FORTRAN, 178
File handling in LISP, 216
File handling in Logo, 242
File handling in Modula-2, 277, 281
File handling in Pascal, 316-319
File handling in PILOT, 338-341
Files, 17
FORTH, 126-159
FORTRAN, 160-196
Functions, 12
Functions in LISP, 198-199

G

Gates, William, 19
GO TO statement, 10
Graphics, 17, 242
Graphics in BASIC, 36
Graphics in C, 71
Graphics in Forth, 149
Graphics in FORTRAN, 180
Graphics in LISP, 217
Graphics in Logo, 242
Graphics in Modula-2, 281
Graphics in PILOT, 341

H

High-level langauges, 2

I

IF-THEN-ELSE construct, 9
Indexed files, 17
Infix notation, 7
Input, 9
Input in BASIC, 21
Input in C, 51
Input in COBOL, 93
Input in Forth, 134
Input in FORTRAN, 163
Input in LISP, 205
Input in Logo, 234
Input in Modula-2, 258
Input in Pascal, 299-303
Input in PILOT, 332
Integer values, 5
Interpreter, 2, 19

K

Kemeny, John, 19

Kurtz, Thomas, 19

L

Language and application, 354
Languages, viii
Languages compared, 350-355
Library modules in Modula-2, 262
Links, 15
LISP, 197-226
Lists, 15
Logical data, 6
Logical expressions, 8
Logical expressions in C, 50
Logical expressions in COBOL, 93
Logical expressions in Forth, 133
Logical expressions in FORTRAN, 163
Logical expressions in LISP, 205
Logical expressions in Logo, 233
Logical expressions in PILOT, 334
Logical operators, 8
Logical statements in BASIC, 21
Logo, 227-253
Loops, 10
Low-level languages, 2
Low-level operations, 354

M

Machine languages, 1
MAKE statement in Logo, 232
Mantissa, 6
Matching the language and the application, 354
MATCH statement in PILOT, 333
McCarthy, John, 197
Microprocessor, 1
Microsoft, Inc., 19
Modula-2, 254-296
Module concept in Modula-2, 254-256
Modules, library (in Modula-2), 262
Moore, Charles H., 126
MOVE statement in COBOL, 91

N

North American geography program in PILOT, 341-348
Notation, infix, 7
Notation, prefix, 8
Numerical computation, 350-352

O

Objectives of the book, 3
Operands, 7
Operators, 7
Operators, logical, 8
Output, 9
Output in BASIC, 21
Output in C, 51

Output in COBOL, 93
Output in Forth, 134
Output in FORTRAN, 163
Output in LISP, 205
Output in Logo, 234
Output in Modula-2, 258
Output in Pascal, 299-303
Output in PILOT, 332

P

Pascal, 297-330
PILOT, 331-349
PL/M, 19
Pointers, 15
Postfix notation, 8
Predicates in LISP, 205
Predicates in Logo, 233
Prefix notation, 8
Program in C, 72-84
Program in COBOL, 110-124
Program in Forth, 149-158
Program in FORTRAN, 180-195
Program in LISP, 217-225
Program in Logo, 246-251
Program in Modula-2, 282-295
Program in Pascal, 319-329
Program in PILOT, 341-348
Program structure in C, 47
Program structure in COBOL, 87

Program structure in Forth, 127-129
Program structure in FORTRAN, 161
Program structure in Modula-2, 254
Program structure in Pascal, 297
Program structure in PILOT, 331
Programs and functions in LISP, 198-199
Programs and procedures in Logo, 228

R

Real values, 5
Records, 17
Recursion, 13
Remark statement, 20
Reverse Polish notation, 8
Ritchie, Dennis, 46

S

Sample program in BASIC, 36-45
Sample program in C, 72-84
Sample program in COBOL, 110-124
Sample program in Forth, 149-158
Sample program in FORTRAN, 180-195
Sample program in LISP, 217-225
Sample program in Logo, 246-251

Sample program in Modula-2, 282-295
Sample program in Pascal, 319-329
Sample program in PILOT, 341-348
Speed, 3
Statement, assignment, 7
Strongly-typed languages, 7
Structure of C programs, 47
Structures, data, 13
Subroutines, 12

T

Turtle graphics, 227

U

UNIX operating system, 46
User friendliness, 354

V

Variables, 6

W

Wirth, Niklaus, 254, 297

Edited by Marilyn L. Johnson